Off Track

RENEWING AMERICAN SCHOOLS:
THE EDUCATIONAL KNOWLEDGE BASE

Series Editors: Henry M. Levin, *Stanford University*, and Jeannie Oakes, *University of California–Los Angeles*

Off Track: When Poor Readers Become "Learning Disabled," Louise Spear-Swerling and Robert J. Sternberg

FORTHCOMING TITLES

The Unfulfilled Promise of Educational Equity, Robert Berne and Leanna Stiefel

Schools for the Twenty-first Century: Linking Child Care and Education, Matia Finn-Stevenson and Edward Zigler

Schooling and Work: The Occupational Role of Education, W. Norton Grubb

Missing a Voice: Critical Pedagogy and the Possibilities of Democratic Teaching, Linda McNeil

The Social Organization of Teaching and Learning, Roland Tharp, Peggy Estrada, Stephanie Dalton, and Lois Yamanchi

Public Education in America, Amy Stuart Wells

Off Track

When Poor Readers Become
"Learning Disabled"

Louise Spear-Swerling
and Robert J. Sternberg

Westview Press
A Member of Perseus Books, L.L.C.

LB1050.5
S636
1996

Renewing American Schools: The Educational Knowledge Base

All rights reserved. Printed in the United States of America. No part of this publication may be reproduced or transmitted in any form or by any means, electronic or mechanical, including photocopy, recording, or any information storage and retrieval system, without permission in writing from the publisher.

Copyright © 1998 by Westview Press, A Member of Perseus Books, L.L.C.

Published in 1996 in the United States of America by Westview Press, 5500 Central Avenue, Boulder, Colorado 80301-2877, and in the United Kingdom by Westview Press, 12 Hid's Copse Road, Cumnor Hill, Oxford OX2 9JJ.

Library of Congress Cataloging-in-Publication Data
Spear-Swerling, Louise.
   Off track : when poor readers become "learning
disabled" / Louise Spear-Swerling and Robert J. Sternberg
      p.   cm. — (Renewing American schools)
   Includes bibliographical references and index.
   ISBN 0-8133-8756-6 (hc). — ISBN 0-8133-8757-4 (pb)
   1. Reading disability—United States.   2. Learning disabilities—
United States.   I. Sternberg, Robert J.   II. Title.   III. Series.
LB1050.5.S636   1996
372.4'3—dc20   95-19900
                                                                                CIP

The paper used in this publication meets the requirements of the American National Standard for Permanence of Paper for Printed Library Materials Z39.48-1984.

10   9   8   7   6   5   4

N. L. TERTELING LIBRARY
ALBERTSON COLLEGE OF IDAHO
CALDWELL, ID 83605

Contents

Tables and Figures

Tables

Figures

Preface

In the 1950s, when each of the coauthors started elementary school, there were few children with "reading disability." Of course, then as now, there were all too many children who were poor readers, children whose reading failure was unexpected in that it could not be accounted for by obvious causes of poor reading, such as mental retardation, hearing or visual impairment, or lack of opportunity for schooling. However, in the 1950s, these poor readers generally were assumed to be either lazy or what was euphemistically called "slow."

In the 1990s, we view the same children through a very different—but unfortunately equally flawed—lens. In the context of learning disabilities, specifically that of reading disability or dyslexia, these poor readers are seen as having a specific disability in learning to read. This disability is assumed to be biological in origin but not to be caused by a lack of motivation to learn or by low intelligence. Indeed, the centerpiece of educational definitions of reading disability is the assumption of a discrepancy between potential for learning, typically measured by means of an IQ test, and actual achievement in reading. In the past thirty years, the numbers of children classified as having reading and other learning disabilities have grown at a rapid pace. These children now constitute the largest category of youngsters who are receiving special-education services in American schools (Torgesen, 1991; U.S. Department of Education, 1991).

Genuine, serious difficulties in learning to read certainly do exist and probably always have. Most educators truly want to help children who have problems in learning to read. In our opinion, however, one of the biggest impediments to helping children with serious reading difficulties is the current tendency of many educators to conceptualize these difficulties in the context of reading disability.

In this book, we advocate another way of thinking about the cognitive difficulties of individuals who have been characterized as having reading disability. In this alternative view, what is important is not the presence or absence of a potential-achievement discrepancy but, rather, the underlying cognitive profile of the poor reader. This, in turn, can be interpreted only by reference to the cognitive profiles of normally achieving readers—that is, to the processes involved in typical reading development. We view children with reading disability as having strayed from the path of typical reading development—as having veered off track—at certain predictable points. This view of children's reading difficulties suggests many ways of addressing these difficulties educationally and, perhaps in some instances, even of preventing them entirely.

The basic elements of this alternative view are far from new; in fact, they are well represented in scientific thinking and research on reading disability. Unfortunately, however, they are not widely represented in educational circles or in popular thinking about reading disability. We hope that this book will contribute to replacement of the traditional concept of reading disability with a different and more productive way of thinking about difficulties in learning to read.

We wrote this book in part because we saw a tremendous gap between what currently is known from scientific investigations of reading disability and what currently is happening in educational practice. Although there are many reasons for this gap between research and practice, closing it requires, in our opinion, a broad view of problems in learning to read. Such a view must consider research not only on reading disability itself but also on related areas such as typical reading development and the effectiveness of different approaches to reading instruction. Consequently, we review scientific findings from a wide variety of disciplines, including cognitive psychology, regular education, special education, reading, neuropsychology, and behavioral genetics. Equally important, this broad view of reading disability must also encompass the day-to-day realities of schooling, a consideration that we have tried to make evident throughout the book.

Now we must say a few words about our terminology. *Learning disability* and *reading disability* are used throughout because these terms are widely employed in educational practice and in the research literature. However, we also show that both terms are highly problematic, given serious flaws in the very concepts underlying them.

In addition, we acknowledge that many contemporary researchers who are interested in reading prefer the terms *literacy* and *literacy acquisition* to *reading* and *reading acquisition*. The concept of literacy is not only broader in scope than that of reading—for instance, literacy includes spelling and written expression as well as word recognition and reading comprehension—but it also is used to convey the idea that becoming a literate person involves participating in a culture of literacy, a culture that includes but is not limited to formal schooling. Because the research on word recognition and reading comprehension is voluminous, and because a full discussion of the other areas of literacy is beyond the scope of this book, we restrict ourselves largely to the area of reading. However, we recognize that reading is embedded in a context that extends far beyond the four walls of a school and that poor reading is closely connected with a constellation of difficulties in areas such as spelling and written expression. Furthermore, although we focus on poor reading, we believe that the concept of "learning disabilities" as it applies to other academic areas—not only spelling and written expression but mathematics as well—is as flawed as that of "reading disability."

Finally, we should point out that our discussions of issues and problems involving educational practice are oriented primarily toward the United States. Other countries, such as Canada and England, also have formal educational programs for children with reading and other learning disabilities, and it would not surprise us if some of the problems found in American schools were found outside the United States as well. Yet there are some important differences between the U.S. educational system and those of other countries. Our focus here is on educational practice in the United States.

This book is intended primarily for an audience of practitioners, including learning-disabilities specialists, regular-classroom teachers, school psychologists, speech and language clinicians, and school administrators. In addition, we have attempted to make the subject matter accessible to nonpractitioners with an interest in reading disability—parents, for instance. For these audiences, we emphasize practical applications of research findings and provide detailed explanations of research methodology and theoretical concepts that are already very familiar to researchers. However, because the book has a strong foundation in theory and in research, both our own and that of other investigators, we believe that it will also interest researchers themselves.

We begin this book by describing exactly what, in our opinion, is wrong with the field of learning disabilities. Toward this end, in Chapter 1, we review research on the difficulties involved in differentiating children with reading disability from other poor readers and discuss the flaws in the traditional concept of reading disability. In Chapter 2, we examine the historical context behind the many contemporary problems in the field. And in Chapter 3, we focus on one particularly important problem: how children with reading disability are defined and identified in schools.

The middle chapters of the book center on our own theoretical model of reading disability, which in turn draws upon the work of many investigators. Chapters 4 and 5 present the model itself, along with the research findings upon which it is based. And in Chapters 6 and 7, we discuss in detail the implications of the model both for identifying and for teaching children with reading disability. These implications must be understood in the context of the continual pendulum swings in education regarding the "best" methods of teaching reading. Thus, in these chapters, we also review research on the effectiveness of different approaches to reading instruction.

Chapters 8, 9, and 10 explore the issues of causation and possible prevention of reading disability. In Chapter 8, we review research on potential biological as well as environmental causes of reading disability. We then present an interactive view of causation. In Chapter 9, we discuss the relationship among reading disability, mental retardation, and broad cognitive characteristics such as intelligence and intellectual styles. And in Chapter 10, we consider a number of early intervention programs in reading and examine the possibility of preventing reading disability.

Finally, the research we review in this book leads to the inescapable conclusion that the traditional concept of reading disability is the wrong way to frame the problems of the children to whom it is applied. Chapter 11 presents another way of conceptualizing reading difficulties. This alternative approach is applicable not only to individuals with the cognitive profiles typical of reading disability but to other poor readers as well.

We wish to acknowledge the individuals who provided valuable feedback during the writing of this book, including Keith Stanovich and Linda Siegel, who made very helpful comments on an earlier draft; Joseph Torgesen and Richard K. Wagner, who commented upon the ideas in the original prospectus; Hank Levin and Jeannie Oakes, the coeditors for the series of which this book is a part; and Dean Birkenkamp, senior editor at Westview Press. We also must thank the many teachers and other professionals working in schools who shared with us their insights and experiences and, in so doing, helped to shape the ideas contained herein. Three teachers who were particularly helpful we would like to mention by name: Jim Grandpre, Mary Holt, and Kathy Sutton. And last, but certainly not least, we would like to thank our families, especially our spouses, Robert Swerling and Alejandra Campos, for their unremitting support and encouragement.

Preparation of this book was supported in part under the Javits Act Program (grant number R206R00001), as administered by the Office of Educational Research and Improvement, U.S. Department of Education. Grantees undertaking such projects are encouraged to express their professional judgment freely. This book, therefore, does not necessarily represent the positions or policies of the government, and no official endorsement should be inferred.

References

Torgesen, J. K. (1991). Learning disabilities: Historical and conceptual issues. In B. Y. L. Wong (Ed.), *Learning about learning disabilities* (pp. 3–37). San Diego, CA: Academic Press.

U.S. Department of Education. (1991). *To assure the free appropriate public education of all children with disabilities.* Thirteenth Annual Report to Congress on the Implementation of the Individuals with Disabilities Act. Washington, DC: U.S. Government Printing Office.

1 What Ails the Field of Learning Disabilities

Those of us in psychology and education love to tinker with words. Children who once were "culturally deprived" are now "culturally diverse." Children who once were "trainable" are now "moderately retarded." Children who once were "hyperactive" now have "attention-deficit disorder."

So, in the course of this chapter and in the rest of the book, when we criticize the labels "learning disabled" and "reading disabled" as potentially harmful, some readers may assume that we are criticizing only the words themselves. Indeed, we do think that words and labels are important. However, our criticism of the field of learning disabilities (LD), and specifically of reading disability (RD), runs much deeper than mere dissatisfaction with terminology. In short, our view of what ails the LD field is that it is founded upon a false concept.[1] Not only is the concept of reading disability potentially stigmatizing, but, even more important, it frames the problem of reading difficulties in the wrong way. If we want to make progress in educating children labeled as having reading disability and in advancing scientific knowledge about poor reading, we must abandon the traditional concept of reading disability.

Consider the story of Kim, an undergraduate student in nursing. Kim's experience provides a good example of how the traditional concept of reading disability frames the problem of reading failure in the wrong way and actually may worsen rather than ameliorate the problems of poor readers.

Kim's Story

From her earliest years in school, Kim experienced serious difficulties in learning to read. In the third grade, she was diagnosed with reading disability and began to receive special-education services. She spent the rest of her education through high school primarily in classes for students with learning disabilities. Kim is quite negative about her educational experiences prior to college. She thinks that

1

she was segregated unnecessarily from other children and that her teachers' and parents' expectations of her were much too low. By contrast, Kim's first two years of college were a big improvement over her experiences in elementary school and in high school. With hard work, but without the need for tutorial services or other special help, she maintained a solid "B" average.

Unfortunately, in her junior year in college, Kim again began to have some academic difficulties. The problem involved her clinical work at a local hospital. Kim was very well liked by patients and by staff, and, with considerable effort, she could still keep up with the reading demands of her classes. She also continued to do well on exams and on research papers. However, spelling—especially in spontaneous situations, such as writing notes on patients' charts—was difficult for her, a problem that is not at all unusual among individuals who have a history of reading failure. But when Kim's nursing supervisor admonished her for poor spelling and Kim mentioned her history of reading disability, the supervisor replied that perhaps Kim did not belong in nursing. Kim found this remark devastating. She was deeply worried that her reading disability would preclude a much-wanted career in nursing and perhaps in many other fields as well.

From the traditional perspective on reading disability, Kim was viewed—by her teachers, her parents, her nursing supervisor, and even her own self—as someone afflicted with a special syndrome of poor reading, one caused by an unknown biological abnormality. Kim's elementary school teachers knew that there was a discrepancy between Kim's IQ, which was above average, and her reading achievement, which was well below average. This IQ-achievement discrepancy, in fact, was central to the identification of Kim as reading disabled. Yet it gave Kim's teachers no insight into how to teach her to read; indeed, unbeknownst to Kim's teachers, the discrepancy construct was not even valid in distinguishing Kim from other poor readers.

Like other individuals identified as having learning disabilities in reading (which in turn affect spelling), Kim is someone who, in our opinion, is not qualitatively different from most other individuals with a history of reading problems. It is highly unlikely that her poor reading was caused by a neurological abnormality or other biological disorder. Rather, in our view, Kim is better seen as an individual who somehow strayed from the more typical path of reading development that is followed by normally achieving readers. From this standpoint, the task for Kim's teachers might have been cast as putting Kim back on track developmentally in reading—a task that would involve, among other things, examining the underlying cognitive abilities that are central to learning to read. Obviously, Kim's problems were not framed in this way.

Kim's story is profoundly troubling, because it illustrates so aptly the negative possibilities of LD diagnosis: segregation from other children, lowered expectations, a watered-down educational program, and a belief in an intrinsic, biologically based disability that tends to impose certain limitations on the individual afflicted with it. Ironically, for two years Kim did quite well in college without any supportive services at all. Even her spelling difficulties might well have been no worse than those of other undergraduates who were also poor spellers. However, those poor spellers, not believing themselves to have an immutable disability in learning, could have pursued certain academic strategies, such as specialized dictionaries, without the anguish of wondering whether they were capable of improvement. (We have seen many such poor spellers in our years of university teaching. One particularly memorable undergraduate, who repeatedly misspelled *alphabet* as "alfabit" and *theory* as "thoery," had never been diagnosed as learning disabled and seemed to suffer no anguish whatsoever from his spelling difficulties.) In short, students like Kim pay a heavy price for their LD diagnosis.

Of course, we recognize that there are two sides to the LD classification. Some children may indeed be helped by being identified as learning or reading disabled. For instance, they may receive an excellent educational program, with specialized attention, that would not otherwise have been available to them. It might even be argued that, in spite of her negative perceptions, Kim had indeed benefited from her special-education program, which had prepared her to do well, at least in reading, at the college level. Some adults identified as learning disabled actually describe the LD label as a relief, not as something to be perceived negatively. For these individuals, the label accounts for long years of difficulty in school and serves as an assurance to its wearers that they are not "just stupid." However, a label is not an explanation; by itself, the diagnosis of LD or RD tells us nothing about what causes children's reading problems or about how these problems might be solved. Furthermore, the possibility that even a few children may be seriously harmed, rather than helped, by such a diagnosis is deeply disturbing. Like physicians, those of us who are educators want at least to leave the "patients" no worse off than they were before they met us (Hilliard, 1992).

Unfortunately, more than just a few children may be harmed by LD identification, and the potential for harm may be increasing. Years ago, parents and teachers were generally unaware that a child could be intelligent, yet still have difficulty learning how to read. Such children were usually viewed as lazy or as intellectually slow. The concept of learning disabilities, and its widespread application in the schools, helped to change that view; many people now recognize that poor reading is not necessarily due to low intelligence or to lack of motivation. In the future, there will probably be fewer poor readers who have struggled through school being branded as "just stupid"; yet given the large numbers of schoolchildren who are identified as learning disabled, there will undoubtedly be many more individuals who have gone through school wearing the LD label. If anything, this increase in numbers should arouse our concern about *any* possible negative effects of LD identification.

Most important, we believe that there is a better way to conceptualize the problems of poor readers who have been labeled as having LD. That is, even for those individuals who perceive "disabled" as an improvement over "just stupid," there is an alternative way to think about themselves, a way that is not only more beneficial to their self-esteem but also, in most cases, more psychologically accurate and more educationally useful. Individuals labeled as learning disabled, like Kim, might instead think of themselves as having taken a wrong turn in the process of learning to read, rather like the traveler on a long and unfamiliar journey who chooses the left fork in the road instead of the right. This wrong turn may have occurred for any of a multitude of reasons, but not because of a lack of general intelligence, any more than getting lost on an unfamiliar road means that one is stupid. However, once the wrong turn has been taken, a number of other factors—which we will explore in the course of this book—are set in motion, making it increasingly difficult for the individual to reach the destination of proficient reading. Still, reaching this destination may be possible, with educational help.

An Overview of This Chapter

In the next two sections of this chapter, we explain in detail why we believe that the concept of reading disability is both problematic and even potentially harmful. Children who are labeled as having reading disability are included under the umbrella category of learning disabilities. In fact, most children in the LD category are classified based on problems in reading and related areas, such as spelling (Moats & Lyon, 1993; Smith, 1991). However, we argue that there is as yet little evidence that children categorized as having reading disability differ substantially from poor readers not labeled as learning or reading disabled. And, again, we suggest that youngsters with RD would be better served educationally if they were simply conceptualized as having wandered off the more typical path of reading acquisition.

Thus, our primary population of interest, both in this chapter and in the rest of the book, encompasses those youngsters who are classified as having reading disability in schools. As we will show, there is currently little educational basis for differentiating school-labeled children with RD from other kinds of poor readers. We are not claiming, however, that one cannot find *any* examples of poor readers with distinctive biological abnormalities. Children who have suffered from lead poisoning or from prenatal exposure to alcohol present two examples of the latter; but they are not the focus of this book. We do claim that these relatively clear-cut cases of biological damage are not typical of children classified as having RD in schools.

After discussing some problems with the concepts of LD and RD, we consider, in the fourth part of this chapter, two radically different perspectives that can be seen in the literature on reading disability. Although each of these perspectives is useful in some ways, neither is as helpful to practitioners as is a third perspective. In our opinion, this third perspective is necessary to capture a complete and educationally relevant understanding of reading disability and indeed, of poor reading generally.

In the fifth and final part of this chapter, we explore some of the reasons for which research findings on reading disability have tended to have a limited impact on educational practice. What amounts to a considerable gap between research and practice in many areas of education seems to be a virtual chasm in the field of reading disability. In addition to discussing ways to bridge this chasm, we explain why we believe that translating research findings into practice has been particularly challenging in the reading-disability field.

Let us turn now to a discussion of our reasons for believing that the concept of reading disability is problematic, and why labeling poor readers as learning or reading disabled may, in some instances, compound rather than solve their difficulties.

Some Problems with the Concept of Reading Disability

Distinguishing Between RD and Other Kinds of Poor Reading

Historically, reading disability has been considered a distinctive syndrome of poor reading (e.g., Rutter & Yule, 1975), with its origins in biology. However, distinguishing between reading disability and other kinds of poor reading is at best difficult. For instance, although the presence of a discrepancy between IQ and reading achievement is one of the criteria central to educational diagnoses of RD, this criterion does not appear to differentiate RD as a discrete syndrome separate from other cases of poor reading (Fletcher et al., 1994; Shaywitz, Escobar, Shaywitz, Fletcher, & Makuch, 1992; Siegel, 1988, 1989).

One line of research has attempted to differentiate children with reading disability from "garden-variety" poor readers (Gough & Tunmer, 1986). The latter are youngsters who, unlike children with RD, have a somewhat depressed IQ score that is commensurate with their low achievement in reading. Presumably, garden-variety poor readers, although not mentally retarded, have more generalized problems in learning than do children with reading disability. The results of the studies comparing these two types of poor readers vary depending on the particular abilities examined and on the design of the study. At present, however, youngsters with RD and garden-variety poor readers appear similar with regard to specific cognitive abilities related to reading, especially word recognition. Both groups also seem to have a core of phonological deficits (Stanovich, 1990; Stanovich & Siegel, 1994; Torgesen, 1991). In addition, there is currently little empirical basis for differentiating the two groups of poor readers in terms of the kinds of remedial programs they require (Felton, 1993; Olson, Rack, Conners, DeFries, & Fulker, 1991; Siegel, 1989; Torgesen, 1991). Some of the programs developed for garden-variety poor readers, generally by specialists in the field of reading, might also be highly appropriate for children with reading disability (e.g., Hiebert, Colt, Catto, & Gury, 1992); and remedial-reading specialists have long made use of programs originally designed for individuals with RD, such as the Orton-Gillingham approach (Gillingham & Stillman, 1970).

Illness Models of Reading Disability

Many educators, as well as the general public, tend to think of reading disability—especially its medical-sounding equivalent, dyslexia—as "diseases" that can be objectively diagnosed. According to this view, RD is analogous to an illness such as measles or rheumatoid arthritis: It is a malady that resides within the individual, a person either has it or does not have it, and differential diagnosis can determine the presence or absence of the disease as well as suggest an optimal treatment. However, a number of authors (Ellis, 1985; Fletcher et al., 1994; Shaywitz et al., 1992; Stanovich, 1990) have argued that, unlike many diseases, RD is not an all-or-none phenomenon. In the view of these authors, such medical disorders as obesity or hypertension provide better analogies to reading disability than do all-or-none illnesses like measles. Just as hypertension exists on a continuum with normal blood pressure and can vary from mild to severe, reading disability exists on a continuum with normal reading and can vary greatly in severity. As Keith Stanovich (1990) notes, the fact that a disorder exists on a continuum rather than as a discrete entity, such that the borderline between disordered and normal functioning is somewhat arbitrary, does not necessarily imply that the disorder itself is trivial. Hypertension, for example, clearly puts one at risk for stroke and heart disease.

However, analogies involving medical conditions, whether to hypertension, measles, or some other disorder, fail to capture some crucial aspects of RD diagnosis. Identifying RD is not really like diagnosing a medical ailment, in part because RD identification is not an objective process involving reliable measurements. For example, in the case of hypertension, although physicians might disagree about whether borderline hypertension should be treated, generally they would not disagree about what constitutes borderline hypertension. Nor would there typically be a need to question the reliability or validity of blood pressure readings. Moreover, upon being diagnosed as hypertensive, patients receive the benefit of treatments of documented effectiveness in reducing their risk of stroke and heart attack.

For schoolchildren diagnosed with reading disability, the situation is far different. Guidelines from federal legislation, used for identifying children with reading disability in American public schools, are vague and may be interpreted quite differently from state to state. Even within a state, interpretation may differ widely from one school district to the next or even, depending on the individual professionals involved, within a district, from school to school (Smith, 1991). Thus, a child who is identified as having a reading disability in one state might not qualify for services under the regulations of a different state; a child who is labeled reading disabled in one town might not be considered reading disabled in a neighboring town. As Moats and Lyon (1993) point out, a child may achieve a dramatic "cure" for RD just by moving!

Identification may further depend on the specific tests used, which, like regulations and guidelines, can vary from place to place. To complicate the situation even more, IQ and achievement tests lack the reliability or validity of many measurements employed by physicians, such as weight or blood pressure readings. For instance, although determination of an IQ-achievement discrepancy is central to most school diagnoses of RD, a child who is categorized as having RD based on one reading test might not meet the classification guidelines if a different reading test or a different IQ measure were used. This situation is like having one's diagnosis of hypertension depend upon which blood pressure cuff the doctor happens to have available.

Furthermore, special-education referral and placement tend to be determined, in great part, by factors that may have little to do with the child's intrinsic abilities or disabilities. These factors include gender, race, and classroom behavior (Heller, Holtzman, & Messick, 1982; Hilliard, 1992; Shaywitz, Shaywitz, Fletcher, & Escobar, 1990; Ysseldyke & Algozzine, 1983), and are particularly important in the case of relatively mild handicapping conditions such as RD or LD, mild emotional disturbance, and mild mental retardation. Thus, a youngster who is a behavior problem in the classroom, and who also has reading difficulties, is especially likely to be referred for special help, whereas a youngster with an equally serious reading difficulty, who is quiet and compliant, may go unnoticed. Moreover, although hypertensive patients can expect to derive clear benefits from treatment, the overall treatment benefits for youngsters with reading disability—if *treatment* is defined as special-education placement—are much less clear. Indeed, there is a depressing degree of consensus among researchers that, at least in the past, special education and placement have often been ineffective not only for students with learning disabilities but for other kinds of students as well (Skrtic, 1991)—although there is much less consensus regarding the reasons for this outcome and what to do about them.

The Notion of an Intrinsic Biological Abnormality

Perhaps the most fundamental weakness in analogies between medical ailments and reading disability involves the notion of an intrinsic biological abnormality as the cause of the disorder. For example, although in most cases the exact etiology of hypertension is unknown, this phenomenon is one that can be described in biological terms, with reference to specific biological mechanisms that are consistent across individuals. Some cases of hypertension do have a known biological cause, such as kidney disease. The same cannot be said for the majority of children who are labeled as having RD (Coles, 1987), in spite of the long-standing assumption in the LD field that the difficulties of children with reading disability are biologically caused (e.g., Hammill, Leigh, McNutt, & Larsen, 1981; Orton, 1937). Some children with RD may indeed have problems stemming from an intrinsic biological disorder (Torgesen, 1991), but these children are clearly a minority of children actually *labeled* as disabled readers.

The learning-disabilities field has a long history of self-criticism, as well as criticism from outside the field, on the biological-disorder issue (e.g., Bateman & Haring, 1977; Schrag & Divoky, 1975). An often-cited critique is that of Coles (1987). After reviewing a wide range of evidence, Coles concludes that there is little or no basis for the claim that youngsters who are labeled as learning disabled have an intrinsic biological disorder. He observes that, despite the lack of evidence for a specific biological cause of most cases of LD, the assumption of neurological dysfunction has always been central to the field. He further suggests that this assumption has led those in the learning-disabilities field to ignore evidence from other fields, such as reading and education, regarding the importance of environmental factors in achievement.

Many of Coles's criticisms of the learning-disabilities field, particularly his criticism of the dogged biological-disorder assumption, are apt. His highlighting of the distinction between biologically based individual differences and biological abnormalities is also important; to claim that most children with RD are biologically "normal" is *not* equivalent to claiming that biology plays no role in reading disability. Biology influences all of us, whether we have RD or not.

For instance, there is considerable evidence that most children with reading disability have deficits in phonological processing, for which many investigators suggest a biological base (e.g., Liberman, 1989; Olson et al., 1991; Rapala & Brady, 1990). Still not clear, however, is the extent to which these problems in phonological processing, if they are biologically based, involve actual abnormalities or simply individual differences that might render these youngsters more susceptible to reading difficulties, given the ways that reading is typically taught in schools. In Chapter 8, we will explore in detail the role of biological, as well as environmental, factors in causing reading disability.

To say that the learning-disabilities field has been overzealous in seeking biological explanations for children's learning problems is putting it mildly. In our opinion, the pendulum in the LD field can stand a few good pushes away from the extreme of biological-deficit views. However, in our eagerness to point out the flaws in the biological-disorder assumption, we do not want to swing the pendulum too far in the opposite direction. Both extremes—the one exaggerating the role of biological factors in reading disability, the other exaggerating the role of environmental factors—fail to capture the complexities of reading disability, and so miss some part of the truth. Moreover, neither extreme captures the way that biology and environment continually interact in shaping children's abilities and behavior.

The Overlabeling Problem

Many children who do not necessarily have intrinsic learning problems, or learning problems specific to reading, are identified and labeled as learning or reading disabled in schools (Moats & Lyon, 1993; Skrtic, 1991; Smith, 1991; Torgesen, 1991). There are several reasons for which the LD and RD concepts have been overgeneralized in American educational practice. One is the role of advocacy in the LD movement. Another concerns the palatability of the LD label relative to other labels under which children receive special-education services in the schools (i.e., it is preferable to be called "learning disabled" rather than "mentally retarded" or "emotionally disturbed"). We will discuss these reasons further in Chapter 2. Authorities in the LD field have taken essentially two different views of the overlabeling problem, corresponding to two much broader and opposing perspectives on reading disability. We will discuss these perspectives, as well as what we believe to be a third, more educationally relevant perspective, later in this chapter.

How LD Identification May Aggravate the Problems of Poor Readers

In the preceding section, we discussed at length the ways in which the diagnosis of reading disability, at least in educational settings, may be arbitrary; how differentiating children with RD from other poor readers has been difficult; and why illness models of RD, which imply that RD can be objectively diagnosed, are flawed. These problems, covered in more detail in later chapters, seriously undermine the validity of the traditional concept of reading disability. As noted, not only is the concept of RD problematic, but poor readers diagnosed as having LD or RD may actually be harmed rather than helped. In particular, the diagnosis of reading disability may exacerbate certain phenomena commonly experienced by youngsters who are poor readers. In this section, we discuss some of these phenomena at length, beginning with Keith Stanovich's (1986) concept of Matthew effects.

Reading Disability and Matthew Effects

Stanovich (1986) has developed a theory of Matthew effects in reading, which are experienced by children at both ends of the continuum in reading acquisition—that is, good readers and poor readers. (The term *Matthew effects* refers to the passage in the biblical book of Matthew about the rich getting richer and the poor getting poorer, a very apt description for what seems to happen to children who are at the extremes in reading skill.) Matthew effects work in the following way. Children who experience difficulties in reading read less than do good readers. As poor readers they may lose motivation for reading, thus also negatively affecting the amount of practice they get in reading. In addition, the adults around these children—both teachers and parents—tend to have lower expectations for them in reading. Lowered expectations, motivation, and levels of practice aggravate the children's initial reading difficulties. Furthermore, since certain cognitive abilities, such as vocabulary, appear to be acquired in part through reading, the children's reading difficulties may eventually become more generalized. Thus, children who start off poorly in reading rapidly become even more disadvantaged relative to other readers, whereas the reverse happens for children who have a successful start in reading.

As an example of these opposite ends of the continuum in beginning reading acquisition, consider the contrast between two first-grade youngsters whom we will call Timothy and Evan. Timothy caught on quickly to first-grade reading instruction. In fact, he could already read some words before he entered first grade, and for him much of the formal reading instruction at the beginning of first grade was quite superfluous. Everyone in Timothy's family was proud of his early success; they exclaimed with pleasure over his attempts to read to them and bragged to friends about his achievements. They also continued the trips to the library they had begun when Timothy was a preschooler; these were even more enjoyable now that Timothy could actually read. Not surprisingly, Timothy loved reading, and since reading was a major emphasis in his first-grade classroom, his enjoyment of reading soon cast a favorable glow over his feelings about school in general. By the end of first grade, Timothy was doing a considerable amount of independent reading, both in and out of school. This practice in reading served to increase his reading speed, fluency, and knowledge base even further.

Like Timothy, Evan was a bright and agreeable youngster (at least he was agreeable when he first entered school). Unfortunately, however, Evan seemed to get off on the wrong foot in reading. Not only did he enter school with little knowledge about letters and words—a characteristic of some other first-grade children, not all of whom turned out to be poor readers—but he did not seem to acquire this knowledge quickly when it was presented in school. When nearly all of the other children began to surpass Evan in reading, he became very conscious of his reading problem and increasingly frustrated and embarrassed. He even began to resist going to school in the morning. Although his parents were aware of his difficulties, they didn't know how to help him. Since the whole subject of reading was rapidly taking on negative connotations, his parents, like Evan, tended to avoid it. They certainly were not inclined to bring him to the library, to read to him, or to buy him books as gifts, since he would not have responded enthusiastically to any of these efforts. They were skeptical of, yet eager to believe, his teacher's suggestion that he might "grow out of" his early reading difficulties. However, as Evan approached the end of first grade, he only seemed to be falling further behind the other children.

Now consider what may happen to youngsters who are not simply poor readers but are identified as having a reading disability. These children not only experience the Matthew effects associated with being poor readers but are also typically viewed as having a biologically based disorder in learning. In some cases, the notion of a biologically based disability may intensify the inclination toward lowered expectations on the part of parents and teachers, thereby decreasing the child's motivation even further. Children with RD, like those with a history of academic failure, often demonstrate "learned helplessness" and maladaptive attributions (Diener & Dweck, 1978; Wong, 1991); these tendencies may be increased when children believe they have an intrinsic and irreparable disability in learning.

Further loss of motivation negatively affects practice. At the same time, the emphasis of some special-education classes on basic skill instruction may further decrease the amount of actual practice that children receive in reading-connected text (i.e., sentences and paragraphs).

Richard Allington, Anne McGill-Franzen, and their colleagues (Allington & Li, 1990; McGill-Franzen, 1994; McGill-Franzen & James, 1990) compared the beliefs of a group of elementary-classroom teachers, remedial-reading teachers, and special-education teachers about the children in their classes. They found that one of the most striking differences between special-education and remedial-reading teachers involved the expectations that the teachers had for their students. As compared with remedial-reading teachers, who thought that their students were capable of making at least one year's progress in a year with appropriate instruction (and with a little bit of luck), special-education teachers had very low expectations for their poor readers—no more than six months' progress in a year. They had these low expectations despite the fact that many of the children in their classes were not particularly far behind their peers in reading and were intellectually normal. At times, even good performance on the part of special-education youngsters was dismissed by their teachers as a fluke! Both remedial-reading teachers and special-education teachers tended to emphasize teaching the "basics" (i.e., word recognition) rather than higher-level skills (i.e., ability to read connected text and to engage in inferential comprehension); both groups of teachers also tended to emphasize a slow pace of instruction. However, these tendencies appeared to be particularly pronounced in the special-education teachers. Thus, these findings support the view that, at least in some instances and in some ways, the LD label worsens rather than improves the lot of poor readers.

Unfortunately, RD identification exacerbated Evan's problems in the ways just described. Evan was diagnosed as having a reading disability in the second grade. Although he did not understand exactly what a reading disability was, he knew that his daily visits to the learning-disabilities resource room marked him as different, and he perceived this difference in a negative way. Indeed, the visits only intensified his privately held view, already initiated by his many experiences with reading failure, that he must be "stupid." Furthermore, his resource teacher required him to complete even more worksheets and workbook exercises than did his regular-classroom teacher, and the question of how anyone could actually enjoy reading became still more of a mystery to him. Evan's parents were somewhat relieved by his diagnosis, because it allowed them to conclude that he was not retarded and reassured them that he might get expert help. They also felt that they had been expecting too much of Evan, and so they scaled down their expectations accordingly.

Of course, students like Evan and Kim experienced very real academic problems long before being classified as learning disabled—LD classification did not *cause* those problems. Furthermore, as noted at the outset of this chapter, we certainly do not claim that all youngsters are affected negatively by LD or RD classification. For many children, the implicit promise of LD diagnosis—that the LD label will lead to better understanding, self-esteem, and achievement—may well be realized.

However, we believe that the phenomenon exemplified by Evan's case, in which the LD label magnifies certain negative experiences of poor readers, is by no means rare. Of even greater importance (as we will discuss in detail in future chapters), there is a more psychologically accurate, more educationally useful way to think about the reading problems of children like Evan and Kim than the way embodied in the traditional concept of reading disability.

Segregation of Children with Reading Disability from Other Children

At the middle or secondary level, poor readers may be tracked into separate classes. At the elementary level, however, this kind of total segregation of poor readers is rare. As an alternative, they can be serviced in pull-out remedial programs such as "Chapter 1" or placed into a low-ability group within the regular classroom. In any case, ability grouping has been repeatedly criticized as being particularly detrimental to poor readers (Anderson, Hiebert, Scott, & Wilkinson, 1985).

More typically, children who are identified as having RD become part of the special-education system, in which models of service delivery range from total inclusion in a regular-classroom setting to self-contained classes within a regular public school, or even to outside placement in a segregated school. Self-contained classes for students with learning disabilities, even at the elementary level, are not uncommon, particularly in certain states (Danielson & Bellamy, 1989). In spite of the federal mandates (P.L. 101-476 and P.L. 94-142) requiring that children in special education be placed in the least restrictive environment, and in spite of movements such as the regular education initiative (Will, 1986), the likelihood that a child who has been identified as learning or reading disabled will experience increased segregation from other children depends heavily on the philosophy of the school that the child happens to attend. In schools that are strongly oriented toward inclusion of special-education youngsters in the regular classroom, the LD label may have a negligible effect in terms of separation from other children. However, in many other schools, LD diagnosis greatly increases the probability that a child will be segregated from "nondisabled" children for a substantial part of the school day.

Inclinations to Change Educational Practice

The belief that children with reading disability have an intrinsic disability in learning may reduce inclinations to change educational practice, since locating the learning problem within the child diverts attention from environmental and instructional factors that may be critically important in achievement. For example, some regular-classroom teachers may automatically view children with RD as needing specialized and expert attention that cannot be provided in the regular classroom, whether or not this is actually true in an individual case. Skrtic (1991) has suggested that the very existence of special education as a field has reduced the motivation of regular education teachers to be innovative, because special education removes from regular education the children who might create the need for change. Special educators are also not immune to resistance toward changing educational practice. For instance, some special educators may attribute the failure of children with RD to progress in reading to an intrinsic, immutable deficit in the children themselves, rather than seeing the lack of progress as an impetus for altering instruction.

Ethical Issues

Finally, we come to the important matter of ethical issues involved in diagnosing children as learning or reading disabled. As we will later discuss in more detail, researchers interested in reading disability, especially those in the field of cognitive psychology, are often not oriented toward the issue of ultimate causation—and, indeed, such an orientation is not necessary for scientific advances to be made. However, as any practitioner knows, when parents are told that a child has a reading disability, their questions often center on causation: What causes reading disability? Does the child have brain damage? Are we as parents at fault? Will the child's reading problems ever go away?

Parents and children have the right to honest answers to their questions. This right includes being told "we don't know." It also includes, of course, being given genuine evidence of neurological abnormality. However, in our opinion, it is just plain wrong to suggest that a child has a neurological abnormality or other biological disorder causing poor reading when—as in the vast majority of school-identified cases of reading disability—there is no real evidence of such a disorder. Furthermore, it strikes us as ethically questionable, at the very least, to segregate poor readers in learning-disabilities programs—especially when these programs continue to be pervaded by unfounded notions about the children placed in them.

Perspectives on Reading Disability

As readers may have decided by this point (if they didn't already know from personal experience), many issues in the field of reading disability are being hotly disputed—and not the least of these is the extent to which reading disability itself actually exists. Opinions on this latter point range from unquestioning faith in the LD and RD constructs to total and equally unshakable skepticism. How can we make sense out of all this contentious confusion?

One way to approach the literature on reading disability is to examine the overall philosophical and theoretical viewpoints represented in it. Roughly speaking, the literature can be sorted into two major perspectives on the problem of RD. Adherents of each perspective have very different approaches to and solutions for reading disability. In this section, we describe and give examples pertaining to both perspectives, which are summarized in Table 1.1, along with a third, and, we believe, more useful perspective.

The Intrinsic Perspective

Here, the focus is on deficits within, or intrinsic to, the child. Theoretically, these deficits could be either biologically or environmentally determined, but most who hold to this perspective assume biological causation. The intrinsic perspective, of course, represents the traditional position of the LD field as well as the perspective of many researchers in other fields. Those with an intrinsic perspective address the overlabeling problem in the schools, along with a variety of research considerations, by attempting to ferret out the "real" cases of reading disability. These "real" cases might be determined in any of several different ways, depending on the specific version of the intrinsic perspective that is involved. For example, one researcher might require subjects with RD to show a discrepancy between math achievement and reading achievement, whereas another might require subjects to show evidence of a particular kind of processing disorder. These "real" cases of RD, however they are defined, represent the true population of interest in the intrinsic perspective.

Hammill (1993), who believes that "the contributions of neuropsychologists underscore the appropriateness of the earlier notion that learning disabilities are most likely due to central nervous system dysfunction" (p. 302), provides a good example of the intrinsic perspective. As we have already indicated, we are considerably less sanguine than Hammill is about the appropriateness of the idea that LD and RD are due to CNS dysfunction, the contributions of neuropsychology notwithstanding. Nevertheless, let us put that argument aside for the moment, and see what Hammill has to say about the overlabeling problem in schools. After discussing some contributions made by educators to the field of learning disabilities, Hammill remarks:

> Not so beneficial is the educator's tendency to conceptualize learning disabilities in terms of problems of a mild or moderate degree, to downplay the role of etiology, to fixate on the school-age child, and to focus on remediation of specific problems rather than on treatment of the whole child. These ideas as implemented in the schools combine to blur the distinctions between students with learning disabilities on the one hand and remedial and slow learning students on the other. . . . This confusion has resulted in an ever-increasing number of students erroneously being classified as learning disabled and in turning learning disabilities into a catchall category. (p. 300)

TABLE 1.1 Three Perspectives on Reading Disability

	Intrinsic	*Extrinsic*	*Interactive*
Focus of perspective	Deficits within the child	Factors outside the child that could account for poor reading	Interaction between child and environment
Population of interest	"Real" cases of RD	School-labeled cases of RD	Both "real" and school-labeled cases of RD
Cause of reading disability	Biological causation usually assumed	Environmental causation emphasized	RD is a result of interaction between biological and environmental factors
View of overlabeling problem in schools	Schools need to find the "real" cases of RD	Overlabeling illustrates flaws in RD construct	Overlabeling illustrates how within-child characteristics interact with contextual variables
Examples of prominent concerns	Neuropsychology and genetics of RD; differentiating RD and "garden-variety" poor reading	Labeling; sociology and politics of RD	Specifying how children's intrinsic processing characteristics might develop and might interact with environment
Role of LD/RD field	Diagnosing and treating "real" cases of RD	No role or vastly different role	Different role
Research base	LD and special-education fields; neuropsychology; cognitive psychology; behavioral genetics	Reading and regular education; sociology; social and developmental psychology	Both intrinsic and extrinsic lines of research

In other words, the overlabeling problem results from confusion over who is "really" RD and who is a slow learner (i.e., a garden-variety poor reader). Moreover, in Hammill's view, this confusion is somehow the fault of educators; evidently educators are insufficiently adept at finding the "real" cases of RD, and are being too easily duped by the fakes. But unfortunately, as we have seen, the distinctions between these two groups of poor readers are indeed blurred. If educators are confused, there is ample reason for them to be so.

Not surprisingly, some of the clearest examples of the intrinsic perspective come from the field of behavioral genetics. As Pennington et al. (1991) point out regarding research on possible genetic bases of reading disability:

> The possibility of autosomal dominant transmission of dyslexia remains an intriguing, elusive, and controversial possibility. Such a mode of transmission would provide a parsimonious explanation for the consistently high familial recurrence rates reported for this disorder (35% to 45%), which are several times higher than the estimated population base rates of 3% to 10%. (p. 1528)

But the situation of a parent or parents who are poor readers—and therefore who are not likely to read extensively to their children, to model reading as a leisure activity, or to have a wide variety of books at home—provides an equally parsimonious explanation for a high familial recurrence rate of reading disability. Environmental factors and genetic-environmental interaction, though certainly acknowledged by Pennington et al. and other behavioral geneticists, are rarely given serious consideration as explanations for poor reading by those with an intrinsic perspective—at least, not for the "real" cases of reading disability.

Let us consider a final example of the intrinsic perspective, this time from our own field of cognitive psychology. Nearly all of the work in cognitive psychology represents an intrinsic perspective, because the focus of such work involves what is going on inside children's heads. Moreover, although intrinsic cognitive processes might be shaped by environmental as well as by biological factors, many cognitive psychologists, like other researchers with an intrinsic perspective, are inclined to emphasize biological factors in the causation of reading disability. For instance, investigators from the Haskins Laboratories group (e.g., Liberman, 1989; Shankweiler & Crain, 1986; Shankweiler, Crain, Brady, & Macaruso, 1992) link reading disability with a broader theory of language acquisition that is strongly nativist (i.e., biological) in orientation.

Bear in mind that, like most other work in cognitive psychology, the research of the Haskins Laboratories investigators occurs at the level of psychological description and does not actually focus on ultimate causes—biological or environmental—of reading disability. As we will elaborate, cognitive psychological research has important implications for both RD and educational practice; thus, we are not suggesting that the research is somehow flawed because it doesn't address the issue of ultimate causation. Moreover, as we will discuss in Chapter 8, research evidence from other fields does provide some key insights about the ultimate causation of reading disability—although unfortunately this evidence is often misinterpreted, especially in the popular press.

What is most noteworthy for our present purpose of illustrating the intrinsic perspective is the focus on the cognitive processes occurring inside the child's head. This emphasis is legitimate in a laboratory situation. But as any practitioner knows, in everyday life what goes on inside the child's head interacts with innumerable contextual variables, such as the nature of reading instruction, the personality of the child's teacher, and the characteristics of the child's home. Thus, talking about cognitive processes in isolation is a bit like talking about gravity in theoretical terms. Theoretically, a stone and a feather dropped from a height are supposed to fall at the same rate; but in reality, of course, a stone and a feather do not fall at the same rate, because they are differentially affected by air currents. Children are not like objects dropped in a vacuum. They need to be viewed in context.

The Extrinsic Perspective

Those with an extrinsic perspective emphasize factors outside, not within, the child as possible determinants of reading disability. These possible extrinsic causes include inadequate instruction, the nature of the home environment, and the way that schools are structured. Rather than pursuing the quest for the "real" cases of reading disability, researchers with an extrinsic perspective are interested in how the concepts of LD and RD are applied in educational practice. Since schools are social as well as educational institutions, and since social reality is often considerably messier than laboratory science, these writers emphasize the social and political underpinnings of the LD field, as well as the many issues arising from the way that the LD and RD concepts have been implemented educationally (such as the overlabeling problem). Whereas the intrinsic perspective charges the LD field with properly sorting out and treating the "real" cases of RD, the extrinsic perspective gives the LD field no separate role at all in identifying and remediating poor reading; or if it does, that role is vastly different from the one currently in place.

Senf (1986) provides one example of an extrinsic perspective on the overlabeling problem and its political implications:

> When one considers that three-quarters of learning-disabled youngsters have problems in the area of reading (Kirk & Elkins, 1975; Norman & Zigmond, 1980), it becomes apparent that what might have been seen earlier as corrective or remedial reading cases had been reclassified as learning disabled. The implications for hiring new personnel and for distributing funds within school districts were direct. (p. 30)

Those with an extrinsic perspective would not necessarily deny that there are "real" instances of reading disability or that the child's intrinsic characteristics are important in reading acquisition. However, just as the intrinsic view acknowledges the importance of the environment, and then ignores it, acknowledgement of the importance of within-child variables by those with an extrinsic perspective, or of the importance of the interaction between the child and the environment, is generally only cursory. Labeling issues also are frequently prominent in the writing of those with an extrinsic perspective. Senf (1986), who refers to school-labeled LD youngsters as "sociological casualties," points out that "how we conceive of something inextricably alters how we deal with it" (p. 30).

Other extrinsic writers view the phenomenon of overlabeling as yet another example of the LD field's wrongheaded emphasis on problems within children, rather than on problems with ineffective teaching. For instance, Christensen (1992) asserts that "the learning disabilities construct deflects attention from the nature of schooling and instruction as a source of failure and locates it clearly within the child. Thus, learning disabilities serve to mask the true nature of reading failure and hinder a more productive search for effective reading instruction" (p. 278).

Skrtic (1991) expresses a similar view with regard to the field of special education as a whole, clearly including the LD field in his criticism: "Structurally, special education is not a rational system; it is a nonrational system, an institutional practice that functions as a legitimizing device. Culturally, it distorts the anomaly of school failure and thus preserves the prevailing paradigm of school organization" (p. 170). In other words, the field of special education, including the LD field, serves to justify children's school failure by locating the source of that failure firmly within the child, rather than within the school, thus avoiding any need to alter the current system of schooling. Skrtic (1991) advocates radical school restructuring via an "adhocratic" system.

In our experience, practitioners usually find the extrinsic perspective to be ultimately as unsatisfying as the intrinsic perspective. Surely, therefore, a "more productive search for effective reading instruction" (Christensen, 1992) must consider not only the instructional methods involved but also the child's intrinsic characteristics. These intrinsic characteristics are not irrelevant to academic success or failure. Analyses such as Skrtic's, though thought provoking, can be equally frustrating from a practitioner's point of view, because they undermine the integrity of what practitioners are currently doing without offering anything concrete or immediate that is feasible for most practitioners to change. After one's consciousness has been raised, what does one do tomorrow in the classroom?

The Need for a Different Perspective

We do not intend to disparage the work of any of the researchers we have quoted here, all of whom have contributed a great deal to the LD field and have influenced our own thinking considerably. We also acknowledge that all of these researchers have more complex views than we can do justice to in a series of brief quotations. Nevertheless, we think that it should be apparent by now that there are serious flaws, especially from a practitioner's point of view, in both the intrinsic and extrinsic perspectives. The intrinsic perspective, in emphasizing within-child characteristics, ignores the importance of looking at children in context. Moreover, the propensity of those who hold an intrinsic perspective to assume a biological disorder as the cause of reading disability is troubling, not only because this assumption appears to be largely unfounded but also because it has the po-tential to do serious harm, as we illustrated in our opening story about Kim, the undergraduate nursing student. The extrinsic perspective is equally flawed be-cause it ignores or drastically downplays the significance of within-child charac-teristics in learning to read and in academic achievement generally.

As an illustration of the flaws in each perspective, consider an experience that one of the coauthors had involving his son Seth. Seth changed schools in the third grade, and on his first day in the new school, he was given a reading test. In his old school, Seth had been in the top reading group, but he did poorly on the new reading test because he was nervous about being in another school, with new teachers, classmates, and so on. Based on the reading test results, he was placed in the bottom reading group. However, it eventually became clear from Seth's day-to-day performance that he did not belong in the bottom reading group, so the school retested him and placed him in the middle reading group. After spending some time in the middle reading group, he was tested once again and performed at the level of the top group. Yet, as his parents were told, he could not join the top reading group because he was now "too far behind." Seth's parents then proposed that Seth's book be sent home so that they could help him catch up, but they were told that sending books home was "not allowed."

Now, we think that most people who have worked in schools can appreciate this kind of story, because they are familiar with the frustrations of trying to get things done in an educational bureaucracy, where they sometimes feel they've gone through the looking glass with Alice or stepped into a pedagogue's version of *Catch-22*. It is easy to view this story from an extrinsic perspective. Educational practices such as ability grouping and inappropriate use of testing clearly can contribute to, or even create, some youngsters' problems. Ultimately, Seth's story did have a happy ending, but the outcome might have been different if his parents not been strong advocates for him. Furthermore, Seth's mother is the associate commissioner of education for her state, and Seth's father is a Yale professor, so they are not exactly novices at negotiating the educational system. But more gen-erally, it is not difficult to imagine situations in which children are inappropri-ately placed in low reading groups and end up staying there for the remainder of their school careers.

An analysis of Seth's story solely from an extrinsic perspective would be flawed, however, because it overlooks the intrinsic characteristics that Seth himself brought to the situation. Obviously, if Seth really had been a poor reader, merely placing him in a higher reading group would not have solved his problems. It is also clear that Seth required a high degree of motivation to "catch up," especially given the muddle the new school had made of his introduction to its program. Conversely, whereas an intrinsic perspective would include Seth's reading skill and motivation in its account, it would miss the equally important contextual aspects of the story.

Finally, and most important, neither the intrinsic nor extrinsic perspective al-lows for the way the child and the environment interact with one another. For ex-ample, a child with certain cognitive characteristics that do not bode well for reading acquisition—say, an impulsive cognitive style or a relative deficit in an area such as phonological processing—might nevertheless succeed with the right kind of reading instruction or the right kind of teacher. A reading program that is disastrous for poor readers might be quite adequate for children without reading problems. From this perspective, the overlabeling problem in the schools might be seen not merely as the failure of practitioners to sort out the "real" cases of RD, nor merely as evidence of the flawed nature of the RD construct, but rather as a product of the interaction between genuine differences in children's abilities and contextual variables. Children labeled as having RD usually do have actual deficits in reading, but factors such as the nature of instruction and the teacher's perception of the child's problem also heavily influence the identification process. As we will discuss further in Chapter 11, the interactive perspective, like the extrinsic perspective, envisions a considerably different role for the LD field in identifying and remediating poor reading than the one currently in place.

As Coles (1987) notes, although psychological and educational theories both inside and outside of the LD field commonly pay lip service to the importance of the interaction between the child and the environment, this interaction is rarely addressed in actual research. Nevertheless, there certainly are examples of interactive theories and research in the fields of learning disabilities and reading. Keith Stanovich's (1986) theory of Matthew effects in reading, which we discussed earlier, provides one example of an interactive theory. Another example is situated action theory (e.g., Chinn, Waggoner, Anderson, Schommer, & Wilkinson, 1993), which maintains that the behavior of both teachers and students—as during an oral reading lesson—is linked to a "dynamic interplay of factors that converge at particular moments" (p. 390). These factors include the teacher's goals for the lesson, the difficulty of the text, the types of errors made by students, and the behavior of other students in the oral reading group. Lipson and Wixson (1991) provide a third example of an interactive view of reading and reading disability.

Coles (1987), who prefers the term *interactivity* to *interaction*, summarizes his theory as follows:

> The interactivity theory of LD proposes that while various features of an individual (including neurology), groups, and institutions, and social, economic, and cultural forces each have their own characteristics, identity, activity, degree of influence, and interdependencies, at the same time they all combine to create the processes and products of learning and disabled learning. One might think of this interactivity as a "polyphony," a musical term for melodic parts that are both independent and interdependent. (p. 209)

Thus, in Coles's theory, a learning "disability" is produced by a complex interplay of factors, including home environment, schooling, and, within the individual, biological differences (not dysfunctions). Coles emphasizes the way in which broader contextual factors—for example, changes in family life and industrial pollution—affect children, schools, and teachers. He also emphasizes the role that children themselves may play in the process of becoming "disabled":

The children do not merely accept a label ascribed by others and then acquire the self-concept of being powerless and act accordingly. Rather, in the activity of failing, of being unable to accomplish academic tasks, and in having their activity defined as one exuding intellectual powerlessness, the child becomes powerless. . . . Being intellectually powerless means that the individual's actions will display learning-disabled behavior that will lead important overseers, such as teachers and parents, to respond to the child in ways that increase the learning disability. (p. 172)

Coles's theory has been criticized as providing a better account of more generalized problems in learning—such as garden-variety poor reading—than of reading disability (Stanovich, 1989; Torgesen, 1991). However, his interactivity theory does capture some crucial aspects of reading disability, such as the importance of setting the phenomenon of reading disability in a larger social context, and the issue of how school failure may cause children to act in ways that exacerbate their problems, an idea similar in some respects to Stanovich's (1986) notion of Matthew effects. We think that Coles's theory nevertheless falls short of being a truly interactive theory, because it disproportionately emphasizes context. As Coles himself puts it, "According to the interactivity theory, systemic economic, social, and cultural conditions are the *principal* influences contributing to learning failure" (p. 209, emphasis added).

Coles has little to say about specific characteristics within children that might contribute to or cause their school failure, other than to observe that school failure causes children to act and to become intellectually powerless. This observation is important, but it does not explain why children fail in school in the first place. Of course, children might initially fail because of poor instruction or inadequate preparation at home (two possibilities that Coles discusses at great length), but such environmental explanations do not address *within-child* characteristics. Coles certainly acknowledges the existence of these characteristics, but he does not elaborate on what they are or emphasize them in his theory. Although he freely acknowledges that a small number of school-identified youngsters with LD may indeed have a neurological dysfunction, and although he takes pains to point out that he is not substituting social reductionism for biological reductionism, it may be his overwhelming emphasis on context that explains why he is nevertheless generally perceived as claiming that LD does not exist (e.g., Moats & Lyon, 1993) and as having a social-environmental theory (e.g., Torgesen, 1991). It seems to us that Coles comes closer to having an extrinsic perspective than a truly interactive one.

In our view, what goes on inside the child's head is as important as, and interacts with, the context surrounding the child—both the immediate classroom context and the larger social context emphasized by Coles. We also believe that cognitive psychological research has crucial educational implications because it yields important insights about what is going on inside a child's head during successful reading acquisition as well as during reading failure. However, Coles—who accurately points out that this line of research focuses largely on the child and not the context, and that it has little to say about the ultimate cause or causes of RD—is skeptical about its usefulness:

> What has all of this contributed to knowledge about reading disabilities? Without denigrating some of the better research . . . [I must point out that] this body of work has not moved beyond earlier erroneous LD explanations. When examined as a whole, this forefront of the long LD march, with its emphasis on the role of phonemic skills, has done little more than rediscover that "phonics" is important in learning to read. (p. 55)

Coles implies that the fact that psychological research often assumes brain dysfunction in children with RD, and generally does not even address the issue of ultimate causation, makes the work educationally useless. But it is helpful for practitioners to know what kinds of deficits children with RD have—for example, word-recognition or phonological deficits—even if they do not know the ultimate sources of those deficits. If practitioners know that children with RD lack certain kinds of cognitive skills and that those skills are crucial to reading acquisition, then this knowledge has clear implications for planning instruction, even when the issue of ultimate causation is unclear. Further, if practitioners know that certain cognitive skills are predictive of early reading acquisition, this knowledge is educationally useful because it tells them which children are especially likely to be at risk educationally and thus need extra attention as well as, perhaps, a different type of instruction. We readily assent that it is even *more* educationally useful to know the ultimate sources of the cognitive deficits—and, as we will see, there is at least suggestive evidence concerning this very issue. Nevertheless, practitioners frequently have to teach children skills that they are lacking without knowing exactly why the lack is there. The idea that knowledge about cognitive deficits is utterly useless without definitive knowledge about ultimate causation strikes us as a matter of throwing the proverbial baby out with the bath water.

Further, Coles's statement that cognitive psychological research has done "little more than rediscover that 'phonics' is important in learning to read" is, we think, just not true. First, although word decoding deficits do appear to be a central feature of reading disability, cognitive psychological research has implications for many areas of reading acquisition and reading disability, well beyond the area of word decoding (i.e., "phonics"). Second, there are multiple ways to approach decoding, or phonics, instruction. Should decoding skills be taught in conjunction with reading stories, or in (decontextualized) isolation? Should they be taught in an analytic manner, focusing on whole words, or in a synthetic manner, requiring the child to blend parts of words? Is one type of approach more beneficial for a certain kind of youngster and a different approach better for another kind of youngster? And so on. Adams (1990) discusses these kinds of issues in considerable detail. Her work, and that of others, makes it clear that the specific ways in which decoding instruction is actually implemented are crucial, and that psychological research provides important insights into how such implementation should be achieved.

In our view, what is needed is a more truly interactive perspective on reading disability, one that draws not only from the work of researchers such as Coles and others with a more extrinsic perspective but also from the work of those with a more intrinsic perspective on RD, such as cognitive psychologists. The interactive perspective is the one we will adopt in this book. We argue that such a perspective is crucial for a complete understanding of reading disability as well as for the ability to effect educational change, both in the classroom and at the broader systemic level.

Why Have Research Findings on Reading Disability Had a Limited Impact on Educational Practice?

In the recent past, Vellutino (1979) noted the long-standing lack of well-articulated theory-driving research and practice in the RD field. As the preceding discussion suggests, this situation has changed dramatically, thanks not only to the efforts of Vellutino and his colleagues (e.g., Vellutino & Scanlon, 1987; Vellutino, Steger, Moyer, Harding, & Niles, 1977) but also to the work of many other investigators from a number of different fields, including the Haskins Laboratories group (e.g., Liberman, 1989; Mann & Liberman, 1984; Shankweiler & Crain, 1986; Shankweiler et al., 1992); Stanovich (1986, 1989, 1990); Torgesen (1990, 1991); Wong (1991); Shaywitz and her colleagues (Shaywitz et al., 1990; Shaywitz et al., 1992); Ehri (1991, 1992); and Gough and his colleagues (e.g., Gough & Juel, 1991; Gough & Tunmer, 1986). Much is now known about reading acquisition in normally achieving readers, and about patterns of deficits typically associated with reading disability and with poor reading generally. As we argued earlier, these research findings have crucial implications for educational practice.

Although there have been some changes in the right direction, educational practice in the LD field has not exactly been revolutionized by these research findings and theoretical advances. Numerous examples leap to mind. For instance, visual perception and visual-motor tests are still used frequently to diagnose RD or to screen kindergarten youngsters for potential problems in reading—even though, as we will discuss in Chapter 3, research indicates that language skills are much more highly correlated with reading than are visual-processing skills. (Any visual-processing differences that might exist between children with reading disability and normally achieving readers could not readily be detected, anyway, with the kinds of measures typically employed in educational settings.) One language skill, phonological awareness, is an excellent predictor of future reading ability; yet, though not particularly difficult to measure in classroom settings, it is conspicuously absent from many RD diagnostic and kindergarten screening tests. Furthermore, many of the tests that continue to be used in identification of RD are characterized by inadequate reliability, validity, and norms (Moats & Lyon, 1993).

Instructional practices directed to children labeled as having RD have also, in many cases, remained relatively impervious to scientific advance. For instance, as already mentioned (and as we will discuss in more detail in Chapter 3), research has consistently documented that word-recognition and decoding skills are lacking in children with reading disability. Yet the current instructional vogue in some schools is to deemphasize, or even to forgo altogether, systematic instruction in decoding skills. As is known by anyone who has read the literature on methods of reading instruction, the whole topic of which method of instruction is "best" has become highly controversial, eliciting a level of emotion usually reserved for subjects such as abortion. For this reason, we hasten to point out that instructional practices also often err in the opposite direction: by *over*emphasizing decoding skills. For example, as noted earlier, some programs for children with RD (especially at the elementary level) focus almost entirely on isolated skill instruction (e.g., having children complete endless phonics worksheets), even though research demonstrates that reading in meaningful contexts is critical to developing reading skill. What, then, is going on? Don't practitioners *want* to do the right thing?

We believe they do, or we wouldn't be writing this book. The difficulty in translating research findings into educational practice in the RD field is part of a more general problem involving not only educational reform movements and the way that schools are structured (Sarason, 1990) but also teacher preparation issues (Moats & Lyon, 1993). In our opinion, however, there are at least two reasons for which the translation of research findings into practice has proven particularly problematic in the RD field. We will attempt to address both reasons definitively in this book.

First, the field is interdisciplinary in nature, drawing from other fields as diverse as cognitive psychology, reading, education, linguistics, and neurology. Accordingly, many of the research findings on RD from a specific discipline are esoteric and not readily comprehensible to practitioners or to others outside that discipline. For example, in our own discipline of cognitive psychology, much of the research is replete with phrases such as "impaired lexical access affects text representation in working memory" and "the phonological code serves as input to an articulatory-motor module," language that is not highly accessible to most practitioners, to say the least. (By the same token, we ourselves are hard-pressed to decipher research on the genetics of learning disabilities, which is filled with phrases like "the transmission probability of the heterozygote.") To say that such language is difficult for practitioners to understand is not, of course, to demean either the research or practitioners. We make the point only to illustrate one of the difficulties of translating research findings into practice in this area.

Second, the research in the RD field is especially contradictory and confusing. It seems as though one can locate isolated research findings to support almost any position one wishes to take: that RD is environmentally determined, that RD is biologically determined, that RD is associated with a phonological deficit, that RD is associated with a visual-processing deficit, and so on. This confusion can be remedied in two ways, however: through attention to methodological issues in interpreting the various research findings, and by means of a broad, integrative model of RD across the age and grade span. Such a model would also have to show how reading disability relates to the process of reading acquisition in normally achieving children. In the absence of this kind of broad, integrative model, the meaning of specific deficits, and their educational implications, would be unclear.

This book is an attempt to bridge the chasm between research and practice in the field of reading disability. We hope to encourage practitioners to apply important scientific findings in educational practice, but also to encourage cognitive researchers who are not already doing so to become involved in educational applications of their work. In addition, we describe a theoretical model of reading disability that, in our opinion, integrates the most reliable research findings on reading disability and, at the same time, provides an educationally useful framework for viewing the problems of poor readers who typically are categorized as having RD. However, before discussing the model itself, we must provide some important background information. Two questions present themselves in this regard: First, what is the historical context behind contemporary problems in the LD field? Second, exactly how are children with RD commonly defined and identified? These issues form the subject matter of the next two chapters.

Notes

1. We use the term *LD field* to include research on, identification of, and treatment of reading disability, because RD is included under the broader category of LD, and because the term *LD* is more common in schools than *RD*. As most children with LD are identified based on reading problems, the two terms are frequently synonymous in educational practice.

References

Adams, M. J. (1990). *Beginning to read: Thinking and learning about print.* Cambridge, MA: MIT Press.

Allington, R., & Li, S. (1990). *Teacher beliefs about children who find learning to read difficult.* Paper presented at the National Reading Conference, Miami, FL.

Anderson, R., Hiebert, E., Scott, J., & Wilkinson, I. (1985). *Becoming a nation of readers: The report of the Commission on Reading.* Champaign, IL: Center for the Study of Reading.

Bateman, B., & Haring, N. (1977). *Teaching the learning-disabled child.* Englewood Cliffs, NJ: Prentice-Hall.

Chinn, C. A., Waggoner, M. A., Anderson, R. C., Schommer, M. & Wilkinson, I. A. G. (1993). Situated actions during reading lessons: A microanalysis of oral reading error episodes. *American Educational Research Journal, 30,* 361–392.

Christensen, C. A. (1992). Discrepancy definitions of reading disability: Has the quest led us astray? A response to Stanovich. *Reading Research Quarterly, 27,* 276–278.

Coles, G. S. (1987). *The learning mystique: A critical look at "learning disabilities."* New York: Pantheon Books.

Danielson, L. C., & Bellamy, G. T. (1989). State variation in placement of children with handicaps in segregated environments. *Exceptional Children, 55,* 448–455.

Diener, C., & Dweck, C. (1978). An analysis of learned helplessness: Continuous changes in performance, strategy, and achievement cognitions following failure. *Journal of Personality and Social Psychology, 35,* 451–462.

Ehri, L. C. (1991). Learning to read and spell words. In L. Rieben & C. A. Perfetti (Eds.), *Learning to read: Basic research and its implications* (pp. 57–73). Hillsdale, NJ: Lawrence Erlbaum Associates.

————. (1992). Reconceptualizing the development of sight word reading and its relationship to recoding. In P. B. Gough, L. C. Ehri, & R. Treiman (Eds.), *Reading acquisition* (pp. 107–143). Hillsdale, NJ: Lawrence Erlbaum Associates.

Ellis, A. W. (1985). The cognitive neuropsychology of developmental (and acquired) dyslexia: A critical survey. *Cognitive Neuropsychology, 2,* 169–205.

Felton, R. H. (1993). Effects of instruction on the decoding skills of children with phonological-processing problems. *Journal of Learning Disabilities, 26,* 583–589.

Fletcher, J. M., Shaywitz, S. E., Shankweiler, D. P., Katz, L., Liberman, I. Y., Stuebing, K. K., Francis, D. J., Fowler, A. E., & Shaywitz, B. A. (1994). Cognitive profiles of reading disability: Comparisons of discrepancy and low achievement definitions. *Journal of Educational Psychology, 86,* 6–23.

Gillingham, A., & Stillman, B. (1970). *Remedial training for children with specific disability in reading, spelling, and penmanship.* Cambridge, MA: Educator's Publishing Service.

Gough, P. B., & Juel, C. (1991). The first stages of word recognition. In L. Rieben & C. A. Perfetti (Eds.), *Learning to read: Basic research and its implications* (pp. 47–56). Hillsdale, NJ: Lawrence Erlbaum Associates.

Gough, P. B., & Tunmer, W. E. (1986). Decoding, reading, and reading disability. *Remedial and Special Education, 7,* 6–10.

Hammill, D. D. (1993). A brief look at the learning disabilities movement in the United States. *Journal of Learning Disabilities, 26,* 295–310.

Hammill, D. D., Leigh, J. E., McNutt, G., & Larsen, S. C. (1981). A new definition of learning disabilities. *Learning Disability Quarterly, 4,* 336–342.

Heller, K. A., Holtzman, W. H., & Messick, S. (1982). *Placing children in special education: A strategy for equity.* Washington, DC: National Academy Press.

Hiebert, E. H., Colt, J. M., Catto, S. L., & Gury, E. C. (1992). Reading and writing of first-grade students in a restructured Chapter 1 program. *American Educational Research Journal, 29,* 545–572.

Hilliard, A. G. (1992). The pitfalls and promises of special education practice. *Exceptional Children, 59,* 168–172.

Kirk, S. A., & Elkins, J. (1975). Characteristics of children enrolled in the child service demonstration centers. *Journal of Learning Disabilities, 8,* 630–637.

Liberman, I. Y. (1989). Phonology and beginning reading revisited. In C. von Euler (Ed.), *Wenner-Gren international symposium series: Brain and reading* (pp. 207–220). Hampshire, England: Macmillan.

Lipson, M. Y., & Wixson, K. K. (1991). *Assessment and instruction of reading disability: An interactive approach.* New York: HarperCollins.

Mann, V. A., & Liberman, I. Y. (1984). Phonological awareness and verbal short-term memory. *Journal of Learning Disabilities, 17,* 592–599.

McGill-Franzen, A. (1994). Compensatory and special education: Is there accountability for learning and belief in children's potential? In E. H. Hiebert & B. M. Taylor (Eds.), *Getting reading right from the start: Effective early literacy interventions* (pp. 13–35). Boston, MA: Allyn and Bacon.

McGill-Franzen, A., & James, I. (1990). *Teacher beliefs about remedial and learning disabled readers.* Paper presented at the National Reading Conference, Miami, FL.

Moats, L. C., & Lyon, G. R. (1993). Learning disabilities in the United States: Advocacy, science, and the future of the field. *Journal of Learning Disabilities, 26,* 282–294.

Norman, C. A., & Zigmond, N. (1980). Characteristics of children labeled and served as learning disabled in school systems affiliated with child service demonstration centers. *Journal of Learning Disabilities, 13,* 542–547.

Olson, R. K., Rack, J. P., Conners, F. A., DeFries, J. C., & Fulker, D. W. (1991). Genetic etiology of individual differences in reading disability. In L. V. Feagans, E. J. Short, & L. J. Meltzer (Eds.), *Subtypes of learning disabilities: Theoretical perspectives and research* (pp. 113–135). Hillsdale, NJ: Lawrence Erlbaum Associates.

Orton, S. T. (1937). *Reading, writing, and speech problems in children.* New York: W. W. Norton.

Pennington, B. F., Gilger, J. W., Pauls, D., Smith, S. A., Smith, S. D., & DeFries, J. C. (1991). Evidence for major gene transmission of developmental dyslexia. *Journal of the American Medical Association, 266,* 1527–1534.

Rapala, M. M., & Brady, S. (1990). Reading ability and short-term memory: The role of phonological processing. *Reading and Writing: An Interdisciplinary Journal, 2,* 1–25.

Rutter, M., & Yule, W. (1975). The concept of specific reading retardation. *Journal of Child Psychology and Psychiatry, 16,* 181–197.

Sarason, S. B. (1990). *The predictable failure of educational reform.* San Francisco, CA: Jossey-Bass.

Schrag, P., & Divoky, D. (1975). *The myth of the hyperactive child.* New York: Pantheon.

Senf, G. M. (1986). LD research in sociological and scientific perspective. In J. K. Torgesen & B. Y. L. Wong (Eds.), *Psychological and educational perspectives on learning disabilities* (pp. 27–53). San Diego, CA: Academic Press.

Shankweiler, D., & Crain, S. (1986). Language mechanisms and reading disorder: A modular approach. *Cognition, 24,* 139–168.

Shankweiler, D., Crain, S., Brady, S., & Macaruso, P. (1992). Identifying the causes of reading disability. In P. B. Gough, L. C. Ehri, & R. Treiman (Eds.), *Reading acquisition* (pp. 275–305). Hillsdale, NJ: Lawrence Erlbaum Associates.

Shaywitz, S. E., Escobar, M. D., Shaywitz, B. A., Fletcher, J. M., & Makuch, R. (1992). Evidence that dyslexia may represent the lower tail of a normal distribution of reading ability. *New England Journal of Medicine, 326,* 145–150.

Shaywitz, S. E., Shaywitz, B. A., Fletcher, J. M., & Escobar, M. D. (1990). Prevalence of reading disability in boys and girls: Results of the Connecticut Longitudinal Study. *Journal of the American Medical Association, 264,* 998–1002.

Siegel, L. S. (1988). Evidence that IQ scores are irrelevant to the definition and analysis of reading disability. *Canadian Journal of Psychology, 42,* 201–215.

———. (1989). IQ is irrelevant to the definition of learning disabilities. *Journal of Learning Disabilities, 22,* 469–478.

Skrtic, T. M. (1991). The special education paradox: Equity as the way to excellence. *Harvard Educational Review, 61,* 148–206.

Smith, C. R. (1991). *Learning disabilities: The interaction of learner, task, and setting.* Needham Heights, MA: Allyn and Bacon.

Snow, C. E., Barnes, W. S., Chandler, J., Goodman, J. F., & Hemphill, L. (1991). *Unfulfilled expectations: Home and school influences on literacy.* Cambridge, MA: Harvard University Press.

Stanovich, K. E. (1986). Matthew effects in reading: Some consequences of individual differences in the acquisition of literacy. *Reading Research Quarterly, 21,* 360–406.

———. (1989). Learning disabilities in broader context. *Journal of Learning Disabilities, 22,* 287–297.

———. (1990). Explaining the differences between the dyslexic and the garden-variety poor reader: The phonological-core variable-difference model. In J. K. Torgesen (Ed.), *Cognitive and behavioral characteristics of children with learning disabilities* (pp. 7–40). Austin, TX: Pro-Ed.

Stanovich, K. E., & Siegel, L. S. (1994). Phenotypic performance profile of children with reading disabilities: A regression-based test of the phonological-core variable-difference model. *Journal of Educational Psychology, 86,* 24–53.

Torgesen, J. K. (1990). Studies of children with learning disabilities who perform poorly on memory span tasks. In J. K. Torgesen (Ed.), *Cognitive and behavioral characteristics of children with learning disabilities* (pp. 41–57). Austin, TX: Pro-Ed.

———. (1991). Learning disabilities: Historical and conceptual issues. In B. Y. L. Wong (Ed.), *Learning about learning disabilities* (pp. 3–37). San Diego, CA: Academic Press.

Vellutino, F. R. (1979). *Dyslexia: Theory and research.* Cambridge, MA: MIT Press.

Vellutino, F. R., & Scanlon, D. M. (1987). Phonological coding, phonological awareness, and reading ability: Evidence from a longitudinal and experimental study. *Merrill-Palmer Quarterly, 33,* 321–363.

Vellutino, F. R., Steger, J. A., Moyer, B. M., Harding, S. C., & Niles, C. J. (1977). Has the perceptual deficit hypothesis led us astray? *Journal of Learning Disabilities, 10,* 54–64.

Will, M. (1986). Educating children with learning problems: A shared responsibility. *Exceptional Children, 52,* 411–415.

Wong, B. Y. L. (1991). The relevance of metacognition to learning disabilities. In B. Y. L. Wong (Ed.), *Learning about learning disabilities* (pp. 231–258). San Diego, CA: Academic Press.

Ysseldyke, J. E., & Algozzine, B. (1983). LD or not LD: That's not the question! *Journal of Learning Disabilities, 16,* 29–31.

2 The History of LD: Variations on a Theme

I T IS OFTEN SAID that knowledge about the past is indispensable for understanding the present. If this statement is true, then nowhere is the study of history more indispensable than in the field of learning disabilities, where Santayana's warning that "those who do not remember the past are condemned to repeat it" ought to receive a little more attention. The history of the LD field is a series of variations on a single theme—namely, the intrinsic view that the problems of children with learning disabilities, including reading disability, are caused exclusively by a defect within the children themselves. None of these variations on the intrinsic perspective has provided a real solution to the problems of children with RD.

Furthermore, although the extrinsic perspective on LD has long coexisted with the intrinsic perspective, it too has failed to provide a real solution to LD. An examination of the history of LD further buttresses the claim of the previous chapter, that both the intrinsic and extrinsic perspectives are fundamentally flawed, and that a third perspective is needed. In addition, an examination of history helps to illuminate some of the many contemporary problems of the LD field, such as the vague and inconsistent nature of current school-identification procedures.

First, let us highlight a distinction made by others who have written about the history of LD (e.g., Torgesen, 1991)—specifically, that between LD as a field of educational practice and LD as a field of scientific research. Our discussion in this chapter emphasizes the history of LD as a field of educational practice. However, we also discuss clinical research that was conducted prior to the formal establishment of the LD field in the 1960s as well as the more recent influence of information-processing research from cognitive psychology on the LD field. As we argued in the previous chapter, much of the latter research is just beginning to influence educational practice. Indeed, the history of LD, as a field of educational practice, is more the story of a powerful social and political movement than one about the triumph of scientific progress.

Our discussion of history will focus primarily on the LD movement in the United States. LD and RD are far from exclusively American concepts; in fact, a great many contemporary studies of RD have been performed in other countries (J. Lerner, 1993; Torgesen, 1991). However, little literature is available regarding actual LD or RD programs and educational policies in other nations (Moats & Lyon, 1993). Furthermore, some countries, such as Japan, clearly have not developed a concept analogous to the American concept of reading disability, although reading failure certainly exists in these countries (Stevenson et al., 1982). Thus, whereas reading problems appear to be culturally universal, explaining those problems with the concept of RD is not.

We organize our discussion of history in terms of the three major perspectives discussed in Chapter 1: the intrinsic perspective, the extrinsic perspective, and the interactive perspective. Because the intrinsic perspective has always characterized most practitioners within the LD field itself, and because it pertains to the bulk of what is generally regarded as the "history" of LD, most of our chapter is devoted to this perspective. Recall that the intrinsic perspective encompasses a variety of theoretical paradigms or models, all of which share the central belief that LD results from a deficit within the child. Historically, the most important of these paradigms were the medical paradigm, the underlying-abilities paradigm, and the direct-instruction paradigm.

The Intrinsic Perspective in the History of LD

The Medical Paradigm

The medical paradigm is the oldest theoretical view of learning disabilities. In fact, this paradigm existed long before the formal establishment, in the 1960s, of learning disabilities as a field of educational practice. The medical paradigm grew out of clinical work done by physicians and psychologists interested in brain function and in the effects of brain injury on cognitive abilities, in both children and adults.

Medical Antecedents of the LD Field. Nineteenth-century brain research by scientists such as Broca and Wernicke is usually viewed as a foundation for the LD field (e.g., J. Lerner, 1993; Smith, 1991; Torgesen, 1991). These scientists were interested in localizing a variety of human abilities, such as language or spatial abilities, to specific areas of the brain, using clinical and autopsy studies of adults who had suffered strokes and other brain injuries. Their work forms part of a long and continuing line of research in psychology and medicine. It also constitutes a substantial improvement over the then-popular "science" of phrenology, which held that information about brain function could be deduced from the measuring of bumps on a person's head and the shape of a person's skull.

Clinical research more directly relevant to the study of LD and RD began around the turn of the twentieth century and continued into the 1950s. The early researchers frequently cited (e.g., Gearheart & Gearheart, 1989; J. Lerner, 1993; Smith, 1991) as being among the forefathers (and foremothers) of the LD field include W. P. Morgan, James Hinshelwood, Alfred Strauss and his colleagues, Samuel Orton, and Grace Fernald. Nearly all of these early figures were physicians or psychologists; at this time, educators played little or no role in the LD field. Indeed the term *learning disabilities* was not coined until the 1960s (Hammill, 1993)—although *reading disability* was used long before then, by authorities such as Orton and Fernald.

The fact that the early guiding lights of the LD field were physicians and psychologists is important. Particularly at that time, physicians and psychologists tended to be oriented toward intrinsic explanations of poor reading (and of other learning problems) rather than toward extrinsic explanations. Furthermore, there was a natural tendency for physicians, at least, to frame their intrinsic view specifically in biological terms, whereby children with RD were seen as having something akin to an illness or disease. Not surprisingly, many of the labels used by the early authorities for what we would now call "reading disability" or "learning disabilities" have a distinctly medical, if not downright grim, cast: "congenital word-blindness" (Hinshelwood, 1917; Morgan, 1896); "brain-injured" and "cripple-brained" (Strauss, 1943; Strauss & Lehtinen, 1947); and "strephosymbolia" (Orton, 1937). Compared to this older terminology, labels such as "reading disabled" sound almost laudatory.

Because the concept of LD was not widely imported into the public schools until the 1960s, the early authorities worked largely with children in clinical settings or in residential schools. As a group, these youngsters may have represented a somewhat more impaired population than the children typically labeled as LD or RD in the public schools today. Also keep in mind that during this time period, and indeed as late as 1975, American public schools had the right to exclude children who were viewed as unmanageable or incapable of being educated.

Like their nineteenth-century counterparts, these twentieth-century progenitors of the LD field made use of case study and anecdotal evidence, for there was little controlled experimental research involving large groups of children at this time. In addition, authorities such as Hinshelwood and Orton drew many inferences from acquired reading disorders (such as those afflicting adults who had lost the ability to read after a stroke) and developmental reading disorders in children, most of whom had no known brain injury. They reasoned that, if injury to a specific part of the brain caused reading problems in previously unimpaired adult readers, then similar reading problems in children were also caused by brain injury or dysfunction, though perhaps of a more subtle type than that seen in adults.

However, there are numerous problems with this line of thought, not the least of which is its basic lack of logic—a bit like arguing that because brain tumors cause headaches, everyone who experiences a headache has a brain tumor. Moreover, as others have noted (e.g., Smith, 1991), children's developing brains have a great deal more plasticity than do those of adults; thus, brain injury that could have severe consequences in an adult might have a much milder effect or even no effect on a child. Eventually, concern about the lack of concrete evidence of brain injury in most children with developmental reading disorders, coupled with concern about the negative effects of labels such as *brain-injured* (not to mention *cripple-brained*), led the LD field away from brain-injury *terminology*—though not away from the belief in an intrinsic neurological base for LD and RD (Coles, 1987).

The Importance of Orton's Ideas. Of these early authorities, Orton (1928, 1937, 1966), a neurologist, has continued to be especially influential on the subject of reading disability. Orton helped to popularize an idea found in many of the earliest case studies of reading disability (e.g., Hinshelwood, 1917; Morgan, 1896): that RD could occur not just in intellectually normal individuals but even in those who were unusually bright:

> The more rapid learners in this field of education are no brighter on the average than are some of the reading disability cases, and indeed some of our very severe strephosymbolics when measured by all available tests rank high in intelligence. The writer, for example, has studied one boy who was reading almost nothing and spelling less, after three years in school, who passed intelligence tests with a quotient of 145 and gave every evidence in every other field except his reading, spelling and writing of being a "near genius." (Orton, 1937, p. 73)

The still-prevalent idea that reading disability is characterized by frequent letter reversals and inversions of words (e.g., reading *b* for *d* or *was* for *saw*), and by problems with laterality (e.g., establishing handedness), was also popularized by Orton. Indeed, Orton believed that reading disability resulted from a delay in or from a failure of the brain to establish hemispheric dominance for language. Letter reversals, word inversions, and confused or mixed laterality were, in Orton's view, outward symptoms of incomplete hemispheric dominance. One of his terms for reading disability, *strephosymbolia,* means "twisted symbols," a reference to these supposedly distinctive letter reversals and word inversions. (Other early figures in the field, such as Morgan and Hinshelwood—who were ophthalmologists—also noted errors involving letter reversals and word inversions in children with RD, but they emphasized a possible visual basis for RD much more than did Orton.)

Although Orton's theory, at least in its original form, is no longer accepted, it has driven a tremendous amount of research (Vellutino, 1979). Orton's remedial program, developed with Gillingham and Stillman, and generally known as the Orton-Gillingham approach (Gillingham & Stillman, 1970; Orton, 1966), has also been highly influential. Orton and his followers believed that children with RD need a highly structured phonetic approach to reading, combined with multisensory activities (e.g., learning a new letter by looking at it, tracing it, and saying the letter name, all at the same time). Many of the phonetic programs currently in use in the schools are based in part on Orton's program, and the Orton-Gillingham approach itself is still widely used by both remedial-reading specialists and special-education teachers. As we will discuss in subsequent chapters, effective instruction in decoding does appear to be essential for youngsters with RD, although there are other, and for some children better, ways to teach decoding than through a purist version of the Orton-Gillingham approach. Moreover, phonetic instruction and multisensory techniques, though frequently helpful, probably did not work for the reasons that Orton believed they did. Nevertheless, Orton was certainly on the right track in emphasizing the importance of word-decoding skills to children with RD and in eschewing the sight-word approach to teaching reading so common in his day.

Differences and Similarities Among the Early Authorities. Even within the medical paradigm, there were substantial differences among the early authorities, not all of whom believed Orton's theory of reading disability or agreed with his remedial methods. Rather, different authorities developed different terminology, identification procedures, and remedial methods, most of which (except, perhaps, for Orton's) were not well founded theoretically. The general lack of a strong theoretical base in the early years of the LD field had important consequences. In particular, the absence of well-articulated theories of RD made it difficult to accumulate scientific knowledge about reading disability, because scientific observations can be interpreted only with reference to some kind of theory; thus, for example, even when remedial procedures seemed to work, no one knew quite why.

In addition to the medical paradigm for LD and RD they shared, the early authorities had in common at least three basic ideas about RD, ideas that are central to contemporary educational definitions of the concept. First, they shared the notion of a "leftover" group of children who did not fit existing categories of mental retardation, sensory impairment, and so on, and yet who nevertheless had great difficulty in learning to read. This notion still can be seen in the nearly universal (e.g., Frankenberger & Harper, 1987) use of exclusionary criteria in diagnosis of RD, which require that the child's reading difficulties not be primarily attributable to some other disability or to environmental factors. Second, the early authorities believed that the reading achievement of children with RD was well below their actual potential for learning. In time, this idea was operationalized as an IQ-achievement discrepancy. Finally, of course, the early authorities shared the idea that children with reading disability had an intrinsic deficit in learning, one that was not caused by inadequate instruction, inadequate home environment, or lack of educational opportunity. However, the "adequacy" factor received little serious scrutiny by the early authorities, who were inclined to overlook even obvious indications of inept instruction or other possible environmental causes of poor reading. (See Coles, 1987, for a more detailed discussion.)

The Underlying-Abilities Paradigm

We have already noted that concern about the stigma of brain-injury labels, as well as the lack of evidence of brain injury in most youngsters with learning disabilities, gradually turned authorities in LD away from brain-injury terminology. This major paradigm shift was the first in the nascent field of LD, and it was well under way by 1963, the generally accepted date for the formal foundation of LD as a field of educational practice. By the same year, professionals and researchers interested in learning disabilities had begun to abandon the medical paradigm in favor of one positing underlying abilities.

In the underlying-abilities paradigm, a variety of abilities were hypothesized to underlie academic learning. For instance, reading achievement was thought to depend heavily on underlying visual-perceptual, auditory-perceptual, memory, and even motor abilities. Identification of RD and LD included extensive testing of these areas. Moreover, many of the remediation programs associated with this paradigm emphasized not direct instruction in academics, as had most authorities from the medical paradigm, but training of underlying perceptual and memory abilities.

It is important to keep in mind that, like the medical paradigm, the underlying-abilities paradigm had an intrinsic view of learning disabilities, because it ascribed the cause of LD to an intrinsic deficit within the child. However, whereas the medical paradigm saw this deficit as biological in nature (i.e., as the result of brain injury or brain dysfunction), the underlying-abilities paradigm was framed in psychological terms (i.e., in relation to perceptual, language, or memory deficits)—a different level of analysis. Yet the underlying-abilities paradigm was a logical outgrowth of the medical paradigm, in that authorities from the medical paradigm had viewed children with LD and RD as having perceptual and memory problems. For instance, Orton (1937) viewed visual-perceptual and motor confusions as symptomatic of RD, although his remediation program emphasized direct instruction in academics. Strauss and his colleagues (e.g., Strauss & Lehtinen, 1947; Strauss & Werner, 1942), whom many writers (e.g., J. Lerner, 1993; Torgesen, 1991) regard as the most direct progenitors of the LD field, also emphasized the importance of underlying abilities to learning and even made some attempts at training these abilities. Note, however, that the adherents of the medical paradigm saw perceptual, linguistic, and memory problems as symptoms of brain injury or brain dysfunction, whereas the adherents of the underlying-abilities paradigm deemphasized the notion of brain injury and focused on the underlying-abilities deficits themselves as potential causes of poor reading.

In the 1960s, professionals in learning disabilities greatly increased the emphasis on testing and training underlying abilities. However, just as adherents of the medical paradigm differed in their views, so did those who adhered to the underlying-abilities paradigm. For example, some authorities emphasized the importance of visual deficits in LD and RD and developed visual perception tests and training programs (e.g., Frostig & Horne, 1964; Frostig, Lefever, & Whittlesey, 1964). Others emphasized a link between perceptual and motor skills (e.g., Roach & Kephart, 1966). Still others emphasized auditory perception and language, in addition to visual perception and motor skills (e.g., Kirk, McCarthy, & Kirk, 1968). These authorities also varied in the extent to which they included direct instruction in academics along with training in underlying abilities. Nevertheless, throughout the 1960s and well into the 1970s, underlying-abilities testing and training were largely the niche of professionals in LD, whereas direct instruction in reading continued to be primarily the purview of reading specialists.

During the heyday of the underlying-abilities paradigm, and immediately following this period, there were a number of important historical developments involving LD, including the formal foundation of LD as a field of educational practice, the passage of legislation relevant to learning disabilities, and the growth of public-school programs for children with learning disabilities. We consider some of these historical developments next.

The Formal Foundation of the LD Field. As noted, many writers cite 1963 as the year in which the LD field was formally founded (e.g., Gearheart & Gearheart, 1989; Hammill, 1993; Moats & Lyon, 1993; Torgesen, 1991). By this time, the idea that perceptual disturbances were common among youngsters with LD and RD was widely believed, whereas the notion of brain injury as a cause of LD was receiving much less emphasis. The term *perceptually handicapped* was now occasionally being used to describe children with LD or RD. And Samuel Kirk popularized the contemporary term *learning disabilities* when he referred to it in his keynote address at a conference sponsored by the Fund for Perceptually Handicapped Children in 1963. This organization quickly became the Association for Children with Learning Disabilities (ACLD), now the Learning Disabilities Association of America (LDA), one of the many influential organizations and lobbying groups in the LD field (Hammill, 1993; Smith, 1991).

In retrospect, the 1960s was indeed a pivotal decade for the LD field. As an area of educational practice, the field clearly began to "take off" at this point, although little controlled experimental research on learning disabilities had been performed by then. The involvement of educators and public schools in the LD field, which previously had been minimal or nonexistent, increased greatly in the 1960s; funds for educational programs and for research became increasingly available; and research interest in the subject of LD, as indicated by an explosion of journals and books about the topic, began a steep rise that continues to this day. Also in the 1960s, gradually escalating numbers of children began to be identified as LD in the public schools, most on the basis of reading problems (J.

Lerner, 1993; Senf, 1986; Smith, 1991). This number would skyrocket in the 1970s and 1980s, from just under 800,000 in the school year 1976–1977 to over 2,000,000 in the school year 1989–1990 (U.S. Department of Education, 1991).

The Education for All Handicapped Children Act of 1975. The passage of legislation played a key role in the burgeoning level of interest in the LD field that began in the 1960s. Although many federal and state laws affecting the field were passed in the 1960s and early 1970s, by far the most significant piece of legislation was the Education for All Handicapped Children Act of 1975 (P.L. 94-142), now amended as the Individuals with Disabilities Education Act of 1990 (P.L. 101-476). P.L. 94-142 federally mandated that states provide a free and appropriate public education to *all* youngsters, including those with learning disabilities and other special needs. It made federal reimbursement to the states for education contingent on the states' compliance with this mandate (Smith, 1991). Although Moats and Lyon (1993) note that federal funding levels for special education now are much lower than those intended by Congress when P.L. 94-142 was first passed, the law was revolutionary in a number of ways, the most important being that public schools could no longer relieve themselves of the responsibility of educating children with learning or behavior problems. (The public schools could continue to refer children with serious problems to private or residential placements, although they now had to foot the bill for this outside schooling or provide an appropriate placement within the public-school setting.) Other important provisions of P.L. 94-142 include the requirement that special-education services be provided in the least restrictive environment; the requirement that all children receiving special-education services have a written Individualized Education Plan, or IEP; strong protection of parental rights to involvement in educational decision making; and the provision that all testing must be linguistically and culturally unbiased. (Unfortunately, the means of accomplishing this particularly difficult last task are not spelled out in the law.)

Contemporary researchers (e.g., Moats & Lyon, 1993; Stanovich, 1991; Torgesen, 1991) have suggested that many of the current problems of the LD field stem from the fact that the field "got ahead of itself"—that educational practice and popular acceptance of LD escalated before there was an adequate scientific base for the field. Undoubtedly, the passage of legislation such as P.L. 94-142 and the provision of funds for research and for educational services contributed to this escalation (e.g., Senf, 1986). However, in our opinion, neither the passage of legislation nor the existence of funding fully explains the dramatic growth of the LD field. For one thing, in order for the legislation to be passed and the funds to be made available, interest in the concepts of LD and RD already had to exist. So how else to explain the rapidly accelerating growth and popularity of the LD field during the 1960s? We consider this question next.

Reasons for the Rapid Growth of the LD Field. A number of authors (Hammill, 1993; Moats & Lyon, 1993; Smith, 1991) have noted the importance of advocacy groups—that is, parent and professional organizations such as the LDA, which lobby for increased funding of educational services and research on learning disabilities—in driving the LD field. Moats and Lyon (1993) link the LD advocacy movement to an even more basic root—namely, genuine need on the part of a large group of youngsters. In other words, there is a significant number of children who are failing to learn to read in American schools, and, given the nature of the American educational system and its funding practices (e.g., Kozol, 1991), one of the most effective ways for parents to get help for their children is to use the political system to lobby for educational services. Coles (1987) further suggests that it was specifically the educational failure of *middle-class* children, whose failure was viewed as "unexpected," that drove the LD field, inasmuch as the academic failure of poor children was all too readily anticipated.

The LD field's strong historical basis in advocacy helps to explain some of the vagueness in educational definitions of LD and RD (Moats & Lyon, 1993; Stanovich, 1992) and, hence, some of the confusion in contemporary school-identification practices. Advocacy organizations have an incentive to keep definitions as broad and vague as possible, in order to include more affected individuals under those definitions, and thereby amass a larger popular base. Historically, in the LD field, vague definitions that commanded more popular support and gave educators more latitude in providing educational services have always superseded more restrictive scientific definitions of LD and RD.

McGill-Franzen (1994) suggests some other, somewhat less noble reasons for the rapid increase in the number of children classified as LD in the 1970s and 1980s. She notes that as funds for special education were becoming more plentiful, funds for compensatory education programs such as "Chapter 1" were declining, thus giving schools a financial incentive to classify youngsters as learning disabled rather than as remedial readers. She also suggests that the increasing emphasis on large-scale standardized testing to evaluate school districts and the concomitant pressure for high test scores have created an incentive for schools to classify low achievers as LD, because in many schools special-education youngsters are excluded from this kind of testing.

All of these factors—lobbying from advocacy organizations, the existence of a group of children who genuinely need help, and certain practical incentives—do go a long way toward explaining the explosion in the numbers of children classified as LD. Still, we think that they do not tell the whole story. Another crucial factor is the appeal of the concepts of LD and RD themselves.

In the first chapter, we raised a number of concerns about the effects of labeling poor readers as "disabled" and viewing them as having a biologically based deficit. We argued that these concerns are serious, especially given the lack of evidence for a biological cause of most cases of school-labeled learning disabilities. Nevertheless, when considered in historical context, it is clear that labels like *learning-disabled* and *reading-disabled* were vastly preferable to older special-education labels such as *mentally retarded* or *emotionally disturbed*. Moreover, the early shift away from brain-injury terminology in the LD field greatly facilitated public acceptance of the concepts of LD and RD; it is unlikely that either parents or teachers would have shown great enthusiasm for terminology such as *cripple-brained* or *strephosymbolic*. The learning-disabilities terminology relieved schools and parents of any responsibility for children's learning problems, without stigmatizing children as egregiously as older special-education terminology had done. It was as though naming a pattern of behavior somehow explained that pattern.

In addition to the palatability of such terms as *LD* and *RD*, there is the popular conception of RD as the "affliction of geniuses" (Adelman & Adelman, 1987; Coles, 1987; Stanovich, 1991). According to this view, RD not only *can* occur among the highly intelligent but is actually *more common* in intellectually brilliant individuals. Stanovich (1991) notes that the typical "media dyslexic" is a very bright rather than an intellectually average youngster. And prominent historical figures, such as Einstein and Edison, have occasionally been offered as examples of the supposed connection between RD and high intelligence. (Recently, some of these prominent figures have been reclassified in the popular press as suffering from yet another overdiagnosed and conceptually problematic condition, attention-deficit hyperactivity disorder, or ADHD. See Wallis, 1994, for some examples of ADHD as the "affliction of geniuses," and Pellegrini & Horvat, 1995, for a discussion of flaws in the ADHD construct.)

Of course, the diagnosis of RD is complicated enough among the living; so posthumous diagnosis is a risky endeavor at best, and the conclusions are often suspect, as Coles (1987) and others have shown. Although children with reading disability can be highly intelligent, there is no evidence to support the idea that RD disproportionately afflicts the intellectually brilliant. But the popular image of the extremely bright youngster with RD, combined with the palatability of the RD and LD labels compared to other labels under which children receive educational services in the schools, have made the LD and RD categories appealing to many people.

Evidence Against the Underlying-Abilities Paradigm. In the early 1970s, there began a thin trickle, and soon an avalanche, of research evidence against the underlying-abilities paradigm, at least as it was then being implemented in the schools (e.g., Coles, 1978; Hammill, 1972; Hammill & Larsen, 1974; Newcomer & Hammill, 1975; Vellutino, 1979; Vellutino, Steger, Moyer, Harding, & Niles, 1977). These experiments and literature reviews were among the first large-scale, controlled studies of learning-disabilities practice, and their conclusions were overwhelmingly negative. The research suggested, among other things, that many of the underlying-abilities tests then in use lacked reliability and validity; thus, a youngster might have a visual-perceptual "problem" today, but not tomorrow. In addition, many of the tests did not correlate with reading skill. For instance, a child might do poorly on an underlying-abilities test but still be a good reader, or do well on an underlying-abilities test but still have reading problems. Further, some of the abilities tapped—none too adequately—by the tests did not respond to training, at least not to the kinds of training efforts then employed in the schools. For example, attempts to train memory by having children practice memorizing lists of words or digits did not appear to have the intended effect. Most damaging of all, but not surprising given the nature of the preceding evidence, efforts at training underlying abilities usually did not result in improvements in reading achievement.

Note that the nature of this evidence leaves in question the legitimacy of the underlying-abilities paradigm itself. For instance, it might have been flaws in the tests, or in the training programs, that resulted in the apparent failure of the model. Hence the basic idea behind the underlying-abilities paradigm—that important cognitive abilities underlie academic performance, and that these abilities can and should be trained—might still have some validity. What is beyond dispute from the research evidence of the 1970s is that the *implementation* of the underlying-abilities model then popular in the schools did not work. In reaction to the avalanche of research evidence against the underlying-abilities paradigm, professionals in the LD field gradually turned to a third paradigm, the direct instruction paradigm. That is, rather than emphasizing the testing of underlying abilities such as visual perception in poor readers, and rather than training underlying abilities, they assessed specific reading skills such as letter-sound knowledge and word recognition, and taught these skills directly in their remediation programs.

However, this second paradigm shift, from underlying abilities to direct instruction, was not accomplished without a great deal of metaphorical bloodshed. Hammill (1993) has aptly dubbed this paradigm shift the "process wars." Advocates of the old underlying-abilities (i.e., "process") tests and teaching programs did not quietly lie down to be buried in the avalanche of opposing research evidence. As a first-year teacher in an elementary LD classroom in 1977, one of the coauthors can clearly recall both the contentious atmosphere of the time and the problems associated with the underlying-abilities paradigm. A good example of the latter is provided by one particular youngster.

The presence of this boy in the class for students with LD was puzzling. Keith (a pseudonym) did not appear to have difficulties in any academic area, and he did not have a history of academic problems. Unlike many of the children in the class, he had not even been a behavior problem in the regular classroom. It turned out that Keith had been diagnosed as LD on the basis of poor performance on the Purdue Perceptual-Motor Survey (Roach & Kephart, 1966), specifically one particular subtest involving "crossing the midline." In this subtest, children have to draw a line from left to right, thus crossing the midlines of their bodies with their arms. Evidently Keith had failed to perform this test properly and was therefore diagnosed as having a "midline problem." No one could explain how Keith's "midline problem" related to his academic performance—which, in any case, was good—or what was supposed to be done about it. It made little sense that Keith, who did not seem to need extra help, was in the class, whereas other children, who were failing miserably in the regular classroom, could not "qualify" for the class because they were doing too well on underlying-abilities tests! Yet most teachers, administrators, and even Keith's parents seemed reluctant to question the authoritative-sounding nature of Keith's diagnosis. Furthermore, a few people—those with a particularly strong underlying-abilities orientation—were quite upset by the coauthor's tentative suggestions that there might be something just a bit spurious about Keith's "midline problem."

The Direct-Instruction Paradigm

Task Analysis and Precision Teaching. In the 1970s, the direct-instruction paradigm was heavily oriented toward task analysis and precision teaching (e.g., Bateman, 1971; Bateman & Haring, 1977; Engelmann & Bruner, 1974, 1975), or what Hammill (1993) has called an "atomistic" approach. These instructional philosophies were strongly influenced by behaviorism in psychology. They emphasized the importance of writing instructional objectives in behavioral terms, the use of behavioral techniques in classroom management, and the teaching of reading by breaking down various reading tasks, such as decoding, into a series of small, specific steps:

> Task analysis is the procedure of determining all of the subskills which lead to performance of instructional objectives. When the task analysis is complete, a checklist of test items corresponding to all the subskills can be used to determine where to begin instruction and children can be grouped according to the skills they need to learn. The task analysis approach to curriculum, diagnosing instructional needs, grouping children, and sequencing instruction offers great promise to classroom teachers. (Bateman, 1971, p. 48)

Bateman's description of precision teaching has an even more behavioristic flavor. Keep in mind that when Bateman uses the term *behavior*, she refers to academic performance as well as to conduct:

1. Pinpoint the behavior to be changed, so it is a countable movement cycle.
2. Record the *rate* (per minute) at which the behavior is occurring. Time during which the movement cycle is counted may vary from all day to a minute or less. Rate is recorded on six-cycle paper.
3. Change something (the events which follow the behavior or the stimuli preceding it).
4. Evaluate the effect of the change on the behavior chart and, if necessary, try a different change.

One of the distinguishing features of precision teaching is the use of six-cycle, logarithmic charts on which behavior rates of zero to 1,000 per minute can be recorded. This encompasses the full range of human behaviors. (Bateman, 1971, p. 84)

In general, the direct-instruction approaches of the 1970s were remarkable for their utter lack of attention to mental processes—to what was transpiring in children's heads. For instance, in Bateman's description of precision teaching, try substituting the word *rat* or *pigeon* for the word *human;* the description reads just as well. The survivors of the "process wars" seem to have emerged from battle with a complete distrust of mental-abilities models, and behaviorism held a strong appeal for them, at least for a while.

It is important to note, however, that by adopting a direct-instruction paradigm, professionals in the LD field did not repudiate a belief in the intrinsic nature of learning disabilities. For instance, Hammill and his colleagues (e.g., Hammill, 1972, 1993; Hammill & Larsen, 1974; Newcomer & Hammill, 1975), who were among the most vocal critics of the underlying-abilities paradigm and whose work was instrumental in the paradigm shift to direct instruction, continued to believe in the intrinsic biological nature of LD and RD. They simply argued that direct instruction in academics was the most efficient way to remediate the learning problems of these youngsters.

Of course, there were versions of the direct-instruction paradigm that did not involve task analysis or precision teaching. For instance, some professionals in LD made use of remedial programs that had been developed by authorities from the medical paradigm, such as the Orton-Gillingham approach, without being aware of or being converted to other theoretical views of the medical paradigm, such as Orton's view that RD was caused by incomplete hemispheric dominance for language. In the 1980s, the LD field increasingly turned away from strongly task-analytic versions of direct instruction, in favor of other versions, such as those that Hammill (1993) has termed "holistic" (e.g., in reading, a whole-language approach). A direct-instruction paradigm continues to be the dominant paradigm among practitioners in the LD field. The adoption of this paradigm was a logical response to the outpouring of negative research evidence on the underlying-abilities paradigm, and direct instruction is certainly a more effective way to address the academic problems of youngsters with LD and RD than was the underlying-abilities training of the 1960s. Nevertheless, as we will discuss in the concluding section of this chapter, the adoption of the direct-instruction paradigm has created another kind of problem for the LD field.

Remnants of Older Paradigms. Although direct instruction is currently the favored paradigm among LD practitioners, remnants of the older medical and underlying-abilities paradigms do exist. These remnants include the continued use of underlying-abilities tests (both the older ones and some newer ones), along with more academic kinds of tests, in diagnosis of RD and LD. Current school-identification guidelines often require, or are interpreted as requiring, the use of underlying-abilities tests. Professionals in fields other than LD also espouse the older paradigms. For instance, some optometrists continue to use visual-training programs to improve reading, although these programs have long been criticized by many organizations, including the American Academy of Ophthalmology

(1981), on the grounds that such training is ineffective (as well as costly). Finally, some contemporary researchers in LD (e.g., Galaburda, 1986) clearly espouse a medical paradigm for reading disability and other learning disabilities.

The Rise of Information-Processing Models of Cognition and Reading

While the LD field waged the "process wars" in the 1970s, the field of psychology saw the rise of information-processing models of cognition and reading (e.g., LaBerge & Samuels, 1974; Newell & Simon, 1972; Sternberg, 1977), which liken human thinking to the functioning of a computer. Information-processing models of cognition are similar to the old underlying-abilities paradigm in that they emphasize the importance of underlying abilities—or, in this case, underlying processes—to academic learning.

In the 1980s, the information-processing approach greatly influenced researchers interested in reading disability. We argued in Chapter 1 that most of these researchers have an intrinsic view of reading disability, inasmuch as they focus on deficits within the child as the cause of RD. However, as we also discussed at the end of that chapter, this newer research in cognitive psychology and reading has had a relatively limited impact on educational practice in the LD field. We suggested several reasons for this limited impact, including the esoteric language of the research and its multidisciplinary nature. Against the historical background, we can now suggest another possible reason for the failure of cognitive research to be translated into educational practice: Some practitioners in LD tend to be skeptical of underlying-abilities models, whether old or new—at least partly as a consequence of unhappy experiences with them.

There are certainly a number of lessons to be learned from the practitioners' experiences with the underlying-abilities paradigm. First, any cognitive model must be well articulated theoretically and must have a strong empirical research base. Some researchers (e.g., Torgesen, 1991; Wong, 1986) have argued that the cognitive models of the 1980s and 1990s are doing a much better job meeting these theoretical and empirical requirements than did the old underlying-abilities paradigm of the 1960s.

A second lesson to be learned from the past involves the need for specific kinds of research findings in order for the cognitive models to be educationally useful. For example, the research must document the reliability and validity of tests of hypothetical cognitive processes; the tests themselves must be usable in educational settings; and the tests must correlate significantly with academic achievement. Furthermore, if the intent is to use the tests to diagnose processes to be trained, rather than solely for predictive purposes (e.g., to screen kindergarten children for potential reading problems), the research must show that the processes are indeed trainable, and that training them will improve academic ability to a greater extent than with direct instruction in academics alone. In other words, the processes have to be the right ones; unlike ports in a storm, when it comes to teaching, not just any process will do. We believe that some cognitive processes identified by contemporary researchers, such as phonological awareness, do meet the requirements outlined here, as will be discussed further in subsequent chapters.

Finally, the newer information-processing models of cognition have some serious flaws, the most obvious of which relates to the fact that human beings are not computers (Sternberg, 1988). The analogies that can be drawn between human thinking and the functioning of computers are limited, because human beings are affected by a host of variables, such as emotions, past experiences, and interaction with the environment, that do not affect computers. After all, computers do not experience Matthew effects or have personality clashes with their teachers. Thus, the central flaw in information-processing models of reading disability is the same malady that afflicts other versions of the intrinsic perspective: an overemphasis on children's intrinsic deficits in isolation.

Unlike computerized information processing, the information-processing characteristics of children with RD must be examined in social, historical, and educational contexts. In our view, information-processing research *does* provide vital insights into RD. However, it is necessary to look beyond this body of work as well in order to understand reading disability fully.

The Extrinsic Perspective in the History of LD

Thus far we have focused on the intrinsic perspective in the history of LD, because this perspective has always characterized the LD field itself. The intrinsic perspective, in its three major paradigms—medical, underlying abilities, and direct instruction—comprises most of what is usually regarded as the "history" of the LD field, as told, for example, by textbooks on learning disabilities (e.g., Gearheart & Gearheart, 1989; J. Lerner, 1993; Smith, 1991). However, it is important to realize that the extrinsic perspective on learning disabilities also has a long history.

Before the formal inception of learning disabilities as a field of educational practice in the 1960s, many professionals in education were doubtful about the medical paradigm of reading disorders and other learning problems. For example, both Coles (1987) and Torgesen (1991) note that in the 1940s and 1950s, reading specialists and educators in the public schools (who had not yet been converted to the LD point of view) did not subscribe to intrinsic brain dysfunction theories of reading failure such as Orton's. Rather, they attributed most reading failure to environmental, instructional, or motivational causes. Indeed, well after the foundation of the LD field had been laid in the 1960s, reading authorities remained somewhat skeptical of the intrinsic view of reading disability. Consider the following statement from a text on the diagnosis and remediation of reading difficulties by Bond, Tinker, and Wasson (1979):

In general, the writers believe that most disability cases are created and are not inherent. Reading disabilities are sometimes the result of unrecognized, predisposing conditions within the child, but for the most part, they are caused by elements of the child's environment at home, at play, and in school. Without appropriate guidance or without proper instruction given at the right time, the child will fail to acquire the skills needed to develop normal reading ability. (p. 14)

Many critiques of the LD field emerged in the 1970s. Some, though certainly not all, of these critiques came from an extrinsic perspective. They took the position that insufficient attention had been accorded to possible environmental determinants of reading failure, including poor or inappropriate instruction. For instance, Divoky (1974) and Schrag and Divoky (1975) suggested that schools and society, not neurological dysfunction, were to blame for learning "disabilities." And Coles (1978) not only criticized both the medical and underlying-abilities paradigms of LD but also suggested that the problems of youngsters with LD were the result of social and instructional factors.

Bateman and Haring (1977) maintained that most school-labeled youngsters with learning disabilities were better conceptualized as having "instructional disabilities." In their view, these children were more handicapped by instructional practices—such as sight-word methods of reading instruction and lack of effective decoding instruction—than by intrinsic neurological dysfunction. Bateman and Haring did not deny the existence of some "real" cases of learning disabilities, but they suggested that these cases constituted only a fraction of children actually labeled as having LD:

Many children who are labeled "learning disabled" are in truth instructionally disabled. That is, they are children who have no neurological disorder at all, but who have had a series of unfortunate, usually inadvertent, experiences in learning preacademic and academic tasks. . . . On the other hand, although a child may have no clinically observable signs of neurological disorders, he or she certainly may have very subtle learning disabilities that cannot be readily accounted for by poor instruction. These learning problems seem to persist in a very small number of children, even though their curriculum has been individualized and they have received systematic instruction. (Bateman & Haring, 1977, p. 4)

Bateman and Haring suggest that even these rare "real" cases of LD respond to appropriate instruction, and that practitioners in LD should therefore focus on making instructional modifications for children with learning problems, rather than on searching for neurological or perceptual disorders.

Researchers with an extrinsic perspective played a role in converting LD professionals to a direct-instruction paradigm during the "process wars." It was logical for these researchers to espouse such a paradigm because the extrinsic perspective emphasized the role of instructional factors in achievement. However, although the extrinsic perspective helped to convert LD professionals to a direct-instruction paradigm, it did not succeed in changing the more fundamental belief of those within the LD field that LD and RD were due to an intrinsic deficit, perhaps because this belief was foundational to the field (Torgesen, 1991).

Criticism of the LD field is as old as the field itself. More contemporary criticism, such as that of Christensen (1992) and Coles (1987), has not sprung from sudden new insights but, rather, is essentially what critics of the field have been saying for decades. As an area of educational practice, the LD field "took off" not for the lack of such criticism but in spite of it—a takeoff that, as we have seen, was fueled much more by social and political factors than by scientific advances. Furthermore, these repeated critiques of the LD field seem to have had little success in stemming the growth of the field, and even less success in altering its intrinsic perspective.

The Interactive Perspective in the History of LD

The interactive perspective emphasizes the way that characteristics within the child interact with the surrounding environment to produce a particular outcome in learning. This perspective views the child in context, taking into account not only the way the environment shapes children but also the way children shape their environment. In Chapter 1, we argued that the interactive perspective holds the most promise for educational practitioners working with children with LD.

The existing literature certainly contains examples of interactive theories of poor reading (e.g., Stanovich, 1986). Even outside the domain of reading, there are numerous examples of interactive views of human development and learning (e.g., R. Lerner, 1978; Plomin, 1989; Thomas & Chess, 1977). Unfortunately, however, most of these interactive views seem thus far to have had little impact on educational practice in the LD field—again, because those in the field always have been strongly inclined toward an intrinsic view of learning disabilities.

Nevertheless, one example of a somewhat interactive view from within the LD field itself is the modality-method interaction (MMI) approach. This approach holds that children learn best if the method of instruction is matched to each individual's putatively preferred modality (e.g., visual, auditory, or kinesthetic). For example, a child who is assessed as a "visual" learner based on visual-perceptual and auditory-perceptual testing would be said to need a sight-word approach to reading, whereas for an "auditory" learner a phonetic approach would be prescribed. A modern incarnation of MMI can be found in the "reading styles" approach of authors such as Carbo, Dunn, and Dunn (1986) and Dunn (1988).

However, historically in the LD field, many versions of the MMI approach did not view children's learning problems as the result of an interaction between the children's intrinsic characteristics and instructional approaches (as in a truly interactive view); instead, they focused on selection of the appropriate instructional method as a way to *compensate* for children's intrinsic deficits. In other words, the emphasis was still primarily on children's intrinsic problems; so this was the same old intrinsic perspective again, dressed up in new clothes. For instance, Johnson and Myklebust (1967), who present an early example of the MMI approach, categorized children with reading disability as either "visual dyslexics" or "auditory dyslexics," and recommended remedial procedures matched to the child's "stronger" (as opposed to "weak" or "deficient") modality.

A great deal of evidence has been mounted against the old modality-method interaction approach (Arter & Jenkins, 1977; Tarver & Dawson, 1978) as well as against its more contemporary equivalents (Snider, 1992; Stahl, 1988). Indeed, researchers have suggested a number of possible reasons for the failure of MMI, including the unreliability of tests of modality preference and inappropriate matching procedures. At least with regard to reading, it is likely that the MMI approach was misconceived from the start, in that modality preference was the wrong characteristic to select for making instructional decisions. We base our argument against the MMI approach in the area of reading on two major lines of evidence, both of which we will describe in more detail in Chapters 4 and 5. Here, we briefly summarize the argument.

First, individual differences in linguistic, especially in phonological (i.e., "auditory"), processing seem to account for much more of the variance in reading achievement than do individual differences in visual processing. Thus, with reliable tests of modality preference, it is not likely that one would find many youngsters whose reading problems were truly associated with "visual dyslexia" or, conversely, many youngsters whose reading success was specifically related to a strong visual modality, regardless of reading approach. A second and related point is that research on typical reading acquisition shows that reading is built on a foundation of oral language competence—in other words, not just on phonology but also on vocabulary, grammar, and so on. The idea that reading can be taught exclusively or even primarily through the visual modality, without regard to these foundational linguistic skills, is not consistent with what is known about the process of reading development.

A frequent example offered to show the folly of the idea that reading can be taught "visually" involves the plight of those profoundly deaf from birth. If it were really possible to learn to read in a purely visual manner, then profoundly deaf individuals should have little difficulty learning how to read through a "visual," or sight-word, approach. In fact, however, most profoundly deaf people, who have great difficulty acquiring oral language competence, have similarly great difficulty learning how to read; when these individuals do succeed in reading, their success appears to be related to their ability to develop linguistic knowledge in spite of their deafness, not to the adoption of a "visual" approach to reading (Hanson, 1989).

The Lessons of History

Some people like Perlman's rendition of a classical violin piece, whereas others prefer Menuhin's; some people enjoy the contemporary reggae rendition of an old Elvis Presley hit, whereas others like Elvis's version better. Still, in either case, the music itself remains the same. If the music isn't good, it probably won't matter much who is doing the playing.

Similarly, the history of the LD field is a series of different renditions of the same music—namely, the intrinsic "tune" that says the problems of children with LD can be attributed to a defect within the children themselves. None of these different renditions—medical, underlying abilities, or direct instruction—has been successful in finding the source of most of these children's learning problems. Rather, old paradigms are abandoned and new ones adopted, but the new ones have the same fundamental flaw as the old—an exclusive focus on deficits within the child. Moreover, the extrinsic viewpoint on LD, which has been around nearly as long as the intrinsic viewpoint, has not proved particularly effective, either in eliminating children's learning problems or in changing the LD field. If decades of debate between the intrinsic and extrinsic viewpoints have done little to solve the learning problems of children classified as having LD, or to alter the LD field itself, it seems unlikely that more of the same will be helpful in the future.

As a field of educational practice, the LD field has been driven more by social, educational, and political factors than by scientific progress, a point that has frequently, and accurately, been made by those with an extrinsic perspective. As long as there are individual differences in learning among children, as long as children need to be labeled to receive intensive educational services, and as long as the "LD" label is the most appealing one available, the LD field will be popular. Those with an extrinsic viewpoint have frequently made cogent criticisms about the LD field as well as about society and the nature of schooling. However, at least for educational practitioners, cogent criticisms cannot substitute for a specific plan of action. Those with an extrinsic perspective have been largely unsuccessful in changing or in stemming the growth of the LD field, because they often have given short shrift to the role played by children's intrinsic characteristics in learning; and because, in most cases, they have not offered a feasible or effective way for practitioners to address very real individual differences among children in these characteristics.

The lessons of history also suggest some caveats about an interactive perspective. Obviously, this interactive perspective needs to be framed around theoretically relevant characteristics—not, for example, modality preference or "visual" versus "auditory" instructional approaches. The MMI approach was fatally flawed in that, among other things, it failed to take into account the individual differences most relevant to reading achievement as well as the abilities central to reading acquisition in nondisabled readers. Research on individual differences in reading and on typical reading development must be a base for any educationally effective model of reading disability.

In the 1990s, the LD field, like those of special education and general education, faces a number of important issues. These issues include the regular education initiative, or REI (Will, 1986), which urges a greater sharing of responsibility on the part of regular educators in teaching children with disabilities; a variety of direct-instruction issues, such as whether to adopt more "atomistic" or "holistic" (Hammill, 1993) approaches to instruction; increased cultural diversity in the schools; and new conceptualizations of intelligence, such as those of Robert Sternberg (1985, 1988) and Howard Gardner (1983). However, none of these issues is unique to the LD field. One that *is*—indeed, its most pressing issue—is to provide a theoretical and empirical justification for LD as a separate field of education (Torgesen, 1991).

As we discussed in the previous chapter, research does not support many of the foundational tenets of the field, such as the belief in neurological dysfunction as a cause of LD for most school-labeled children with LD; nor does it support a distinction between children with reading disability and other kinds of poor readers, in terms of either the educational interventions they require or the reading-related cognitive characteristics of these children. The direct-instruction paradigm to which LD professionals turned after the "process wars" is educationally more effective, and more appealing to most practitioners, than are the older paradigms, but it does not provide a rationale for LD as a separate field of education. For example, why should poor readers be labeled as "LD" and go to LD classes, when they could receive similar remedial help from a reading specialist? Indeed, as we have already pointed out, placement decisions of this type often are highly arbitrary in educational practice. Furthermore, as we will elaborate in the next chapter, educational decisions about whether or not to label a particular poor reader as "LD" often have less to do with diagnosing an intrinsic "syndrome" than with other factors, such as finding a way to provide necessary educational services.

We believe that the learning-disabilities field can and should continue as an area of education, but not without undergoing some fundamental changes: In its current configuration, it rests on extremely shaky ground. We will discuss our recommendations for the future of the LD field in the last chapter of this book.

References

Adelman, K. A., & Adelman, H. S. (1987). Rodin, Patton, Edison, Wilson, Einstein: Were they really learning disabled? *Journal of Learning Disabilities, 20,* 270–279.

American Academy of Ophthalmology. (1981). *Policy statement: Learning disabilities, dyslexia, and vision.* San Francisco, CA: Author.

Arter, J., & Jenkins, J. (1977). Differential diagnosis: Prescriptive teaching—A critical appraisal. *Review of Educational Research, 49,* 517–555.

Bateman, B. (1971). *The essentials of teaching.* San Rafael, CA: Dimensions Publishing Company.

Bateman, B., & Haring, N. (1977). *Teaching the learning-disabled child.* Englewood Cliffs, NJ: Prentice-Hall.

Bond, G. L., Tinker, M. A., & Wasson, B. B. (1979). *Reading difficulties: Their diagnosis and correction* (4th ed.) Englewood Cliffs, NJ: Prentice-Hall.

Carbo, M., Dunn, R., & Dunn, K. (1986). *Teaching students to read through their individual learning styles.* Reston, VA: Reston Publishing Co.

Christensen, C. A. (1992). Discrepancy definitions of reading disability: Has the quest led us astray? A response to Stanovich. *Reading Research Quarterly, 27,* 276–278.

Coles, G. S. (1978). The learning disabilities test battery: Empirical and social issues. *Harvard Educational Review, 48,* 313–340.

———. (1987). *The learning mystique: A critical look at "learning disabilities."* New York: Pantheon Books.

Divoky, D. (1974). Education's latest victim: The "LD" kid. *Learning, 3,* 20–25.

Dunn, R. (1988). Teaching students through the perceptual strengths or preferences. *Journal of Reading, 31,* 304–309.

Engelmann, S., & Bruner, E. (1974). *Distar Reading Level I.* Chicago, IL: Science Research Associates.

———. (1975). *Distar Reading Level II.* Chicago, IL: Science Research Associates.

Frankenberger, W., & Harper, J. (1987). States' criteria and procedures for identifying learning disabled children: A comparison of 1981/82 and 1985/86 guidelines. *Journal of Learning Disabilities, 20,* 118–121.

Frostig, M., & Horne, D. (1964). *The Frostig program for the development of visual perception.* Chicago, IL: Follett.

Frostig, M., Lefever, D. W., & Whittlesey, J. R. B. (1964). *The Marianne Frostig developmental test of visual perception.* Palo Alto, CA: Consulting Psychologists Press.

Galaburda, A. M. (1986). Animal studies and the neurology of developmental dyslexia. In G. Pavlidis & D. F. Fisher (Eds.), *Dyslexia: Its neuropsychology and treatment.* New York: John Wiley & Sons.

Gardner, H. (1983). *Frames of mind: The theory of multiple intelligences.* New York: Basic Books.

Gearheart, B. R., & Gearheart, C. J. (1989). *Learning disabilities: Educational strategies.* Columbus, OH: Merrill Publishing Company.

Gillingham, A., & Stillman, B. (1970). *Remedial training for children with specific disability in reading, spelling, and penmanship.* Cambridge, MA: Educator's Publishing Service.

Hammill, D. D. (1972). Training visual perceptual processes. *Journal of Learning Disabilities, 5,* 552–559.

———. (1993). A brief look at the learning disabilities movement in the United States. *Journal of Learning Disabilities, 26,* 295–310.

Hammill, D. D., & Larsen, S. C. (1974). The effectiveness of psycholinguistic training. *Exceptional Children, 41,* 5–14.

Hanson, V. L. (1989). Phonology and reading: Evidence from profoundly deaf readers. In D. Shankweiler & I. Y. Liberman (Eds.), *Phonology and reading disability: Solving the reading puzzle* (pp. 69–89). Ann Arbor, MI: University of Michigan Press.

Hinshelwood, J. (1917). *Congenital word-blindness.* London: H. K. Lewis & Company.

Johnson, D. J., & Myklebust, H. R. (1967). *Learning disabilities: Educational principles and practices.* New York: Grune & Stratton.

Kirk, S. A., McCarthy, J. J., & Kirk, W. D. (1968). *The Illinois test of psycholinguistic abilities* (rev. ed.). Urbana, IL: University of Illinois Press.

Kozol, J. K. (1991). *Savage inequalities: Children in America's schools.* New York: Crown.

LaBerge, D., & Samuels, S. J. (1974). Toward a theory of automatic information processing in reading. *Cognitive Psychology, 6,* 293–323.

Lerner, J. W. (1993). *Learning disabilities: Theories, diagnosis, and teaching strategies.* Boston, MA: Houghton Mifflin Company.

Lerner, R. (1978). Nature, nurture, and dynamic interactionism. *Human Development, 21,* 1–20.

McGill-Franzen, A. (1994). Compensatory and special education: Is there accountability for learning and belief in children's potential? In E. H. Hiebert & B. M. Taylor (Eds.), *Getting reading right from the start: Effective early literacy interventions* (pp. 13–35). Boston, MA: Allyn and Bacon.

Moats, L. C., & Lyon, G. R. (1993). Learning disabilities in the United States: Advocacy, science, and the future of the field. *Journal of Learning Disabilities, 26,* 282–294.

Morgan, W. P. (1896). A case of congenital word-blindness. *British Medical Journal, 2,* 1378.

Newcomer, P., & Hammill, D. D. (1975). The ITPA and academic achievement. *The Reading Teacher, 28,* 731–741.

Newell, A., & Simon, H. A. (1972). *Human problem solving.* Englewood Cliffs, NJ: Prentice-Hall.

Orton, S. T. (1928). Specific reading disability—strephosymbolia. *Journal of the American Medical Association, 90,* 1095–1099.

———. (1937). *Reading, writing, and speech problems in children.* New York: W. W. Norton.

———. (1966). The Orton-Gillingham approach. In J. Money & G. Shiffman (Eds.), *Disabled reader.* Baltimore, MD: Johns Hopkins Press.

Pellegrini, A. D., & Horvat, M. (1995). A developmental contextualist critique of attention deficit hyperactivity disorder. *Educational Researcher, 24,* 13–19.

Plomin, R. (1989). Environment and genes: Determinants of behavior. *American Psychologist, 11,* 105–111.

Roach, E. G., & Kephart, N. C. (1966). *The Purdue perceptual-motor survey.* Columbus, OH: Merrill.

Schrag, P., & Divoky, D. (1975). *The myth of the hyperactive child.* New York: Pantheon.

Senf, G. M. (1986). LD research in sociological and scientific perspective. In J. K. Torgesen & B. Y. L. Wong (Eds.), *Psychological and educational perspectives on learning disabilities* (pp. 27–53). San Diego, CA: Academic Press.

Smith, C. R. (1991). *Learning disabilities: The interaction of learner, task, and setting.* Needham Heights, MA: Allyn and Bacon.

Snider, V. E. (1992). Learning styles and learning to read: A critique. *Remedial and Special Education, 13,* 6–18, 30–33.

Stahl, S. (1988, December). Is there evidence to support matching reading styles and initial reading methods? *Phi Delta Kappan,* 317–327.

Stanovich, K. E. (1986). Matthew effects in reading: Some consequences of individual differences in the acquisition of literacy. *Reading Research Quarterly, 21,* 360–406.

———. (1991). Discrepancy definitions of reading disability: Has intelligence led us astray? *Reading Research Quarterly, 26,* 7–29.

———. (1992). Response to Christensen. *Reading Research Quarterly, 27,* 279–280.

Sternberg, R. J. (1977). *Intelligence, information processing, and analogical reasoning: The componential analysis of human abilities.* Hillsdale, NJ: Lawrence Erlbaum Associates.

———. (1985). *Beyond IQ: A triarchic theory of human intelligence.* New York: Cambridge University Press.

———. (1988). *The triarchic mind: A new theory of human intelligence.* New York: Viking.

Stevenson, H. W., Stigler, J. W., Lucker, G. W., Lee, S. Y., Hsu, C. C., & Kitamura, S. (1982). Reading disabilities: The case of Chinese, Japanese, and English. *Child Development, 53,* 1164–1181.

Strauss, A. A. (1943). Diagnosis and education of the cripple-brained, deficient child. *Exceptional Children, 9,* 163–168.

Strauss, A. A., & Lehtinen, L. (1947). *Psychopathology and education of the brain-injured child.* New York: Grune & Stratton.

Strauss, A. A., & Werner, H. (1942). Disorders of conceptual thinking in the brain-injured child. *Journal of Nervous and Mental Disease, 96,* 153–172.

Tarver, S. G., & Dawson, M. M. (1978). Modality preference and the teaching of reading: A review. *Journal of Learning Disabilities, 11,* 5–17.

Thomas, A., & Chess, S. (1977). *Temperament and development.* New York: Brunner/Mazel.

Torgesen, J. K. (1991). Learning disabilities: Historical and conceptual issues. In B. Y. L. Wong (Ed.), *Learning about learning disabilities* (pp. 3–37). San Diego, CA: Academic Press.

U.S. Department of Education. (1991). *To assure the free appropriate public education of all children with disabilities.* Thirteenth Annual Report to Congress on the Implementation of the Individuals with Disabilities Act. Washington, DC: U.S. Government Printing Office.

Vellutino, F. R. (1979). *Dyslexia: Theory and research.* Cambridge, MA: MIT Press.

Vellutino, F. R., Steger, J. A., Moyer, B. M., Harding, S. C., & Niles, C. J. (1977). Has the perceptual deficit hypothesis led us astray? *Journal of Learning Disabilities, 10,* 54–64.

Wallis, C. (1994, July 18). Life in overdrive. *Time,* 42–50.

Will, M. (1986). Educating children with learning problems: A shared responsibility. *Exceptional Children, 52,* 411–415.

Wong, B. Y. L. (1986). Problems and issues in the definition of learning disabilities. In J. K. Torgesen & B. Y. L. Wong (Eds.), *Psychological and educational perspectives on learning disabilities* (pp. 3–26). San Diego, CA: Academic Press.

3 What Is Reading Disability?

To this point, the most basic question about reading disability remains unanswered: What is it? We already know what it isn't—or at least, what it isn't supposed to be—mental retardation, emotional disturbance, sensory impairment, environmental disadvantage. But this definition by exclusion tells us nothing about what RD actually is, other than unexplained reading difficulty. In this chapter, we discuss in detail the multitude of problems with the ways in which RD is defined and identified in schools. As we will show, many of these problems are not easy to repair.

Contemporary definitions of RD come from the intrinsic perspective and are an outgrowth of earlier historical views of reading disability. From an intrinsic perspective, solving definitional problems is simply a matter of coming up with better—more precise, more stringent, or more scientific—definitions. However, years of wrangling about definitions on the part of those from various paradigms within the intrinsic perspective have not been fruitful, at least not with regard to educational practice in the LD field, where definitions of RD have changed little since the days of Hinshelwood and Orton. Contemporary educational definitions of LD and RD continue to be vague for the same reason that they have always been vague: because there are practical incentives to keep definitions broad, in order to make educational services available to more children and to include more individuals in the LD advocacy movement. In addition, only relatively recently has basic research begun to provide a more detailed picture of reading disability.

To those with an extrinsic perspective, "What is reading disability?" is simply the wrong question to ask. This view sees little need to differentiate "types" of poor readers. Rather, in the extrinsic view, the right question is something like, "What are the environmental and instructional determinants of reading failure, and how can we solve them?" However, the extrinsic view, as we discussed at the end of the previous chapter, has had little impact on schools, where identification of children with LD and RD continues to flourish.

Although we strongly disagree with the traditional concept of reading disability, we do not think that ignoring children's intrinsic characteristics and individual differences in learning is ever going to be educationally effective. To suggest that all poor reading is attributable purely to environmental factors such as inadequate instruction is, in our view, much too simplistic. Moreover, poor readers may indeed differ in terms of the cognitive underpinnings of their poor reading, and these differences may be important for a variety of reasons—for instance, in designing instruction.

School definitions group reading disability under the umbrella term of *learning disabilities.* Therefore, in the first part of this chapter, we will discuss current educational definitions of both LD and RD. We should note that, although our emphasis here, as elsewhere, is on schools, other definitions of RD have often mirrored those used in schools. For example, until recently, many researchers defined RD on the basis of essentially the same criteria still used by the schools. As the problems with these school criteria have become more widely recognized among scientific investigators, and as a more detailed picture of the cognitive deficits associated with RD has emerged, researchers have begun adopting more specific identification criteria, as we will discuss later in this chapter.

In the second part, meanwhile, we will look at the ways in which definitions of RD are applied in educational practice—in other words, at school-identification procedures for RD. We will begin with a case example. This case example illustrates, among other things, that school-identification practices are influenced by a host of variables that have nothing to do with the technical adequacy or inadequacy of definitions, such as the pragmatic need to provide intensive educational help to a youngster who needs it. Next, we will detail some of the problems with current school-identification procedures, ranging from problems that are relatively easy to fix, such as the use of inappropriate kinds of test scores, to problems that are much more fundamental and difficult to remedy. We will then discuss the suggestions of some contemporary researchers regarding how RD should be defined.

In the third and final part of this chapter, we will summarize the alternative perspectives on the problems in defining and identifying RD, and on the solutions to those problems. We will then offer our own conclusions about what is needed for a more complete understanding of reading disability.

Contemporary Definitions of Reading Disability

Contemporary educational definitions of reading disability contain the three elements that historically have been central to definitions of the concept. These three elements are the notion that children with RD are achieving well below their true potential for learning; the assumption that RD is due to an intrinsic deficit (sometimes described in psychological terms as a "disorder in processing" but assumed to have a biological cause); and exclusionary criteria, which rule out other disorders (e.g., mental retardation, emotional disturbance, or sensory impairment) and the environment as the primary causes of RD. Although many definitions of RD and LD have been advanced, and considerable dispute has attended each "new" definition, the differences among educational definitions have been more hairsplitting than substantive. (Of course, should the suggestions of contemporary researchers be implemented in educational practice, the definition of RD would have to change more dramatically.)

The Federal Definition

The most important definition of RD being used in schools is the federal definition (P.L. 101-476 and its earlier version, P.L. 94-142), which includes RD under the category of learning disabilities. The federal definition has two parts. The first part is a paragraph that states:

> "Specific learning disability" means a disorder in one or more of the basic psychological processes involved in understanding or in using language, spoken or written, which may manifest itself in an imperfect ability to listen, think, speak, read, write, spell, or to do mathematical calculations. The term includes such conditions as perceptual handicaps, brain injury, minimal brain dysfunction, dyslexia, and developmental aphasia. The term does not include children who have learning problems which are primarily the result of visual, hearing, or motor handicaps, of mental retardation, of emotional disturbance, or of environmental, cultural, or economic disadvantage. (*Federal Register*, December 29, 1977, p. 65083)

This first part of the federal definition of LD contained in P.L. 101-476 and P.L. 94-142 is virtually identical to an even earlier definition of learning disabilities formulated by the National Advisory Committee on Handicapped Children (U.S. Office of Education, 1968).

The second part of the federal definition requires that children with learning disabilities have a "severe discrepancy between achievement and intellectual ability" (p. 65083) in at least one of seven specified areas: basic reading skill (i.e., word recognition), reading comprehension, listening comprehension, oral expression, written expression, mathematics calculation, or mathematics reasoning. Federal law does not specify what constitutes a "severe discrepancy" but, rather, leaves this judgment to the multidisciplinary team that evaluates the child. (This team generally includes, among others, the child's classroom teacher, a learning-disabilities teacher, and a school psychologist.) Furthermore, federal law does not specify how "intellectual ability" should be measured; but in educational practice, individually administered IQ tests are typically used to determine intellectual ability.

Thus, in the federal definition, one can see all three of the elements that have been historically central to the concepts of LD and RD. Exclusionary criteria are listed in the last sentence of the paragraph that forms the first part of the definition; the idea of an intrinsic handicap is implicit in the statement that children with learning disabilities have "a disorder in one or more of the basic psychological processes involved in understanding or in using language" as well as in the exclusionary criteria involving "environmental, cultural, or economic disadvantage"; and the requirement of a discrepancy between potential and achievement is spelled out in the second part of the definition. However, in educational diagnosis the overwhelming emphasis is on the discrepancy requirement, rather than on the exclusionary criteria or on the notion of an intrinsic processing disorder (Frankenberger & Harper, 1987; Stanovich, 1991). This emphasis probably stems, at least in part, from the fact that IQ-achievement discrepancies can be quantified, whereas processing disorders and many of the exclusionary criteria are less easily quantifiable and, in some cases, difficult to measure at all.

It is also important to note that children with reading disability may qualify for educational services in *either* of two areas, basic reading or reading comprehension. Frequently, of course, children qualify in both areas, but according to the federal definition, children can qualify based on either basic reading (i.e., word recognition) or reading comprehension deficits alone. Furthermore, a child may qualify for educational services in reading as part of a much broader array of problems involving receptive oral language ("listening comprehension") or expressive oral language ("oral expression"). However, typical school-labeled youngsters with RD—and the ones who are the focus of this book—do not have obvious or severe spoken language deficits, although they usually do have language difficulties of a subtle nature. As we will discuss more extensively in Chapters 4 and 5, for most children with RD, these subtle language deficits appear to center on phonological processing—that is, processing of the phonemes or sounds in the language—rather than on processing of meaning or grammar.

Some Other Definitions

State Definitions. Individual states provide their own definitions of LD and RD to school districts. However, federal guidelines on LD and RD take precedence over state guidelines, so the latter may not be more restrictive than the former (Smith, 1991).

Many states attempt to quantify what constitutes a "severe discrepancy between achievement and intellectual ability" by specifying a minimum amount of discrepancy that the student should have in order to qualify for educational services. For example, Connecticut suggests a minimum discrepancy of one and one-half standard deviations between IQ and achievement, when standard scores from both kinds of tests are used. Because most tests employed in identification of LD have a standard deviation of 15 points (and a mean of 100 points), a discrepancy of one and one-half standard deviations usually translates into a 22.5-point difference between IQ score and standard score in achievement. Thus, a child with an IQ of 94, a standard score of 80 in basic reading, and a standard score of 70 in reading comprehension could qualify for learning-disabilities services in the area of reading comprehension, because of an IQ-achievement discrepancy of 24 points; but technically, that child would not qualify in the area of basic reading, where the discrepancy is only 14 points.

The NJCLD Definition. Another frequently cited definition is that of the National Joint Committee on Learning Disabilities (NJCLD). The NJCLD is a committee composed of representatives from a variety of influential learning-disabilities organizations and professional groups. Its definition explicitly states that learning disabilities are intrinsic and biologically based, elaborates on the meaning of exclusionary criteria, and uses more contemporary language. It also addresses the issue of social-skills deficits, which are often noted among youngsters with LD:

> *Learning disabilities* is a general term that refers to a heterogeneous group of disorders manifested by significant difficulties in the acquisition and use of listening, speaking, reading, writing, reasoning, or mathematical abilities. These disorders are intrinsic to the individual, presumed to be due to central nervous system dysfunction, and may occur across the life span. Problems in self-regulatory behaviors, social perception, and social interaction may exist with learning disabilities but do not by themselves constitute a learning disability. Although learning disabilities may occur concomitantly with other handicapping conditions (for example, sensory impairment, mental retardation, serious emotional disturbance) or with extrinsic influences (such as cultural differences, insufficient or inappropriate instruction), they are not the result of those conditions or influences. (National Joint Committee on Learning Disabilities, 1988, p. 1)

From the preceding discussion it is clear that definitions of RD and LD have not changed substantially since the earliest days of the LD field. Educational definitions of reading disability continue to be purely descriptive, exceedingly vague, and almost hypnotic in their circularity. For example, the NJCLD definition describes RD as a disorder "manifested by significant difficulties in the acquisition and use of . . . reading . . . abilities." The point is that, in educational practice, RD continues to be defined more in terms of what it isn't than in terms of what it is. However, as we will see, there are possibilities for redefining RD in more specific terms.

School Identification of Reading Disability

In this section, we discuss how definitions of RD are commonly applied in schools, beginning with a case example of school identification of reading disability. Next, we consider some of the problems with school-identification procedures as well as solutions to these problems. We conclude the section by examining the ideas of some contemporary researchers regarding how RD should be defined, and how those ideas, if implemented in educational practice, would affect school identification of reading disability.

A Case Example

As an illustration of the ways in which definitions of LD and RD are typically applied in educational practice, let us consider Evan, the youngster we mentioned in

Chapter 1 in our discussion of Matthew effects. We have already noted that Evan struggled in reading from his earliest days in the first grade. However, Evan's first-grade teacher, who had seen other children have initial difficulties in reading but then improve, thought that Evan might "grow out of" his reading problems. Unfortunately, spontaneous recovery did not happen in Evan's case, and Evan's initial reading problems were soon complicated by a variety of other factors, such as lowered motivation.

These complications became even worse after Evan started second grade. Other second-graders were acquiring skill at decoding two- and three-syllable words, whereas Evan still could not consistently recall many letter sounds, such as the sound for short *a*. Evan's decoding problems kept him from reading all but the simplest text, while his classmates were beginning to read more advanced (and more interesting) stories and to concentrate more on comprehension rather than on the mechanics of word recognition. The increasing disparity between Evan's reading skill and that of his classmates made it extremely difficult for his second-grade teacher to group him with other children for reading instruction. The teacher also found that Evan's poor reading caused him to become restless and inattentive during reading group as well as at other times during the school day, such that he was becoming something of a behavior problem.

Evan's school district required that teachers document certain prereferral steps—that is, before formally referring a child for special-education evaluation. The prereferral stage, in which a regular-classroom teacher seeks advice from supportive personnel in working with or in making modifications for individual youngsters, can significantly reduce the numbers of children who have to be referred for evaluation (Lloyd, Crowley, Kohler, & Strain, 1988). Prereferral is important, because once children have been referred for evaluation, there is a high probability that they will subsequently be identified as needing special-education services (Foster, Ysseldyke, Casey, & Thurlow, 1984); thus, the prereferral stage can potentially reduce the numbers of youngsters classified as LD or RD.

Evan's second-grade teacher consulted with the learning-disabilities specialist in the school about Evan's problems. The learning-disabilities teacher observed Evan in the regular classroom and looked at a file containing samples of his work as well as at results of group achievement testing routinely administered to children in the school. She suggested that Evan's teacher arrange preferential seating for Evan near the teacher's desk, both to increase the amount of individual attention the teacher could give him and to help improve his behavior. She also suggested that, if possible, Evan be grouped with one or two other very low achievers for additional help with decoding. Evan's second-grade teacher did implement these and some other suggestions, but to little avail. The main problem was that Evan was already functioning so far below the other children—even well below the other two poor readers with whom he was grouped—that his classroom teacher felt she could not give him the intensity of instructional help that he required. Thus, about midway through second grade, she referred him for a formal learning-disabilities evaluation. Evan's parents, who were well aware of his poor reading, readily gave their consent for the evaluation—consent that is required by law.

An IQ test, the WISC-III (*Wechsler Intelligence Scale for Children,* Third Edition, 1991), was administered to Evan by the school psychologist, who also gave him the *Bender Visual-Motor Gestalt Test* (Bender, 1946), a visual-motor test that requires the child to copy nine geometric forms. Subsequently, the learning-disabilities specialist administered a battery of academic tests: the *Woodcock Reading Mastery Tests—Revised* (Woodcock, 1987), a formal test of a variety of reading subskills; an oral reading inventory, in which the child has to read a series of graded paragraphs aloud and answer oral questions about them; and the *Wide Range Achievement Test—Revised,* or WRAT-R (Jastak & Wilkinson, 1984), which features subtests for word recognition, spelling, and math.

When the testing had been completed and analyzed, about a month from the time Evan's parents first agreed to it, the school convened a meeting with the parents. This was termed the Planning and Placement Team (PPT) meeting. Those present were Evan's parents, Evan's second-grade teacher, the school psychologist, the learning-disabilities specialist, and the principal of the school. Results of testing indicated that Evan met the discrepancy requirement for receiving learning-disabilities services in the areas of basic reading and reading comprehension. Evan's full-scale WISC-III IQ score was 106 (within the average range), whereas his standard scores on the formal reading tests he had taken were in the low 70s, nearly two standard deviations below average, for both word recognition and reading comprehension. Evan's school district required a discrepancy of two standard deviations (30 points) between IQ and achievement, so his reading scores met this requirement. His performance on the oral reading inventory also showed that, as expected, he could read only the easiest text from a beginning first-grade level. In addition, Evan met the discrepancy requirement for written expression, based on his WRAT-R spelling score of 70. He did not meet the discrepancy requirement in math, as his score of 98 placed him at an average level and his IQ-achievement discrepancy was much less than the necessary 30 points.

In order for Evan to be classified as LD, his school district required, in addition to the IQ-achievement discrepancy, that Evan show evidence of a processing disorder and that exclusionary criteria be satisfied. Evan's low score on the Bender (one year below age level) and his low scores on two of the WISC-III subtests, Digit Span (a measure of short-term memory) and Coding (a measure of both short-term memory and visual-motor facility), were viewed by the team as evidence of a processing disorder. Evan had already been screened by the school nurse for vision and hearing; these screenings, along with the prereferral documentation of alternative instructional strategies from his second-grade teacher, were considered to satisfy the exclusionary criteria.

Based on the results of testing, and with the agreement of his parents, Evan was scheduled to begin regular visits to the learning-disabilities specialist. The service-delivery model used in Evan's school, once children were formally classified as needing learning-disabilities services, was a resource model. Children went to the resource room individually or in small groups for remedial instruction for part of the school day, spending the remainder of the school day in the regular classroom. Evan was scheduled to receive resource help for one and one-half hours per day in the areas of reading, spelling, and written expression, whereas for instruction in math, the content areas (e.g., science and social studies), and "specials" (e.g., art and music) he was present in the regular classroom.

At the PPT meeting, the team also developed an IEP, or individualized education plan, for Evan. Among other things, the IEP documented Evan's need for learning-disabilities services and outlined how much time Evan would be spending in the resource room. In addition, the IEP set Evan's goals for the coming year—for example, the kinds of words he would learn to decode and the level of text he would be able to read by the end of the school term. Evan's parents were told they had to sign the IEP before it could be implemented; they did so.

Three points about this case example should be highlighted. First, the particulars of the referral and identification process may vary considerably. Some of these particulars—for instance, whether or not there is a prereferral stage, and the amount of discrepancy required for a child to qualify for learning-disabilities services—can make a substantial difference in the numbers of children identified as LD in any given school. Other basic elements of the process, however, are mandated by law and must be consistent across school districts. These elements include specific parental rights, such as the right to consent to testing and to be present at meetings where educational decisions are being made; the need for school personnel to document specific kinds of deficits, such as an ability-achievement discrepancy (whatever its size), in order for the child to qualify for learning-disabilities services; and the requirement for a written IEP.

A second point concerns the relatively heavy weight given to the IQ-achievement discrepancy in the decision as to whether Evan should receive learning-disabilities services. Although the personnel at his school did not ignore the issue of exclusionary criteria, relative to the determination of a discrepancy these criteria actually carried very little weight in the identification process. As we have already noted, the emphasis on the discrepancy requirement is both typical and understandable. After all, this requirement is quantifiable, whereas the adequacy of Evan's home environment or of his first-grade instruction is not. In short, whatever environmental factors may have contributed to or even caused his reading problem, these factors were subtle and not easily measurable, especially from the viewpoint of Evan's teachers, who had not been trained to consider that subtle environmental factors might have a substantial influence on the learning of individual children.

Finally, the personnel at Evan's school had a pragmatic choice to make about how best to help him. It was clear that Evan was not doing well in the regular classroom and that just leaving him there was not going to solve any of his problems. Evan might have seen a remedial-reading specialist, but he also had serious problems in spelling and written expression. The reading specialist felt that her program would not be intensive enough for Evan in these other areas. In addition, the other children with whom Evan would have been grouped for remedial reading were all functioning significantly above him, so the school personnel felt that this program would not be the most appropriate one for him. Special-education placement was the only other alternative for providing substantial extra help—and among the special-education categories, the LD category was not only the most appropriate but also the most appealing. Typically, even in more borderline cases (where one must ask, for example, Is the child learning disabled or mentally retarded? learning disabled or emotionally handicapped?), school personnel opt for the learning disabilities category because it is the least pejorative. Thus, Evan's classification as learning disabled was governed not merely by a straightforward "diagnosis" but also by a host of pragmatic considerations.

Some Problems in School Identification of LD and RD

It is evident from the example of Evan, as well as from the earlier discussion, that there are numerous problems with the identification of learning disabilities in general and—because it is most often the kind of learning disability identified— reading disability in particular. All of the problems with identification of RD are serious, but some are relatively less so because there are ways to address them. Others, however, appear so broad or so fundamental that it is not clear how to address them, or even if they can be addressed at all. In this section, we begin by discussing some of the potentially remediable problems; the more fundamental ones we reserve for the end.

Use of Inappropriate Scores and Tests. Many practitioners continue to make use of grade- or age-equivalent scores in reporting test data, especially from certain kinds of tests. For example, some of the older tests in the field do not yield anything other than grade or age equivalents, so in these cases practitioners do not have a choice about which kind of score to report. In addition, practitioners sometimes report grade or age equivalents even on tests that yield other kinds of scores, because such equivalents are more meaningful to parents. For instance, a grade equivalent of 4.1 on a standardized reading test is more comprehensible to most parents than is a standard score of, say, 82. However, grade and age equivalents tend to be inaccurate types of scores, because, among other things, they do not take into account the standard error of the test or the greater variability of scores at upper age ranges (Cronbach, 1960; Hargrove & Poteet, 1984; Smith, 1991). Scores that are comprehensible but inaccurate are not of much use. Therefore, authorities on testing agree that practitioners should report and interpret standard scores or percentile ranks rather than grade or age equivalents (e.g., Brown, 1980).

Grade or age equivalents also should not be used in formulas attempting to calculate IQ-achievement discrepancies (Cone & Wilson, 1981). Instead, standard-score comparisons—that is, between an IQ score, which is a standard score, and a standard score on an achievement measure—often are used. (This approach was the one used in Evan's school district.) Standard-score comparisons constitute an improvement over formulas employing grade or age equivalents, although, as we will see below, the use of such comparisons poses some serious problems of its own.

In addition, many researchers and authorities have expressed concern about the use of tests with inadequate norms, reliability (i.e., consistency in measurement), or validity (i.e., the extent to which the test measures what it claims to measure) in the diagnosis of learning disabilities (e.g., Moats & Lyon, 1993; Salvia & Ysseldyke, 1991). Indeed, norming, reliability, and validity are often flawed in tests used to measure disorders in processing. The validity of IQ measures is an especially important problem, which we will discuss in further detail below. Yet many of the newer achievement tests do have adequate norms, reliability, and validity. Obviously, it is important for practitioners to use tests that are as adequate as possible in these areas. Equally important, all formal test results should be interpreted with caution, because, at best, they represent performance at only one point in time.

The Discrepancy Concept. We have already mentioned two problems with the way the discrepancy concept is frequently implemented in educational practice. First, different states, different school districts within a state, and sometimes even different schools within a district employ different cutoffs for what constitutes a "severe" discrepancy, such that the question of whether children are diagnosed as LD may depend largely on where they live. For instance, the discrepancy requirement of two standard deviations that was used in Evan's school district is a conservative criterion. Evan was sufficiently far behind in reading to be diagnosed as LD, but many other children with serious reading deficits would not qualify for LD services in Evan's district, whereas they might well qualify in a district with a one or one-and-a-half standard deviation cutoff. Second, some school districts continue to use discrepancy formulas involving grade- or age-equivalent scores, which are not highly accurate. Both of these problems can be addressed—the first by the adoption of a consistent cutoff, at least within states and school districts, and the second through the use of standard-score comparisons in determining discrepancies.

However, all of the methods of calculating IQ-achievement discrepancies, including standard-score comparisons, are based on the assumption that IQ is a perfect predictor of achievement. For instance, youngsters with an IQ of 120 are assumed to have an expected standard-score achievement of 120, and those with an IQ of 80 are assumed to have an expected achievement of 80. Unfortunately, this tacit assumption is just plain wrong (Siegel, 1989). Particularly as a predictor of reading achievement in the early elementary grades, IQ is in fact far from perfect, usually accounting for only 10 to 25 percent of the variance in reading achievement; even among adults, IQ typically accounts for no more than 50 percent of such variance (Stanovich, Cunningham, & Feeman, 1984).

For readers of all ages, inaccuracies in prediction become more acute at the extremes of IQ, because of a phenomenon known as "regression to the mean." Regression effects were first studied by Sir Francis Galton in the nineteenth century (McCall, 1980). Galton was interested in predicting certain biological and behavioral traits from other traits—for example, predicting sons' heights from their fathers' heights. He noticed that the sons of very short fathers tended to be shorter than average height, but not as short as their fathers; and similarly, that sons of very tall fathers also tended to be taller than average, but not quite as tall as their fathers. In other words, he found that in predicting one variable from another, extreme scores on one variable (e.g., father's height) tended to predict somewhat less extreme scores on the other variable (e.g., son's height).

Now let's return to the question of predicting reading achievement from IQ. Given the statistical phenomenon of regression, those with IQs higher than average—for example, 120—can be expected to score somewhat lower in reading achievement, or somewhat closer to the mean. Thus, it is *not* reasonable to expect that children with IQs of 120 will necessarily have comparable scores for reading achievement. Similarly, those with IQs around 80 can actually be expected to have reading achievement somewhat higher than 80—again, closer to the mean. Thus, the standard-score comparison method of determining discrepancy tends to overidentify high-IQ youngsters, and to underidentify low-IQ youngsters, as LD. High-IQ youngsters are thought to have discrepancies when they really don't, and low-IQ youngsters are thought not to have discrepancies when they really do. Furthermore, the less reliable the test, the more problematic are the regression effects. As we have already noted, many of the tests used in the LD field exhibit inadequate reliability.

It turns out that the problem of regression can be addressed by calculating discrepancies through a method known as regression analysis (Cone & Wilson, 1981; Hargrove & Poteet, 1984; Lerner, 1993; Smith, 1991). However, this method requires knowledge of all the correlations between the specific IQ test used, on the one hand, and the specific achievement tests used, on the other. Furthermore, the correlations must be known for a sample comparable to the one being tested in age, socioeconomic status, sex, and number of years of schooling (Pennington, 1986). In educational practice, these various correlations are usually unknown, so most schools do not use regression analysis (Frankenberger & Harper, 1987; Smith, 1991).

An even more fundamental problem with IQ-achievement discrepancies has to do with the legitimacy of the discrepancy concept itself. Historically, as we have seen, the idea that children with reading disability are not functioning up to their potential for learning is an old one. This idea was widely operationalized in the schools as an IQ-achievement discrepancy after the passage of the Education for All Handicapped Children Act of 1975, P.L. 94-142 (Senf, 1986). Schools employed IQ tests as a measure of overall potential for learning, or general intelligence, in children with LD and RD. However, as Stanovich (1991) points out, many psychologists and psychometricians long ago abandoned the idea that IQ really measures intelligence! Indeed, as we will discuss in Chapter 9, many contemporary researchers have a multidimensional view of intelligence. According to this view, intelligence as one broad, all-encompassing general ability does not even exist. Thus, the outdated assumption that IQ measures the true overall potential for learning of children with LD and RD is one of the most fundamental flaws in the discrepancy construct.

Of course, it is possible that, despite these problems with the use of IQ, some other measure might be used as an indicator of potential, specifically in the area of reading. For instance, some researchers argue that verbal IQ and listening comprehension are more realistic indicators of potential in reading than is nonverbal IQ (Hessler, 1987; Rack, Snowling, & Olson, 1992; Stanovich, 1991), which is not highly predictive of school achievement. These investigators have suggested that the use of verbal IQ or measures of listening comprehension in identification of RD is preferable to the use of a global or nonverbal IQ score. Keep in mind that listening comprehension is actually a discrepancy area in which children can qualify for LD services under federal guidelines. However, the researchers we have mentioned would not view children with broad listening-comprehension problems as having RD (nor would we).

Unfortunately, there is yet another fly in the ointment of the discrepancy construct. Even if one believes that verbal IQ can be used to predict potential in reading, or even if one uses some other predictor of potential, such as listening comprehension, the phenomenon of Matthew effects poses a problem (Stanovich, 1986, 1991). Matthew effects suggest that the difficulties of children with reading disability may become more generalized over time, in part because many of the cognitive skills measured by IQ and listening comprehension tests, such as vocabulary, are actually acquired through reading. Therefore, what starts out as a relatively circumscribed problem in word recognition may eventually generalize to many cognitive areas, including those tapped by IQ tests, listening-comprehension assessments, or other measures of potential in reading. Thus, a child with RD may gradually become more and more like a garden-variety poor reader. Although this decline in IQ over time is clearly not inevitable (Bruck, 1990), it is enough of a possibility to seriously undermine the discrepancy concept, especially when applied to older children and adults.

Finally, the discrepancy concept does not provide any insight into what reading disability actually *is*. It merely reiterates the historical conceptualization of RD as unexpected reading difficulty—unexpected because the child's reading achievement is significantly lower than his or her estimated potential in reading. In the absence of more specific knowledge about the kinds of reading deficits and underlying cognitive characteristics associated with RD, accurate identification and, hence, optimal remediation are impossible.

Exclusionary Criteria. As we have seen, exclusionary criteria receive fairly cursory attention in diagnosis of LD and RD, and an important reason for this relative lack of attention is that many of the exclusionary areas are themselves difficult to define or to measure. For instance, exactly what constitutes "emotional disturbance" or "cultural disadvantage"? Most of us would not have difficulty recognizing extreme examples of these conditions, but youngsters who are candidates for LD diagnosis are unlikely to present with childhood psychosis or extreme disadvantage.

Unlike theoreticians, practitioners come face-to-face with children whose problems are embedded in a complicated context. For instance, children with academic difficulties frequently have other problems as well. They may be behaviorally difficult; they may have trouble getting along with their teachers, parents, or classmates; and, in some cases, they may have experienced inappropriate teaching or may come from culturally different backgrounds. Disentangling these factors is sometimes impossible because of the ways in which they interact with one another. For example, academic failure and frustration may cause a child to develop behavior problems, which then exacerbate the child's difficulties in learning. The direction of causality may also be reversed, but with a similar outcome: A child may start out with behavioral or emotional difficulties that result in academic failure, and the frustration of failing may contribute to further emotional problems as well as to further academic failure.

In LD diagnosis, when youngsters have difficulties in multiple areas, practitioners are theoretically supposed to determine the "primary" disability. According to federal and (most) state guidelines, a child with sensory impairment, emotional disturbance, cultural and economic disadvantage, and so on, may be diagnosed as LD, but only if these factors are not the primary causes of the child's learning problem. However, with the exception of sensory impairment, all of the exclusionary areas—like LD itself—are defined only vaguely. In many cases, then, trying to determine the "primary" disability is like attempting to sift out the flour after the cake batter has been mixed. Indeed, as we will discuss further in the next section, some of these supposedly exclusionary variables clearly *do* influence whether or not children are identified as LD or RD, sometimes even more than do children's actual cognitive abilities.

The Importance of Noncognitive Variables in RD Identification. In the previous chapters, we argued that the medical paradigm of reading disability, which likens the identification of RD to the diagnosis of a disease, is misleading for a number of reasons. One reason is that school identification of RD is heavily influenced by factors that have little or nothing to do with a child's intrinsic cognitive abilities (or disabilities). These factors may include gender; socioeconomic status, race, and ethnicity; the child's classroom behavior; characteristics of the classroom teacher; and pragmatic considerations of how best to provide extra help to that particular child. For advocates of the intrinsic perspective, these other influences on the identification of RD are a problem. Given the foundational assumptions of the field—namely, that RD is a distinctive and biologically based syndrome and that children with RD meet exclusionary criteria—such influences undermine the soundness of the entire endeavor of RD identification.

For example, consider the characteristic of gender, which, as it turns out, is also linked to the characteristic of classroom behavior. It has long been noted that more boys than girls are identified as having RD, in ratios of 2:1, 3:1, and even higher (Lerner, 1993; Smith, 1991). Not surprisingly, some researchers with an intrinsic perspective suggest a biological basis for this unequal sex ratio. For example, Galaburda (1986) argues that an excess of testosterone may adversely affect left-hemisphere brain development in male fetuses. And Pennington et al. (1991) suggest that RD may be a genetic disorder involving a sex difference in "penetrance"—that is, in the extent to which the gene is expressed. In other words, both girls and boys might inherit the gene for RD, but the gene might be expressed more or less strongly depending upon whether the affected individual is a boy or a girl.

However, recent evidence has indicated that sex ratios for RD are more nearly equal than was previously thought (Rumsey, 1992). For instance, Shaywitz, Shaywitz, Fletcher, and Escobar (1990), in a longitudinal study of over 400 elementary-age boys and girls, found that the two sexes met their criteria for RD in essentially equal numbers. (Their criteria were similar to those employed in school identification of RD, with heavy emphasis on an IQ-achievement discrepancy in reading.) Yet boys were identified by the schools much more often than were girls. The apparent mediating variable was behavior: School-identified children with RD were more likely to be rated by teachers as having behavioral problems or as having a high activity level than were nonschool-identified children, and in general, boys were more likely than girls to be viewed as having behavior problems. Shaywitz et al. (1990) suggest that the unequal sex ratio in school identification of reading disability is not "real" but, rather, is the result of a referral bias. In other words, teachers were more likely to refer boys than girls for testing, because boys were perceived to constitute more of a behavior problem in the classroom.

Interestingly, in the study by Shaywitz et al., *over half* of the school-identified children with RD did not meet the discrepancy criterion employed by the researchers. The researchers' criterion, like state guidelines on learning disabilities, involved an IQ-achievement discrepancy of at least one and one-half standard deviations; however, the researchers, unlike most school districts, employed the regression-analysis method rather than the standard-score comparison method of determining discrepancy. The difference in method—regression analysis versus standard-score comparison—likely explains why many of the school-identified children did not meet the researchers' discrepancy criterion. In addition, some children may have been classified by schools as having RD less on the basis of an IQ-achievement discrepancy than on that of other characteristics, such as behavior.

A brief look at research on gender differences in the classroom, involving normally achieving children, provides some further insights into the issue of referral bias. In a literature review of research on this subject, Sadker, Sadker, and Klein (1991) concluded that teachers respond differently to boys and girls in subtle but important ways. This differential response can occur regardless of whether the teacher is male or female and is typically quite unconscious. (Teachers usually deny that they treat boys and girls differently until the evidence is pointed out to them in videotapes). The basic findings are that teachers give boys more attention than girls in ways both positive (more praise) and negative (more criticism), with regard to academics as well as conduct. Teachers seem to give boys more attention at least partly out of anticipation that boys are more likely than girls to have learning and behavior problems. In fact, girls often have particularly severe academic deficits by the time they are identified as needing LD services (Vogel, 1990).

Thus, the apparent referral bias in RD identification is only one manifestation of a much broader pattern of differences in the ways that teachers typically interact with boys and girls in the classroom. In line with this view, the findings of Shaywitz et al. (1990) showed that teachers were more likely to rate *normally achieving* boys than girls as having behavioral or academic problems, even though there were no significant group differences between genders in either cognitive abilities or academic performance. Similarly, Snow, Barnes, Chandler, Goodman, and Hemphill (1991), in a detailed longitudinal study of the literacy acquisition of a group of low-income youngsters, found that teachers were more likely to contact boys' parents rather than girls' parents regarding academic problems, although again there were no overall differences in academic performance between the girls and boys.

Moats and Lyon (1993) suggest that teachers' beliefs about their ability to teach individual youngsters also play an important role in identification of LD. Teachers tend to refer children for special-education testing and placement when they believe that they cannot effectively help those children. This was clearly the case with Evan's second-grade teacher, who, after making many sincere attempts to help him, resorted to special-education referral only when she believed that there was little else she could do. Ironically, however, the constructs of LD and RD may in some cases actually weaken teachers' confidence in their abilities to effectively teach certain children—as, for example, when regular-classroom teachers view children with reading disability as having an unusual syndrome that requires expert, specialized attention.

Note, too, that socioeconomic status, race, and ethnicity are not irrelevant in diagnosing LD and RD. For example, although authors such as Coles (1987) have pointed out the strong middle-class orientation of the LD field, other investigators (e.g., McGill-Franzen, 1994) suggest that the LD category increasingly involves poor children, as a result of the decline in funds available for compensatory education programs such as "Chapter 1." The relationship of race and ethnicity to LD identification is linked in part to historical events involving children labeled as mentally retarded (MR). Historically, the overrepresentation of minority youngsters in classes for the mentally retarded resulted in a number of court cases under civil rights law (Lerner, 1993). Because of these court cases, in 1973 the American

Association on Mental Deficiency (AAMD) revised its guidelines on identification of mental retardation, making them more stringent (Smith, 1991). For example, children with IQs in the 70s, who once would have been labeled as mentally retarded, now could no longer be given the MR label in states that adopted the AAMD guidelines. The numbers of children being identified as LD skyrocketed in the 1970s and 1980s, but the number identified as MR fell by about 38 percent in the same period (U.S. Department of Education, 1991). Clearly, some children who at one time were labeled as MR are now being labeled as LD, and a significant number of these children appear to be minority youngsters (Ysseldyke, Algozzine, & Thurlow, 1992).

For practitioners seeking to help poor or minority children who have serious learning problems, placing these children in LD classes may be a pragmatic choice, as there may be few immediate alternatives for offering them intensive academic help. However, from a broader standpoint, there is something ironic about the inappropriate placement of some minority children in LD classes. The point of the civil rights litigation of the 1960s and 1970s was that minority youngsters should receive equal educational opportunity rather than be disproportionately labeled as retarded. Instead, it appears that, rather than receiving equal educational opportunity (Kozol, 1991), some minority children are simply being given a different label.

Finally, one might take the purely pragmatic stance that identifying children as RD and LD, whether or not they are poor or minority youngsters, is simply a way to provide them with much-needed educational services. We can understand why practitioners sometimes adopt this point of view, as there are often so few options for providing children with extra help. But the pragmatic stance does not justify saddling youngsters with the misconception that they have an intrinsic and unique "disability," when they really don't. In fact, many of the practitioners we know are troubled by this issue. They see themselves, in some cases, as making a "lesser of two evils" kind of choice—diagnosing children with spurious "disabilities" in order to provide educational services—when what they would prefer is to have another option altogether. Indeed, as we will discuss in the last chapter of this book, another option is possible, one in which children do not need to be diagnosed as "disabled" in order to receive educational help.

Some Suggestions from Researchers

Contemporary researchers have made a number of suggestions regarding the ways that identification of RD might be improved. First, many researchers have agreed that RD should be defined as a disorder primarily involving word-recognition processes rather than comprehension processes (e.g., Moats & Lyon, 1993; Rack, Snowling, & Olson, 1992; Siegel, 1985, 1988, 1989; Stanovich, 1991; Vellutino, 1979), although, of course, poor word recognition may lead to impaired comprehension. Second, as we discussed earlier, some researchers argue that discrepancy determinations should use verbal IQ or listening-comprehension measures, rather than a full-scale or a nonverbal IQ score, to assess potential in reading—although other investigators (e.g., Siegel & Heaven, 1986) have argued against using listening comprehension in the identification of reading disability. Finally, some researchers have suggested shelving the discrepancy construct altogether (e.g., Moats & Lyon, 1993; Siegel, 1988, 1989; Stanovich, 1991). This last suggestion would necessitate major alterations in current educational procedures, in which discrepancy determinations typically form the cornerstone of LD identification.

We certainly agree with the ideas that word-recognition processes are central to RD and that the discrepancy construct needs to be scrapped. However, we do not think that these ideas by themselves will solve the problems with learning disabilities *as a field of educational practice.* For one thing, because word-recognition problems tend to lead to a variety of other reading problems, such as reading-comprehension problems, identification and educational assessment of children with RD require more than just testing word recognition. In fact, in older students with RD, the most salient problem is frequently reading comprehension.

Nevertheless, many older students with RD do manifest word-recognition difficulties relative to normally achieving readers (e.g., Bruck, 1990). These difficulties are often of a subtle nature; for example, they might be detected with tests consisting of carefully constructed pseudowords (nonsense words) or reaction-time measures (i.e., measures involving *speed* of word recognition), though not with many common measures of word-recognition *accuracy* involving real words. Thus, identification of RD through the measurement of word-recognition difficulties would, in some cases, require significant changes in testing practices and perhaps the development of new tests. Moreover, some students with RD may overcome their initial word-recognition difficulties and have only comprehension problems. For these students, identification would require a detailed reading history.

Second, the suggestions about redefining RD as a word-recognition disorder and dropping the discrepancy concept do not address an even more fundamental problem: the flawed nature of the RD construct as a whole. Although the discrepancy concept is central to educational definitions of reading disability, there is more to the construct of RD than discrepancy criteria. In particular, the RD construct includes the idea that RD is a unique syndrome of poor reading caused by a biological disorder. Whether RD is defined in terms of current IQ-achievement discrepancy criteria or as a word-recognition disorder, there is no evidence to support the other assumptions that are embedded in the RD construct. Thus, in our opinion, not only the discrepancy concept, but the traditional construct of reading disability as a whole, needs to be abandoned in favor of another way of thinking about reading difficulties.

A third and crucial issue for the learning-disabilities field, as we discussed at the end of the previous chapter, involves providing a justification for the field as a separate area of education. Merely redefining RD as a word-recognition disorder, without abandoning the other cherished but invalid foundational assumptions of the field, would not bring about such a justification. For instance, this redefinition would not identify a group of poor readers who need separate, distinctive educational treatment, because poor readers in general are characterized by problems with word recognition (Stanovich & Siegel, 1994).

As we have discussed, one alternative to the current IQ-achievement discrepancy construct involves replacing IQ tests with a different measure of potential, such as listening comprehension. In this scenario, practitioners would seek to identify children with listening comprehension-achievement discrepancies—rather than those with IQ-achievement discrepancies—as having RD. The basic idea here is that listening comprehension is an indicator of how well children with RD would be able to read, in the event that their word-recognition problems were remediated (Stanovich, 1991). Note that in this approach, children with listening-comprehension deficits would not be considered to have RD, but if their nonverbal abilities were relatively high, they might still be grouped under the learning disabilities umbrella and considered, for example, "language disabled." Development of reliable and valid measures of listening comprehension is a significant, but probably not insurmountable, measurement problem. (See Stanovich, 1991, for a more detailed discussion.)

This approach may indeed identify a group of poor readers who are somewhat different from other poor readers in terms of their underlying cognitive profiles. For example, Fletcher et al. (1994) found that using listening comprehension rather than IQ as a measure of potential did distinguish a group of youngsters with more generalized language and cognitive impairments relative to youngsters of the same age who had listening comprehension–reading comprehension discrepancies. In other words, children lacking in listening comprehension–reading comprehension discrepancies were more like "garden-variety poor readers" than were children lacking in IQ-achievement discrepancies. However, even when the measure of potential was listening comprehension, the differences in the cognitive profiles of the two groups—those with discrepancies and those without discrepancies—were not large.

Of course, we are still left with the issue of Matthew effects, which, in some children with RD, might gradually erode an initial discrepancy between listening comprehension and reading achievement. In this event, only a detailed educational history, with longitudinal information about both listening and reading skills, would allow practitioners to ascertain whether or not a child with reading problems once had a discrepancy. Unfortunately, such comprehensive assessment information is not currently routine in schools, especially for children who have not been placed in special education.

The study of different types of poor readers, such as those with and without listening comprehension–reading achievement discrepancies, clearly is scientifically legitimate. Furthermore, this scientific study ultimately may pay off in practical ways, inasmuch as the specific instructional needs of different types of poor readers may indeed vary. However, as Siegel (1989) points out, there is no evidence to indicate that children without discrepancies benefit any less from remediation than do children with discrepancies. *All* poor readers need educational help. We know of no basis for singling out one group of poor readers as somehow more deserving of help than the rest.

In short, we do not think that the use of listening comprehension–reading achievement discrepancies in identifying RD—or the redefinition of RD as a word-recognition disorder—will solve the problems with learning disabilities as a field of educational practice. In order to justify their existence in a separate area of education, those in the LD field must either confine themselves to helping a group of stringently defined low achievers who require separate classification and distinctive treatment—or dramatically redefine not only reading disability but also their roles as professionals.

Where Do We Go from Here?

It may be tempting to dismiss the ceaseless definitional disputes surrounding LD and RD as empty exercises, somewhat like medieval theological arguments about how many angels can dance on the head of a pin. And in any case, whether or not these disputes are resolved, practitioners have to get on with the business of teaching children to read. Still, without some insight into the underlying cognitive difficulties of poor readers, practitioners can never be entirely effective, either in identifying children who are at risk of reading failure or in helping these children.

Like so much else in the learning-disabilities field, the proposed answers to the problems of defining reading disability depend largely upon whom one asks. On the one hand, some advocates of the extrinsic perspective would argue that trying to improve definitions of and identification of RD is like trying to find better methods of bloodletting—a hopeless enterprise that simply ought to be abandoned. For instance, Christensen (1992) maintains:

> After 30 years of fruitless endeavour, surely it is morally and ethically encumbent upon researchers to acknowledge that the way ahead does not lie in the continued search for the "true" learning disabled child, but rather in a search for specific instructional solutions to reading failure regardless of whether the child is developmentally delayed, economically disadvantaged, or from a racial or cultural minority, or is a white, middle-class male. (p. 278)

On the other hand, those who maintain a strong belief in RD as an intrinsic, biologically based disorder tend to view refinements in definitions, and eventual improvement in both school-identification practices and remediation, as a straightforward outcome of scientific progress. This view is the position of most textbooks on LD and RD. For example, Lerner (1993) says that "neuroscientific research holds the promise of furthering our understanding of the enigma of learning disabilities, even though the findings may not have an immediate application for teaching" (p. 217). And Smith (1991) touts the possible practical benefits of neuroscientific research:

> Neuropsychological research was initially met with excitement because knowledge of how the brains of individuals with disabilities are electroneurologically unique had the potential to direct the teaching strategies used with a student. More recently, enthusiasm has heightened even further as evidence has emerged regarding the potential for altering abilities by direct stimulation of various brain regions. (p. 91)

We have argued repeatedly that neither the extreme of the intrinsic perspective nor the extreme of the extrinsic perspective has been particularly useful to educational practitioners; nor is either likely to be useful in the future. Even a quick perusal of the history of the LD field should make us highly suspicious of the suggestion that children's learning problems can ever be fully explicated, let alone solved, simply through the straightforward march of brain research. Yet it is also important to acknowledge that individual differences in children's intrinsic characteristics have a real impact on how children learn. Ultimately, it is the interactive view that sets the intrinsic characteristics of children with RD in a broader social and educational context. It considers not only the intrinsic processing characteristics of children with RD but also how they interact with and are shaped by environmental variables, such as the nature of instruction; equally important, it considers how identification of RD is influenced by other forces, such as the pragmatic need to provide educational help to children who are struggling in the regular classroom.

Finally, of course, we need to know what reading disability *is*, not just what it isn't. Fortunately, the work of numerous researchers in cognitive psychology and in related fields has provided an increasingly clear picture of what reading disability is, especially at a psychological level. For instance, as we have mentioned, and as we will discuss further in Chapter 5, one cognitive characteristic that has been very consistently associated with RD is a deficit in word-recognition skill. Obviously, however, a complete understanding of reading disability, even at the psychological level, entails much more than just knowing that children with RD have a word-recognition problem. What cognitive characteristics presage difficulties with word recognition? How do the word-recognition difficulties of young children with RD become transformed into the reading problems typical of older children with RD? Is there more than one pattern of difficulties associated with RD, or only a single pattern? These are the kinds of questions to which cognitive research provides, if not definitive answers, at least some strongly suggestive clues.

In our view and that of many other cognitive investigators, problems in learning to read should be related, first and foremost, not to IQ or to listening comprehension but to *reading*—specifically, to the processes involved in typical reading development. The meaning of cognitive characteristics associated with reading disability can be interpreted only with reference to reading acquisition in normally achieving readers. Therefore, an educationally useful model of reading disability must describe how characteristics associated with RD change over time and must *also* relate these characteristics to those seen in normally achieving readers. We believe that our model of reading disability, which is described in the next two chapters, provides the kind of broad and educationally relevant framework that is needed. This model is our answer to the question "What is reading disability?"

References

Bender, L. (1946). *Visual motor gestalt test.* New York: American Orthopsychiatric Association.

Brown, F. G. (1980). *Guidelines for test use: A commentary on the standards for educational and psychological tests.* Washington, DC: National Council on Measurement in Education.

Bruck, M. (1990). Word-recognition skills of adults with childhood diagnoses of dyslexia. *Developmental Psychology, 26,* 439–454.

Christensen, C. A. (1992). Discrepancy definitions of reading disability: Has the quest led us astray? A response to Stanovich. *Reading Research Quarterly, 27,* 276–278.

Coles, G. S. (1987). *The learning mystique: A critical look at "learning disabilities."* New York: Pantheon Books.

Cone, T. E., & Wilson, L. R. (1981). Quantifying a severe discrepancy: A critical analysis. *Learning Disability Quarterly, 4,* 359–371.

Cronbach, L. J. (1960). *Essentials of psychological testing,* 2nd ed. New York: Harper & Row.

Federal Register (1977, December 29) (65082–65085), Washington, DC.

Fletcher, J. M., Shaywitz, S. E., Shankweiler, D. P., Katz, L., Liberman, I. Y., Stuebing, K. K., Francis, D. J., Fowler, A. E., & Shaywitz, B. A. (1994). Cognitive profiles of reading disability: Comparisons of discrepancy and low achievement definitions. *Journal of Educational Psychology, 86,* 6–23.

Foster, C. G., Ysseldyke, J. E., Casey, A., & Thurlow, M. L. (1984). The congruence between the reason for referral and placement outcome. *Journal of Psychoeducational Assessment, 2,* 209–217.

Frankenberger, W., & Harper, J. (1987). States' criteria and procedures for identifying learning disabled children: A comparison of 1981/82 and 1985/86 guidelines. *Journal of Learning Disabilities, 20,* 118–121.

Galaburda, A. M. (1986). Animal studies and the neurology of developmental dyslexia. In G. Pavlidis & D. F. Fisher (Eds.), *Dyslexia: Its neuropsychology and treatment.* New York: John Wiley & Sons.

Hargrove, L. J., & Poteet, J. A. (1984). *Assessment in special education.* Englewood Cliffs, NJ: Prentice-Hall.

Hessler, G. L. (1987). Educational issues surrounding severe discrepancy. *Learning Disabilities Research, 3,* 43–49.

Jastak, S., & Wilkinson, G. S. (1984). *Wide Range Achievement Test—Revised.* Wilmington, DE: Jastak Associates.

Kozol, J. K. (1991). *Savage inequalities: Children in America's schools.* New York: Crown.

Lerner, J. W. (1993). *Learning disabilities: Theories, diagnosis, and teaching strategies.* Boston, MA: Houghton Mifflin Company.

Lloyd, J. W., Crowley, E. P., Kohler, F. W., & Strain, P. S. (1988). Redefining the applied research agenda: Cooperative learning, prereferral, teacher consultation, and peer-modulated interventions. *Journal of Learning Disabilities, 21,* 43–52.

McCall, R. B. (1980). *Fundamental statistics for psychology.* New York: Harcourt Brace Jovanovich.

McGill-Franzen, A. (1994). Compensatory and special education: Is there accountability for learning and belief in children's potential? In E. H. Hiebert & B. M. Taylor (Eds.), *Getting reading right from the start: Effective early literacy interventions* (pp. 13–35). Boston, MA: Allyn and Bacon.

Moats, L. C., & Lyon, G. R. (1993). Learning disabilities in the United States: Advocacy, science, and the future of the field. *Journal of Learning Disabilities, 26,* 282–294.

Naglieri, J. A., & Reardon, S. M. (1993). Traditional IQ is irrelevant to learning disabilities—Intelligence is not. *Journal of Learning Disabilities, 26,* 127–133.

National Joint Committee on Learning Disabilities. (1988). Letter to NJCLD member organizations.

Pennington, B. F. (1986). Issues in the diagnosis and phenotype analysis of dyslexia: Implications for family studies. In S. D. Smith (Ed.), *Genetics and learning disabilities* (pp. 69–96). San Diego, CA: College Hill Press.

Pennington, B. F., Gilger, J. W., Pauls, D., Smith, S. A., Smith, S. D., & DeFries, J. C. (1991). Evidence for major gene transmission of developmental dyslexia. *Journal of the American Medical Association, 266,* 1527–1534.

Rack, J. P., Snowling, M. J., & Olson, R. K. (1992). The nonword reading deficit in developmental dyslexia: A review. *Reading Research Quarterly, 27,* 28–53.

Rumsey, J. M. (1992). The biology of developmental dyslexia. *Journal of the American Medical Association, 268,* 912–915.

Sadker, M., Sadker, D., & Klein, S. (1991). The issue of gender in elementary and secondary education. *Review of Research in Education, 17,* 269–334.

Salvia, J., & Ysseldyke, J. (1991). *Assessment* (5th ed.) Boston, MA: Houghton Mifflin Company.

Senf, G. M. (1986). LD research in sociological and scientific perspective. In J. K. Torgesen & B. Y. L. Wong (Eds.), *Psychological and educational perspectives on learning disabilities* (pp. 27–53). San Diego, CA: Academic Press.

Shaywitz, S. E., Shaywitz, B. A., Fletcher, J. M., & Escobar, M. D. (1990). Prevalence of reading disability in boys and girls: Results of the Connecticut Longitudinal Study. *Journal of the American Medical Association, 264,* 998–1002.

Siegel, L. S. (1985). Psycholinguistic aspects of reading disabilities. In L. S. Siegel & F. J. Morrison (Eds.), *Cognitive development in atypical children* (pp. 45–65). New York: Springer-Verlag.

———. (1988). Evidence that IQ scores are irrelevant to the definition and analysis of reading disability. *Canadian Journal of Psychology, 42,* 201–215.

———. (1989). IQ is irrelevant to the definition of learning disabilities. *Journal of Learning Disabilities, 22,* 469–478.

Siegel, L. S., & Heaven, R. K. (1986). Categorization of learning disabilities. In S. J. Ceci (Ed.), *Handbook of cognitive, social, and neuropsychological aspects of learning disabilities* (Vol. 1, pp. 95–121). Hillsdale, NJ: Erlbaum.

Smith, C. R. (1991). *Learning disabilities: The interaction of learner, task, and setting.* Needham Heights, MA: Allyn and Bacon.

Snow, C. E., Barnes, W. S., Chandler, J., Goodman, J. F., & Hemphill, L. (1991). *Unfulfilled expectations: Home and school influences on literacy.* Cambridge, MA: Harvard University Press.

Stanovich, K. E. (1986). Matthew effects in reading: Some consequences of individual differences in the acquisition of literacy. *Reading Research Quarterly, 21,* 360–406.

———. (1991). Discrepancy definitions of reading disability: Has intelligence led us astray? *Reading Research Quarterly, 26,* 7–29.

Stanovich, K. E., Cunningham, A., & Feeman, D. (1984). Intelligence, cognitive skills, and early reading progress. *Reading Research Quarterly, 19,* 278–303.

Stanovich, K. E., & Siegel, L. S. (1994). Phenotypic performance profile of children with reading disabilities: A regression-based test of the phonological-core variable-difference model. *Journal of Educational Psychology, 86,* 24–53.

Torgesen, J. K. (1991). Learning disabilities: Historical and conceptual issues. In B. Y. L. Wong (Ed.), *Learning about learning disabilities* (pp. 3–37). San Diego, CA: Academic Press.

U.S. Department of Education. (1991). *To assure the free appropriate public education of all children with disabilities.* Thirteenth Annual Report to Congress on the Implementation of the Individuals with Disabilities Act. Washington, DC: U.S. Government Printing Office.

U.S. Office of Education. (1968). *First Annual Report, National Advisory Committee on Handicapped Children.* Washington, DC: U.S. Department of Health, Education, and Welfare.

Vellutino, F. R. (1979). *Dyslexia: Theory and research.* Cambridge, MA: MIT Press.

Vogel, S. (1990). Gender difference in intelligence, language, visual-motor abilities, and academic achievement in students with learning disabilities: A review of the literature. *Journal of Learning Disabilities, 23,* 44–52.

WISC-III Manual. (1991). *Wechsler Intelligence Scale for Children, Third Edition.* San Antonio, TX: Psychological Corporation.

Woodcock, R. W. (1987). *Woodcock Reading Mastery Tests—Revised.* Circle Pines, MN: American Guidance Service.

Ysseldyke, J., Algozzine, B., & Thurlow, M. (1992). *Critical issues in special education.* Boston, MA: Houghton Mifflin Company.

4 The Road to Proficient Reading

FIRST-TIME PARENTS are famous for worrying about each stage of their new child's development. Is the child learning to walk on schedule? Talk on schedule? Is he or she "normal"? With subsequent children, however, parents are usually more relaxed, in part because they now know more about how children typically develop. Knowledge about development gleaned from experience with previous children may also make second-, third-, or fourth-time parents quicker to catch genuine problems in development than are first-time parents.

Of course, what is "normal" in a given domain may vary widely. Still, some generalizations are possible. A two-year-old who speaks only in short phrases, who refuses to use the toilet, and who routinely treats his parents to ear-splitting tantrums probably is developmentally appropriate; a six-year-old who does these things is not. Problems in development can be interpreted only with reference to what is, broadly speaking, "normal."

Similarly, problems in learning to read require reading acquisition in non-disabled readers as a reference point. Most teachers are familiar with what constitutes typical reading development in academic terms. That is, they have a clear idea of what it means to read at a first-grade level as opposed to a third-grade level or a sixth-grade level. However, practitioners often are much less familiar with the cognitive underpinnings of this academic sequence. For instance, which cognitive skills are most important to beginning reading acquisition, and are these skills different from those most crucial to later reading acquisition? Which cognitive skills predict future reading achievement in preschoolers? How are the cognitive skills important to reading acquisition related to one another?

Why Knowledge About "Normal" Reading Development Is Important

Knowledge about the cognitive underpinnings of reading acquisition in normally achieving readers is especially important for understanding reading disability, for at least two reasons. First, although the academic deficits of children with RD are glaringly apparent, the cognitive underpinnings of these academic deficits are usually much less obvious. Information about these cognitive underpinnings is necessary for a deeper understanding of RD. However, the cognitive characteristics of children with RD can be interpreted only with reference to the cognitive characteristics of normally achieving readers. Among other things, knowledge about reading acquisition in nondisabled readers can clarify which of the many cognitive deficits in youngsters with RD are more causally central to RD (for it is all too easy to find evidence of cognitive deficits in reading disability) and which are offshoots of poor reading itself.

Consider, for example, the common view of reading disability as associated with frequent letter reversals and inversions of words in reading. The traditional interpretation of these errors has been that they are evidence of a visual-perceptual deficit (the view of early authorities such as Morgan and Hinshelwood) or evidence of incomplete hemispheric dominance for language (Orton's view). However, a look at reading acquisition reveals that normally achieving readers, when they are at the earliest stages of reading acquisition, also make errors involving letter reversals and inversions of words in reading (Mann, Tobin, & Wilson, 1987). In fact, children with RD do not make more of these kinds of errors than do other poor readers or than do younger, normally achieving readers (Shankweiler, Crain, Brady, & Macaruso, 1992). The reversal and inversion errors made by children with RD appear to be associated with their low reading level, not with poor visual perception of letters and words, and not with a distinctive syndrome of poor reading. Thus, proper interpretation of the cognitive characteristics of children with RD—in this example, a particular type of error pattern—requires a comparison to reading development in normally achieving readers.

The second reason why knowledge about reading acquisition, framed in cognitive terms, is important for practitioners interested in RD is that this knowledge yields implications about how to design educational programs for children with RD. We must emphasize that these implications are not necessarily simple or straightforward. In particular, they do not mandate a single teaching approach or method. However, they do suggest some constraints. For example, if certain cognitive skills are prerequisites for success in reading, and if children with RD lack those skills, then it is important to develop those skills in youngsters with RD. Nevertheless, there might be many different ways to develop the same cognitive skill. We might draw an analogy here between reading and many other kinds of complex skills, such as learning to play the piano or learning to play tennis. There is more than one acceptable way to teach someone to play the piano or to play tennis. Then again, one simply cannot learn to play the piano without understanding how the keys work or without achieving a certain degree of manual dexterity; one cannot learn to play tennis without knowing how to hold a racket.

In this chapter, as a prelude to discussing our model of reading disability in Chapter 5, we present our model of reading acquisition. This model is similar in some respects to another model familiar to many educators, that of Jeanne Chall (1983; Chall, Jacobs, & Baldwin, 1990). Like Chall and her colleagues, we conceptualize reading acquisition in terms of a sequence of phases of development, whereby word recognition is more prominent in the early phases and comprehension more prominent in the later ones. However, Chall's model is framed primarily in academic terms whereas ours is framed primarily in cognitive terms. For instance, Chall emphasizes certain reading and writing skills—naming letters of the alphabet, printing one's name, decoding common one-syllable words, reading narrative and expository text, and so on—learned in each phase of development, whereas we emphasize the cognitive processes involved in the various phases, such as phonological processes and strategic processes. Thus, our model has a different, and specifically more cognitive, focus than does Chall's. As we have explained, we believe that a cognitive focus is particularly useful for understanding reading disability.

In addition, our model of reading acquisition has been strongly influenced by a particular line of work in psychology, that of information-processing research. We have already discussed some limitations of the information-processing approach, especially its tendency to ignore the influence of contextual variables, such as the nature of instruction, on information-processing abilities. Nevertheless, information-processing research offers some valuable insights, about both typical reading acquisition and reading disability.

Finally, a word about the three perspectives—intrinsic, extrinsic, and interactive—discussed in previous chapters. For normally achieving readers, no less than for children with reading disability, reading acquisition is the result of a unique interaction between children's intrinsic characteristics and the features of the environment. In our view, reading acquisition is not merely the spontaneous flowering of innate aptitudes, nor is it the sole product of instruction or of other environmental variables. Thus, with regard to reading acquisition in nondisabled readers, and to reading disability itself, we have an interactive view.

We will begin our discussion of reading acquisition with an overview presenting some generalizations about reading and the research findings that support these generalizations. Next, we will describe in detail our model of reading acquisition, which involves a series of six cognitive phases and integrates the work of numerous investigators of reading. We will conclude this chapter by comparing our model to other cognitive models of reading acquisition.

An Overview of Reading Acquisition

To say that the precise nature of reading acquisition is controversial is a considerable understatement (see, for example, Adams et al., 1991). Ever mindful of this controversy, we nevertheless think that current data clearly warrant some generalizations about reading acquisition. Here, we discuss at length three of these generalizations: the idea of reading as a developmental process; the idea of a common road to proficient reading, with a focus on the role played by phonological processes in children's progress along this route; and the idea of emergent literacy.

Reading as a Developmental Process

Like many other researchers (e.g., Adams, 1990; Chall, 1983; Chall et al., 1990; Frith, 1985; Gough & Juel, 1991), we have a developmental view of reading acquisition. According to this view, what constitutes "reading" changes with the age and proficiency level of the reader. Reading is not the same act for a beginning reader or for an intermediate-level reader as it is for a proficient adult reader.

For example, David, the son of one of the coauthors, consistently recognized the *Coca-Cola* logo on the side of a truck at the age of twenty-five months, even though he could not yet name any letters and indeed had no idea what a "letter" was, of either the alphabetic or the postal variety. Now, this is word recognition of a sort, and it seems fairly impressive in a twenty-five-month-old; at least, it impressed the coauthor. Nevertheless, we do not think that anyone would equate this kind of reading with an adult's reading of, say, *Crime and Punishment,* or even with a first-grader's decoding of a primer.

Because the nature of reading changes with development, it is reasonable to assume that the cognitive processes implicated in reading differ with age and reading level. One would not expect exactly the same cognitive processes to be implicated in recognizing the *Coca-Cola* logo as in reading *Crime and Punishment* with a high level of comprehension and appreciation. Thus, our model of reading acquisition involves a sequence of developmental phases in which the cognitive processes most crucial to reading acquisition shift over time. The defining feature of each phase is different, although some phases may share certain characteristics. For instance, children in the earliest phase of reading acquisition, like the coauthor's son David, rely on visual cues, such as a distinctive logo, to recognize words, whereas children in the next phase, which entails what we call phonetic-cue word recognition (after Ehri, 1991, 1992), make use of some letter-sound correspondences in word recognition. What distinguishes the two phases is children's use of visual versus phonetic cues; the two phases have some characteristics in common, such as heavy reliance on context to aid word recognition. We view the transitions between these phases as gradual, not as abrupt or sharply distinct.

There is compelling evidence that children do go through different cognitive phases in learning to read and that the sequence of these phases is similar across children, at least across those who are learning an alphabet (Adams, 1990; Chall, 1983; Chall et al., 1990; Ehri, 1991, 1992; Gough & Juel, 1991). To what factors are these different phases linked? In part, they are linked to the changing task demands of schooling. For instance, reading curricula tend to emphasize word-recognition skills in the early grades but to emphasize reading comprehension in the later grades. The kinds of comprehension demands that schools and teachers make also vary depending on age and grade level. Older students are expected to read an increasing range of technical and expository text, and to read narratives with deeper comprehension and appreciation, than are younger students. A group of ninth graders, say, would be expected to read Shakespeare at a level of comprehension different from that of college students.

However, it would be a mistake to regard the different phases of reading acquisition as linked only to educational curricula. In part, these phases also are linked to broad changes in cognitive development that occur with age. Indeed, recognition that these changes occur is one reason that reading curricula are structured the way they are. We expect deeper comprehension from college students than from ninth-graders because college students are (we hope, anyway) cognitively more mature and have a broader base of experience and knowledge. In addition, the phases appear to be linked not only to broad changes in cognitive development but also to certain cognitive skills more specific to reading acquisition itself. For instance, as we will discuss in detail later, certain phonological-processing skills are necessary for the development of accurate word recognition; and fast, accurate word recognition is necessary for the development of higher-order reading comprehension.

A Common Road to Proficient Reading

As the preceding discussion implies, we believe there is a common route that normally achieving readers typically take in becoming proficient readers. Investigators disagree considerably about the number and precise nature of the phases involved in reading acquisition. Nevertheless, most contemporary models of reading acquisition are phase or stage models, which assume that all children— normally achieving ones, at least—pass through the same phases (e.g., Chall, 1983; Chall et al., 1990; Ehri, 1991, 1992; Frith, 1985; Gough & Juel, 1991). This sequence of phases is what we will call the route to proficient reading.

To say that there is a common or typical route in normal reading acquisition is not to suggest that there are *no* variations, other than rate of development, among normally achieving readers. Obviously, there are. For instance, readers may vary in the strategies they employ in word recognition, with some youngsters relying more on whole-word strategies (e.g., drawing an analogy between an unfamiliar word such as *vat* and a known word such as *cat*) and others relying more on parts-to-whole phonetic strategies (e.g., reading an unfamiliar word such as *vat* by sounding out and blending individual letters or groups of letters). Not surprisingly, children's choices of strategies are influenced by, among other things, the nature of instruction (Vellutino & Scanlon, 1991). Children who have been taught to read via a sight-word or other whole-word approach will be more likely to use whole-word strategies in word recognition, whereas children who have been taught via a parts-to-whole phonetic approach will be more likely to use parts-to-whole phonetic strategies.

Nevertheless, although children's strategies in word recognition may vary, the development of fast and accurate word recognition is critical to progress in reading acquisition (Adams, 1990; Perfetti, 1985, 1992; Stanovich, 1986, 1991). Furthermore, the development of word-recognition skills is clearly tied to the development of phonological-processing skills—that is, to processing skills involving the sound structure of the language. (We will have more to say about these skills in a moment.) As already indicated, in the earliest phases of reading acquisition it is typical—and perfectly "normal"—for children to adopt purely visual strategies in word recognition or for children to rely heavily on contextual cues to guess at words, in either case not attending closely to the actual sequence of letters in a word. The point is that children cannot *progress* in reading by persisting in such strategies. Rather, progress in reading is tied to the development of word-recognition and phonological skills.

We should acknowledge at this point that considerable dispute still exists among researchers regarding the role of phonological processes in proficient *adult* word recognition. However, most authorities agree that phonological processes play a role in the reading comprehension of adults, and that these processes are crucial to children's acquisition of word-recognition skills (Perfetti, 1985; Stanovich, 1992). Indeed, it has been said that "specification of the role of phonological processing in the earliest stages of reading acquisition is one of the more notable scientific success stories of the last decade" (Stanovich, 1992, p. 12).

What exactly are these phonological processes that are so important in reading acquisition? Researchers have studied several such processes and have given them a variety of names. Four of the most commonly studied phonological processes are discussed in the following subsections.

Phonological Awareness. Phonological awareness, which has also been termed phonemic awareness, phonological sensitivity, or phonemic segmentation, probably has been the most intensively studied of the phonological processes related to reading acquisition. Phonological awareness means awareness of the sound structure of spoken language. Thus, phonological-awareness tasks involve spoken rather than written words. Researchers interested in phonological awareness have employed a variety of tasks, ranging from those that are relatively easy for young children, involving only a rudimentary level of phonological awareness, to those that are extremely difficult for young children. For example, alliteration tasks, in which children have to identify spoken words that start with the same sound— *farm, funny, phone, food,* and so on—are relatively easy. Phoneme-deletion tasks, in which children are asked to delete a sound from a spoken word (e.g., "Say 'goat' without the /t/," where the children are supposed to answer "go"), are among the most difficult of phonological-awareness tasks, especially for young children. And phoneme-counting tasks, in which children count the number of phonemes (or sounds) in a spoken word—"fish" has three phonemes, "eat" has two phonemes, and so on—also are quite difficult for young children. A few of the more rudimentary phonological-awareness tasks, such as those involving alliteration and rhyme, are familiar to many educators as traditional "reading readiness" activities.

Keep in mind that phonological awareness is different from simple perception of phonemes. A child might have perfectly normal perception of speech but still have difficulty with phonological-awareness tasks. Indeed, some investigators (e.g., Liberman & Liberman, 1990) argue that because children are born with the capacity to process phonemes in spoken language, and because this spoken language processing is automatic, or below the level of conscious awareness, there is ordinarily little need for youngsters to pay attention to phonemes in speech—until, of course, they begin to learn to read in an alphabetic language, where letters map onto (i.e., roughly correspond to) sounds in the spoken language. Although the fact that "fish" contains three phonemes seems obvious from an adult's point of view, it turns out that this fact is not at all obvious to young children, particularly before they learn to read.

Phonological Reading. In contrast to phonological-awareness tasks, which involve spoken words, measures of phonological reading entail the reading of written words in isolation. Phonological-reading skill is simply what teachers call "word decoding" or "word attack." To measure phonological-reading ability, some experimenters have compared subjects' skill at reading phonetically regular words, such as *gave* and *cat,* to their skill at reading phonetically irregular or exception words, such as *have* and *what.* However, because the interpretation of this task can be problematic, a different task, one that involves reading pseudowords, is a better measure of phonological-reading skill (Rack, Snowling, & Olson, 1992). Pseudowords, also called nonwords, are made-up words such as *sark* or *felmit.* Because pseudowords are not real words, yet are pronounceable to someone who understands the workings of the English alphabet, subjects cannot recognize the words "by sight" but instead must decode them. Laboratory measures of pseudoword reading usually involve not only accuracy of reading but also latency—that is, the time it takes for the subject to respond to the word.

A reader's ability to decode pseudowords does not necessarily mean that the reader has a set of explicit phonic rules in his or her head. For instance, rather than decoding words by applying a set of phonic rules, one might decode an unfamiliar word by analogy with a known word, such as by comparing *sark* with *dark.* Of course, the ability to decode pseudowords also requires detailed knowledge about how the alphabet works.

Phonological Coding in Working Memory. Here it is helpful to begin by defining some terms. Working memory, similar to the older concept of short-term memory, is important for long-term retention of information. In other words, information gets into long-term memory via working memory. Coding involves the way that information is mentally represented; a speech-based code, or phonological coding, seems to play an especially important role in working memory.

Consider the following common example. Suppose that you call the operator for a phone number but do not have a pencil handy to write it down. How would you remember the number until you find a pencil? You might use a visual code in memory, such as forming a mental picture of the number in your head. It is more likely, however, that you would mentally *say* the number, over and over, until you're able to write it down. The latter is an example of verbal rehearsal, which involves phonological coding.

Experimentally, phonological coding in working memory is typically measured through the use of a short-term memory task involving phonetically confusable strings of items, such as *t, b, z, v, g* or *man, fan, ran, ban, tan.* The items may be spoken or written, and they may involve phonetically confusable sentences as well as words or letters. Memory for the phonetically confusable strings of items is contrasted with memory for phonetically nonconfusable strings of items, such as *o, x, r, y, q* or *boy, green, with, fast, down.* Poorer performance on the phonetically confusable as compared with the phonetically nonconfusable strings is interpreted as demonstrating that the subject was making use of a phonological code in memory, because if the subject were using some other type of code, such as a visual code, then it should not have mattered whether the items were phonetically confusable.

The use of phonological coding in working memory appears to be especially important during reading. For instance, in reading a sentence such as *The cat, who playfully nudged the sleeping old dog on the sofa, was small and black,* readers need a way to maintain the words from the beginning of the sentence in memory; otherwise, by the time they reach the end of the sentence, they will not remember whether it was the dog, the cat, or the sofa that was small and black. Phonological coding seems to be a particularly useful way of maintaining information in memory during ongoing reading and therefore plays an important role in reading comprehension, in skilled adult readers as well as in children (Perfetti, 1985; Stanovich, 1992).

Phonological Processes in Lexical Access. The role of phonological coding in working memory, and its significance in reading comprehension, is acknowledged for readers of all ages and skill levels, including proficient adult readers. However, the role of phonological processes in lexical access is much more controversial (Stanovich, 1992; Wagner & Torgesen, 1987). Here the question involves the role of phonological processes not in reading comprehension but, rather, in word recognition. What the controversy centers on is the role of phonological processes in the word recognition of proficient adult readers, given that, in reading acquisition (especially early reading acquisition), phonological processes are generally agreed to play a role in lexical access.

Lexical access means accessing the mental representation of a word in memory. To put it most simply, in recognizing a word such as *pond,* can readers go directly from the written word to its meaning in memory, or is phonological mediation necessary? This is the question being disputed by researchers, especially with regard to proficient adult readers.

The role of phonological processes in lexical access has most commonly been measured through two kinds of tasks, lexical-decision tasks and rapid-naming tasks (Wagner & Torgesen, 1987). In a lexical-decision task, the subject has to decide whether or not a string of letters is a word. For example, when shown the letter string *train,* the subject pushes a "yes" button, whereas when shown the letter string *mukj,* the subject pushes a "no" button. In rapid-naming tasks, the subject is shown pictures of objects, colors, numbers, letters, or written words and must name them as rapidly as possible.

Until recently, most models of word recognition have been dual-route models (e.g., Coltheart, 1978). Here the word *route* refers not to a sequence of development in reading (as we have used it) but, rather, to a mental pathway for recognizing words. In dual-route models of word recognition, there is a direct visual route for recognizing words without phonological mediation, as well as a phonological route in which phonological mediation is required. Dual-route models have varied in numerous respects, but they all subscribe to the idea that there are two alternative, and at least partially independent, ways to recognize words. Which route the reader employs depends upon, among other things, the nature of the word and the reader's skill. For example, a highly regular word such as *sat* might be recognized via the phonological route by a beginning reader but via the direct visual route by a more accomplished reader. By contrast, an irregular word that cannot be easily phonologically decoded, such as *ocean,* might be recognized via the direct visual route even by beginning readers.

One of the strongest lines of evidence supporting dual-route models of word recognition involves studies of acquired dyslexia, whereby an individual who once was a normally achieving reader loses the ability to read after a brain injury or stroke. These studies appear to show selective impairments to either a visual or phonological route in word recognition (Patterson, Marshall, & Coltheart, 1985; Rayner & Pollatsek, 1989).

However, recently, and with the advent of connectionist models of word recognition, dual-route models have fallen into some disfavor (Ehri, 1992; Rack, Snowling, & Olson, 1992; Stanovich, 1991). Some researchers have argued that the distinction between the two routes is artificial. For instance, a word such as *ocean* is not completely arbitrary, phonologically speaking, but might be recognized through the use of both phonological processes and direct visual recognition. In any case, however the scientific dispute may eventually be resolved with regard to proficient adult readers, there is convincing evidence that beginning readers initially need to rely on phonological processes to read words (Adams, 1990; Perfetti, 1985; Stanovich, 1991, 1992; Wagner & Torgesen, 1987).

Some General Comments. Three general points can now be made about the role of phonological processes in reading acquisition. First, the tasks that have been used to measure phonological processing sometimes tap more than one kind of process. For example, phonological-awareness tasks, such as phoneme deletion (e.g., "Say 'goat' without the /t/"), tap the ability to use phonological codes in memory as well as actual awareness of phonemes. Phonological-reading tasks may also tap phonological-coding skills, especially in beginning readers, because the child may use phonological codes to hold letter sounds in memory before blending them.

Second, although we have referred to phonological processes as being speech or sound based, we must note that they do not *literally* involve sounds. Readers do not literally have to hear voices in order to read well. Rather, phonological processes are more abstract than is literal speech. Perhaps the best example of the abstract nature of phonological processes comes from research with congenitally deaf readers (e.g., Hanson, 1989; Hanson & Fowler, 1987; Hanson, Liberman, & Shankweiler, 1984). The work of Hanson and her colleagues demonstrates that, like reading skill in hearing readers, reading skill in profoundly deaf readers involves phonological-processing skills—despite the fact that the latter have never heard speech! How can this be? Hanson (1989) suggests that congenitally deaf individuals who become successful readers are able to acquire linguistic, and specifically phonological, knowledge from sources other than auditory experience with speech, such as lip reading.

Finally, phonological-processing skills can be viewed as intrinsic characteristics that children bring to reading acquisition. Although some investigators seem to assume that these intrinsic phonological-processing skills are biologically determined, there is also considerable evidence, which we will explore later, that phonological-processing skills are affected by experience. In any case, it is clear that children do begin formal reading instruction with individual differences in phonological processing. These individual differences may influence, among other things, children's capacities to profit from a given instructional approach in reading. For example, a child with strong phonological-processing skills may be able to profit from a variety of reading programs, whereas a child with weak phonological-processing skills may require an educational program with more emphasis on phonological skills.

Emergent Literacy

In recent years, the concept of emergent literacy has strongly influenced both practitioners and researchers in reading. Yet authorities have seemed to give somewhat different shades of meaning to the concept. For example, Holdaway (1979)—whose usage we prefer—uses the term to mean a particular stage of development in reading, one that involves very young children who have not yet learned to identify words, but who have become fascinated with books and reading. For other authorities (e.g., Goodman, 1986), the concept of emergent literacy seems to include not only the idea of a particular stage of development but also an implicit theory of reading acquisition: specifically, the theory that, if children are given sufficient experience with books, learning to read will be as natural and as effortless as learning to speak.

Researchers interested in emergent literacy (e.g., Clay, 1979; Ferreiro & Teberosky, 1982; Holdaway, 1979; Mason, 1992; Sulzby, 1985; Teale & Sulzby, 1987) have made important discoveries about the beginnings of reading acquisition. Above all, it is clear that young children, especially those from homes with highly literate parents, already know quite a lot about reading before they ever enter school. At least for these children, reading acquisition is not initiated upon entrance to school but, rather, is already well under way by the onset of formal reading instruction. Young children's knowledge about reading may include such things as knowing how to hold a book and turn its pages; knowing that spaces separate printed words; knowing the direction in which print is read (left to right and top to bottom); being able to identify letters and words; and understanding the language and structure of stories.

Young children glean their knowledge about reading from a variety of sources. In particular, researchers interested in emergent literacy have emphasized the importance of storybook reading in initiating children into literacy and in introducing them to the differences between oral and written language. Mason (1992) reviews some of these differences. For instance, written language ordinarily is more decontextualized than is oral language. Speakers can use gestures and facial expressions to communicate meaning, and they can repeat or paraphrase themselves if the listener fails to understand; but these supports for comprehension are not available in reading. Furthermore, written language employs words and syntactic structures that may not be used often in oral language. When children are read to frequently, they tend to develop a "book language" way of speaking (Sulzby, 1985) and to increase their vocabularies (Robbins & Ehri, 1994). Mason (1992) suggests that storybook reading in the preschool years contributes to later success in reading by improving children's comprehension of text, which in turn may allow the children in the early grades to focus their mental resources on decoding and thus to excel in reading comprehension in the later grades.

Moreover, storybook reading is typically mediated by a caring adult, such as a parent, who is familiar with the child's abilities and prior knowledge. Because of this familiarity with the child, the adult can bridge gaps in the child's background knowledge or reword parts of the story that may not be comprehensible. Shared storybook reading with a caring adult also provides a highly positive emotional and motivational context for future or continued reading acquisition.

Other sources for young children's learning about literacy include exposure to environmental print, such as signs and labels; games, such as playing with magnetic letters; and children's earliest attempts at writing. Researchers and practitioners interested in emergent literacy tend to stress the importance not only of reading storybooks but also of immersing children in an environment rich in print and encouraging children's writing. These experiences are a foundation for later formal instruction in reading. Conversely, a lack of exposure to books, print, and writing does not bode well for later reading acquisition, particularly if schools fail to compensate for this lack (Anderson, Hiebert, Scott, & Wilkinson, 1985).

However, we must take issue with the view, held by some researchers in the area of emergent literacy, that reading development unfolds naturally and automatically with sufficient exposure to literacy experiences. Research evidence does not support the idea that most children will learn to read naturally (i.e., without formal instruction) if only they have enough exposure to books and print. For one thing, much of the research on emergent literacy involves case studies of children from middle-class homes, with highly literate parents (Delpit, 1988). As Adams (1990) points out, these youngsters may have literally thousands of hours of exposure to activities such as being read to, playing with letters, writing, and so on, before they ever enter school. Obviously, however, not all children have such a high level of exposure to literacy experiences in the preschool years. Furthermore, even among children from homes that do provide such exposure, there are individual differences in the extent to which children "emerge" as readers, as many parents will attest (Stahl, 1990).

Authorities with the "reading-is-natural" view often draw comparisons between oral language acquisition and reading acquisition. However, these comparisons are misleading, not only because oral language and written language differ in important ways, as we discussed earlier, but also because the acquisition processes for each domain are dissimilar. Some informal observations suggest that these differences between oral language acquisition and reading acquisition do exist. For instance, most children do not have to attend school to learn how to speak. Furthermore, oral language is universal among cultures, whereas writing systems are not. Most cultures that are literate have formal systems of schooling to develop literacy in the young.

Liberman and Liberman (1990) argue that the reason that reading acquisition appears to be so much less "natural" than oral language acquisition has to do with the phonological processes we discussed earlier, especially with phonological awareness. Although both oral speech and a written alphabet involve phonemes, the phonemes in oral speech are processed automatically, below the level of conscious awareness. Moreover, phonemes in oral speech are co-articulated; that is, they are not distinct but overlapped.

For instance, imagine that the word *big* is recorded on a tape recorder. Because of co-articulation, it would be impossible to isolate the separate phonemes /b/, /i/, /g/ from the word on the tape, no matter how slowly the tape is played. Without co-articulation, oral speech would be painfully slow. However, the existence of co-articulation, along with the processing of phonemes in oral language below a level of conscious awareness, makes awareness of phonemes a skill that is not "natural" for preschool children. Yet, this awareness is necessary in an alphabetic language such as English, where letters map onto phonemes in the oral language. If the child does not achieve at least a rudimentary level of phonological awareness, learning how to do this mapping (i.e., how to decode), and indeed the whole point of an alphabet, will remain incomprehensible.

In order to progress in reading, children need to acquire specific kinds of print-related knowledge, including both phonological awareness and letter-sound knowledge. Exposure alone, both to environmental print and to books, does not appear to be sufficient for the acquisition of this knowledge. For instance, Masonheimer, Drum, and Ehri (1984) found that preschool youngsters who were good environmental print readers did not attend closely to the print itself and thus failed to notice letter changes in familiar signs, such as *Xepsi* for *Pepsi*. In addition, Ehri and Sweet (1991) examined fingerpoint-reading of text in children aged four to six. Fingerpoint-reading, in which children learn to point word by word as they recite a text from memory, requires children to pay closer attention to print than does mere exposure to books and signs. Nevertheless, Ehri and Sweet found that children did not progress to independent word recognition from fingerpoint-reading and, indeed, had difficulty even doing fingerpoint-reading, unless skills such as letter-name knowledge and phonological awareness were already in place.

Practices such as reading aloud to children and fingerpoint-reading are valuable in their own right. However, such practices, by themselves, do not ensure that children will figure out independently how the alphabet works; for most children, this knowledge about the alphabet is acquired through formal schooling. The point, then, is not that children have to be taught to read via any one particular method, nor even that they have to go to school to acquire word-recognition skills. Rather, the point is that learning to read generally requires interaction with an adult who systematically draws the child's attention to letters and to the alphabetic code (as well as to other matters, of course, such as word meanings). Usually this adult is a teacher, but he or she could also be a parent. In colonial America, for example, children generally were expected to learn their "ABCs" and basic reading skills at home, under the tutelage of their mothers (S. Wolf, 1993).

Indeed, many advocates of shared storybook reading and fingerpoint-reading (e.g., Clay, 1979; Holdaway, 1979; Mason, 1992) acknowledge the importance of structured adult guidance and support for children to profit from these activities. For instance, in shared storybook reading, adults can draw children's attention to letters and to similarities in spelling among different words. It is important that this message regarding the need for guidance from adults, especially in understanding the workings of the alphabet, not get lost in the translation of research on emergent literacy into educational practice.

Staying on the Road to Proficient Reading

In this section, we present our own model of reading acquisition, which involves a sequence of six phases: visual-cue word recognition, phonetic-cue word recognition, controlled word recognition, automatic word recognition, strategic reading, and proficient adult reading. Table 4.1 lists the various phases of reading acquisition, their defining features, and the approximate age and grade levels at which they occur. Table 4.2 gives a more complete listing of the cognitive characteristics of each phase, including those that may be shared by more than one phase.

Before beginning our description of each of the six phases, we wish to emphasize several points. First, as suggested above, the age and grade levels for each phase are only approximations, based on research involving mostly middle-class, English-speaking youngsters. As we will discuss, attainment of each phase of reading depends on factors such as the child's level of cognitive development, the nature of the child's home environment, and the nature of the instructional curriculum—all of which may vary widely, both within and across socioeconomic levels.

TABLE 4.1 Phases of Reading Acquisition

Phase	Defining Feature(s)	Approximate Grade	Approximate Age
Visual-cue word recognition	Child uses visual cues (e.g., word shape, color, a logo), rather than phonetic cues, in word recognition	Preschoolers and some kindergartners	Two to five years
Phonetic-cue word recognition	Child uses partial phonetic cues in word recognition	Kindergarten and first grade	Five to six years
Controlled word recognition	Child makes full use of phonetic and orthographic cues in word recognition, but is not automatic in recognizing words	Second grade	Six to seven years
Automatic word recognition	Child recognizes common words accurately and automatically	Second to third grade	Seven to eight years
Strategic reading	Child routinely uses strategies to aid comprehension	Beginning at third to fourth grade	Beginning at eight to nine years
Proficient adult reading	Individual has higher-order comprehension skills	Beginning at later high school or college level	Beginning in later adolescence

Second, we make no claims of cultural universality for our model. Indeed, research has suggested that the cognitive correlates of reading acquisition differ to some extent across cultures and orthographies (e.g., Mann, 1985; Read, Zhang, Nie, & Ding, 1986). For example, whereas a rudimentary level of phonological awareness appears to play a crucial role in learning to read an alphabetic language such as English, phonological awareness is not crucial for learning to read a logographic language such as Chinese, in which the written symbols primarily map onto units of meaning rather than onto units of sound. Thus, children from other cultures, especially those involving nonalphabetic languages, may follow a sequence of development that differs from the one proposed here. Obviously, many factors other than orthography, such as the nature of schooling and cultural attitudes toward literacy and academic achievement, vary across cultures. These other factors may also contribute to differences across cultures in the nature of reading acquisition.

TABLE 4.2   Cognitive Characteristics of Each Phase of Reading Acquisition

	Phase					
	Visual Cue	*Phonetic Cue*	*Controlled*	*Automatic*	*Strategic*	*Highly Proficient*
Uses only visual cues in word recognition	x					
Has partial or full letter-sound knowledge		x	x	x	x	x
Has rudimentary phonological awareness		x				
Has relatively advanced level of phonological awareness			x	x	x	x
Has achieved alphabetic insight		x	x	x	x	x
Uses only partial phonetic cues to recognize words		x				
Relies heavily on context to aid or speed word recognition	x	x	x			

(continues)

We should point out, however, that researchers have found many similarities in children's reading acquisition of a wide variety of alphabetic languages, including English, Swedish, French, Russian, and Italian. Even across different orthographies, there are many similarities in reading acquisition. For example, Harold Stevenson and his colleagues (1982, 1987), who compared the reading achievement of children in the United States, Japan, and Taiwan, emphasized that there appeared to be more similarities than differences among the poor readers in these three cultures. These investigators found that there were always some children who experienced difficulty in learning how to read, no matter what the orthography. Poor readers across cultures were similar in, among other things, their attitudes toward reading and in the amount of time they spent reading. Furthermore, different writing systems did not seem to cause large differences in the rates at which most children learned to read.

TABLE 4.2 (continued)

	Phase					
	Visual Cue	Phonetic Cue	Controlled	Automatic	Strategic	Highly Proficient
Makes full use of orthographic information to recognize words			x	x	x	x
Has acquired accurate word-recognition skills			x	x	x	x
Has automatic word-recognition skills				x	x	x
Routinely uses some strategies to aid comprehension					x	x
Has higher-order comprehension abilities						x

Finally, our model draws upon the work of a multitude of investigators who are interested in the cognitive processes involved in reading acquisition. Although we do of course cite specific studies, we also wish to acknowledge from the beginning some of the researchers whose work has been particularly influential in shaping our model. These include Brian Byrne, Linnea Ehri, Ruth Garner, Philip Gough, Connie Juel, Isabelle Liberman, Scott Paris, Charles Perfetti, Keith Stanovich, Joseph Torgesen, and Richard Wagner. Both our model of typical reading acquisition and our model of reading disability (to be presented in the next chapter) owe much to the research of these and other cognitive investigators. We now turn to a description of the six phases in our model.

Visual-Cue Word Recognition

A number of investigators (e.g., Ehri, 1991, 1992; Gough & Juel, 1991) have shown that reading acquisition begins with a phase of paired-associate learning in which children do not make use of letter-sound relationships in recognizing words but, rather, make use of some salient visual cue, such as the shape of the word or a distinctive logo. We call this first phase of reading acquisition visual-cue word recognition, after Ehri (1991, 1992). Our earlier example of David's recognition of the *Coca-Cola* sign is an instance of visual-cue word recognition. Another familiar example would be the youngster who recognizes the *McDonald's* sign based on the golden arches. Visual-cue word recognition is most characteristic of preschool children and many, though not all, kindergartners—in other words, children approximately two to five years old.

Gough and Juel (1991) present a particularly memorable example of visual-cue word recognition, for which they use the term *selective association*. In two unpublished experiments, Gough trained a group of four- and five-year-olds to recognize four words randomly presented on flash cards. One of the flash cards had a conspicuous thumbprint on it. Not only did all of the children learn the word on the thumbprinted card faster than they learned the other three words, but when they were shown the same word on another card without the thumbprint, most of the children did not recognize it. Moreover, when a different word was accompanied by a thumbprint, most of the children incorrectly identified it as the first word they had learned to associate with the thumbprint. In short, these children not only focused on the thumbprint, but they did so to the exclusion of attending to the letters.

Clearly, children in the phase of visual-cue word recognition do not understand that the letters within words carry important information. In particular, they have not yet discovered the alphabetic principle—the idea that letters represent sounds in a systematic way. Children in this phase may recognize some letters or know some letter names but still not apply this knowledge in reading words, because they lack alphabetic insight.

We agree with Byrne (1992) that children's discovery of the alphabetic principle is an insight, a sudden leap of understanding in which children grasp a general principle. (This insight also may involve a series of smaller insights, as discussed in Stahl & Murray, 1994.) To have alphabetic insight, children do not have to know *how* all of the letters and sounds map onto each other—only that they do. For example, there is a memorable scene at the end of the movie *The Miracle Worker* in which Helen Keller's teacher, Annie Sullivan, finger-spells *water* while holding Helen's hand under a water pump. Suddenly, Helen grasps not only the finger-spelling for *water* but also the general principle that finger-spellings mean something, that they represent words. A similar phenomenon applies to children in general. Before they can decode large numbers of words, they have to understand that there *is* a meaningful, systematic code—one that, in the case of reading, involves mapping letters onto sounds.

For children in the phase of visual-cue word recognition who are receiving formal reading instruction, a number of instructional variables may interact with reading development. One of these variables involves the structural nature of the first words being taught. If the first words in the instructional curriculum are structurally highly dissimilar (e.g., *dinosaur, swamp, big, footprints*), then the children may be quite successful in learning the words, because it is relatively easy for them to find a distinctive visual cue for each word, such as length or shape. Of course, as more words are introduced into the curriculum, it will become progressively more difficult for the children to recognize them based on a distinctive visual cue. Conversely, if the initial words in the curriculum are structurally similar (e.g., *sat, sit, bat, bit*), the children will probably be much less successful initially in recognizing them, but their lack of understanding of the alphabetic principle also will be readily revealed to the teacher. (Complicating the issue is the fact that, at first blush, the "dinosaur" story seems a lot more appealing than the "sat-sit-bat-bit" story, a distinction we will address in Chapter 6.)

A related point is that children in the phase of visual-cue word recognition appear to have great difficulty in deducing the alphabetic principle from whole-word instructional approaches alone—that is, without additional training in phonological awareness and in letter-sound relationships. For example, Byrne (1991, 1992) trained a group of preschool youngsters who were nonreaders and who knew no letter-sound correspondences to recognize two words by sight, *fat* and *bat*. However, when the children were shown a word such as *fun* and told that the word said either *fun* or *bun*, they could not pick the correct choice above chance expectancy. In other words, they had not deduced from learning the two sight words that the letter *f* corresponds to the phoneme /f/ and that the letter *b* corresponds to the phoneme /b/.

Seymour and Elder (1986) examined the reading skills of a group of children who had learned to read via a strong sight-word approach, with no formal decoding instruction. Although the children varied considerably in their abilities to learn sight words, most of them failed to acquire phonological-reading skills; even after a year of instruction, they could read only words that they had been taught and were unable to decode unfamiliar words. These findings support the conclusion that deducing the alphabetic principle from whole-word learning alone is extremely difficult for young children.

Phonetic-Cue Word Recognition

Ehri (1991, 1992) identified a second phase of reading acquisition. We will use her term, *phonetic-cue word recognition,* for this phase. In phonetic-cue word recognition, children begin to use partial phonetic cues to recognize words—often, but not always, involving the initial or final letters. For instance, children in this phase might recognize the word *boat* based on the initial *b* and the final *t;* but because they cannot fully decode words, they might confuse *boat* with *beat, boot,* and so on. To put it another way, children use some, but not all, of the letter information in a word, so their word recognition is still inaccurate. Therefore, they need to rely on context to facilitate word recognition. For example, the child who is reading a sentence such as *The boy sailed a toy boat* can use context to identify the last word as *boat* rather than *boot* or *beat.*

In order to reach the phase of phonetic-cue word recognition, children must attain alphabetic insight. And attaining alphabetic insight, in turn, appears to depend upon at least two other things (Byrne, 1991, 1992). First, children must be able to remember at least some letter-sound relationships. In the *boat* example, they must know that the letter *b* can represent /b/ and that the letter *t* can represent /t/. Second, children must achieve at least a rudimentary level of phonological awareness. In the *boat* example, they must be aware that the spoken word *boat* begins with the sound /b/ and ends with the sound /t/. Children in this phase are capable of accomplishing other relatively easy phonological-awareness tasks as well, such as rhyming and alliteration.

The relationship between early reading acquisition and phonological awareness is complex. For one thing, the causality is bidirectional (e.g., Ehri & Sweet, 1991; Perfetti, Beck, Bell, & Hughes, 1987; Stanovich, 1986; Wagner & Torgesen, 1987; Wagner, Torgesen, & Rashotte, 1994). In other words, phonological awareness both causes and is caused by reading skill. On the one hand, although phonological skills, including phonological awareness, do correlate significantly with general intelligence (Torgesen, Wagner, & Rashotte, 1994), phonological awareness predicts later reading achievement even when both IQ and prior knowledge of decoding are controlled (Mann & Liberman, 1984; Vellutino & Scanlon, 1987; Wagner & Torgesen, 1987; Wagner et al., 1994). Indeed, among preschool children, phonological awareness is a *better* predictor of future reading skill than is IQ (Stanovich, 1992). Ehri and Sweet (1991), whose study we mentioned in our discussion of emergent literacy, found that phonological awareness, as measured by a phoneme-segmentation task, was an important predictor of fingerpoint-reading performance. Furthermore, there is evidence that phonological awareness can be trained, and that phonological-awareness training can improve reading skill (Bradley & Bryant, 1985; Lundberg, Frost, & Peterson, 1988). All of this evidence suggests that phonological awareness is an important cause of later reading achievement.

On the other hand, learning to read itself, especially in the context of an alphabetic orthography, develops phonological awareness (e.g., Byrne & Ledez, 1986; Perfetti et al., 1987; Wagner & Torgesen, 1987; Wagner et al., 1994). Illiterate adults do not spontaneously develop more advanced levels of phonological awareness in the absence of experience with an alphabet (e.g., Morais, Bertelson, Cary, & Alegria, 1986), and individuals who learn to read nonalphabetic orthographies, such as Chinese, may also lack phonological awareness (e.g., Read et al., 1986). It appears that rudimentary levels of phonological awareness enable beginning reading acquisition in an alphabetic orthography. Furthermore, as children acquire some reading skill, they develop even more phonological awareness—which may in turn facilitate further gains in reading (e.g., Perfetti et al., 1987).

Treiman (1991, 1992) has studied the ability of children to achieve awareness of onsets and rimes, which are intrasyllabic units—that is, linguistic units at a level intermediate between syllables and phonemes. For instance, in the word *cat,* the onset is represented by the letter *c* and the rime by the letters *at;* in *flash,* the onset is represented by *fl* and the rime by *ash.* Children can become aware of these intrasyllabic units more easily than they can become aware of phonemes. In fact, many rudimentary phonological-awareness tasks, such as alliteration and rhyming, can be accomplished with awareness only of onsets and rimes. Treiman suggests that onsets and rimes may be a more natural entry point for reading instruction in young children than are phonemes, and also that awareness of onsets and rimes may play a role in spelling acquisition.

In their study of a group of kindergartners and first-graders, Stahl and Murray (1994) found that onset-rime awareness—for instance, the ability to segment the onset and rime within a one-syllable word such as *fan*—appeared to be particularly essential to early reading acquisition. That is, onset-rime awareness may constitute the kind of minimal level of phonological awareness necessary for beginning to learn to read in an alphabetic language. However, even onset-rime awareness may not be independent of reading-related knowledge and, specifically, of letter knowledge; Stahl and Murray argued that knowledge of letter names was necessary but not sufficient for children to manipulate onsets and rimes. Thus, this study reinforces the picture of complex and reciprocal relationships among skills such as onset-rime awareness, more advanced forms of phonological awareness, letter knowledge, and simple word recognition. (For further discussion of onsets, rimes, and phonological awareness, see Adams, 1990.)

Some children, especially those from homes with highly literate parents, may enter school already in the phase of phonetic-cue word recognition. Children who have been read to extensively, who have had their attention drawn to letters and written words, who have learned at least some letter names, and who have been exposed to activities that appear to promote phonological awareness, such as hearing nursery rhymes (e.g., Maclean, Bryant, & Bradley, 1987), may achieve alphabetic insight in the preschool years. However, for many children, alphabetic insight, and the phase of phonetic-cue word recognition, will be attained only through formal schooling, generally in either kindergarten or first grade, at the age of five or six.

The nature of the kindergarten program may influence attainment of phonetic-cue word recognition. Kindergarten programs vary in the extent to which they focus on language and specifically, phonological skills. They also vary in the extent to which they introduce formal academic instruction, as opposed to pre-academic (e.g., language and social) skills. In this connection, Elkind (1987) argues that there has been a tendency in recent years for kindergartens to become increasingly "academic." And Bryant, Clifford, and Peisner (1991), in an evaluation of kindergarten programs, found that a significant number of kindergarten programs were not developmentally appropriate.

How does this variation in kindergarten programs influence reading acquisition? Children who enter kindergarten already in the phase of phonetic-cue word recognition may be able to profit from formal instruction in reading—in other words, from a more "academic" program. However, children without alphabetic insight, who are in the phase of visual-cue word recognition, need to be prepared to develop this insight when they are enrolled in kindergarten, through programs that stress, among other things, phonological awareness and letter knowledge. In the absence of such preparation, these latter children might have considerable difficulty with formal reading instruction.

Controlled Word Recognition

In this third phase of reading, children have acquired accurate word-recognition skills. That is, the children are able to make use of all the letter information in a word, rather than relying only on partial phonetic cues, as in the previous phase. Because children in this phase have acquired accurate word recognition, they do not confuse similarly spelled words. However, we use the word *controlled* for this phase to indicate that word recognition is still relatively effortful. Controlled processes are those that are consuming of mental resources—in other words, not yet automatic. Children with controlled word recognition, like those in earlier phases of reading, may continue to rely on context to speed word recognition, especially when reading more difficult texts.

Just as alphabetic insight is crucial to the attainment of phonetic-cue word recognition, orthographic knowledge is crucial to the attainment of controlled word recognition. Orthographic knowledge is knowledge about spelling patterns that occur in English. This knowledge is necessary for fully accurate recognition of most words, because in English, groups of letters frequently map onto a single sound. For instance, in the word *boat,* the *oa* must be recognized as a unit that maps onto the long *o.* Other examples of common orthographic patterns in English include *igh* as in *light, eer* as in *cheer,* and *augh* as in *caught.*

Orthographic knowledge also includes knowledge about word-specific spelling patterns. For instance, readers with orthographic knowledge recognize *shert* as an incorrect representation of *shirt,* even though both representations are phonologically the same. Orthographic knowledge allows readers to discriminate between common homophones, such as *to* versus *two* or *there* versus *their.*

Some researchers include in the concept of orthographic processing the idea that words are recognized on a direct visual basis (as in the visual route of dual-route theory), without phonological mediation. By contrast, we use the term *orthographic knowledge* in a manner similar to that of Perfetti (1985), to mean knowledge about spelling patterns and word-specific spellings, as outlined above. We do not use the term to mean that words necessarily are recognized on a direct visual basis, although orthographic knowledge does appear to play a role in more rapid processing of words, especially in connected text (Barker, Torgesen, & Wagner, 1992).

What factors influence the development of orthographic knowledge? One involves phonological-processing skills, which we have already discussed. That is, in order to achieve a level of reading in which orthographic skills come into play, children must also have developed some phonological-processing skills. However, research indicates that the development of orthographic knowledge involves more than just phonological-processing skills. Differences in phonological processing do not completely account for differences in orthographic processing, and each kind of processing makes an independent contribution to word recognition (Barker et al., 1992; Cunningham & Stanovich, 1990; Olson, Wise, Conners, Rack, & Fulker, 1989).

Another factor that influences the development of orthographic knowledge is exposure to text. Even when differences in phonological processing and overall intelligence are accounted for, variations in exposure to text partially explain variations in orthographic processing (Barker et al., 1992; Cunningham & Stanovich, 1990). In other words, children who read more receive repeated exposure to words in text, which in turn helps them to remember spellings of words and of common letter strings such as *igh* and *augh*. In the studies just cited, the measure of exposure to text involved children's ability to recognize titles of popular children's books that were not used in the school curriculum.

We stated that variations in exposure to text *partially* explain variations in orthographic processing, inasmuch as these studies typically find residual variance in orthographic processing that is not accounted for by differences in exposure to text. There are numerous possible explanations for this residual variance in orthographic processing. One possibility is that there really is no residual variance, but that current measures of exposure to text simply are incomplete. For example, the title-recognition measure mentioned above would be sensitive to differences in reading experience incurred outside of school but not inside of school (Barker et al., 1992). A second possibility is that individual differences in some kind of visual-processing skill, such as the ability to visualize words in memory, contribute to individual differences in orthographic processing. As yet, however, researchers have not been successful in finding this visual-processing skill, if in fact it exists (Cunningham & Stanovich, 1990; Olson et al., 1989).

When do children usually achieve controlled word recognition? Juel, Griffith, and Gough (1986) found that orthographic knowledge makes little contribution to word-recognition skill in first-graders but contributes much more to word-recognition skill in second-graders. Ehri and Sweet (1991) also suggest that orthographic knowledge emerges in second grade. Other authorities, too, have pointed out that instruction in basic word-decoding skills can be completed by the end of second grade for most normally achieving readers (Anderson et al., 1985). Thus, achievement of controlled word recognition, at least in the case of common words, probably occurs for most children by the end of second grade, or at about the age of seven. Obviously, however, the exact point at which children reach this phase may be influenced by a number of other variables, including the children's exposure to text, both in and outside of school, and the nature of the instructional curriculum, such as the extent to which the children are given explicit instruction and practice in spelling words and commonly occurring units within words.

Automatic Word Recognition

In this phase of word recognition, children can recognize words not only accurately but also with relatively little effort—in other words, automatically. Thus, what distinguishes this phase from the previous one is ease rather than accuracy of word recognition. A number of researchers (e.g., LaBerge & Samuels, 1974; Perfetti & Lesgold, 1977; Sternberg & Wagner, 1982) have emphasized the importance of automatic word recognition to reading comprehension. On the one hand, when children have to expend mental resources in word recognition, they have fewer resources left over for comprehension. On the other hand, achievement of automatic word recognition sets the stage for rapidly increasing reading comprehension, because the children can now focus their mental resources on understanding the text rather than on deciphering the words. At this point, reading can increasingly be used as a tool for acquiring new concepts and information.

We should note here that accurate, automatic word recognition appears to be necessary, but not sufficient, for good reading comprehension. That is, in order to develop good reading-comprehension skills, children must have automatic word recognition, but automatic word recognition is not a *guarantee* of good reading comprehension. Obviously, children may have poor reading comprehension for reasons other than deficient word recognition, such as poor listening-comprehension skills. However, even in proficient adult readers, and even after differences in listening comprehension and general intelligence have been controlled for, variance in word-recognition skill accounts for variance in reading-comprehension ability (Stanovich, 1991). Eye-movement studies of reading indicate that proficient readers do not generally skip over words in text, as some theories of reading have claimed (Smith, 1973), but rather attend closely to individual words and letters (Rayner & Pollatsek, 1989). Thus, skill in word recognition is a hallmark of good reading, and it does not become irrelevant to reading comprehension at any age.

Examples of automatization, and of its role in freeing up mental resources for other pursuits, can be found in many domains. Consider, for example, the process of learning how to drive an automobile with standard transmission. Initially, the novice driver has to employ controlled processing—to think consciously about when to shift, when to depress the clutch, how to keep the car from rolling backward on a hill, and so on. Most of us would not be able, say, to drink a cup of coffee at the same time that we were contending with learning to drive the car. However, as the details of operating the car become automatized, we can not only sip coffee as we are driving but can also fiddle with the radio or have a lively conversation with a passenger, and scarcely be aware of shifting or working the clutch at all. Automatization is also important in academic domains other than reading. For instance, in written expression, automatization of handwriting and spelling enable the writer to concentrate on content.

We must acknowledge, however, that in recent years the concept of automatization has come into criticism from some researchers. It turns out that the different tasks that have been used to measure automatization do not yield the same developmental curves but, rather, appear to be measuring somewhat different things (Stanovich, 1990). For instance, some experimental tasks have equated automatization with obligatory processing (the assumption being that automatic word recognition is not under the conscious control of the reader). These tasks have yielded different developmental curves from tasks measuring automatization through resource allocation (i.e., automatic word recognition is believed to consume few or no mental resources). Because of these problems with measurement, some reading theorists (e.g., Ehri, 1992; Perfetti, 1992; Stanovich, 1990) have recently reformulated the concept of automatization in other terms that are related to, but not synonymous with, automatization. These other terms include references to the quality of mental representations of words, the number of mental connections to words in memory, and modularity.

Although we continue to favor the concept of automatization over these other terms, we also recognize the importance of elaborating on what we mean by automatization. We define *automatic word recognition* as word recognition that consumes few mental resources. Other characteristics tend to occur along with automatization of word recognition, and one of the most important of these is modularity. Modular processes are self-contained and independent of higher-level processes. In reading, these higher-level processes include the use of prior knowledge and contextual cues. Thus, word recognition is modular when it is *not* guided by prior knowledge or by context. Prior knowledge and the ability to use contextual cues play an important role in reading *comprehension*. However, they do not play a role in automatic *word recognition*. Unlike children in previous phases of reading, those with automatic word recognition do not need to rely on prior knowledge or contextual cues to guess at words, or to speed word recognition, because their skill at recognizing words, in or out of context, is both fast and accurate.

Both controlled word recognition and automatic word recognition can be domain-specific; that is, they can vary depending upon the types of words being read. For example, even a first-grader might recognize many short words automatically but still need to rely on controlled processing for multisyllable words. And a proficient adult reader would recognize automatically the vast majority of words. However, even adults might need to rely on controlled processing for highly technical or unusual words from an unfamiliar domain.

Clearly, the development of automatization is a complicated process to track. Nevertheless, we can come to some broad conclusions about when automatic recognition of common words usually occurs. Chall's (1983) model of reading development places achievement of fluency in word recognition at a second- to third-grade level, or at roughly seven to eight years of age. And Perfetti (1992) suggests that when the measure of automatization is resource allocation, automatization of familiar words may occur even earlier, largely between the first- and second-grade levels. The important point here is that normally achieving readers seem to progress rapidly from accurate recognition of words to automatic recognition of words, and that this progression occurs primarily in the early elementary years. By the middle-elementary level, if not sooner—that is, by approximately eight years of age—good readers will be able to recognize automatically most words that are in their spoken vocabularies.

Some investigators (e.g., Bowers, 1993; Wolf, 1991) have suggested that naming speed—the speed with which one can name simple symbols such as digits, letters, and so on—plays a role in the development of automatic word recognition. Like phonological awareness, naming speed (also known as speed of lexical access) is an important predictor of reading achievement (Torgesen et al., 1994). Indeed, it might represent an intrinsic limit for the speed of reading words in text. In this view, children with slow word recognition but with rapid naming speed would have greater potential for improving their speed of word recognition than would children with slow word recognition and slow naming speed.

Another factor that appears to be particularly important in the development of automatization is practice, especially practice without mistakes (Sternberg, 1986). Children who read widely outside of school, or who attend schools where independent reading is encouraged and where classroom time is devoted to independent reading, will develop automatic word recognition sooner than if they did not do much independent reading. Furthermore, it is specifically practice without mistakes that appears to be important, because frequent mistakes seem to interfere with the development of automatization. Thus, certain classroom practices other than those involving independent reading may facilitate the transition to automatic word recognition. These other classroom practices include having children do repeated readings of the same material and ensuring that children are not given written materials that are too difficult in terms of word recognition. (For further discussion, see Anderson et al., 1985, and Chinn, Waggoner, Anderson, Schommer, & Wilkinson, 1993.)

Strategic Reading

The central feature of the fifth phase of reading acquisition, strategic reading, involves the regular use of strategies to aid *reading comprehension* (not word recognition). For example, when children fail to understand something in a text, there are a number of "fix-up" strategies that they may use (Anderson et al., 1985). Among other things, they may look for an unfamiliar word in the dictionary; reread a passage to see if it is more understandable the second time around; or read ahead to see if an apparent inconsistency may be resolved later in the text. The regular use of strategies contributes to further growth in reading comprehension.

We are not claiming that children in earlier phases of reading are completely incapable of using strategies. For example, even children as young as six, at the first-grade level, may be able to apply strategies when they are listening rather than reading, and when the subject matter is familiar (Vosniadou, Pearson, & Rogers, 1988). However, in the early phases of reading, children are in the process of acquiring efficient word-recognition skills. It is not until these skills are acquired that children can devote most of their mental resources to comprehension and to comprehension strategies. Thus, in our view, strategy use does not become more routine in reading until this fifth phase of strategic reading.

"Fix-up" strategies are general strategies, in that they can be applied across a wide variety of tasks and domains. Another example of a general strategy involves making acronyms to aid recall, as when readers form a word using the first letters of a list of items they want to remember. However, other strategies are domain-specific (Alexander & Judy, 1988; Garner, 1990; Garner, Alexander, & Hare, 1991). For instance, some of the strategies useful for reading narratives, such as strategies for remembering the plot or keeping track of characters, would not be applicable to many expository texts. A strategy for remembering the relationships among characters in a Russian novel probably would not be very helpful in reading physics. Even among expository texts themselves, strategies helpful in one domain might not be applicable in another; for instance, a strategy for locating countries in geography might get little use in chemistry.

The transition to strategic reading appears to be facilitated by several factors. As we have already mentioned, one important factor is the development of automatic word recognition, which enables children to focus their mental resources on comprehension. Children who are still expending considerable effort on basic word recognition will not have many mental resources available for generating or applying strategies. In addition, the transition to strategic reading is aided by children's increasing metacognitive development—that is, by their ability to understand and manage their own learning.

A third factor important in the transition to strategic reading involves the nature of the academic demands that children experience. Paris and Lindauer (1982) point out that, among normally achieving readers, strategies typically are learned not so much through direct instruction as in the service of meeting academic demands. Chall and her colleagues (1983; Chall et al., 1990) note that there is usually a sharp increase in these demands at the fourth-grade level, when children are expected to read text involving much more challenging concepts and vocabulary than at previous grade levels. Even normally achieving readers experience a temporary "fourth-grade slump" in reading as they adjust to these increased text demands. However, in our view, these demands may be critical to the acquisition of many comprehension strategies. For example, if children read only text that is easy for them in terms of its demands on comprehension, then their comprehension will rarely fail—and in that case, there would be little need for them to generate or to use "fix-up" strategies.

Prior knowledge influences strategy use (Alexander & Judy, 1988; Chan, Burtis, Scardamalia, & Bereiter, 1992; Garner, 1990). In some cases, when readers have a great deal of prior knowledge about a domain, they do not use certain strategies because they have less need for them. Consider again the case of "fix-up" strategies. If a youngster who happens to be an expert on snakes is reading a text about snakes, he or she is unlikely to encounter unfamiliar vocabulary or to experience a breakdown in comprehension—a situation that obviates the need for "fix-up" strategies. However, in other situations, prior knowledge is *necessary* for strategy use, in which case a lack of prior knowledge could interfere with the use of strategies. For instance, in order to use a summarizing strategy, readers must have knowledge about text structure. Indeed, as Garner (1990) notes, children who are unfamiliar with the structure of expository text have difficulty applying a summarizing strategy to this kind of text, not necessarily because they cannot summarize but, rather, because they do not know where to look for the important information.

Strategies also appear to be quite context-dependent (Garner, 1990). That is, children may have strategic knowledge that they reveal in one setting but not in another. For example, Ceci and Bronfenbrenner (1985) recruited children to engage in activities that required them to keep track of time (e.g., baking cupcakes) and compared their time monitoring in the home with their time monitoring in the laboratory. They found that the children were much more likely to use a complicated time-conserving strategy in the home than in the laboratory. These investigators suggest that, when children are in an unfamiliar setting, they may be more anxious and less likely to use some strategies. Many teachers also know how difficult it can be to get children to generalize strategies across tasks and settings.

Depending on the nature of the comprehension strategy and the experimental procedure, researchers usually find children beginning to use strategies routinely at a middle to ending elementary level—that is, roughly around the age of eight to eleven years. One study found that older elementary children are much more likely to employ "fix-up" strategies than are beginning readers (Anderson et al., 1985). And when Myers and Paris (1978) compared second-grade children with sixth-grade children, they found that the older readers had much more knowledge about strategies such as how to skim a text than did the younger readers. Some strategic abilities, however, may be weak even in older readers. For instance, older readers engage in better comprehension monitoring—usually measured by the readers' ability to detect inconsistencies in a text—than do younger readers, but even older readers display faulty comprehension monitoring at times (Garner, 1987; Markman & Gorin, 1981).

Like the previous transition to automatic word recognition, the transition to strategic reading may occur quickly in normally achieving readers. Furthermore, strategy acquisition may continue throughout life. Although the phase of strategic reading is the one during which children *begin* to make efficient and routine use of comprehension strategies, obviously adults, too, can continue to acquire strategies.

Proficient Adult Reading

Older children have developed many of the same reading skills possessed by adults. For instance, seventh-graders, like adults, have automatic word-recognition skills, at least for most words, and make use of strategies to aid comprehension. Indeed, older children can comprehend many texts just as well as adults can. Stanovich (1992) points out that much of the reading done by adults involves mundane expository material, such as *Take two tablets every four hours. May cause drowsiness. Do not drive or operate heavy machinery while taking this medication.* The reading skills of the average seventh-grader are more than adequate for reading this kind of material, as well as for reading a great deal of fiction. Nevertheless, most of us would not characterize a seventh-grader as a highly proficient reader in the same sense that an adult is a highly proficient reader. What, then, is the difference between the phase of strategic reading and the phase of proficient adult reading?

The defining feature of proficient adult reading involves highly developed comprehension abilities, which depend in part on highly skilled word-recognition abilities (Bell & Perfetti, 1994). (The other factors they depend on will be discussed later.) Highly proficient readers are insightful, analytical, and reflective. They make higher-order connections, both within and across texts, and integrate knowledge from a wide variety of sources. In formal psychological terms, these comprehension abilities might be viewed as higher-order integration within a schema (Rumelhart, 1975) or as higher-order selective combination (Davidson & Sternberg, 1984). Although strategic readers can readily understand many texts, including those encountered in school situations, they lack these higher-order comprehension abilities. Higher-order comprehension abilities probably do not develop in many readers until later adolescence.

The following example may help to clarify what we mean by proficient reading. One of the coauthors teaches a course in which students must select a contemporary issue in the field of learning disabilities (e.g., the inclusion of students with LD in regular classrooms), do a literature review on the selected topic, and write a paper. The paper is supposed to be an integrative one; that is, instead of doing a "book report" that summarizes one study after another, students are urged to take a stand on the issue at hand and then to defend that stand by referring to relevant research.

Some students have a very difficult time with this assignment, especially with its integrative nature. In other words, these students may understand individual studies, but they have trouble with a higher-order level of analysis that requires them to resolve inconsistencies across studies and to see how findings that initially appear disparate may actually fit together in a logical way. Other students carry out the assignment with ease, even though, in some cases, they have no more formal knowledge of research about learning disabilities than do the students previously described. What they do have are higher-order comprehension skills that the other students lack.

Although we have used an example involving expository text from one particular domain, examples involving other domains and other kinds of texts, including narratives, could easily be generated. Indeed, many narratives require readers to make higher-order connections and to integrate information from a variety of sources. This is one reason why many classic books can be read by younger students with one level of comprehension and by adults with an entirely different level of comprehension and appreciation.

What determines the transition from strategic reading to proficient reading? In part, the higher-order abilities implicated in proficient reading are linked to general intelligence (Chall, 1967; Stanovich, 1986). The attainment of proficient reading is also facilitated by increases in knowledge base and vocabulary (Stanovich, 1986). Consider our previous example about the learning-disabilities assignment. Obviously, those students who already know something about educational research and have at least a passing familiarity with terms such as *multiple regression* would have some advantage over students without this knowledge. In turn, these two areas—general knowledge and vocabulary—are, like orthographic knowledge, affected by exposure to text, even after variables such as reading comprehension, nonverbal reasoning ability, age, and educational level are controlled for (Stanovich & Cunningham, 1992; West, Stanovich, & Mitchell, 1993). In other words, sheer volume of reading appears to benefit vocabulary and general knowledge as well as spelling, and the resultant advantage is not just a function of intelligence, reading-comprehension skill, or education.

Finally, we think that the transition to proficient reading, like the previous transition to strategic reading, is heavily influenced not only by sheer volume of reading but also by the specific nature of the comprehension demands experienced by the reader. For instance, if readers never experience the kinds of academic demands that require them to employ higher-order comprehension skills, then they may be much less likely to develop those skills, even though they may have the potential to do so. Indeed, some higher-order comprehension abilities may not develop spontaneously but, rather, may require the stimulus of a certain kind of reading experience. For example, Snow, Barnes, Chandler, Goodman, and Hemphill (1991) found that wide reading, as measured by a "favorite author" question, did not correlate highly with reading comprehension in a group of low-income adolescents. These students tended to select undemanding materials for independent reading and to be in relatively unchallenging courses in high school. Snow et al. argue that

> literacy skills show the increasing influence of explicit instruction in and exposure to content areas as students advance into secondary school. Out-of-school reading, particularly of the undemanding kind engaged in by even the brightest of our subjects, cannot make up for the lack of exposure to higher level reading tasks and various content areas in school. (pp. 211–212)

As adults, most of us have a greater knowledge base and more reading experience in some domains than in others. Thus, as we advance in reading acquisition, the various phases may become more domain-specific. Some of the students who did not appear to be proficient readers on the learning-disabilities assignment might well have been proficient readers in some other domain. We ourselves would probably perform no better than at the strategic-reading level in a domain such as economics or physics! Far from being a static end state, then, proficient reading involves a set of cognitive abilities that continue to develop throughout life.

A Word About Instance-Based Theories

In recent years, some cognitive researchers have become oriented toward in-stance-based theories of cognition and reading (see, e.g., Logan, 1988; Perfetti, 1992; Stanovich, 1990). Instance-based theories do not emphasize mental processes or an age-related progression of phases in reading acquisition. Rather, such theories focus on the words themselves—specifically, on the number and quality of mental representations of words. (Recall that we touched on instance-based views in our earlier discussion of automatization and modularity.) Of course, the number and quality of mental representations vary with the age and skill level of the reader. For example, proficient adult readers have complete and high-quality mental representations for most—but not all—words.

We have not framed our model of reading acquisition in terms of instance-based views because, among other reasons, these views are not easily communi-cated to nonspecialists. However, we do wish to emphasize a point about our own model that is consistent with instance-based views—namely, that within a given phase a reader's approach to reading is not an all-or-nothing phenomenon but, rather, may vary somewhat depending upon the specific words or text being read. For example, as we have mentioned, readers in the phase of automatic word recog-nition, strategic reading, and proficient adult reading can recognize most words rapidly and automatically; however, even these readers may sometimes need to use controlled processing or context for certain words from very unfamiliar domains.

Suppose you are reading a text on tropical diseases, a subject about which you know little. You encounter the following sentence: *Onchocerciasis, also known as river blindness, is caused by a parasite carried by blackflies.* All of the words except the first one you probably would recognize automatically. However, for the word *onchocerciasis,* you would be likely to use controlled processing; you might even avoid complete processing of the the word altogether and use context to equate *onchocerciasis* with *river blindness.*

Conversely, a youngster in the phase of, say, phonetic-cue word recognition is unable to decode most words fully but, nevertheless, might have automatic recog-nition of a handful of highly familiar words, such as *man* and *an.* Thus, the phases in our model describe a reader's general approach to most words and reading tasks, but they are not completely independent of the words or tasks themselves.

Comparing Our Model to Other Models

A number of investigators have developed cognitive models of reading acquisi-tion, most of which involve stages or phases. These investigators include Ehri (1991, 1992), Frith (1985), and Gough and Juel (1991). As noted, our thinking has been influenced a great deal by these and other researchers. For example, the first two phases in our model are virtually identical to the first two in Ehri's model. The first four phases in our model roughly map onto the three phases—logographic, alphabetic, and orthographic—in Frith's model. And the first phase in our model is similar to Gough and Juel's initial phase of paired-associate learning. In our opinion, this similarity across models speaks to the current level of knowledge about early reading acquisition.

However, our model of reading acquisition is also different from those of other researchers in ways that we believe are important to educational practitioners in general, and especially to those interested in reading disability. First, the cognitive models of many other investigators are intended to be models of *early* reading acquisition; they end with the acquisition of word-recognition skills. From an educator's perspective, these models take us about as far as the third-grade level; but of course a great deal happens in reading between third grade and adulthood. It seems to us that cognitive models of reading acquisition, if they are to be educationally useful, must address the period following successful acquisition of word-recognition skills; yet relatively few models have attempted to do this. (The work of Keith Stanovich and his colleagues—for example, Stanovich and Cunningham, 1992, and West, Stanovich, and Mitchell, 1993—is a notable exception.)

Word-recognition problems do appear to be causally central to reading disability, as we have already noted. However, the long-term as well as immediate impacts of these problems on other reading skills, such as comprehension, must be considered if we are to have a complete picture of RD, particularly in older individuals. Thus, a broad cognitive model of reading acquisition is needed not only by educators who work with normally achieving youngsters but also by educators who work with individuals with RD.

A second difference between our model of reading acquisition and those of other investigators is that our model distinguishes phases that are not separate in some other models. For example, models such as that of Gough and Juel (1991) do not appear to make a distinction between accurate word recognition and automatic word recognition. These models seem to assume that, once children can read a specific word or a given class of words with complete accuracy, they have also attained automatization for those words. However, although the transition from controlled (i.e., accurate) word recognition to automatic word recognition may pass so quickly as to be almost unnoticed in normally achieving readers, we still think it is useful to distinguish the two phases as separate. This distinction is especially important in the case of reading disability. We have observed that children with RD, if given appropriate instruction, can acquire orthographic knowledge and accurate word-recognition skills, yet still fail to be automatic in applying this knowledge. This observation, as well as the widespread applicability of the concepts of controlled and automatic processing in many domains other than reading, convinces us that the distinction between controlled and automatic word recognition is appropriate.

A third difference between our model and those of other investigators involves the interactive perspective of our model. Researchers interested in the reading acquisition of normally achieving readers have not been as relentlessly intrinsic in their perspectives as have many of the researchers interested in reading disability.

For instance, the former typically have been more concerned with the possible impact of instructional variables on the acquisition of word-recognition skills than have the latter. Nevertheless, few models of reading acquisition have attempted to specify how children's intrinsic cognitive characteristics (e.g., their phase of reading acquisition) might *interact* with either home or school variables. An interactive perspective suggests many ways that children can go off track developmentally in reading, down roads that may eventually lead them to be classified as having RD. In the next chapter, we will take a closer look at these roads to reading disability.

References

Adams, M. J. (1990). *Beginning to read: Thinking and learning about print.* Cambridge, MA: MIT Press.

Adams, M. J., Allington, R. L., Chaney, J. H., Goodman, Y. M., Kapinus, B. A., McGee, L. M., Richgels, D. J., Schwartz, S. J., Shannon, P., Smitten, B., & Williams, J. P. (1991). Beginning to read: A critique by literacy professionals and a response by Marilyn Jager Adams. *Reading Teacher, 44,* 370–395.

Alexander, P. A., & Judy, J. E. (1988). The interaction of domain-specific and strategic knowledge in academic performance. *Review of Educational Research, 58,* 375–404.

Anderson, R. C., Hiebert, E. H., Scott, J. A., & Wilkinson, I. A. G. (1985). *Becoming a nation of readers: The report of the Commission on Reading.* Champaign, IL: Center for the Study of Reading.

Barker, T. A., Torgesen, J. K., & Wagner, R. K. (1992). The role of orthographic processing skills on five different reading tasks. *Reading Research Quarterly, 27,* 335–345.

Bell, L. C., & Perfetti, C. A. (1994). Reading skill: Some adult comparisons. *Journal of Educational Psychology, 86,* 244–255.

Bowers, P. G. (1993). Text reading and rereading: Determinants of fluency beyond word recognition. *Journal of Reading Behavior, 25,* 133–153.

Bradley, L., & Bryant, P. E. (1985). *Rhyme and reason in reading and spelling.* Ann Arbor, MI: University of Michigan Press.

Bryant, D. M., Clifford, R. M., & Peisner, E. S. (1991). Best practices for beginners: Developmental appropriateness in kindergarten. *American Educational Research Journal, 28,* 783–803.

Byrne, B. (1991). Experimental analysis of the child's discovery of the alphabetic principle. In L. Rieben & C. A. Perfetti (Eds.), *Learning to read: Basic research and its implications* (pp. 75–84). Hillsdale, NJ: Erlbaum.

———. (1992). Studies in the acquisition procedure for reading: Rationale, hypotheses, and data. In P. B. Gough, L. C. Ehri, & R. Treiman (Eds.), *Reading acquisition* (pp. 1–34). Hillsdale, NJ: Erlbaum.

Byrne, B., & Ledez, J. (1986). Phonological awareness in reading-disabled adults. *Australian Journal of Psychology, 35,* 185–197.

Ceci, S. J., & Bronfenbrenner, U. (1985). "Don't forget to take the cupcakes out of the oven": Prospective memory, strategic time-monitoring, and context. *Child Development, 56,* 152–164.

Chall, J. (1967). *Learning to read: The great debate.* New York: McGraw-Hill.

———. (1983). *Stages of reading development.* New York: McGraw-Hill.

Chall, J., Jacobs, V. A., & Baldwin, L. E. (1990). *The reading crisis: Why poor children fall behind.* Cambridge, MA: Harvard University Press.

Chan, C., Burtis, P. J., Scardamalia, M., & Bereiter, C. (1992). Constructive activity in learning from text. *American Educational Research Journal, 29,* 97–118.

Chinn, C. A., Waggoner, M. A., Anderson, R. C., Schommer, M. & Wilkinson, I. A. G. (1993). Situated actions during reading lessons: A microanalysis of oral reading error episodes. *American Educational Research Journal, 30,* 361–392.

Clay, M. M. (1979). *The early detection of reading difficulties.* Portsmouth, NH: Heinemann.

Coltheart, M. (1978). Lexical access in simple reading tasks. In G. Underwood (Ed.), *Strategies of information processing* (pp. 151–216). London: Academic Press.

Cunningham, A. E., & Stanovich, K. E. (1990). Assessing print exposure and orthographic processing skill in children: A quick measure of reading experience. *Journal of Educational Psychology, 82,* 733–740.

Davidson, J. E., & Sternberg, R. J. (1984). The role of insight in intellectual giftedness. *Gifted Child Quarterly, 28,* 58–64.

Delpit, L. D. (1988). The silenced dialogue: Power and pedagogy in educating other people's children. *Harvard Educational Review, 58,* 280–298.

Ehri, L. C. (1991). Learning to read and spell words. In L. Rieben & C. A. Perfetti (Eds.), *Learning to read: Basic research and its implications* (pp. 57–73). Hillsdale, NJ: Erlbaum.

———. (1992). Reconceptualizing the development of sight word reading and its relationship to recoding. In P. B. Gough, L. C. Ehri, & R. Treiman (Eds.), *Reading acquisition* (pp. 107–143). Hillsdale, NJ: Erlbaum.

Ehri, L. C., & Sweet, J. (1991). Fingerpoint-reading of memorized text: What enables beginners to process the print? *Reading Research Quarterly, 26,* 442–462.

Elkind, D. (1987). *Miseducation: Preschoolers at risk.* New York: Alfred A. Knopf.

Ferreiro, E., & Teberosky, A. (1982). *Literacy before schooling.* Portsmouth, NH: Heinemann.

Frith, U. (1985). Beneath the surface of developmental dyslexia In K. Patterson, J. Marshall, & M. Coltheart (Eds.), *Surface dyslexia* (pp. 301–330). London: Erlbaum.

Garner, R. (1987). *Metacognition and reading comprehension.* Norwood, NJ: Ablex.

———. (1990). When children and adults do not use learning strategies: Toward a theory of settings. *Review of Educational Research, 60,* 517–529.

Garner, R., Alexander, P. A., & Hare, V. C. (1991). Reading comprehension failure in children. In B. Y. L. Wong (Ed.), *Learning about learning disabilities* (pp. 283–307). San Diego, CA: Academic Press.

Garner, R., & Reis, R. (1981). Monitoring and resolving comprehension obstacles: An investigation of spontaneous text lookbacks among upper-grade good and poor comprehenders. *Reading Research Quarterly, 16,* 569–582.

Goodman, K. S. (1986). *What's whole in whole language: A parent-teacher guide.* Portsmouth, NH: Heinemann.

Gough, P. B., & Juel, C. (1991). The first stages of word recognition. In L. Rieben & C. A. Perfetti (Eds.), *Learning to read: Basic research and its implications* (pp. 47–56). Hillsdale, NJ: Erlbaum.

Hanson, V. L. (1989). Phonology and reading: Evidence from profoundly deaf readers. In D. Shankweiler & I. Y. Liberman (Eds.), *Phonology and reading disability: Solving the reading puzzle* (pp. 69–89). Ann Arbor, MI: University of Michigan Press.

Hanson, V. L., & Fowler, C. A. (1987). Phonological coding in word reading: Evidence from hearing and deaf readers. *Memory and Cognition, 15,* 199–207.

Hanson, V. L., Liberman, I. Y., & Shankweiler, D. (1984). Linguistic coding by deaf children in relation to beginning reading success. *Journal of Experimental Child Psychology, 37,* 378–393.

Holdaway, D. (1979). *The foundations of literacy.* Sidney, Australia: Ashton Scholastic.

Juel, C., Griffith, P. L., & Gough, P. B. (1986). Acquisition of literacy: A longitudinal study of children in first and second grade. *Journal of Educational Psychology, 78,* 243–255.

LaBerge, D., & Samuels, S. J. (1974). Toward a theory of automatic information processing in reading. *Cognitive Psychology, 6,* 293–323.

Liberman, I. Y., & Liberman, A. M. (1990). Whole language versus code emphasis: Underlying assumptions and their implications for reading instruction. *Annals of Dyslexia, 40,* 51–76.

Logan, G. D. (1988). Toward an instance theory of automatization. *Psychological Review, 95,* 492–527.

Lundberg, I., Frost, J., & Peterson, O. (1988). Effects of an extensive program for stimulating phonological awareness in preschool children. *Reading Research Quarterly, 23,* 263–284.

Maclean, M., Bryant, P., & Bradley, L. (1987). Rhymes, nursery rhymes, and reading in early childhood. *Merrill-Palmer Quarterly, 33,* 255–281.

Mann, V. A. (1985). A cross-linguistic perspective on the relation between temporary memory skills and early reading ability. *Remedial and Special Education, 6,* 37–42.

Mann, V. A., & Liberman, I. Y. (1984). Phonological awareness and verbal short-term memory. *Journal of Learning Disabilities, 17,* 592–599.

Mann, V. A., Tobin, P., & Wilson, R. (1987). Measuring phonological awareness through the invented spellings of kindergarten children. *Merrill-Palmer Quarterly, 33,* 365–391.

Markman, E. M., & Gorin, L. (1981). Children's ability to adjust their standards for evaluating comprehension. *Journal of Educational Psychology, 83,* 320–325.

Mason, J. M. (1992). Reading stories to preliterate children: A proposed connection to reading. In P. B. Gough, L. C. Ehri, & R. Treiman (Eds.), *Reading acquisition* (pp. 215–241). Hillsdale, NJ: Erlbaum.

Masonheimer, P. E., Drum, P. A., & Ehri, L. C. (1984). Does environmental print identification lead children into word reading? *Journal of Reading Behavior, 16,* 257–272.

Morais, J., Bertelson, P., Cary, L., & Alegria, J. (1986). Literacy training and speech segmentation. *Cognition, 24,* 45–64.

Myers, M., & Paris, S. G. (1978). Children's metacognitive knowledge about reading. *Journal of Educational Psychology, 70,* 680–690.

Olson, R. K., Wise, B., Conners, F., Rack, J., & Fulker, D. (1989). Specific deficits in component reading and language skills: Genetic and environmental influences. *Journal of Learning Disabilities, 22,* 339–348.

Paris, S. G., & Lindauer, B. K. (1982). The development of cognitive skills during childhood. In B. Wolman (Ed.), *Handbook of developmental psychology* (pp. 333–349). Englewood Cliffs, NJ: Prentice-Hall.

Patterson, K. E., Marshall, J. C., & Coltheart, M. (1985). *Surface dyslexia: Neuropsychological and cognitive studies of phonological reading.* Hillsdale, NJ: Lawrence Erlbaum Associates.

Perfetti, C. A. (1985). *Reading ability.* New York: Oxford University Press.

———. (1992). The representation problem in reading acquisition. In P. B. Gough, L. C. Ehri, & R. Treiman (Eds.), *Reading acquisition* (pp. 145–174). Hillsdale, NJ: Erlbaum.

Perfetti, C. A., Beck, I., Bell, L., & Hughes, C. (1987). Phonemic knowledge and learning to read are reciprocal: A longitudinal study of first grade children. *Merrill-Palmer Quarterly, 33,* 283–319.

Perfetti, C. A., & Lesgold, A. (1977). Discourse comprehension and sources of individual differences. In M. Just & P. Carpenter (Eds.), *Cognitive processes in comprehension* (pp. 141–183). Hillsdale, NJ: Erlbaum.

Rack, J. P., Snowling, M. J., & Olson, R. K. (1992). The nonword reading deficit in developmental dyslexia: A review. *Reading Research Quarterly, 27,* 28–53.

Rayner, K., & Pollatsek, A. (1989). *The psychology of reading.* Englewood Cliffs, NJ: Prentice-Hall.

Read, C., Zhang, Y., Nie, H., & Ding, B. (1986). The ability to manipulate speech sounds depends on knowing alphabetic reading. *Cognition, 24,* 31–44.

Robbins, C., & Ehri, L. C. (1994). Reading storybooks to kindergartners helps them learn new vocabulary words. *Journal of Educational Psychology, 86,* 54–64.

Rumelhart, D. (1975). Notes on a schema for stories. In D. G. Bobrow & A. Collins (Eds.), *Representation and understanding: Studies in cognitive science* (pp. 40–82). San Diego, CA: Academic Press.

Seymour, P. H. K., & Elder, L. (1986). Beginning reading without phonology. *Cognitive Neuropsychology, 3,* 1–36.

Shankweiler, D., Crain, S., Brady, S., & Macaruso, P. (1992). Identifying the causes of reading disability. In P. B. Gough, L. C. Ehri, & R. Treiman (Eds.), *Reading acquisition* (pp. 275–305). Hillsdale, NJ: Erlbaum.

Smith, F. (1973). *Psycholinguistics and reading.* New York: Holt, Rinehart & Winston.

Snow, C. E., Barnes, W. S., Chandler, J., Goodman, J. F., & Hemphill, L. (1991). *Unfulfilled expectations: Home and school influences on literacy.* Cambridge, MA: Harvard University Press.

Stahl, S. A. (1990). Riding the pendulum: A rejoinder to Schickedanz and McGee and Lomax. *Review of Educational Research, 60,* 141–151.

Stahl, S. A., & Murray, B. A. (1994). Defining phonological awareness and its relationship to early reading. *Journal of Educational Psychology, 86,* 221–234.

Stanovich, K. E. (1986). Matthew effects in reading: Some consequences of individual differences in the acquisition of literacy. *Reading Research Quarterly, 21,* 360–406.

———. (1990). Concepts in developmental theories of reading skill: Cognitive resources, automaticity, and modularity. *Developmental Review, 10,* 72–100.

———. (1991). Word recognition: Changing perspectives. In R. Barr, M. L. Kamil, P. Mosenthal, & P. D. Pearson (Eds.), *Handbook of reading research* (Vol. 2, pp. 418–452). New York: Longman.

———. (1992). The psychology of reading: Evolutionary and revolutionary developments. *Annual Review of Applied Linguistics, 12,* 3–30.

Stanovich, K. E., & Cunningham, A. E. (1992). Studying the consequences of literacy within a literate society: The cognitive correlates of print exposure. *Memory and Cognition, 20,* 51–68.

Sternberg, R. J. (1986). *Intelligence applied: Understanding and increasing your intellectual skills.* San Diego, CA: Harcourt, Brace, Jovanovich.

Sternberg, R. J., & Wagner, R. K. (1982). Automatization failure in learning disabilities. *Topics in Learning and Learning Disabilities, 2,* 1–11.

Stevenson, H. W., Lucker, G. W., Lee, S., Stigler, J. W., Kitamura, S., & Hsu, C. C. (1987). Poor readers in three cultures. In C. Super & S. Harkness (Eds.), *The role of culture in developmental disorder* (Vol. 1, pp. 153–177). New York: Academic Press.

Stevenson, H. W., Stigler, J. W., Lucker, G. W., Lee, S., Hsu, C. C., & Kitamura, S. (1982). Reading disabilities: The case of Chinese, Japanese, and English. *Child Development, 53,* 1164–1181.

Sulzby, E. (1985). Children's emergent reading of favorite storybooks: A developmental study. *Reading Research Quarterly, 20,* 458–481.

Teale, W. H., & Sulzby, E. (1987). The cultural practice of storybook reading: Its effects on young children's literacy development. In D. A. Wagner (Ed.), *The future of literacy in a changing world* (pp. 111–130). New York: Pergamon.

Torgesen, J. K., Wagner, R. K., & Rashotte, C. A. (1994). Longitudinal studies of phonological processing and reading. *Journal of Learning Disabilities, 27,* 276–286.

Treiman, R. (1991). The role of intrasyllabic units in learning to read. In L. Rieben & C. A. Perfetti (Eds.), *Learning to read: Basic research and its implications* (pp. 149–160). Hillsdale, NJ: Erlbaum.

———. (1992). The role of intrasyllabic units in learning to read and spell. In P. B. Gough, L. C. Ehri, & R. Treiman (Eds.), *Reading acquisition* (pp. 65–106). Hillsdale, NJ: Erlbaum.

Vellutino, F. R., & Scanlon, D. M. (1987). Phonological coding, phonological awareness, and reading ability: Evidence from a longitudinal and experimental study. *Merrill-Palmer Quarterly, 33,* 321–363.

———. (1991). The effects of instructional bias on word identification. In L. Rieben & C. A. Perfetti (Eds.), *Learning to read: Basic research and its implications* (pp. 189–203). Hillsdale, NJ: Erlbaum.

Vosniadou, S., Pearson, P. D., & Rogers, T. (1988). What causes children's failures to detect inconsistencies in text? Representation vs. comparison difficulties. *Journal of Educational Psychology, 80,* 27–39.

Wagner, R. K., & Torgesen, J. K. (1987). The nature of phonological processing and its causal role in the acquisition of reading skills. *Psychological Bulletin, 101,* 192–212.

Wagner, R. K., Torgesen, J. K., & Rashotte, C. A. (1994). The development of reading-related phonological processing abilities: New evidence of bidirectional causality from a latent variable longitudinal study. *Developmental Psychology, 30,* 73–87.

West, R. F., Stanovich, K. E., & Mitchell, H. R. (1993). Reading in the real world and its correlates. *Reading Research Quarterly, 28,* 35–50.

Wolf, M. (1991). Naming speed and reading: The contribution of the cognitive neurosciences. *Reading Research Quarterly, 26,* 123–141.

Wolf, S. (1993). *As various as their land: The everyday lives of eighteenth-century Americans.* New York: HarperCollins.

5 Roads to Reading Disability

W E BEGIN THIS CHAPTER with some tales of four children: Calvin, Megan, James, and Stacy. These four children are different from one another in many ways. Among other things, they are of varying ages, they come from a wide range of socioeconomic backgrounds, and they exhibit different levels of achievement in reading. However, they also have some basic things in common. Although they are all of normal intelligence, they all strayed early from the road to proficient reading, and they all ended up being classified as learning disabled.

We tell the stories of these four children for two reasons. First, we want to illustrate some of the points that we argued earlier in this book, regarding the flawed nature of intrinsic and extrinsic perspectives on reading disability as well as the fundamental problems with the concept of RD and its application in schools. Second, we tell these stories because they serve as examples in our own model of reading disability, which we believe provides an educationally useful way of looking at these and other youngsters' difficulties.

Accordingly, the first section of this chapter presents the stories of the four children, and the second provides some "morals" of these stories—specifically, by showing how the stories illustrate some problems in the LD field. In the third section of the chapter, we present our model of reading disability in detail. In the fourth section we offer a general discussion of the model. And in the fifth and final section, we compare our model to those of other researchers interested in reading disability, anticipate some possible objections to the model, and discuss its educational usefulness.

Tales of Four Children

Calvin

Calvin is entering the fifth grade. The child of a chemist and an electrical engineer, he comes from an upper-middle-class family. He has one older sibling, who recently graduated as valedictorian of her high school class. However, school and, more specifically, reading have been difficult for Calvin. His kindergarten year apparently went smoothly, but in first grade, he soon fell behind the other children in his ability to recall sight vocabulary and to apply the phonic rules taught in the basal program used in his school. Calvin was retained twice—once in first grade, and again in second grade—so that he'd have a chance to "catch up developmentally." However, in spite of the retentions, his progress in reading was extremely slow, and during his second year in second grade, he was identified as needing learning-disabilities services. Calvin is now twelve years old. Tall for his age, he towers over the ten-year-olds in his fifth-grade class.

For the past three-and-a-half years, Calvin has received all of his language-arts subjects (i.e., reading, spelling, and written expression) in a learning-disabilities resource room, where the resource teacher uses the Orton-Gillingham approach to reading and spelling. Calvin can now accurately decode most words in his oral vocabulary. However, his reading level in text is still about a year below his grade placement and about three years below the grade level that would be predicted by his chronological age, due to his difficulties with reading comprehension. Although Calvin decodes accurately, the process itself—especially the decoding of long words—is effortful for him. His oral reading, though also generally accurate, is slow and disfluent, thereby impairing his comprehension. He is having a particularly difficult time with the transition from the narrative material common in beginning texts to expository material, such as social studies and science texts. However, his listening comprehension for the same material is excellent.

Calvin generally is a cooperative youngster, but he does not like attending the resource room. Although his parents and his resource teacher have tried to explain why he needs to be there, he complains that his friends in the regular classroom make fun of him for having to go to the "dummy class," and his embarrassment is becoming more acute as he grows older. Also, he repeatedly expresses concern about missing lessons and activities in the regular classroom, although he has been reassured that his regular-classroom teacher will not hold him accountable for material he has missed. The fact is that Calvin *does* sometimes miss important or interesting material in the regular classroom, due to the exigencies of scheduling in the resource room.

Calvin's lack of enthusiasm for reading is obvious. When asked to name a favorite book, he cannot think of one. His parents report that Calvin never chooses reading as a free-time activity, and their attempts to continue reading to him, as they did when he was a preschooler, have been tolerated by Calvin only grudgingly. He would rather watch television or play with his model cars, two favorite pastimes. Calvin's parents cannot understand why he has had so much difficulty in school, and they are very worried about his future.

Megan

Megan, who is entering the third grade, is eight years old. She lives with her mother and one younger sister, who is an average student. Megan's parents were divorced three years ago, but she has regular visits with her father. The family is middle class.

Megan was identified as needing learning-disabilities services at the end of last year. An especially sweet and likable child, she initially brought home report cards filled with comments like "a joy to have in the classroom" and "making gradual progress in reading." Nevertheless, the testing from last year, at the end of second grade, revealed that Megan was virtually a nonreader and knew few letter-sound correspondences, not even many of those for single consonants such as *m* and *g*. Although she recognized a few sight words, she was unable to read connected text, even at the preprimer level. Her decoding skills were essentially nonexistent. She even had difficulty with some kindergarten-level reading-readiness tasks, such as listening for initial and final consonant sounds. Because of her very low level of academic functioning in the language-arts areas, she has been placed in a self-contained class for children with learning disabilities.

Megan's school employs a whole-language program, with considerable emphasis on the use of children's literature for the children to read as well as on early writing. The teacher also frequently reads to the children—and, indeed, Megan loves being read to. However, although her listening comprehension is good, her enthusiasm and good listening abilities have not translated into progress in independent reading. Megan remains a very agreeable and sweet child, and she clearly needs the kind of intensive instruction provided in the self-contained LD class, but her teachers are a little concerned about how she will fare there. She is the youngest child in the LD class, and many of the other children have behavioral as well as academic problems.

James

James, who is nine years old and entering the fourth grade, comes from a family that can best be described as "working poor." He lives with his maternal grandparents, both of whom work at low-paying jobs. The family lacks medical insurance and must struggle to make ends meet. However, James's grandparents are loving and very involved in his schooling.

James's early life was a chronicle of repeated loss. His father abandoned the family when James was an infant. An older brother died after being hit by a car when James was four. The following year, when James was five, his mother simply vanished; she dropped him off at his grandmother's and took what was supposed to be a quick trip to the supermarket, a trip from which she never returned. The family believes she was murdered, but her body has not been found. After that, James went to live with his grandparents.

Throughout kindergarten and first grade, James was a very quiet, withdrawn, sad little boy. Projective testing by the school psychologist revealed—in what probably required no leap of diagnostic insight—that James felt "afraid," "vulnerable," and "unable to control his environment." No serious academic problems were noted at this time, and James seemed to be progressing adequately in *Distar* (Engelmann & Bruner, 1974), the synthetic-phonic reading program used in his school. However, because of his emotional problems, he was placed in a self-contained classroom for socially and emotionally handicapped youngsters at the end of first grade.

In this classroom, and after moving in with his grandparents, James gradually became more outgoing. Unfortunately, however, his initial progress in reading seemed to level off. By the end of third grade, he was still reading only at a beginning second-grade level, due to problems with reading comprehension as well as with decoding. He can decode some, but not all, one-syllable words. Words of more than one syllable are very difficult for him; he does not even know how to attempt them. In fact, his inclination is to guess at them based on the first few letters, reading, for instance, *play* for *planet* or *fan* for *family*. However, James is good at using contextual cues during reading and thus does somewhat better at recognizing words in context than might be expected from his word-recognition skills in isolation. Although he is not a serious behavior problem in the classroom, he dislikes reading and will try any diversionary tactic—rambling on at length about an unrelated topic, making repeated trips to the bathroom or the pencil sharpener, and so on—in order to avoid it.

Concerned that James might have learning disabilities, his special-education teacher referred him for a formal evaluation last year. She also believed that the learning-disabilities class would be a better environment for James than her own classroom, where most of the children were much more aggressive and behaviorally difficult than James. James did qualify for learning-disabilities services in reading and written expression. This year will be James's first in a self-contained class for children with learning disabilities.

Stacy

Stacy, fourteen years old, is entering the ninth grade. She lives with her mother, a single parent, and two younger siblings. One sibling has also been identified as needing LD services, but the other is an average student. Stacy has had no contact with her father for many years. The family is on welfare.

Stacy was first identified as needing learning-disabilities services in the fifth grade. However, like those of the other children in our tales, Stacy's problems in reading date from the beginning elementary grades. She entered school with little or no experience with books or letters. She had never been read to regularly, never played games with letters or words, and rarely ever used crayons or a pencil, even to draw pictures. Stacy happened to attend a middle-class school where many of the children came from homes with highly literate parents, and where the kindergarten program was geared more toward these higher achieving youngsters. Although Stacy seemed verbally bright, she always lagged behind most of the other children in reading. She inevitably ended up in the bottom reading group in her regular classroom, where a basal reading program was used. Her difficulties in reading comprehension, spelling, and written expression escalated sharply in the fourth and fifth grades, eventually resulting in her diagnosis as LD.

After four years of special-education services, Stacy's oral reading is quite good. She now reads grade-appropriate material fluently. However, her reading comprehension, especially in content areas such as science and history, remains a problem. She seems to find the increasing reading demands of the upper grades overwhelming and has little idea how to approach them. When she fails to understand something she reads, she is inclined to abandon the reading rather than to try to figure things out. She also continues to have serious difficulties with written expression.

Stacy's grades in middle school, particularly those she received in mainstreamed courses, were generally poor. The low grades were the result not only of her genuine academic difficulties but also of what her teachers referred to as "attitude" problems—failure to complete homework, mouthing off to the teacher, mediocre attendance, and so on. Stacy has grown very accustomed to the individualized attention she receives in special education and is having a hard time adjusting to being just another student in a class of twenty or thirty. When she has difficulty with an assignment in class but cannot get immediate attention from the teacher, she quickly becomes frustrated and gives up—or, worse, gets into trouble.

In high school, Stacy will be mainstreamed in most areas, spending one class period a day with a learning-disabilities teacher. She is already looking forward to the day when she can quit school, although she has no specific plans for the future.

Some Morals of the Tales

Our stories of four children illustrate a point that we have repeatedly argued throughout this book—that in the "real-life" context of schools, identifying poor readers as LD and providing them with appropriate educational services are considerably more complex than theoretical discussions of LD and RD might suggest. Our opening tales illustrate, among other things, our claim that school identification of LD is not a straightforward scientific process akin to diagnosing hypertension or diabetes. For instance, all four of the children in our tales had relatively long-standing reading difficulties by the time they were identified as having RD. And for the most part, they were identified not because they had problems that were strikingly different from those of other poor readers but, rather, because those problems had reached a level of severity that could be accommodated instructionally only through special-education placement.

Theoretically, of course, the problems of children with RD are not supposed to be primarily attributable to conditions such as emotional disturbance or economic disadvantage. Many authorities might therefore argue that youngsters like James or Stacy do not represent "true" cases of reading disability. Researchers in RD understandably select certain populations depending on their basic perspectives; those with an intrinsic perspective would undoubtedly drop James and Stacy from the subject pool, because the economic disadvantage of both children, as well as James's history of emotional problems, represents confounding variables in the interpretation of research findings.

Of course, we could have chosen to tell the stories of four middle-class children with no obvious history of traumatic events or emotional problems. However, we wanted to make the point that practitioners and researchers face different sets of issues. Practitioners have to find a way to help youngsters with reading problems, whether or not the children's lives are "confounded" by issues such as economic disadvantage or emotional difficulties. In fact, many children's lives are confounded by one circumstance or another, a situation that some authorities (e.g., Hewlett, 1991) would argue is not only common but increasingly so. For example, 20 percent of children live below the poverty line, a significant increase over the past twenty years (U.S. Bureau of the Census, 1990). As practitioners will attest, in some school districts there are many more children like James and Stacy than like Calvin and Megan, both inside and outside of LD placements.

One such confounding issue, divorce, crosses economic and class boundaries and is not confined to lower-class or impoverished children. Indeed, approximately half of all children now grow up in divorced families. According to some statistics, nearly half of those children have little or no contact with their fathers; and some authorities have expressed concern about the long-term emotional consequences of divorce for many, though certainly not all, children of divorce (Furstenberg & Nord, 1985; Hewlett, 1991). Theoretically, one can conceptualize a syndrome of reading failure that is independent of these other problems, such as economic disadvantage, emotional difficulties, or the trauma of divorce. In practice, however, many children's lives are confounded by just those kinds of other problems, whether they are labeled LD or not.

An overemphasis on environmental factors, as with an extrinsic perspective, is also inadequate for understanding the problems of the four children in our stories. Clearly, all of these youngsters currently bring certain intrinsic cognitive characteristics to reading instruction that interfere with their abilities to profit from instruction that is generally effective for other children. For example, Megan has very weak phonological skills, whereas Stacy has serious strategic weaknesses. These intrinsic weaknesses may have been shaped at least as much by environmental factors as by innate biological ones. Nevertheless, for a complete understanding of these children's reading difficulties, these intrinsic cognitive characteristics, whatever their ultimate sources, must be addressed. An educational program that ignores Megan's very real weaknesses in phonological processing or Stacy's strategic weaknesses is not likely to be effective.

Trying to assign a single cause, whether intrinsic or extrinsic, to reading failure is virtually impossible in most school-identified cases of reading disability. Were Megan's reading problems initially caused by an intrinsic biological deficit, by the nature of an instructional program that did not emphasize decoding, by subtle emotional difficulties occasioned by her parents' divorce, or by the failure of the school to address her minor academic difficulties immediately? Were Stacy's initial problems in reading related more to lack of parental involvement and economic disadvantage than to an inappropriate early educational program? Obviously, economically disadvantaged children can have biologically based learning problems, too; perhaps Stacy's reading failure was really caused by a biological deficit. Who knows? Real life is a lot messier than either an intrinsic or extrinsic perspective allows for.

Now, the preceding discussion is not meant to suggest that causes are unimportant, simply because it is often difficult or impossible to figure out the causes of children's learning problems. Clearly, causes *are* important. Ultimately, long-term solutions to children's learning problems, as well as prevention of those problems, depend in part on an understanding of causes. And, indeed, there is a place for both environmentally and biologically oriented research on causation.

However, there is another way to understand the reading failure of children like Calvin, Megan, James, and Stacy—a way that is *educationally more useful.* All four of these youngsters can be seen as children who went developmentally off track in reading. The pattern of reading failure demonstrated by each child is related to the point at which the child went astray; for instance, a child who went astray very early, in the phase of visual-cue word recognition (e.g., Megan), would exhibit a pattern of difficulties different from that of a child who went astray after having acquired some phonological-reading skills (e.g., James). The different patterns have different implications both for educational assessment and for instruction.

In short, we are proposing a "road-map" metaphor for understanding reading disability (see Figure 5.1). In this figure, the road to proficient reading is represented by the vertical line on the left-hand side, marked by the successive phases of reading acquisition; as you can see, these are listed in order from the bottom to the top of the figure. Children may wander off this road in any of the phases, and the paths they take—which may eventually lead them to be characterized as having reading disability—are shown horizontally, leading off to the right-hand side of the figure. In our model, as we will discuss in more detail later, reading disability is characterized by departures from the road of typical reading acquisition in any of the first four phases—that is, at the *word-recognition* level. Children may also go astray in the fifth phase, that of strategic reading. We refer to these youngsters as suboptimal readers, but suboptimal readers would not generally be considered to have RD.

We think that the "road-map" metaphor is an apt one because it captures several important aspects of RD. First, it shows how the phenomenon of reading disability relates to the process of reading acquisition in normally achieving readers. Second, it illustrates the crucial idea that the farther children wander along one of the wrong paths (in other words, the longer they go without appropriate educational intervention), the more difficult it will likely be to get them back on to the road to proficient reading.

FIGURE 5.1 A "Road Map" for Understanding Reading Disability

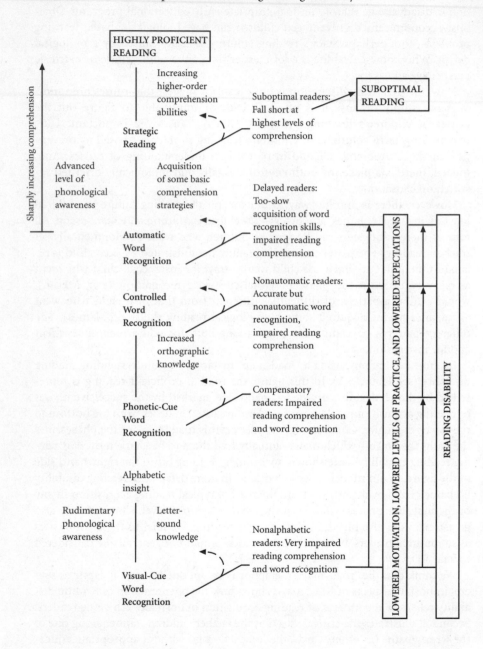

And third, the "road map" metaphorically represents the fact that children with RD do not remain frozen in time at a particular phase but, rather, have other experiences—see other sights, as it were—as a direct result of straying from the road to proficient reading. Unfortunately, these other experiences are mostly negative. They involve, as we discussed in Chapter 1, some negative experiences common to poor readers in general, such as Matthew effects, as well as experiences more specific to poor readers who have been labeled LD, such as the possible stigma of the LD label. In our opening tales, all of the children—except perhaps for Megan, the youngest—obviously had negative experiences as a consequence of reading failure. For example, all except for Megan disliked reading: Calvin never read independently, James tried diversionary tactics to avoid reading even in the classroom, and Stacy could not wait to drop out of school altogether. Of course, these negative experiences exacerbate children's reading problems, making it even more difficult for them to get back on the right path.

In addition, for three of the children in our tales, LD diagnosis itself appeared to exacerbate some of the negative consequences of reading failure. For instance, Calvin was embarrassed about going to the resource room and worried about missing information taught in the regular classroom, a concern that was not totally unjustified. Stacy's pattern of "learned helplessness," as exemplified by her difficulties in working independently, ironically was aggravated by long-term special-education placement. And Megan's teachers were concerned about the possible deleterious effects of the self-contained LD class on her future behavioral and academic development, owing to the characteristics of the other children in the class. Only for James was LD diagnosis something of a step up.

Finally, it is important to note that a child may go astray in a particular phase of reading acquisition for any number of reasons—indeed, what is more likely, for a combination of reasons. Thus, we are *not* proposing an etiological typology of reading disability. Such a typology would imply that each of the different patterns of reading disability has a single distinct cause. For example, Boder (1973) posited an etiological typology of reading disability involving three subtypes: a subtype with a linguistic deficit, another with a visual deficit, and a third with mixed deficits. According to this view, there are different types of reading disability, each caused by different, presumably biological, deficits. As we shall see, the possibility of subtypes of RD certainly cannot be ruled out. However, along with a number of other investigators (e.g., Shankweiler, Crain, Brady, & Macaruso, 1992; Siegel & Heaven, 1986; Torgesen, 1991), we think that current evidence for distinct subtypes of RD is weak.

More important, the whole idea of a single discrete cause of RD, either for all children with RD or for subgroups of them, strikes us as the wrong way to frame the problem of RD, at least for educational purposes. Specifically, the single-cause, or single-cause-per-subtype, idea does not fit with our interactive view of

RD; in this view, an individual's reading problems obviously cannot be reduced just to a single cause. Thus, whether there is a unitary phonological deficit associated with RD, as proposed by the Haskins Laboratories group of researchers (e.g., Liberman & Liberman, 1990; Shankweiler et al., 1992), or multiple deficits, as proposed by investigators such as Boder (1973) and Willows (1991), these deficits develop and operate not in a vacuum but, rather, in conjunction with a host of other variables, both intrinsic (e.g., personality variables) and environmental (e.g., the nature of instruction).

An interactive view explains, among other things, why Stacy could have a sibling who achieved normally in reading even though, like her, he was economically disadvantaged and lacked educational stimulation at home. It also explains why no single instructional program is a guarantee of success for everyone. For instance, all of these children failed in reading, although they were exposed to very different instructional approaches, ranging from strongly code oriented (e.g., *Distar*) to strongly meaning oriented (e.g., whole language). Reading disability, then, results not from just one cause but from a set of causes acting in concert.

Having provided this preamble, we are now ready to discuss the roads to reading disability in our model. Table 5.1 presents the characteristics of the five patterns of reading difficulty predicted by the model. After discussing the four patterns of reading disability (nonalphabetic readers, compensatory readers, nonautomatic readers, and delayed readers), we will briefly discuss suboptimal readers. Suboptimal readers, who would not typically be characterized as having RD, are readers who have gone astray relatively late in the process of reading acquisition.

Straying from the Road to Proficient Reading

Nonalphabetic Readers

In our model of reading acquisition, the first phase of reading is termed visual-cue word recognition (after Ehri, 1991, 1992). Thus, this phase is the first point at which readers may wander off the road to proficient reading. Children who go astray this soon have not yet grasped the alphabetic principle; hence, we refer to them as *nonalphabetic readers*. Without the skills to use any phonological information at all in word recognition, these readers are extremely limited in an alphabetic orthography such as English. They may use visual cues, such as pictures, word shape, or word length, in recognizing words. However, as they encounter more and more words, finding a distinctive visual cue for each word becomes progressively more difficult. Nonalphabetic readers have very limited word-recognition skills, and because of this poor word recognition they also exhibit extremely low comprehension.

TABLE 5.1 Characteristics of Various Patterns of Reading Difficulty

	Characteristics			
	Word Recognition Skills	Reading Comprehension Skills	Use of Comprehension Strategies	Disabled Reader
Nonalphabetic	No phonological reading skills. Uses visual cues to recognize words.	Very low reading comprehension due to poor word recognition.	Very limited or nonexistent.	Yes
Compensatory	Has limited phonological reading skills. Relies on compensatory abilities, such as use of sentence context.	May do well with relatively undemanding materials. Has difficulty when comprehension demands escalate, because word recognition consumes too many mental resources.	Very limited or nonexistent.	Yes

(continues)

Many nonalphabetic readers also appear to lack phonological awareness. As we discussed in the previous chapter, phonological awareness strongly predicts reading skill in the early elementary grades, independent of IQ or of prior decoding knowledge. For example, Mann and Liberman (1984) found that youngsters who performed most poorly on phonological-awareness tasks in kindergarten ended up in the bottom reading group at the end of first grade. Furthermore, some studies have found deficits in phonological awareness among older children with RD, even relative to younger, normally achieving readers matched to them on reading level (Bradley & Bryant, 1978; Olson, Wise, Conners, Rack, & Fulker, 1989; Snowling, 1981). Thus, the phonological-awareness deficits of children with RD do not seem to be exclusively connected to their low reading level or to their lack of experience with reading (unlike, for example, the letter reversals and word inversions discussed in the previous chapter). There is also some evidence that training phonological awareness, especially in conjunction with more formal reading instruction, can benefit youngsters with RD (Alexander, Andersen, Heilman, Voeller, & Torgesen, 1991; Blachman, 1989, 1994; Kennedy & Backman, 1993).

TABLE 5.1 (continued)

	Characteristics			
	Word Recognition Skills	*Reading Comprehension Skills*	*Use of Comprehension Strategies*	*Disabled Reader*
Nonautomatic	Has accurate word-recognition skills, but these are effortful, not automatic. May use sentence context to speed word recognition.	May do well with relatively undemanding materials. Has difficulty when comprehension demands escalate, because word recognition consumes too many mental resources.	Very limited or nonexistent.	Yes
Delayed	Has automatic recognition of words, but lags far behind peers in acquisition.	Impaired comprehension. Was not "ready" for comprehension instruction when it was delivered.	Impaired strategy use.	Yes
Suboptimal	Has automatic word-recognition skills.	Lacks higher-order comprehension skills.	Has at least some basic strategies, but may lack higher-level strategies.	No

At least one factor besides a rudimentary level of phonological awareness is necessary in order for children to achieve alphabetic insight. This other factor is knowledge about letters. Neither phonological awareness nor letter knowledge alone seems to be sufficient for alphabetic insight; rather, Byrne (1992) suggests that the two skills work together in a complementary way to facilitate alphabetic insight. Thus, some nonalphabetic readers may be lacking letter knowledge rather than, or in addition to, lacking phonological awareness. Like phonological awareness, letter-name knowledge is strongly predictive of future reading skill (Share, Jorm, MacLean, & Matthews, 1984).

Although exposure to letters and instruction in letter names are virtually universal in kindergarten, there is evidence that letters must be very well learned in order for children to progress in beginning reading acquisition. For instance, Ehri and Sweet (1991) stress that it is memory of letters, not just the ability to recognize or discriminate letters, that is important to progress in word recognition. And Adams (1990) emphasizes the value of overlearning of letters and of letter-naming speed to beginning reading acquisition. Thus, a child may notice letters in words or even recognize letters by name, yet still become a nonalphabetic reader, if for some reason he or she does not firmly commit letters to memory.

Both a rudimentary level of phonological awareness and letter knowledge are necessary for children to achieve alphabetic insight; nevertheless, in some cases, they may not be sufficient for alphabetic insight to occur. In other words, there may be one or more factors *besides* phonological awareness and letter-sound knowledge that contribute to children's achievement of alphabetic insight. Some children may have a rudimentary level of phonological awareness and know some letter-sound correspondences well, yet still be nonalphabetic readers because they have failed to realize that the letters and sounds in written words map onto each other in a systematic way. Without this realization, such children would have little reason to apply their letter-sound knowledge in decoding words.

Children who continue to be nonalphabetic readers will have very limited reading skills. In our opening stories of four children, Megan was the nonalphabetic reader. Clearly, she had not yet grasped the alphabetic principle. Her difficulty with determining initial and final consonant sounds in spoken words suggests a problem with phonological awareness. Furthermore, she had essentially no decoding skills and did not even remember many letter-sound correspondences, even though she was at the end of second grade—a grade level at which most normally achieving readers are concluding, not beginning, their acquisition of basic decoding skills. Megan could recognize a few sight words, but these were not sufficient to enable her to read much in the way of connected text. Thus, her reading comprehension was also virtually nonexistent. Megan is still relatively young but, like some children, may persist as a nonalphabetic reader for many years. Indeed, even adults can be nonalphabetic readers (Byrne, 1992).

Compensatory Readers

Some children progress to the second phase of reading acquisition, phonetic-cue word recognition, before straying from the road to proficient reading. These youngsters have more skills at their disposal than do nonalphabetic readers, because they have grasped the alphabetic principle and can make use of some phonological information in word recognition. However, their word-recognition skills are not completely accurate. We call these children *compensatory readers,* because they tend to use other abilities, such as sight-word knowledge or contextual skills, to compensate for weak phonological skills.

For example, many researchers (e.g., Perfetti, 1985; Stanovich, 1991) have found not only that poor readers make use of sentence context to aid word recognition but that they frequently make even more use of context than do normally achieving readers. This finding strikes some practitioners as odd. Aren't good readers *better* than poor readers at using contextual cues? As it happens, the finding is not at all strange if one keeps in mind that it is the use of context as an aid to *word recognition,* not comprehension, that is relevant here. Good readers do not need to rely on contextual cues to aid word recognition, because their word-recognition skills are accurate and rapid; rather, poor readers are the ones who need to supplement their weak word-recognition skills with other kinds of cues. Conversely, with regard to the use of context as an aid to *comprehension,* as, for example, in figuring out word meanings based on contextual cues, good readers are indeed better than poor readers (Stanovich, 1991).

A crucial difference between compensatory and nonalphabetic readers is that the former have grasped the alphabetic principle, whereas the latter have not. Compensatory readers can make some use of phonological information in reading and may even have acquired some orthographic knowledge about words. However, their phonological and orthographic skills are not sufficiently developed to allow for fully accurate word recognition. By contrast, nonalphabetic readers have no phonological-reading skills. Although, as we have discussed, some nonalphabetic readers may have a rudimentary level of phonological awareness, they cannot apply this awareness to word recognition because they have not yet achieved alphabetic insight.

In our view, at least some phonological-reading skills are required in order for compensatory skills to come into play in the reading of connected text. Consider, for instance, sight-word compensatory skills. A youngster who relies solely on sight-word abilities without any phonological cues whatsoever (i.e., a nonalphabetic reader) will need to keep finding a distinctive visual cue for each new word that is learned—a process that becomes increasingly difficult with each successive word. In addition, many of the small function words that occur frequently in connected text are visually similar: *what, when, where, were,* and so on. Thus, reading anything but the simplest text will be very difficult if the child is completely lacking the ability to use phonological information in word recognition.

As a second example of compensatory skills, consider the use of sentence context to facilitate word recognition. In order to make use of contextual cues to help in recognizing a specific word, the child already has to be able to read many of the other words in the sentence; otherwise, there is no "context" that the child can use. Nonalphabetic readers probably do not lack the actual ability to make use of sentence context in word recognition. Rather, they have such limited word-recognition skills that there is little opportunity for their contextual abilities to be used during reading of text.

The major problem for compensatory readers is that their continued reliance on compensatory skills eventually results in impaired reading comprehension. As we discussed in the previous chapter, the development of skilled word recognition, which in turn depends on phonological skills, is a necessary though not sufficient condition for good reading comprehension (Stanovich, 1991). A child with skilled word recognition may still have poor reading comprehension due, for example, to deficient listening-comprehension skills; however, a child with poor word-recognition skills cannot also have good reading comprehension. In short, children who rely on contextual abilities to compensate for deficient word-recognition skills may be able to read the words on the page, but they do so at a price: They divert mental resources toward word recognition that, in good readers, would be free for comprehension. Thus, compensatory readers will eventually be disadvantaged in comprehension relative to good readers.

Using sight-word abilities to compensate for weak phonological-reading skills also is not a good long-term strategy for compensatory readers. For example, Byrne, Freebody, and Gates (1992) did a longitudinal study of second- and third-grade children, using a classification system previously developed by Baron (1977), that involves "Chinese" readers and "Phoenician" readers. The "Chinese" readers were children who had at least average sight-word knowledge but poor decoding skills, whereas the "Phoenicians" performed at average levels on tests of decoding but had below-average knowledge of sight words. The children who were classified as "Chinese" readers, but not those classified as "Phoenicians," showed a progressive deterioration in reading skill, for both word reading and reading comprehension.

Keep in mind that, in the very early grades, it is common for children, including normally achieving ones, to rely on compensatory abilities in word recognition. What becomes problematic is a youngster's *continued* reliance on these compensatory skills, to the exclusion of acquiring accurate word-recognition skills. In the early grades, the demands on comprehension are relatively low, and compensatory readers may appear to be performing adequately in reading. However, without accurate word-recognition skills, their performance will deteriorate rapidly in the middle elementary grades, when greatly increasing demands are made on comprehension and on the ability to recognize a large number of unfamiliar words (Chall, 1983; Mason, 1992).

This escalating difficulty is precisely what befell James, our compensatory reader. James had some decoding skills and was also good at using contextual cues to compensate for his weaknesses in word recognition. In addition, the text used at the beginning of his reading program was relatively easy, in terms of both its demands on word recognition and its demands on comprehension. Thus, James initially appeared not to have reading problems. However, when he failed to develop fully accurate word-recognition skills and continued to rely on compensatory skills, and as he was expected to read increasingly difficult texts, his reading comprehension eventually deteriorated.

Nonautomatic Readers

Nonautomatic readers are readers who can recognize words accurately, but only with effort; they have failed to make word recognition automatic. Thus, they have left the road to proficient reading at the point of controlled word recognition, the third phase of reading in our model of reading acquisition. Like compensatory readers, nonautomatic readers may rely on contextual cues to speed word recognition, but this compensatory strategy adversely impacts comprehension, especially that of more difficult text. Thus, nonautomatic readers may also show deteriorating performance in the middle elementary grades, when text demands become more challenging. The main difference between compensatory and nonautomatic readers involves accuracy of word recognition. Nonautomatic readers are accurate in recognizing words, but their word recognition is effortful; compensatory readers are inaccurate in recognizing words and also find word recognition effortful.

Whereas normally achieving readers appear to pass quickly from the phase of controlled word recognition to that of automatic word recognition, for many children with RD this passage is a major stumbling block (Sternberg & Wagner, 1982). Many children with RD do acquire word-recognition skills with direct instruction, but applying those skills in an effortless, automatic way while reading connected text, especially more difficult text, is another hurdle altogether. Calvin is an example of a nonautomatic reader. Although he can recognize words accurately, he still has to devote considerable mental energy to word recognition; therefore, his comprehension is affected, particularly in relatively difficult expository materials such as social studies and science.

A number of factors could account for the problems experienced by children with RD in automatization of word recognition. One factor involves deficits in naming speed, which have been found among some youngsters with RD (Bowers, 1993; Katz, 1986; Wolf, 1991). Young children who have *both* naming-speed deficits and phonological-awareness deficits are at particular risk for failure in reading, as compared with children who have only one type of deficit (Felton, 1993). Moreover, naming-speed deficiencies may be especially important in limiting reading achievement in the middle elementary grades (Blachman, 1994)— that is, when automatization of word recognition begins to be crucial to progress in reading.

As we mentioned in the previous chapter, some authorities view naming speed as a possible limiting factor for fluency in reading. In other words, perhaps we all have an intrinsic limit for how quickly we can name words, and no matter how good our decoding skills are, we cannot exceed this natural limit. According to this view, the automatization problems of youngsters with RD might be construed as an intrinsic deficit in naming speed, one that has in turn been connected to phonological deficiencies (e.g., Katz, 1986).

However, as we also discussed in the previous chapter, there is another factor strongly related to the development of automatization, and this factor is practice (Sternberg, 1985, 1986). It is clear that children with RD get less practice in reading, both in and outside of school, than do normally achieving readers. Differences in amount of practice in school between good and poor readers begin very early. For example, even at the first-grade level, there are large differences between high and low reading groups in amount of practice reading in school (Stanovich, 1986). Practice in reading outside of school also consistently relates to gains in reading achievement (Anderson et al., 1985). Most children with RD, like Calvin, do little reading outside of school and prefer television to reading as a pastime. Indeed, one large cross-cultural study (Stevenson et al., 1987) found that poor readers in the United States, Japan, and Taiwan were all highly similar in their disinclination to choose reading as a free-time activity.

Motivation is another factor that is related to both practice and automatization. The more motivated children are to read, the more practice they are likely to get in reading. Although levels of motivation can vary even among youngsters without apparent reading difficulties, children who are struggling in reading will be especially likely to lose motivation for reading. Stevenson et al. (1987) found that, in Japan and Taiwan as well as in the United States, poor readers were significantly less positive about reading than were good readers, and that attitudes toward reading were established very early in schooling. Children's ratings of how well they liked reading did not change significantly between the first and the fifth grades.

Delayed Readers

Some children with RD finally do seem to acquire accurate and automatic word-recognition skills, but much more slowly and with much more difficulty than do normally achieving readers. These youngsters lag so far behind others of their age in the acquisition of word-recognition skills that we refer to them as *delayed readers*. Delayed readers lose their way to proficient reading at the point of automatic word recognition.

Unfortunately for these children, their reading problems do not vanish with the acquisition of word-recognition skills, because their normally achieving peers have moved far ahead of them on the road to proficient reading. For instance, while delayed readers were struggling with basic word-recognition skills, their normally achieving peers were not only beginning to use reading as a tool to acquire new concepts and a bigger knowledge base but also learning how to use strategies to aid comprehension, areas in which delayed readers continue to be deficient. Thus, we use the word *delayed* to refer specifically to word-recognition skills, not to overall reading achievement. As the word implies, delayed readers do eventually catch up in word recognition, but not necessarily in other areas of reading.

Reading-comprehension deficits, pertaining even to text that has been controlled for decoding level, are well-documented among children with RD (Garner, Alexander, & Hare, 1991; Smiley, Oakley, Worthen, Campione, & Brown, 1977; Wong, 1991). These deficits can occur even when children have been selected based on an ability measure involving verbal IQ or listening comprehension. Thus, reading-comprehension deficits in RD are due not to poorer general-language comprehension skills (provided, of course, that the appropriate ability measure is used) but, rather, at least partially to strategic deficits. That is, children with RD are less skilled at using strategies to aid comprehension than are nondisabled readers. Children with RD do have some strategic knowledge, but this knowledge is less sophisticated than that of their normally achieving peers (Paris, Jacobs, & Cross, 1987; Wong, 1991). For example, children with RD are both less sensitive to passage organization (Wong & Wong, 1986) and less efficient at scanning text (Garner & Reis, 1981).

Keep in mind that delayed readers do have the potential to learn more advanced comprehension skills and strategies. They lack these skills as a consequence, rather than as a cause, of their years of poor reading. For example, delayed readers may fail to use strategies to aid comprehension, not because they are intrinsically incapable of using strategies but because they have not had the kinds of reading experiences that would encourage them to generate strategies. In addition, delayed readers may fail to use the strategic knowledge that they do possess, for a variety of reasons (Garner, 1990). One reason is that poor readers demonstrate low self-esteem and attributional patterns that are not conducive to strategy use (Borkowski, Carr, & Pressley, 1987). In other words, when poor readers experience a breakdown in comprehension, they tend to attribute that breakdown to lack of ability ("I'm just stupid") rather than to lack of effort ("I have to find another way to figure this out"). The belief that one is "just stupid" is more conducive to giving up than to using strategies.

There is ample evidence to support the position that strategy deficits, though common among youngsters with RD, are not causally central to reading disability. First, strategy training does not necessarily eliminate group differences in comprehension between children with RD and nondisabled readers but, rather, tends to benefit both groups of children (Worden, 1983). Second, children with reading disability are not necessarily deficient in strategy knowledge when matched to younger nondisabled readers on reading level (e.g., Taylor & Williams, 1983).

Finally, as we and others have noted (e.g., Spear & Sternberg, 1987; Stanovich, 1986), strategic abilities are too closely linked to broader intellectual abilities to serve as a good explanation for reading disability. Whereas contemporary theorists (e.g., Sternberg, 1985) view strategic abilities as central to intelligence, reading disability has always been conceptualized as a disorder that is different from mental retardation or from generally low intellectual abilities. Thus, invoking strategic deficits as a primary cause of reading disability is highly problematic to the traditional view of RD as a disorder distinct from mental retardation. Yet this traditional view can still accommodate the idea of strategic deficits as a *secondary* problem, a position increasingly espoused by investigators in the field. For example, Wong (1991) suggests that strategic deficits in reading disability are a product of loss of motivation for reading, learned helplessness, and deficient reading experiences.

Among youngsters with RD, delayed readers are frequently seen at the middle or secondary school level. In our opening tales of four children, Stacy was the delayed reader. Although Stacy had always lagged behind other children in acquiring word-recognition skills, she did eventually learn to decode accurately and fluently. However, by the time she had acquired accurate, automatic word recognition, she was completely out of step with normally achieving readers of her age. She had missed out on the higher-level aspects of reading, such as higher-level comprehension and strategic abilities, because it took her so long to acquire the lower-level skills. And due in part to her lack of strategic abilities, she felt overwhelmed by the reading demands of the regular classroom.

It is possible to teach strategic skills, as well as certain other higher-level reading skills, directly (Paris et al., 1987; Worden, 1983). However, delayed readers are further handicapped by three factors that complicate the problems of all youngsters with reading disability. These factors are lowered motivation for reading; lowered levels of practice; and lowered expectations, on the part of both the children themselves and the adults around them. Although, as we have discussed, motivation and practice are particularly relevant to the development of automatic word recognition, decreases in motivation and practice also contribute to the Matthew effects experienced by all youngsters with RD, whether they are nonalphabetic, compensatory, nonautomatic, or delayed readers. We discuss these three negative factors next.

Negative Factors Affecting All Children with RD

On the right-hand side of Figure 5.1, we represent these three factors—lowered motivation, lowered levels of practice, and lowered expectations—as a set of complicating difficulties cross-cutting all of the roads to reading disability. One might think of these factors, collectively, as a kind of swamp; once children become enmired, it is extremely difficult for them to get out. Of course, these three factors affect poor readers in general, not just those who have been diagnosed with reading disability.

Consider, for instance, the findings of Allington and McGill-Franzen (1989), who compared special-education programs and "Chapter 1" programs for poor readers in six school districts of New York State. They found that both kinds of programs tended to emphasize drill-and-practice worksheet activities, not the reading of stories or content-area texts. In fact, in both cases, less than *two minutes* of every hour of instructional time went to teacher-directed reading of connected text with an emphasis on comprehension. What did this lack of emphasis on reading stories and books, as opposed to worksheets, mean for poor readers?

For one thing, even in school, poor readers were getting much less practice reading words as a part of coherent, naturalistic text than were normally achieving readers. Because there are usually many more words in a story than on a worksheet, or even several worksheets, poor readers were probably getting much less practice reading words, period. So the special programming received by poor readers, whether in "Chapter 1" or in special education, did little to offset the differences in practice between good and poor readers in the regular classroom, and perhaps even widened the gap. Second, at least in the programs examined in this study, poor readers were receiving relatively little instruction in higher-level comprehension areas, a situation that might be expected to affect their eventual performance in these areas. Third, the worksheets probably did not stimulate students to generate the kinds of strategies required for reading stories and content-area texts; thus, poor readers' acquisition of appropriate comprehension strategies may also have suffered. And finally, it is likely that the emphasis on worksheet and drill activities, as opposed to the reading of interesting stories or books, did little to increase the already sagging motivational levels of poor readers.

In a review of research on reading comprehension instruction, Dole, Duffy, Roehler, and Pearson (1991) point out that students frequently infer unintended meanings from the nature of teachers' reading instruction and of the academic work they do in class. Indeed, students' very concept of what reading is may be shaped by such instruction and academic work. For instance, if a teacher's instruction frequently involves situations similar to those in which literate people typically use reading, students make different inferences about what reading is than when the instruction frequently involves contrived tasks such as workbook exercises. Similarly, if a teacher's instruction emphasizes finding the "right answers" to literal comprehension questions, then students will draw different inferences about what reading is than if the teacher emphasizes the use of strategies in reading or the use of Socratic dialogue. In other words, instruction that focuses largely on worksheets, low-level comprehension tasks, and contrived activities— as in the programs examined by Allington and McGill-Franzen (1989)—is not likely to produce strategic, motivated readers who view reading in the same way that most literate people do.

We have argued that, in some cases, labeling poor readers as LD and putting them in the special-education system actually may aggravate some of the negative consequences of poor reading. Allington and McGill-Franzen (1989) found some evidence to support this position. For instance, their study revealed that poor readers in special-education programs sometimes received less instructional time in reading than did either regular-classroom students or "Chapter 1" children. Even when instructional time was equivalent, the children in special-education programs engaged in more seatwork and in fewer teacher-directed activities in reading than did children in either "Chapter 1" or regular education. Thus, poor readers in special education may be particularly likely to suffer decreases in practice, to benefit less from direct instructional interaction with a teacher, to engage in unmotivating instructional activities, and to draw maladaptive conclusions about what reading is.

Of course, not all special-education programs emphasize drill and seatwork. For instance, Allington and McGill-Franzen (1989) have noted wide variability in the nature of the reading instruction experienced by the youngsters in the special-education programs that they studied. And we ourselves have seen some fine special-education programs in which higher-level reading skills are emphasized and worksheets and workbooks are eschewed. Even in cases where special-education teachers do emphasize lower-level skills and drill-and-practice activities, they generally have good intentions, in that they believe that this emphasis is what the children need. And indeed, as we have seen, children with RD typically *are* lacking in lower-level areas of reading such as word recognition. Unfortunately, however, the road to proficient reading needs to be paved with more than just good intentions. Although children with RD generally do need considerable instruction in word-recognition skills, if this instruction occurs at the expense of higher-level-reading skills, then the children's reading achievement will continue to suffer.

Leaving One Road for Another

When a youngster initially strays from the road to proficient reading, onto one of the roads leading toward reading disability, he or she is not necessarily on a one-way street without exits. Rather, when a "wrong turn" is taken, one of three things may happen. First, children with RD may start out on one road to reading disability, for example, as nonalphabetic readers, and end up on one of the other roads, such as that of compensatory reading. In Figure 5.1, we represent this mobility by the two solid vertical lines, with arrows pointing upward, on the right side of the figure.

Consider Megan, our example of a nonalphabetic reader. On the one hand, with appropriate instruction Megan might well achieve alphabetic insight and develop some phonological-reading skills. However, if these phonological-reading skills did not become fully accurate, she would then be a compensatory reader. On the other hand, if her word-recognition skills were accurate, but not automatic, she would be a nonautomatic reader. Finally, even if she eventually acquired both accurate and automatic word-recognition skills, her acquisition of word-recognition skills would have lagged far behind that of her peers, and she would be a delayed reader.

In short, children may fit into multiple patterns of reading disability over time. However, they can move only upward, not downward, between paths. For instance, a delayed reader cannot become a nonautomatic reader; and a child who is a compensatory reader cannot suddenly "forget" the alphabetic principle and become a nonalphabetic reader.

Returning to the example of Megan, we find that there is yet another, more pessimistic scenario. Megan might fail to develop alphabetic insight entirely and thus *remain* on the road of nonalphabetic reading. This failure could occur for a number of reasons, such as an inappropriate instructional program or particularly severe phonological-processing deficits.

Third, it is also possible for children to stray from the road to proficient reading but, eventually, to find their way back to it and become good readers. This possibility is represented by the dashed lines, with curved arrows, in Figure 5.1. However, in our view, for most children this possibility is unlikely without active educational intervention. In particular, once children have become mired in the "swamp" of limited practice, low motivation, and low expectations—an entanglement that may occur as early as the first grade—it may be extremely difficult for them to get back to the road to proficient reading, and some kind of active educational intervention will almost certainly be needed.

Calvin is an example of a youngster who started out on one path to reading disability and ended up on a different path. Because his reading difficulties began in the first grade, and because they initially involved problems with accuracy, not speed, of word recognition, it is likely that Calvin first went astray in the phase of either visual-cue or phonetic-cue word recognition—that is, as either a nonalphabetic or a compensatory reader. With intensive instruction in decoding skills, Calvin did eventually acquire accurate word recognition. Unfortunately, however, his word recognition remained slow and effortful, and he became a nonautomatic reader.

Suboptimal Readers

There is at least one other phase of reading acquisition in which readers may wander off the road to proficient reading. This is the phase of strategic reading. Readers who go astray at this point have acquired accurate, automatic word-recognition skills, as well as routine use of at least some strategies to aid comprehension; nevertheless, they fall short in terms of higher-level comprehension skills. We refer to these individuals as *suboptimal readers*. Although suboptimal readers have not quite attained highly proficient reading, their reading achievement usually is not so impaired as to present a serious problem in schooling, at least not below a high school or college level.

As normally achieving readers progress in reading acquisition, there is a tendency for the various phases to become more domain-specific, such that a student may be a proficient reader in some domains but not in others. In the previous chapter, we used economics and physics as examples of domains in which we ourselves would not live up to our own definition of proficient reading. However, suboptimal readers are not proficient in any domain; rather, they lack higher-level reading comprehension skills in all domains. The generality of this lack of higher-level comprehension skills is what differentiates suboptimal readers from proficient readers who merely are reading in an unfamiliar domain.

Suboptimal readers do not have the kinds of reading problems typical of children who are classified as having reading disability. First, the overall reading achievement of suboptimal readers usually is not sufficiently impaired for them to be classified as having RD. Second, the evidence we have reviewed strongly suggests that reading disability is linked specifically to problems in word recognition and, hence, manifests itself early in schooling. However, suboptimal readers do not have, nor (unlike delayed readers) have they ever had, problems in word recognition. For that matter, the difficulties of suboptimal readers may not become apparent at all until well into high school, or even college, because their reading skills generally are adequate for success at previous levels.

Because suboptimal readers generally would not be classified as having RD in schools, and because their profile of poor reading differs from the profile typical of RD, we will not discuss suboptimal readers at length in this book. However, we should point out that, although suboptimal readers are much less impaired in reading than are most children with RD, suboptimal reading may nevertheless cause problems. For instance, a suboptimal reader who is in a highly competitive academic environment, or who wants to continue his or her schooling beyond high school, will probably begin to experience significant academic difficulties. Because we live in a culture that values literacy, suboptimal reading would tend to cut this individual off from a wide range of educational and professional choices in adulthood.

The Five Patterns over Time

To conclude our discussion of the five patterns of reading difficulty, we would like to indulge in some speculation about the different developmental courses of these patterns over time. Suppose, for instance, that Megan, James, Calvin, and Stacy do not find their way back to the road to proficient reading but instead remain on their current paths. What might happen to them with the passage of time? Keep in mind that our knowledge base for comparing the developmental trajectories of the five patterns is limited at best, leading us to emphasize our choice of the word *speculation*.

In our view, many individuals who remain nonalphabetic readers will be virtually illiterate. The attainment of alphabetic insight is essential for even a very low level of achievement in an alphabetic language such as English; without this insight, an individual will find it extremely difficult to progress beyond a small sight vocabulary in reading. Thus, most nonalphabetic readers are unlikely to achieve even a functional level of literacy that would enable them to read directions, job applications, newspapers, and so on.

Compensatory and nonautomatic readers will have persistent word-recognition deficits but may be partially able to compensate for these deficits. Many of them may attain at least functional literacy and perform well in work situations that do not place high demands on literacy skills. Indeed, as we will see shortly, there is evidence to suggest that these kinds of readers may be found at the university level. In short, some compensatory and nonautomatic readers can function even at a relatively high reading level if they are able (and willing) to compensate for their word-recognition difficulties.

Consider, for example, a nonautomatic reader such as Calvin. Although, without remediation, Calvin's slow reading is likely to continue causing him serious problems in school, there are ways in which he can compensate for these problems, even at the college level—by taking a reduced course load each semester, by putting in longer hours studying, and so on. Especially if Calvin has strengths in cognitive areas other than reading—as well as the motivation to work much harder than many other students to graduate from college—then he might perform relatively well despite his nonautomatic word recognition.

Of the four patterns of reading disability, only delayed readers have both accurate and automatic word recognition. Delayed readers' difficulties revolve around reading comprehension rather than word recognition. Like compensatory and nonautomatic readers, delayed readers may be able to function at a relatively high level of achievement with compensation. Also, because delayed readers no longer are plagued by word-recognition deficits, they may have better spelling skills than do other individuals with RD. However, if delayed readers have limited ability or motivation to compensate for their strategic deficits, or if the reading material is very demanding, then their deficits may continue to pose serious problems.

Finally, as we have indicated, suboptimal readers are much less impaired in reading than are most individuals with RD. Like delayed readers—but unlike nonalphabetic, compensatory, or nonautomatic readers—suboptimal readers have adequate word recognition and may have adequate spelling skills. Although suboptimal readers lack higher-order comprehension skills, they have better strategic knowledge than do delayed readers. Thus, of the five patterns of reading difficulty that we have described, suboptimal readers would be likely to function at the highest level of reading achievement. However, as we have also indicated, suboptimal reading can cause serious problems, especially in educational or professional situations that demand a very high level of literacy.

A General Discussion of the Model

In this general discussion of our model, there are five major points we wish to emphasize. In condensed form, these five points involve the interactive perspective of the model; its emphasis on verbal abilities, both in reading acquisition and in reading disability; some comments on comparing children with RD to younger, normally achieving readers; the relationship between the four patterns of reading disability and age; and the variability of reading performance within a given pattern. We now discuss each of these five points in more detail.

An Interactive Perspective

To begin, we reiterate our view that the particular road to reading disability taken by a youngster with RD is determined by the interaction of intrinsic factors (e.g., cognitive-processing abilities, overall intelligence, motivation, temperament) and extrinsic factors (e.g., home environment, the nature of instruction). Thus, each pattern of reading disability does not involve a single discrete "cause." For example, children with severe phonological-processing deficits—deficits that may be shaped by environmental as well as biological factors—might do especially poorly in an instructional program in which phonological skills are not stressed, and thereby end up as nonalphabetic readers. Yet an appropriate instructional program might enable some of these youngsters to grasp the alphabetic principle and to remain on the road to proficient reading, or at least to remain on it longer before going astray on some other path to reading disability.

Of course, instructional variables certainly are not the only factors important in determining which route a given reader takes. Certain characteristics of the home environment appear to be very important in reading achievement, thus exerting a strong influence on that route. For instance, a child with highly literate parents, who emphasize books, reading, and writing at home, may be less affected by intrinsically weak phonological-processing skills or by an instructional approach that does not teach phonological skills than would a youngster from a less literate home environment.

Furthermore, it appears that, even among highly literate families, there is variability in the extent to which children are prepared for reading acquisition. Some rather specific factors that may vary even among middle-class, literate families— such as the kinds of questions parents ask their children while reading to them (Anderson et al., 1985), or the extent to which children are involved in rhyming activities (Goswami & Bryant, 1992; Maclean, Bryant, & Bradley, 1987)—are associated with successful reading acquisition. Thus, not all children from literate families are necessarily equally well-prepared for reading acquisition. In addition, note that, even within a family, these factors could well vary from child to child. We will discuss this idea of within-family environmental influences in Chapter 8.

Verbal Versus Visual Deficits

In our model as a whole, with regard to both reading acquisition and reading disability, we have emphasized the role of verbal, and especially phonological, factors. We have already reviewed evidence that we think strongly supports this emphasis. Although visual-deficit views of RD were especially popular prior to the 1970s, the flood of negative research evidence on visual-perceptual testing and training in the schools has led many researchers to turn their attention to verbal rather than to visual factors in RD. However, in recent years, a number of research findings (e.g., Eden, Stein, Wood, & Wood, 1995; Lovegrove & Slaghuis, 1989; Martin & Lovegrove, 1988) have breathed new life into ailing visual-deficit views of reading disability. We would be remiss if we did not discuss these findings, at least briefly.

Willows (1991) provides a lengthy review of evidence on the role of visual-processing deficits in reading disability. She argues that more than one kind of processing deficit is implicated in the disorder. Thus, Willows represents a multiple-deficit rather than a unitary-deficit view of RD; she acknowledges the role of verbal deficits in reading disability, but, in addition, she maintains that at least some children with RD also have visual deficits. The evidence for visual-processing deficits is strongest for young children with RD—those seven years old or younger—and under conditions in which stimuli are presented very rapidly—

that is, at short exposures. These deficits, however, would not be detected by the kinds of visual-perceptual tests commonly employed in schools, because they do not involve brief exposure times or rapid presentation of stimuli.

Other investigators (e.g., Fletcher & Satz, 1979) have theorized that the nature of the processing deficits exhibited by children with RD changes developmentally, with younger children exhibiting primarily visual deficits and older children exhibiting primarily verbal deficits. Thus, only research involving young children would be expected to uncover visual-processing deficits. In addition, as we discussed in the previous chapter, some researchers have suggested that visual-processing skills play a role in the acquisition of orthographic knowledge—that is, knowledge about common spelling patterns and word-specific spellings. As yet, however, researchers have not been successful in identifying a specific visual-processing skill that accounts for variance in orthographic knowledge.

We think it unlikely that visual-processing deficits will turn out to play a significant role in most cases of reading disability. For one thing, as Stanovich (1992) points out, phonological problems are extremely common among children with reading disability, whereas visual-processing deficits are much more elusive. This observation suggests that, if visual-processing deficits are involved in reading disability, they play a lesser role or affect many fewer youngsters than do phonological deficits.

Second, as our review of research evidence in Chapter 4 indicates, verbal factors generally appear to be much more important than visual factors in reading acquisition. Here, it may be helpful to distinguish between skills that are needed in reading acquisition and skills that account for meaningful *variance* in reading acquisition. Obviously, in some sense, visual perception is necessary for reading acquisition, but it does not seem to account for a meaningful proportion of the variance in reading achievement, at least not by comparison with verbal abilities. Breathing is necessary for reading, too, but because everyone who reads also breathes, breathing does not account for variance in reading achievement.

Finally, although the findings reviewed by Willows (1991) appear reliable, it is not clear how these laboratory measures of visual processing—involving both rapid presentations of stimuli and brief exposures—relate to the actual task of reading. Some researchers argue that such measures are particularly sensitive. However, because reading does not necessarily involve the kind of brief exposure times used experimentally (e.g., the reader can reread text or can fixate on words for varying lengths of time), the impact of very subtle visual-processing deficits on actual reading is uncertain.

Comparisons Between Children with RD and Younger Nondisabled Readers

Although our model links reading disability with developmental deviations from the path of typical reading acquisition, we do not claim that children with RD are exactly like younger nondisabled children, or that they have a disorder that will be

remedied by the simple passage of time. Clearly, there are many similarities between children with RD and younger, normally achieving readers, and observations of these similarities are important for interpreting many of the difficulties of
children with RD. Certain error patterns in reading, such as letter reversals and
word inversions, provide one example of these similarities, as we have already discussed.

However, in other ways, children with RD are very different from younger, normally achieving readers. For instance, we have reviewed evidence suggesting that
children with RD are deficient even relative to younger nondisabled readers in
some cognitive areas, such as those involving certain phonological-processing
skills. In addition, children with RD do not remain arrested in time; rather, they
tend to have a host of other negative experiences associated with their initial reading failure, such as decreases in motivation, practice, and expectations, which
complicate their reading problems but generally do not affect younger normally
achieving children.

Time also does not stop for the normally achieving peers of children with RD;
the former are progressing rapidly along the road to proficient reading while the
latter are struggling with basic word-recognition skills. Thus, children with RD
diverge increasingly from normally achieving readers of their own age. All of
these factors make it highly unlikely that children with RD will just catch up
spontaneously in overall reading achievement. Even with intensive educational
intervention, catching up may be an extremely difficult enterprise, especially for
older children with reading disability.

The Four Patterns and Age

Each of the four patterns of performance in reading disability may be more common at certain age or grade levels than at others. For example, as we discussed
earlier, when children initially make a "wrong turn" on one of the four roads to
reading disability, one of three things may happen: They may remain on the first
wrong road; they may take a connecting route that leads them to one of the other
roads to reading disability; or, on rare occasions, they may find their way back to
the road to proficient reading. Thus, for example, more nonalphabetic readers
will be found at an early elementary level than in high school, because over time,
and with educational intervention, some nonalphabetic readers will become compensatory, nonautomatic, or delayed readers, or may even return to the path of
normal reading acquisition.

However, assuming that the appropriate point in reading acquisition has been
passed, any of the patterns potentially could be found at any grade level. For instance, one obviously cannot find nonautomatic readers with RD at the beginning of first grade, because even normally achieving readers lack automatic word
recognition at that point. But an adult with RD theoretically could be a delayed,
nonautomatic, compensatory, or even nonalphabetic reader.

Bruck (1990) studied the reading skills of a group of college students who had been identified as having reading disability in childhood. She found that they continued to be characterized by word-recognition deficits. These adults with RD performed especially poorly on tests of phonological reading (as measured by reading of pseudowords), speed of word recognition, and spelling. They relied on context to supplement their faulty word-recognition skills, and many remarked that they had to read slowly or their comprehension was affected. Although the individual differences Bruck found among her subjects were not large, they appeared to involve accuracy of word recognition rather than speed. In short, some of the adults with RD had word recognition that was accurate but slow, whereas others were both slow and inaccurate.

Many of Bruck's subjects appeared to be compensatory readers. They used contextual and sight-word abilities, among other things, to compensate for weak phonological skills. The individual-difference data also suggested the possibility that some of the subjects—those with accurate but slow word recognition—were nonautomatic readers. Clearly, none of the subjects were nonalphabetic readers; but this finding is not surprising in a group of college students, because nonalphabetic readers would be highly unlikely to achieve a level of reading achievement that would enable them to function in college. Also, none of the subjects appeared to have been delayed readers; all were characterized by some kind of significant word-recognition deficit.

In this study, however, certain measures involved in uncovering word-recognition deficits were quite subtle by educational standards. For instance, Bruck acknowledges that some of the subjects achieved high scores on a standardized test of word recognition (the *Wide Range Achievement Test—Revised;* see Jastak & Wilkinson, 1984) and would not be classified as having RD on the basis of this test. Rather, the measures that were most consistent in showing deficits were those assessing pseudoword reading as well as *latency* of word recognition, for both pseudowords and real words. Latency refers to the amount of time the subject takes to respond to the word—that is, to the speed of word recognition. In this regard, practitioners may recall that the WRAT-R is a timed measure, involving a ten-second time limit per word. However, the differences in latency between adults with RD and nondisabled college students ranged from an average of over a second per word (for pseudowords) to an average of about a fifth of a second per word (for common regular words). The point is that, although these differences are statistically reliable (in fact, some of them are very large for this kind of research), they are not of an order of magnitude that would be detected in educational testing.

One interesting result of this study concerns the finding that some of the adults with RD achieved high levels of comprehension in spite of their word-recognition problems. This finding appears to contradict a large body of other evidence, which we have already reviewed, suggesting that accurate, automatic word recognition is necessary for higher-level comprehension. Here too, however, the measure of comprehension involved a standardized test (the *Stanford Diagnostic*

Reading Test; see Karlsen, Madden, & Gardner, 1974), which may not have been sufficiently sensitive to detect comprehension differences between normally achieving college students and the relatively high comprehenders among the students with RD. Indeed, other authors (e.g., Anderson, Hiebert, Scott, & Wilkinson, 1985) have criticized standardized tests of reading comprehension for, among other things, their emphasis on lower-level aspects of comprehension. Thus, as Bruck (1990) herself points out, had more naturalistic measures of comprehension been used in the study—for example, answers to open-ended essay questions—comprehension differences between the two groups of students might have been revealed. We think that this outcome would have been very likely.

Bruck also suggests an alternative explanation for these findings. The alternative explanation involves the possibility of a minimum threshold for word recognition: Beyond a certain level of accuracy and speed of word recognition, other skills—such as language comprehension skills—may be more important in accounting for variance in reading comprehension than is word recognition. At the same time, it is not entirely clear what some of these relatively subtle (from an educator's, not a researcher's, point of view) word-recognition deficits mean in practical terms—that is, for everyday performance in reading comprehension. In any case, Bruck's results demonstrate that it is important to differentiate between commonly used educational measures and the kinds of measures that are used in research.

Lovett and her colleagues (Lovett, 1987; Lovett, Ransby, Hardwick, Johns, & Donaldson, 1989) have classified children with RD as either accuracy disabled or rate disabled based upon their performance on standardized educational tests. The subjects in these studies, who ranged in age from eight to thirteen years, were considerably younger than the population studied by Bruck (1990). The accuracy-disabled children demonstrated significant difficulties with word-recognition accuracy, whereas the rate-disabled children had grade appropriate accuracy of word recognition but were deficient in terms of speed. In other words, like Bruck's adult subjects, some of Lovett's subjects had both slow and inaccurate word recognition, whereas others were just slow. In our model, the former subjects would be conceptualized as compensatory or, in extreme cases, nonalphabetic readers, whereas many of the latter subjects might be seen as nonautomatic readers. However, we should point out that Lovett's educational measures were different from, and probably less sensitive than, some of the measures employed by Bruck (1990). Thus, among the children classified as rate disabled, there may have been youngsters with relatively subtle deficits in word-recognition accuracy that were not revealed by standardized educational tests.

Variations Within Patterns

Finally, just as intrinsic individual differences interact with extrinsic variables to determine which roads children will take to reading disability, children's performance within a given pattern may vary somewhat, depending both on these intrinsic individual differences and on extrinsic variables. For example, a very bright, highly motivated compensatory reader will do a better job of compensating for weak phonological-reading skills than will a compensatory reader who is less bright or less motivated. Among the college students with RD studied by Bruck (1990), those who were good comprehenders had better vocabulary knowledge and higher childhood IQ scores than did the poor comprehenders. Similarly, Rack, Snowling, and Olson (1992), in a review of phonological-reading deficits in RD, conclude that, although most children with RD appear to have persistent deficits in phonological reading, many of them acquire word-recognition skills that exceed the level that would be predicted by their phonological skills. These authors suggest that factors such as the nature of remediation, the amount of practice reading, and underlying cognitive and linguistic abilities (e.g., orthographic-processing skills and vocabulary) may influence the extent to which children can compensate for weak phonological skills.

Other evidence indicates that, for school-identified children with LD generally, factors that are especially important for predicting academic success are IQ, socioeconomic status (SES), motivation, and a supportive home environment (Vogel, Hruby, & Adelman, 1993)—in addition, of course, to on-task classroom behavior (McKinney, Osborne, & Schulte, 1993). Obviously, strengths in these areas can offset some of the basic skill deficits among children with LD, helping them to achieve a much higher level of academic functioning than would otherwise be possible. Nevertheless, strengths in areas such as motivation can go only so far in ameliorating the academic effects of word-recognition deficits. Thus, we would argue that, without at least a threshold level of accurate and automatic word-recognition skills, children will find themselves on roads to reading disability. Only by finding their way back to the road to proficient reading, or by being helped to do so, can any of these youngsters escape being seriously disadvantaged in reading.

Comparing Models of Reading Disability

How Our Model Relates to Other Cognitive Models

Our model of reading disability is relatively compatible with the cognitive models of many other researchers who emphasize the importance of word-recognition processes, especially phonological processes, in reading disability. In our model, the four patterns of reading disability all involve departures from the road to proficient reading at the word-recognition level, and phonological processes play a prominent role in these departures. Furthermore, like most of these other investigators, we view the broad higher-level deficits that are found in RD—such as deficits in strategic knowledge and reading comprehension—as consequences rather than causes of RD. As we have discussed, deficits in these higher-level areas may be directly caused by the lower-level deficits (as when problems in word recognition cause poor reading comprehension) or may be a consequence of lack of appropriate reading experiences (as in the case of strategic deficits). These causal distinctions are important for discriminating between RD and mental retardation.

However, although our model is relatively compatible with these other views, we believe that it goes beyond them in most instances, to provide a broader picture of reading disability across the age and grade span. For example, researchers such as Wong (1991) have studied the strategic deficits of children with RD; the phonological deficits of children with RD have been intensively studied by a multitude of investigators, such as the Haskins Laboratories group of researchers (e.g., Liberman & Liberman, 1990; Mann & Liberman, 1984; Shankweiler et al., 1992); and the possible role of orthographic deficits in poor reading is receiving increasing attention (e.g., Barker, Torgesen, & Wagner, 1992; Cunningham & Stanovich, 1990). Our model integrates these bodies of work to provide a comprehensive picture of reading disability.

Two other cognitive models that are relatively similar to ours are those of Lovett (1987) and Frith (1985). These models are similar to ours not only in emphasizing the centrality of lower-level verbal processes to reading disability but also in linking reading disability to normal reading development. As we have discussed, Lovett (1987) classifies children with RD as either accuracy disabled or rate disabled. In turn, Frith's (1985) model of reading acquisition involves three stages—the logographic, alphabetic, and orthographic stages. Frith conceptualizes reading disability as involving a developmental "arrest" at the logographic stage of reading, a stage similar to our phase of visual-cue word recognition. Attributing this arrest at the logographic stage to phonological deficiencies, Frith thus views children with RD in terms of our pattern of most severely impaired reading, that of nonalphabetic reading.

According to our model, however, reading disability also involves the other patterns we have discussed, patterns that may be shaped by environmental as well as biological factors. For instance, our model can accommodate Frith's idea that most children with RD have a phonological deficit that creates problems for children in making the transition from visual-cue to phonetic-cue (or, in Frith's terms, logographic to alphabetic) word recognition. Nevertheless, we believe that phonological deficits do not develop in a vacuum but, rather, may be shaped or modified by environmental factors. For example, the right kind of instructional program might permit a child with intrinsic phonological problems to progress further in reading acquisition, such as to the phase of controlled word recognition, before straying from the road to reading proficiency. It is even possible that, in some cases, an appropriate instructional program might keep a youngster from going astray at all, a possibility we discuss at length in Chapter 10. Furthermore, the possible involvement of deficits other than phonological ones in some cases of reading disability, as suggested by the multiple-deficit views of researchers such as Willows (1991), cannot be completely dismissed.

In addition, we believe that the notion of developmental arrest does not capture fully what happens to youngsters with RD. As we and many others have noted (e.g., Gough & Juel, 1991; Spear & Sternberg, 1992; Stanovich, 1986), initial failure in reading brings about a cascade of negative consequences for poor readers—loss of motivation, lack of practice, and so on—that exacerbate the initial reading problems. Moreover, we have argued repeatedly in this book that these negative consequences, in some cases, may be more severe when poor readers are categorized as having RD. Children with RD are not just arrested at a particular point in development; rather, they have developed a wide range of additional problems—a phenomenon that, in our view, is more accurately captured by the "road-map" metaphor than by the notion of developmental arrest.

Thus far, we have focused on discussing models of RD that are similar to ours in emphasizing verbal, and especially phonological, processes as central to reading disability. However, some cognitive models view broader cognitive deficits as causally implicated in reading disability. Examples of the latter include the model of Morrison and Manis (1982), who ascribe RD to a general rule-learning difficulty; that of Tunmer (1991), who associates RD with a developmental lag in a Piagetian ability, namely the ability to decenter; and that of Wolford and Fowler (1984), who suggest that RD involves a failure to make use of partial information. These views of RD are particularly different from ours. Although broad cognitive deficits may eventually be consequences of reading disability, we do not think that they can be *causally* involved, because they undermine the idea that RD differs from mental retardation.

Possible Objections and Responses

In this section, we attempt to anticipate and respond to some possible objections to our model. Undoubtedly, for example, some people will argue that our model does not address the "real" cases of reading disability, those youngsters who, in the intrinsic view, have always been thought to suffer from a unique biological deficit. However, as we explained at the outset of this book, our population of interest involves the kinds of youngsters who typically are identified as having reading disability in the schools, and it is this population for whom we have developed our model. There is little evidence that most of these children suffer from a biological abnormality or a distinctive syndrome of poor reading.

Of course, there are instances of poor reading involving clear-cut biological causation, such as those stemming from lead ingestion or prenatal exposure to alcohol. A small minority of school-identified youngsters with RD does suffer from these—and possibly other, as yet unidentified—kinds of biological abnormalities. Our book is not intended to address this population. However, although this population may have unique kinds of reading problems that are not captured by our model of reading disability, we do think that, even for these children, an interactive perspective is crucial—because biological deficits do not develop in a vacuum. On the contrary, even in clear-cut instances of biological abnormality, the nature of the environment can make a tremendous difference in eventual outcomes. The issue of possible causes of reading disability, including the role of biology in causation of RD, is one to which we will return in Chapter 8.

The possible objection regarding "real" cases of RD raises a second issue, that of "garden-variety" poor reading. Recall that garden-variety poor readers are poor readers who do not exhibit an IQ-achievement discrepancy and whose reading problems are thought to be associated with low overall intellectual ability. So, how are children with reading disability distinguished from garden-variety poor readers in our model? As you may recall, we have emphasized that children with RD do not stray from the road to proficient reading because of low overall intellectual abilities or because of poor listening comprehension. Yet researchers have had considerable difficulty differentiating children with RD from garden-variety poor readers. In particular, both types of poor readers manifest similar kinds of word-recognition deficits and phonological-processing deficits (Fletcher et al., 1994; Stanovich, 1990; Stanovich & Siegel, 1994).

In answer to the question posed above, then, our model proposes that garden-variety poor readers, like children with RD, stray from the road to proficient reading early in reading acquisition, during the phases involving the development of word recognition. However, garden-variety poor readers may stray not only because of weak phonological-processing skills but also because of weak vocabulary and weak listening-comprehension skills. Their reading comprehension is compromised by their deficient word recognition, but also by these other verbal weaknesses, which make them less able to compensate for poor word recognition. Moreover, even with educational intervention that puts them back on the road to proficient reading, some garden-variety poor readers may end up as suboptimal readers, because of broad cognitive and linguistic weaknesses. (However, keep in mind that individuals may become suboptimal readers for many reasons other than broad cognitive weaknesses; one such reason might be deficient experiences with reading.)

In other words, although we have addressed ourselves specifically to the issue of reading disability in this book, we do not think that garden-variety poor readers need a completely different "road map." Rather, garden-variety poor readers are on the same continuum with children with RD, although garden-variety poor readers have other cognitive deficits that may impede their ability to compensate for word-recognition and phonological weaknesses.

The idea that most children with RD are on the same continuum with garden-variety poor readers, instead of suffering from a distinctive syndrome of poor reading, is one that has been advanced by a number of other investigators interested in reading disability (e.g., Fletcher et al., 1994; Shaywitz, Escobar, Shaywitz, Fletcher, & Makuch, 1992; Stanovich, 1990; Stanovich & Siegel, 1994). A widely cited theoretical model that encompasses the notion of a continuum between reading disability and garden-variety poor reading is the phonological-core variable-difference model of Keith Stanovich (1990). In this model, children with RD and garden-variety poor readers are hypothesized to be on the same continuum and to share a core of phonological deficits. However, as we move along the continuum from children with a potential-achievement discrepancy (children defined as having RD) to those without discrepancies (garden-variety poor readers), we see increasing deficits in cognitive and linguistic areas other than phonological processing. These other areas of deficit are the "variable differences." In a test of the phonological-core variable-difference model, Stanovich and Siegel (1994) compared garden-variety poor readers and children with RD who had similar word-recognition levels. They found that the two groups of poor readers did indeed share a core of phonological deficits but also that, as compared with children with RD, garden-variety poor readers had deficits in short-term and working memory, in arithmetic, and in some language-processing tasks. (However, also see Fletcher et al., 1994, who found that when children with IQ-achievement discrepancies were matched to garden-variety poor readers based on *age* rather than on word-recognition level, there were few differences between the two groups of poor readers.)

A third possible objection to our model involves the issue of the persistence of word-recognition deficits in RD. Some researchers who emphasize the role of phonological processes in RD (e.g., Bruck, 1990; Rack et al., 1992) suggest that word-recognition deficits are extremely persistent in reading disability; thus, these researchers may differ with us regarding our concept of delayed readers. We agree, of course, that word-recognition problems are causally central to RD and that, for many individuals, they are long lasting. However, evidence also suggests that, at least for some children with RD, these deficits do respond to appropriate instruction. To assume that word-recognition and phonological deficits are inevitably permanent is to give too little weight to environmental factors in reading disability—a tendency that, in our view, is the principal flaw in the intrinsic perspective, which is shared by many, though certainly not all, cognitive researchers. Thus, although the pattern of delayed reading may be relatively uncommon in reading disability, we suggest that it does exist.

Fourth, with regard to the part of our model involving reading acquisition in normally achieving readers, some authorities in reading will object to our emphasis on word-recognition processes in the early phases, even though this emphasis is also present in most other cognitive models of early reading acquisition. Of course, we do not claim that prior knowledge, vocabulary, and comprehension are ever irrelevant in reading acquisition, even in the earliest phases. However, in our view, the major task confronting beginning readers is to figure out the orthographic system and then to learn to decode that system in an accurate, automatic manner. Comprehension is less crucial in these early phases, for two reasons: Typically the demands of the text on comprehension are relatively low; and until children can recognize some words, there is little opportunity for their abilities in comprehension to come into play. By the same token, some researchers have suggested that improvements in word recognition continue to some extent throughout life (e.g., Perfetti, 1992); however, in the later phases of reading acquisition, it is the development of strategic and comprehension skills, rather than further refinements in word recognition, that is likely to be most crucial to the reading acquisition of normally achieving readers. That is, both word-recognition and comprehension skills are important in reading acquisition, but the former are more crucial in the early phases and the latter are more crucial in the later phases.

Fifth, some investigators may object to our emphasis on phonological processes in both reading acquisition and reading disability. As we have discussed, researchers such as Willows (1991) have espoused multiple-deficit views of reading disability, suggesting that visual as well as phonological deficits play a causal role in the problems of children with RD. We, too, acknowledge that multiple kinds of cognitive deficits may be causally involved in reading disability. However, the research evidence we have reviewed supports our position—which is also, of course, the position of many other researchers—that phonological rather than visual problems play the more crucial role in most cases of RD.

And sixth, although we have taken pains to point out that our model of reading disability is not an etiological typology, perhaps the point is worth reiterating one more time. The four patterns of reading disability in our model are patterns of *performance* in reading and in cognitive processes related to reading, not etiological subtypes. As just indicated, we leave open the possibility that multiple cognitive deficits may be causally involved in reading disability. However, as we discussed in comparing our model to that of Frith (1985), even if there is only one cognitive deficit that is causally involved in reading disability, such as a unitary phonological-processing deficit, this deficit is expressed in conjunction with a host of environmental variables as well as in conjunction with other intrinsic variables such as temperament and motivation. Thus, the four patterns of performance that we have outlined may be produced by the interaction of a single kind of cognitive deficit with environmental factors, or by the interaction of multiple kinds of cognitive deficits with environmental factors. What is surely too simplistic is the idea that reading disability can be reduced either to a single cognitive deficit or to a set of cognitive deficits, without regard to how those deficits develop and interact with the environment.

Educational Usefulness of Our Model

We believe that our model will be useful to educators for several reasons. First, the interactive perspective of the model is especially appropriate for practitioners, who deal with children's cognitive problems not in some idealized theoretical world but, rather, in a complicated real-life context. The intrinsic perspective tends to ignore this context, whereas the extrinsic perspective tends to ignore the intrinsic cognitive abilities that are crucial to reading acquisition. Although valuable insights about RD have arisen from both of these other perspectives, they are not as educationally useful as the interactive perspective.

Second, our model integrates a wide range of research findings on reading disability and shows how the various reading and processing deficits involved in RD develop and change over time. In other words, it provides a more complete picture of RD across the age and grade span. Practitioners frequently work with children who vary widely in age and level of functioning. At the secondary level, for example, a practitioner who works with poor readers may see students who vary from being virtual nonreaders to being only a year or two below grade level. Practitioners need to know how the various deficits involved in reading disability are related to one another, for children of varying ages and varying levels of reading skill. They also must be able to anticipate the kinds of deficits likely to arise in the future if appropriate educational intervention is not forthcoming.

Finally, our model is useful to practitioners in relating reading disability to reading acquisition in normally achieving readers. Practitioners need to make this comparison in order to recognize the deficits of children with RD and to interpret the meaning of these deficits. Thus, this aspect of the model is relevant to educational assessment. In addition, knowledge of typical reading acquisition, and of how children with RD deviate from it, can aid practitioners in making appropriate instructional choices. Just what these choices in assessment and instruction should be—not only for Calvin, Megan, James, and Stacy but also for the many other children like them—is the topic of the next two chapters.

References

Adams, M. J. (1990). *Beginning to read: Thinking and learning about print.* Cambridge, MA: MIT Press.

Alexander, A. W., Andersen, H. G., Heilman, P. C., Voeller, K., & Torgesen, J. K. (1991). Phonological awareness training and remediation of analytic decoding deficits in a group of severe dyslexics. *Annals of Dyslexia, 41,* 193–206.

Allington, R. L., & McGill-Franzen, A. (1989). School response to reading failure: Instruction for Chapter 1 and special education students in grades two, four, and eight. *The Elementary School Journal, 89,* 529–542.

Anderson, R. C., Hiebert, E. H., Scott, J. A., & Wilkinson, I. A. G. (1985). *Becoming a nation of readers: The report of the Commission on Reading.* Champaign, IL: Center for the Study of Reading.

Barker, T. A., Torgesen, J. K., & Wagner, R. K. (1992). The role of orthographic processing skills on five different reading tasks. *Reading Research Quarterly, 27,* 335–345.

Baron, J. (1977). Mechanisms for pronouncing printed words: Use and acquisition. In D. LaBerge & S. J. Samuels (Eds.), *Basic processes in reading: Perception and comprehension* (pp. 75–216). Hillsdale, NJ: Erlbaum.

Blachman, B. A. (1989). Phonological awareness and word recognition: Assessment and intervention. In A. Kamhi & H. Catts (Eds.), *Reading disabilities: A developmental language perspective* (pp. 133–158). Boston, MA: College-Hill.

————. (1994). What we have learned from longitudinal studies of phonological processing and reading, and some unanswered questions: A response to Torgesen, Wagner, and Rashotte. *Journal of Learning Disabilities, 27,* 287–291.

Boder, E. (1973). Developmental dyslexia: A diagnostic approach based on three atypical reading-spelling patterns. *Developmental Medicine and Child Neurology, 15,* 663–687.

Borkowski, J. G., Carr, M., & Pressley, M. (1987). "Spontaneous" strategy use: Perspectives from metacognitive theory. *Intelligence, 11,* 61–75.

Bowers, P. G. (1993). Text reading and rereading: Determinants of fluency beyond word recognition. *Journal of Reading Behavior, 25,* 133–153.

Bradley, L., & Bryant, P. (1978). Difficulties in auditory organization as a possible cause of reading backwardness. *Nature, 271,* 746–747.

Bruck, M. (1990). Word-recognition skills of adults with childhood diagnoses of dyslexia. *Developmental Psychology, 26,* 439–454.

Byrne, B. (1991). Experimental analysis of the child's discovery of the alphabetic principle. In L. Rieben & C. A. Perfetti (Eds.), *Learning to read: Basic research and its implications* (pp. 75–84). Hillsdale, NJ: Erlbaum.

———. (1992). Studies in the acquisition procedure for reading: Rationale, hypotheses, and data. In P. B. Gough, L. C. Ehri, & R. Treiman (Eds.), *Reading acquisition* (pp. 1–34). Hillsdale, NJ: Erlbaum.

Byrne, B., Freebody, P., & Gates, A. (1992). Longitudinal data on the relations of word reading strategies to comprehension. *Reading Research Quarterly, 27,* 140–151.

Chall, J. (1983). *Stages of reading development.* New York: McGraw-Hill.

Chall, J., Jacobs, V. A., & Baldwin, L. E. (1990). *The reading crisis: Why poor children fall behind.* Cambridge, MA: Harvard University Press.

Cunningham, A. E., & Stanovich, K. E. (1990). Assessing print exposure and orthographic processing skill in children: A quick measure of reading experience. *Journal of Educational Psychology, 82,* 733–740.

Dole, J. A., Duffy, G. G., Roehler, L. R., & Pearson, P. D. (1991). Moving from the old to the new: Research on reading comprehension instruction. *Review of Educational Research, 61,* 239–264.

Eden, G. F., Stein, J. F. , Wood, M. H., & Wood, F. B. (1995). Verbal and visual problems in reading disability. *Journal of Learning Disabilities, 28,* 272–290.

Ehri, L. C. (1991). Learning to read and spell words. In L. Rieben & C. A. Perfetti (Eds.), *Learning to read: Basic research and its implications* (pp. 57–73). Hillsdale, NJ: Erlbaum.

———. (1992). Reconceptualizing the development of sight word reading and its relationship to recoding. In P. B. Gough, L. C. Ehri, & R. Treiman (Eds.), *Reading acquisition* (pp. 107–143). Hillsdale, NJ: Erlbaum.

Ehri, L. C., & Sweet, J. (1991). Fingerpoint-reading of memorized text: What enables beginners to process the print? *Reading Research Quarterly, 26,* 442–462.

Engelmann, S., & Bruner, E. (1974). *Distar Reading Level I.* Chicago, IL: Science Research Associates.

Felton, R. H. (1993). Effects of instruction on the decoding skills of children with phonological-processing problems. *Journal of Learning Disabilities, 26,* 583–589.

Fletcher, J. M., & Satz, P. (1979). Unitary deficit hypotheses of reading disabilities. *Journal of Learning Disabilities, 12,* 22–26.

Fletcher, J. M., Shaywitz, S. E., Shankweiler, D. P., Katz, L., Liberman, I. Y., Stuebing, K. K., Francis, D. J., Fowler, A. E., & Shaywitz, B. A. (1994). Cognitive profiles of reading disability: Comparisons of discrepancy and low achievement definitions. *Journal of Educational Psychology, 86,* 6–23.

Frith, U. (1985). Beneath the surface of developmental dyslexia. In K. Patterson, J. Marshall, & M. Coltheart (Eds.), *Surface dyslexia* (pp. 301–330). London: Erlbaum.

Furstenberg, F. F., & Nord, C. W. (1985). Parenting apart. *Journal of Marriage and the Family, 47,* 874.

Garner, R. (1990). When children and adults do not use learning strategies: Toward a theory of settings. *Review of Educational Research, 60,* 517–529.

Garner, R., Alexander, P. A., & Hare, V. C. (1991). Reading comprehension failure in children. In B. Y. L. Wong (Ed.), *Learning about learning disabilities* (pp. 283–307). San Diego, CA: Academic Press.

Garner, R., & Reis, R. (1981). Monitoring and resolving comprehension obstacles: An investigation of spontaneous text lookbacks among upper-grade good and poor comprehenders. *Reading Research Quarterly, 16,* 569–582.

Goswami, U., & Bryant, P. (1992). Rhyme, analogy, and children's reading. In P. B. Gough, L. C. Ehri, & R. Treiman (Eds.), *Reading acquisition* (pp. 49–63). Hillsdale, NJ: Erlbaum.

Gough, P. B., & Juel, C. (1991). The first stages of word recognition. In L. Rieben & C. A. Perfetti (Eds.), *Learning to read: Basic research and its implications* (pp. 47–56). Hillsdale, NJ: Erlbaum.

Hewlett, S. A. (1991). *When the bough breaks: The cost of neglecting our children.* New York: Basic Books.

Jastak, S., & Wilkinson, G. S. (1984). *Wide Range Achievement Test—Revised.* Wilmington, DE: Jastak Associates.

Karlsen, B. M., Madden, R., & Gardner, E. (1974). *The Stanford Diagnostic Reading Test.* New York: Harcourt, Brace, Jovanovich.

Katz, R. B. (1986). Phonological deficiencies in children with reading disability: Evidence from an object naming task. *Cognition, 22,* 225–257.

Kennedy, K. M., & Backman, J. (1993). Effectiveness of the Lindamood Auditory Discrimination in Depth program with students with learning disabilities. *Learning Disabilities Research & Practice, 8,* 253–259.

Liberman, I. Y., & Liberman, A. M. (1990). Whole language versus code emphasis: Underlying assumptions and their implications for reading instruction. *Annals of Dyslexia, 40,* 51–76.

Lovegrove, W., & Slaghuis, W. (1989). How reliable are visual differences found in dyslexics? *Irish Journal of Psychology, 10,* 542–550.

Lovett, M. W. (1987). A developmental approach to reading disability: Accuracy and speed criteria of normal and deficient reading skill. *Child Development, 58,* 234–260.

Lovett, M. W., Ransby, M. J., Hardwick, N., Johns, M. S., & Donaldson, S. A. (1989). Can dyslexia be treated? Treatment-specific and generalized treatment effects in dyslexic children's response to remediation. *Brain and Language, 37,* 90–121.

Maclean, M., Bryant, P., & Bradley, L. (1987). Rhymes, nursery rhymes, and reading in early childhood. *Merrill-Palmer Quarterly, 33,* 255–281.

Mann, V. A., & Liberman, I. Y. (1984). Phonological awareness and verbal short-term memory. *Journal of Learning Disabilities, 17,* 592–599.

Martin, F., & Lovegrove, W. (1988). Uniform and field flicker in control and specifically disabled readers. *Perception, 17,* 203–214.

Mason, J. M. (1992). Reading stories to preliterate children: A proposed connection to reading. In P. B. Gough, L. C. Ehri, & R. Treiman (Eds.), *Reading acquisition* (pp. 215–241). Hillsdale, NJ: Erlbaum.

McKinney, J. D., Osborne, S. S., & Schulte, A. C. (1993). Academic consequences of learning disability: Longitudinal prediction of outcomes at 11 years of age. *Learning Disabilities Research and Practice, 8,* 19–27.

Morrison, F. J., & Manis, F. R. (1982). Cognitive processes and reading disability: A critique and proposal. In C. J. Brainerd & M. I. Pressley (Eds.), *Progress in cognitive development research* (Vol. 2, pp. 59–93). New York: Springer-Verlag.

Olson, R. K., Wise, B., Conners, F., Rack, J., & Fulker, D. (1989). Specific deficits in component reading and language skills: Genetic and environmental influences. *Journal of Learning Disabilities, 22,* 339–348.

Paris, S. G., Jacobs, J. E., & Cross, D. R. (1987). Toward an individualistic psychology of exceptional children. In J. Borkowski & J. Day (Eds.), *Intelligence and cognition in special children: Perspectives on mental retardation, learning disabilities, and giftedness* (pp. 1–49). New York: Ablex.

Perfetti, C. A. (1985). *Reading ability.* New York: Oxford University Press.

———. (1992). The representation problem in reading acquisition. In P. B. Gough, L. C. Ehri, & R. Treiman (Eds.), *Reading acquisition* (pp. 145–174). Hillsdale, NJ: Erlbaum.

Rack, J. P., Snowling, M. J., & Olson, R. K. (1992). The nonword reading deficit in developmental dyslexia: A review. *Reading Research Quarterly, 27,* 28–53.

Shankweiler, D., Crain, S., Brady, S., & Macaruso, P. (1992). Identifying the causes of reading disability. In P. B. Gough, L. C. Ehri, & R. Treiman (Eds.), *Reading acquisition* (pp. 275–305). Hillsdale, NJ: Erlbaum.

Share, D. L., Jorm, A. E., Maclean, R., & Matthews, R. (1984). Sources of individual differences in reading acquisition. *Journal of Educational Psychology, 76,* 1309–1324.

Shaywitz, S. E., Escobar, M. D., Shaywitz, B. A., Fletcher, J. M., & Makuch, R. (1992). Evidence that dyslexia may represent the lower tail of a normal distribution of reading ability. *New England Journal of Medicine, 326,* 145–150.

Siegel, L. S., & Heaven, R. K. (1986). Categorization of learning disabilities. In S. J. Ceci (Ed.), *Handbook of cognitive, social, and neuropsychological aspects of learning disabilities* (Vol. 1, pp. 95–121). Hillsdale, NJ: Erlbaum.

Smiley, S. S., Oakley, D. D., Worthen, D., Campione, J. C., & Brown, A. L. (1977). Recall of thematically relevant material by adolescent good and poor readers as a function of written versus oral presentation. *Journal of Educational Psychology, 69,* 381–389.

Snowling, M. (1981). Phonemic deficits in developmental dyslexia. *Psychological Research, 43,* 219–234.

Spear, L. C., & Sternberg, R. J. (1987). An information-processing framework for understanding reading disability. In S. J. Ceci (Ed.), *Handbook of cognitive, social, and neuropsychological aspects of learning disabilities* (Vol. 2, pp. 3–31). Hillsdale, NJ: Erlbaum.

———. (1992). Information processing, experience, and reading disability. In D. J. Stein & J. E. Young (Eds.), *Cognitive science and clinical disorders* (pp. 313–336). San Diego, CA: Academic Press.

Stanovich, K. E. (1986). Matthew effects in reading: Some consequences of individual differences in the acquisition of literacy. *Reading Research Quarterly, 21,* 360–406.

———. (1990). Explaining the differences between the dyslexic and the garden-variety poor reader: The phonological-core variable-difference model. In J. K. Torgesen (Ed.), *Cognitive and behavioral characteristics of children with learning disabilities* (pp. 7–40). Austin, TX: Pro-Ed.

———. (1991). Word recognition: Changing perspectives. In R. Barr, M. L. Kamil, P. Mosenthal, & P. D. Pearson (Eds.), *Handbook of reading research* (Vol. 2, pp. 418–452). New York: Longman.

———. (1992). Speculations on the causes and consequences of individual differences in early reading acquisition. In P. B. Gough, L. C. Ehri, & R. Treiman (Eds.), *Reading acquisition* (pp. 307–342). Hillsdale, NJ: Erlbaum.

Stanovich, K. E., & Siegel, L. S. (1994). Phenotypic performance profile of children with reading disabilities: A regression-based test of the phonological-core variable-difference model. *Journal of Educational Psychology, 86,* 24–53.

Sternberg, R. J. (1985). *Beyond IQ: A triarchic theory of human intelligence.* New York: Cambridge University Press.

———. (1986). *Intelligence applied: Understanding and increasing your intellectual skills.* San Diego, CA: Harcourt, Brace, Jovanovich.

Sternberg, R. J., & Wagner, R. K. (1982). Automatization failure in learning disabilities. *Topics in Learning and Learning Disabilities, 2,* 1–11.

Stevenson, H. W., Lucker, G. W., Lee, S., Stigler, J. W., Kitamura, S., & Hsu, C. C. (1987). Poor readers in three cultures. In C. Super & S. Harkness (Eds.), *The role of culture in developmental disorder* (Vol. 1, pp. 153–177). New York: Academic Press.

Taylor, M. B., & Williams, J. P. (1983). Comprehension of learning disabled readers: Task and text variations. *Journal of Educational Psychology, 75,* 584–601.

Torgesen, J. K. (1991). Subtypes as prototypes: Extended studies of rationally defined extreme groups. In L. Feagons, E. J. Shaf, & L. J. Meltzer (Eds.), *Subtypes of learning disabilities* (pp. 229–246). Hillsdale, NJ: Erlbaum.

Tunmer, W. E. (1991). Phonological awareness and literacy acquisition. In L. Rieben & C. A. Perfetti (Eds.), *Learning to read: Basic research and its implications* (pp. 105–119). Hillsdale, NJ: Erlbaum.

U.S. Bureau of the Census. (1990). *Money, income, and poverty status in the United States: 1989.* Washington, DC: U.S. Government Printing Office.

Vogel, S. A., Hruby, P. J., & Adelman, P. B. (1993). Educational and psychological factors in successful asnd unsuccessful college students with learning disabilities. *Learning Disabilities Research and Practice, 8,* 35–43.

Willows, D. (1991). Visual processes in learning disabilities. In B. Y. L. Wong (Ed.), *Learning about learning disabilities* (pp. 163–193). San Diego, CA: Academic Press.

Wolf, M. (1991). Naming speed and reading: The contribution of the cognitive neurosciences. *Reading Research Quarterly, 26,* 123–141.

Wolford, G., & Fowler, C. A. (1984). Differential use of partial information by good and poor readers. *Developmental Review, 6,* 16–35.

Wong, B. Y. L. (1991). The relevance of metacognition to learning disabilities. In B. Y. L. Wong (Ed.), *Learning about learning disabilities* (pp. 231–258). San Diego, CA: Academic Press.

Wong, B. Y. L., & Wong, R. (1986). Study behavior as a function of metacognitive knowledge about critical task variables: An investigation of above average, average, and learning-disabled readers. *Learning Disabilities Research, 1,* 101–111.

Worden, P. E. (1983). Memory strategy instruction with the learning disabled. In M. Pressley & J. R. Levin (Eds.), *Cognitive strategies: Developmental, educational, and treatment-related issues* (pp. 101–148). New York: Springer-Verlag.

6 Issues in the Education of Children with Reading Disability

IN THEIR MORE PESSIMISTIC MOMENTS, teachers sometimes express doubts about the extent to which classroom practices actually can make lasting differences in children's lives. Often these doubts are particularly acute when teachers work with children who have academic problems. Many children with academic difficulties are so far behind their classmates, and so turned off to school, that the capacity of teachers to help them can seem very limited. If, in addition to academic problems, there are also serious problems in the child's home life, or if the child is believed to be intrinsically limited by a disability in learning, the situation may appear bleak indeed.

However, at least for educational practitioners, what is most amenable to change is what goes on in the classroom. Teachers and schools can do little to affect children's home lives and certainly even less to affect their biology, but there is evidence that they are able to make a very substantial difference in children's achievement. For instance, in their longitudinal study of the achievement of a group of low-income youngsters, Snow, Barnes, Chandler, Goodman, and Hemphill (1991) found that a wide range of variables, both in the home and at school, contributed to gains in reading comprehension. A strong educational program could compensate to a considerable degree, though not completely, for weaknesses at home. (The reverse was also true: A strong home environment could compensate to a considerable degree, but not entirely, for a weak educational program.) Thus, even when children are biologically compromised in some way (as a result of preterm birth, for instance), environmental factors may make a tremendous difference in eventual outcomes (Beckwith & Rodning, 1991).

We have argued throughout this book in favor of an interactive perspective on reading disability. In our view, reading disability results from an interaction of characteristics inside the child—characteristics that in turn may be shaped both by biology and by environment—with factors outside the child, such as the nature of instruction. However, an interactive perspective does not necessarily render educational practices any less important than they would be in an extrinsic perspective, which attributes nearly all of children's achievement problems to the environment. Because multiple factors interact to produce a reading disability, altering even one of those factors, such as the instructional program, may have an impact on the child's reading achievement. (By analogy, it takes many ingredients to make a cake, but changing just one of them can make a big difference in how the cake turns out.)

In this chapter and the next, we discuss the educational implications of our model as well as of the research that we have reviewed so far. Specifically, we present what appear to be the most effective educational practices for children with reading disability—practices that we believe can make a very substantial difference in the achievement of these youngsters. Like perspectives on reading disability, instructional approaches for teaching reading frequently have been polarized into two extremes, the meaning-emphasis approach and the code-emphasis approach (Chall, 1967), both of which we will describe at length later in the chapter. These two extremes involve not only different instructional methods but also different underlying philosophies and different theoretical views of reading acquisition. Education has cycled back and forth between the two extremes with the predictability of a swinging pendulum. When one version of code emphasis is found to be defective, there is a swing to a meaning-emphasis approach; and when that fails, the pendulum swings back to a new version of code emphasis. However, in our view, just as the extremes represented by the intrinsic and extrinsic perspectives on reading disability are seriously flawed, so is the idea that a single method, whether code emphasis or meaning emphasis, is optimal for children with reading disability—or for nondisabled readers.

In our model, there is a basic route to good reading that normally achieving readers typically follow. We have argued that, at least for educational purposes, children with reading disability are best conceptualized as having strayed from this road to good reading, down paths that may eventually lead them to be classified as having reading disability. Obviously, there are many differences between normally achieving readers and children with RD, and these differences will necessitate some different instructional emphases for the two groups of children. Nevertheless, as we will show, no single method is adequate for either group. Rather, all normally achieving readers need a combination of methods to bring them along the road to proficient reading—and all children with RD need a combination of methods to bring them back to it.

In the next chapter, we will focus on specific educational practices for the four patterns of reading disability: nonalphabetic readers, compensatory readers, nonautomatic readers, and delayed readers. In this chapter, meanwhile, we present a more general overview, examining educational issues and implications of our model that are relevant to most youngsters with reading disability. The first part of the chapter involves educational issues and implications for identification of RD, as well as for ongoing educational assessment. In the second part, we examine issues and educational implications involving reading instruction. The latter section focuses on the reading-methods controversy, contrasting code emphasis with the current version of meaning emphasis—namely, whole language.

Before continuing, we must make several points about the approach we will take throughout this chapter and the next one. First, we will focus on basic implications and principles for teaching, rather than endorsing specific tests or instructional programs—although in the next chapter we will sometimes give examples of specific tests and programs that we think might be useful. A basic principle such as "directly teach decoding skills" might be embodied in many different programs. Furthermore, specific instructional programs can be implemented in numerous ways. A program that is highly effective as implemented by one teacher might be much less effective as implemented by another. In our view, understanding basic principles about how to identify and to teach children with RD, and using these principles to guide one's selection and implementation of specific tests and instructional programs, usually is more important than the test or program itself.

Second, in implementing these (or any other) basic principles, there is always a place for teachers' judgments. In other words, principles cannot be applied in a rigid or absolute way. Decoding instruction provides a good example of a type of instruction that, although very important to children with RD, can be implemented too rigidly. In this chapter, we will argue that most children with reading disability need direct, systematic instruction in decoding—specifically, instruction that promotes both accuracy and automatization of decoding. In our view, the lack of such instruction is likely to be catastrophic for these youngsters. However, it is also true that decoding programs can bog down in nearly infinite teaching of "the 10,000 sounds of the English language" (as one of the coauthors once heard a whole-language advocate derisively refer to phonics instruction). For example, many decoding programs cover letter-sound relationships and phonic rules that children will use only rarely, if at all, because the relationships and rules pertain to relatively few words. In addition, children sometimes get "stuck" in learning skills that are genuinely important, yet difficult for them. Getting children "unstuck" in these cases may require a variety of solutions, but inflexibly hammering away at the same material in the same way day after day usually is not one of them.

Another example of the need for teacher judgment and flexibility involves invented spelling, whereby children are encouraged to use their own knowledge about letter-sound correspondences to spell unfamiliar words. Teachers who encourage invented spelling may try to guide children toward phonetic spelling and, eventually, toward more conventional spelling, but they do not emphasize "correct" and "incorrect" spellings of words. Invented spelling can be very helpful in encouraging children's writing, especially for children with limited spelling skills, because it helps them circumvent their lack of spelling knowledge. In addition, as we will discuss in the next chapter, the use of invented spelling not only may help to promote phonological-reading, or decoding, skills (Clarke, 1988; Uhry &

Shepherd, 1993), but it also provides an informal way to assess children's phonological awareness (Mann, Tobin, & Wilson, 1987).

Teachers who want children to use invented spelling should not be too quick to give them the correct spellings, as some children will avoid attempting to spell words on their own; instead, they will just ask the teacher. Therefore, some practitioners who are advocates of invented spelling make it a general rule not to provide or even to confirm spellings of words for children. The following anecdote is a good example of how this kind of rule, though well motivated, can be too rigidly applied. A colleague of one of the coauthors observed a boy who was involved in making a Mother's Day card. Inside the card, the boy wanted to write, "Mom, you're awesome." His teacher insisted that he use invented spelling, but the word "awesome" was too, well, awesome for him; he did not even know how to begin to spell it. Although the teacher attempted to cue him with some hints about letter-sound relationships, the boy remained genuinely stumped. After the teacher resisted many entreaties to spell the word for him, the boy simply changed the inside of the card to read, "Mom, you're great," which he already knew how to spell. In other words, although he managed to write a message similar in meaning to the one he originally wanted to write, an opportunity to learn something new was missed.

Thus, in implementing the basic principles that we will discuss here and in the following chapter, teachers need to use their own judgment in individual situations. They need to decide when a principle should be amended, as in the case of the anecdote about invented spelling. Our recommendations can guide teachers in selecting specific instructional programs, but no program is perfect in every detail for every youngster. Rather, programs that are generally appropriate still may need modification in specific situations, as in the example about systematic instruction in decoding.

A final point we wish to make involves our focus on children who have the cognitive profiles typical of RD. In this chapter and the next, we discuss assessment and remedial practices for such children, because this population is the one addressed by our model. Certainly, however, we do not mean to imply that only poor readers with the cognitive profiles typical of RD should be provided with educational help. Indeed, most of the educational practices that we discuss are as appropriate for garden-variety poor readers as for children with RD.

Issues in Identification and Assessment

In this first major section of the chapter, we discuss implications of our model and make educational recommendations related to four issues in the identification of reading disability and in ongoing assessment. These four issues involve the reading skills that are central to reading disability; the measurement of listening comprehension and of other broad verbal skills; the types of tests (e.g., norm-referenced or criterion-referenced tests) that may be useful; and the setting of goals and objectives.

Reading Skills Central to Reading Disability

In Chapter 3, we discussed some problems with the way that reading disability, as a subset in the umbrella category of learning disabilities, currently is identified in most schools. The cornerstone of this identification process is the IQ-achievement discrepancy. According to federal guidelines on learning disabilities, in order for a child to be identified as having a learning disability involving reading, achievement must be low, relative to IQ, in at least one of two areas of reading: basic reading (i.e., word recognition) or reading comprehension.

In our model of reading disability as well as in those of many other researchers interested in RD, word-recognition deficits are central. The four patterns of reading disability all involve departures from the road to proficient reading in phases involving the acquisition of word-recognition skills. Thus, it seems logical to emphasize word-recognition deficits in the identification of reading disability and in ongoing assessment. However, despite its apparent simplicity, this logical prescription turns out to be rather complicated to implement in educational practice. For one thing, as our model illustrates, word-recognition deficits lead to a variety of other problems, including difficulties in reading comprehension, especially as children encounter the increased comprehension demands of the texts used in later grades. Furthermore, we have suggested that some individuals with reading disability—those we have called delayed readers—eventually may overcome their word-recognition problems, at least as evidenced on standardized educational tests, and be characterized primarily by reading-comprehension deficits, rather than by word-recognition deficits.

Thus, with regard to the two discrepancy areas for reading mentioned in federal and most state guidelines on learning disabilities, practitioners may observe one of the following three tendencies: Children with RD may have problems in word recognition alone; most commonly, they may have problems both in word recognition and in reading comprehension; or, particularly in the case of adolescents and adults with reading disability, they may have problems in reading comprehension alone, with a history of previous word-recognition deficits. What does *not* characterize RD is a consistent pattern over time of reading-comprehension deficits alone, with no previous history of serious word-recognition deficits.

Practitioners at the elementary level, particularly in the early and middle elementary grades, should look for word-recognition deficits in children with RD; they should also recognize that these deficits are causally central to the children's other problems in reading. Moreover, as we have seen, the specific areas of word recognition that appear troublesome for youngsters with RD involve decoding and phonological skills. That is, a child with average decoding skills and a below-average sight vocabulary probably does not have a reading disability, whereas a child with an average sight vocabulary but poor decoding skills is cause for serious concern.

Although practitioners at the secondary level also may see some students with significant word-recognition deficits, they tend to see more students who are struggling primarily with reading comprehension (i.e., delayed readers). For a student in the latter category, it may be useful to examine his or her elementary school records (if they're available) for a history of serious word-recognition deficits. Indeed, this kind of history is suggestive of reading disability; it may have been the origin of the student's current problems in reading comprehension, even if there are no longer word-recognition problems.

Measurement of Listening Comprehension and Broad Verbal Skills

As we also discussed in Chapter 3, listening comprehension probably is a more realistic indicator of potential in reading than is a nonverbal or global IQ score. On this basis, some investigators have suggested the possibility of replacing the current cornerstone of RD identification, the IQ-achievement discrepancy, with a new one, the listening comprehension-achievement discrepancy. We have argued that not only the discrepancy construct but also the entire construct of RD should be shelved. However, our objection to the discrepancy construct does not mean that we are opposed to the measurement of listening comprehension, or of other broad verbal skills such as vocabulary, in children with reading difficulties. On the contrary, we believe that assessment of these verbal areas is extremely important to the effective design of instruction. Obviously, for example, the specific instructional needs of children with broad listening-comprehension weaknesses and the instructional needs of children with listening-comprehension strengths are not exactly the same. The point is not that there are no underlying cognitive differences among poor readers but, rather, that these differences do not provide a rationale for singling out only one group of poor readers for educational help.

Thus, we would encourage practitioners to evaluate broad verbal skills, including listening comprehension, in poor readers. Unfortunately, although there are numerous standardized tests for measuring areas such as vocabulary, few standardized measures of listening comprehension are currently available. However, listening comprehension may be measured informally. For instance, many practitioners employ listening comprehension tests as part of an informal reading inventory (IRI), in which children read or listen to a series of graded paragraphs and answer comprehension questions about them. (See, for example, Hargrove and Poteet, 1984, for guidelines on developing and interpreting informal reading inventories.) Practitioners should be cautious about interpreting these tests because of their lack of standardization. Nevertheless, if carefully used and interpreted, informal tests of listening comprehension can be helpful in providing a broad profile of a child's reading difficulties.

Keep in mind that children with the cognitive profile typical of reading disability are characterized by significantly better performance on measures of listening comprehension and verbal ability than on measures of reading comprehension. Children who show very broad language deficits—for example, poor listening comprehension that is on a par with poor reading comprehension—probably are better conceptualized as having a "language disability" or "language difficulties" than as having a "reading disability." In the case of reading disability, the linguistic deficits typically are more circumscribed and appear to center largely on the phonological aspects of language. However, particularly in adolescents and adults with reading disability, Matthew effects (e.g., a lack of exposure to new vocabulary through reading) eventually may adversely affect listening comprehension and overall verbal ability. Thus, especially for practitioners who work with older populations, the distinctions between circumscribed and broad language deficits, or between "language disability" and "reading disability," may become a bit murky.

In our model of RD, children stray from the path to proficient reading largely because of problems involving specific reading skills (e.g., decoding and letter-sound knowledge) and linguistic skills (e.g., phonological awareness). In our view, these are the kinds of skills that should be emphasized in identification of reading disability and in ongoing educational assessment—along with other skills, such as listening comprehension, that are areas of relative strength for children with RD. We do not think that measures of visual perception or visual-motor skills, although they are common in educational test batteries, are very useful in identifying reading disability. Granted, we have acknowledged the possibility that visual-processing deficits may play a role in some cases of reading disability; but the evidence that we have reviewed thus far indicates that linguistic skills play the more crucial role in most cases of RD. Furthermore, the kinds of visual-motor and visual-perceptual tests typically used in school identification of reading disability are confounded by language and memory factors, rendering test results difficult or impossible to interpret. More valid laboratory measures of visual processing, involving brief tachistoscopic presentations of visual stimuli, are not yet feasible in most educational settings.

Types of Tests

In the foregoing discussion, we focused on the skills, such as word-recognition and phonological skills, that we think are most relevant to identification of reading disability. Now we also want to say something about the *types* of tests that may be useful, not only in the initial identification of children with RD but also in ongoing educational assessment. As our discussion of listening comprehension indicates, we believe that both formal and informal kinds of measures can be useful in identification and assessment.

Formal standardized tests are required in many school districts in order to identify reading disability and qualify children for learning-disabilities services. Standardized tests also can provide information about how children are doing as compared with a large, nationally normed sample—rather than as compared only with other children in their class or their school district. Thus, standardized tests may be useful for evaluating the overall success of an educational program as well as for identifying and evaluating the progress of individual children. Of course, if a standardized test is to be adequate for these purposes, it must meet minimum requirements for validity and reliability, and it must be normed on an appropriate population. A number of publications offer information on the technical adequacy of specific tests used in education and psychology; one such publication is the *Buros Mental Measurements Yearbook.*

However, standardized norm-referenced tests rarely provide information that is sufficiently detailed for planning an educational program. For instance, a norm-referenced test of word recognition would provide ample information about how a youngster is doing relative to the normative group, but usually little information about the specific word-recognition skills the youngster needs to be taught. Also, norm-referenced test batteries can be time-consuming to administer and generally cannot be given more than once or twice a year, whereas ongoing educational assessment that provides information for day-to-day teaching requires much more frequent measurement.

A number of other kinds of measures may be more useful than standardized norm-referenced tests for developing an educational program and for ongoing educational assessment. These measures include systematic observations of children, trial teaching, criterion-referenced tests, and curriculum-based assessment, or CBA (C. Smith, 1991). Criterion-referenced tests assess specific skills in a relatively circumscribed area of content, such as decoding, and may be commercially published or developed by the teacher. In curriculum-based assessment, the content being measured is tied to the curriculum of a particular school and the tests are developed by the school district.

Criterion-referenced tests that are commercially published generally include information about the technical adequacy of the test, such as reliability and validity data. However, when individual school districts or teachers develop their own tests, they also need to make sure that the tests meet minimum standards for reliability and validity. We suspect that, due to the difficulties involved in obtaining and analyzing the appropriate data, this step—that of ascertaining technical adequacy—is frequently skipped. Thus, although teacher-developed tests and curriculum-based assessment can provide very useful information, a possible drawback is lack of information about the technical adequacy of the tests.

Also, even when these kinds of tests are technically adequate, they can be misleading if not supplemented by information from norm-referenced tests. For example, consider a child who demonstrates average performance on curriculum-based measures of word recognition. If most of the children in the school were functioning two years below grade level according to national norms, then this child's performance would mean something quite different than if the overall level of achievement at the school were very high.

Thus, a combination of both formal and informal approaches to assessment and identification appears warranted. However, the availability of the commercially published tests depends upon the ability one wishes to measure. For example, a considerable number of tests, both norm referenced and criterion referenced, are available for assessing specific areas of reading such as word recognition and reading comprehension. In these areas, teachers might choose to use a combination of formal standardized tests and informal assessment techniques. In contrast, there are few commercially published tests available for some of the cognitive abilities that play an important role in reading disability, such as phonological awareness, naming speed, and strategic knowledge. In these areas, as we will discuss further in the next chapter, teachers will probably have to rely on informal methods of assessment, such as observation and the development of their own tests. However, the potential pitfalls of these methods, such as the need for technical adequacy in teacher-developed tests, must be kept in mind.

Setting Goals and Objectives

When students are identified as having a learning disability and are scheduled to receive special-education services, federal guidelines require a written IEP, or Individualized Education Program, as we discussed in Chapter 3. As part of the IEP, a list of long-term and short-term objectives for each of the areas addressed in special education—such as basic reading and reading comprehension—must be provided. These objectives are used in the ongoing educational assessment of the child's program.

IEPs may vary widely from one school district to the next, with some practitioners writing IEPs as formal narrative reports and others using standardized or computerized forms on which relevant goals and objectives are checked off. Philosophies about goal setting also vary widely, with some school districts setting generally ambitious goals and others setting more conservative ones. In some cases, the goals may be so vague—"to improve word-recognition skills" or "to improve reading comprehension"—as to be almost meaningless.

Obviously, the magnitude of the goals varies according to the individual youngsters. However, in our view, it is crucial not to aim too low in setting goals for children with RD. Especially in the elementary grades, a strong effort should be made to catch children up in reading, before they become seriously enmired in the "swamp" of lowered motivation, lowered levels of practice, and negative expectations. For children in the early and middle elementary years, catching up in reading often is feasible, but as the children become older and progressively further behind in reading and in a host of related areas, the goal of catching up becomes ever more difficult to attain. Note, too, that ambitious goals also can communicate to children the teacher's confidence that they can succeed, whereas very limited goals may communicate a message of low expectations.

Teachers sometimes express the concern that a failure to achieve goals may make them look bad to parents, or that children with RD are not capable of meeting ambitious goals. On other occasions, teachers may say that they receive pressure from administrators to set limited goals for these reasons. However, as we have repeatedly discussed thus far and will discuss further in Chapter 8, there is little evidence that youngsters with RD suffer from intrinsic biological abnormalities that preclude learning to read. In any case, practitioners cannot know what children are capable of attaining without testing the limits of their capabilities.

As for parents, few are impressed favorably by a program that involves only very limited goals, even if they are achieved consistently. Indeed, we would argue that, if every goal is achieved consistently, the goals are probably being set too low, because the search for the limits of children's capabilities necessarily entails finding failure on some occasions. The success of a program, whether for an individual youngster or for a group of children, should be measured by what students actually learn, not by whether each and every goal is achieved.

Issues in Reading Instruction

The expectation that there must be a unique or distinctive educational treatment for reading disability, just as there are distinctive treatments for medical disorders like hypertension and diabetes, is common among the general public and even among educational professionals. However, there is little evidence that children with reading disability require a dramatically different type of instruction in reading than do other poor readers, especially with regard to word-recognition skills. In this section and in the next chapter, we will discuss research findings and instructional programs involving unlabeled poor readers and "at-risk" readers as well as children with reading disability. Given the similarities between children with RD and garden-variety poor readers in terms of word recognition, and given the somewhat arbitrary nature of school identification of RD, we believe that many instructional programs and techniques developed for one group (children with RD) are equally applicable to the other group (garden-variety poor readers). Moreover, as we will see, in some ways the instructional needs of children with RD are not strikingly different even from the needs of normally achieving readers.

In this section, we begin by describing two major instructional approaches that are commonly used to teach reading in the early elementary grades: the code-emphasis approach and the whole-language approach. Next, we discuss the hotly disputed question of which of these two overall approaches is better, and why the question needs to be reframed. Third, using our model to organize the discussion, we consider the kind of instructional approach that appears to be optimal for normally achieving readers as well as what kind of approach, by comparison, is needed for children with reading disability. Finally, we summarize our own views of the code-emphasis versus whole-language debate and of the issues faced by practitioners who teach reading to youngsters with reading disability.

Approaches to Reading Instruction

As noted, specific instructional programs for reading can be viewed as falling into one of two broad approaches: code-emphasis programs and meaning-emphasis programs. The former emphasize learning to decode in initial reading instruction, whereas the latter emphasize meaning (i.e., comprehension). In the regular classroom, meaning-emphasis programs are more commonly used to teach reading than are code-emphasis programs. The current incarnation of meaning emphasis, and one that has been immensely influential, is termed *whole language*. Thus, in this section, we will focus on contrasting the code-emphasis approach with that of whole language.

The question of which of these two approaches is better, and for whom, has been at the heart of much contentious debate in education—a debate that too often has been guided by rhetoric rather than by scientific evidence. Before considering this debate, along with the research evidence that can help to resolve it, we will review some of the major distinctions between the two instructional approaches. (These distinctions are summarized in Table 6.1.) Some of the characteristics that most clearly distinguish code emphasis from whole language include the following: whether the initial instructional emphasis is more on comprehension or more on learning to decode words; the extent to which direct and system-

TABLE 6.1 Two Approaches to Beginning Reading Instruction

	Code Emphasis	*Whole Language*
Initial emphasis	Learning to decode words	Comprehension
Amount of direct instruction in decoding	High	Varies from very low to moderate
Decoding is practiced in isolation as well as in context	Yes	Usually no
Nature of decoding instruction	Highly systematic; may be analytic or synthetic	Not systematic; usually more analytic than synthetic
Reading and spelling instruction are integrated	Yes	Yes
Reading and content instruction are integrated	Usually no	Yes
Nature of beginning texts	Phonetically controlled	Not controlled (although predictable texts may be used)
Underlying view of reading acquisition	Reading acquisition requires formal instruction, especially in decoding	Reading acquisition is "natural"

atic instruction in decoding is provided; the extent to which other subject areas, such as social studies, science, and mathematics, are integrated with reading instruction; and the nature of the beginning texts that children read.

Advocates of a particular approach often accuse their critics of misrepresenting the nature of that approach. Hence, where possible, we have tried to rely on advocates as well as critics of each approach as sources for describing it. Also, we emphasize only the most consistent differences between approaches and discuss common variations within approaches. Our descriptions of approaches draw most heavily from the following sources: Adams (1990); Adams et al. (1991); Anderson, Hiebert, Scott, and Wilkinson (1985); Chall (1967, 1983); Gersten and Dimino (1993); Goodman (1986); Liberman and Liberman (1990); McGee and Lomax (1990); Reid (1993); and Stahl and Miller (1989).

We freely acknowledge that we are presenting rather "purist" versions of each approach. Thus, some teachers who view themselves as, say, whole-language practitioners, may scan the right-hand column in Table 6.1 and feel that not every characteristic applies to them. We recognize—indeed, applaud—the fact that some teachers use a combination of approaches, a point that we will discuss in much more detail later. Code emphasis and whole language are better conceptualized as end points on a continuum than as a dichotomy; some instructional approaches fall in the middle of the continuum rather than at the two extremes. Nevertheless, in order to explain the nature of the controversy surrounding beginning reading instruction, we must highlight distinctions, rather than commonalities, between the approaches. We believe that the distinctions we make—as in Table 6.1—are generally accurate. Furthermore, in our experience, many practitioners do rely on relatively "purist" versions of these approaches.

Code-Emphasis Programs. Although both decoding and comprehension skills are taught in the code-emphasis approach to reading instruction, the initial emphasis is more on learning to decode words than on comprehension. Code-emphasis programs teach decoding in one of two principal ways. Some encourage children to induce decoding knowledge by teaching them highly patterned words (e.g., word families such as *bat, hat, sat,* and so on). In these programs, phonetic analysis of whole words is stressed, and blending of isolated sounds to form words is avoided; hence, the method used to teach decoding sometimes is called analytic phonics. For instance, a youngster might be encouraged to decode a word like *plate* by analyzing familiar units within the word—such as *ate*—rather than by "sounding out" and blending individual letters or groups of letters.

In contrast, other code-emphasis programs involve explicit teaching of phonic rules, letter-sound relationships, and blending of sounds to form words. Because the blending of sounds into words is emphasized, this method sometimes is called synthetic phonics. For example, children might learn that when there is a vowel-consonant-e pattern at the end of a word, again as in *plate,* the vowel generally is long and the *e* is silent; to decode a word like *plate,* then, they would apply the rule, decide that the vowel sound will be long, and "sound out" the word from left to right, blending individual sounds to form the word.

In code-emphasis programs, decoding instruction is highly systematic in that there is a predetermined sequence of rules, sounds, or types of words to be taught, and these skills are practiced in isolation (i.e., on single words) as well as in context. Spelling and reading often are integrated in such programs, with children learning to read and spell the same kinds of words. Typically, however, there is not much integration of other subject areas, such as science or social studies, with reading.

Generally, the texts that children read in code-emphasis programs are phonetically controlled, at least initially. That is, children read, in context, words conforming to the phonetic categories, rules, or sound-symbol relationships that they have been taught in isolation. Phonetic control limits the word-recognition demands of the text and enables children to practice decoding skills in context. Code-emphasis programs vary considerably in terms of how highly the beginning texts are phonetically controlled. However, as Anderson et al. (1985) point out, if the texts are too highly controlled, children may end up reading truly mind-numbing—and, on occasion, barely pronounceable—sentences, such as *Nat the cat sat on a tan mat.*

Whole-Language Programs. In whole-language programs, the initial emphasis is more on comprehension than on learning to decode words. These programs vary greatly in the extent to which there is direct instruction in decoding skills, with some programs involving a considerable amount of instruction in decoding and others involving little or no direct instruction. When decoding instruction is present, it tends more toward analytic phonics than toward synthetic phonics. Also, decoding instruction generally is not systematic, in the sense that it involves neither a predetermined sequence of knowledge to be taught nor practice of decoding skills in isolation. Rather, the emphasis is on teaching decoding skills in context, as the need arises—for example, when a child stumbles on a particular word while reading a story.

Thus, reading and writing in meaningful contexts, not developing skills in isolation, are the focus of whole-language programs. For instance, a writing activity in a whole-language classroom might involve having children write invitations to a class party that they are planning, with punctuation, capitalization, and other basic "rules" taught in the context of that activity. Although critics (e.g., Gersten & Dimino, 1993; Liberman & Liberman, 1990) view whole language as having a bias against basic-skill instruction, whether the basic skills in question involve decoding, spelling, or the mechanics of written expression (e.g., Gersten & Dimino, 1993; Liberman & Liberman, 1990), many whole-language theorists (e.g., Reid, 1993) emphasize that it is *isolated,* out-of-context skill instruction, not skill instruction itself, to which they are opposed.

The whole-language approach to teaching reading also emphasizes a high degree of integration across subject areas (e.g., reading instruction is integrated with instruction in areas such as social studies, science, and math). Children's attempts at writing are strongly encouraged via techniques such as invented spelling. Especially characteristic of this approach is the nature of the texts that children read: Whole-language programs primarily use children's literature, trade books, and texts generated by the children themselves, not phonetically controlled texts.

Basal Reading Programs. Basal reading programs feature sets of prepackaged, commercially published materials—basal textbooks, teachers' manuals, workbooks, tests, and so on—organized by grade level, from kindergarten to approximately the eighth grade. Anderson et al. (1985) observe that the top-selling basal reading programs exert a strong influence not only on how children learn to read in the United States but also on the types of texts that they read, because these programs are widely used to teach reading in elementary classrooms.

However, basal programs do not so much represent a third approach to teaching reading as instances of either code emphasis or meaning emphasis. In recent years, the most popular basal programs have taken a sharp swing toward meaning emphasis; many of these programs have obviously been influenced strongly by the whole-language philosophy, especially in their choices of texts, which are largely selections from children's literature and trade books. Nevertheless, we should point out that the idea of a "whole-language" basal series would be viewed as something of an oxymoron by many whole-language advocates.

For one thing, basal reading programs, by their very nature, involve a predetermined sequence of instruction and a predetermined sequence of texts. These characteristics conflict with some basic tenets of the whole-language philosophy (see, for example, McGee and Lomax, 1990, and Reid, 1993): authenticity and meaningfulness (i.e., the tenet that children should be engaged in personally meaningful acts of reading and writing, which typically will not be congruent with a predetermined sequence of instruction) and choice (i.e., the tenet that children should be given choices of what to read and write). Also, most basal reading programs, even the ones that have a very strong meaning emphasis, provide at least some isolated instruction in decoding, whereas many whole-language programs do not. Finally, the children's literature in basal programs often is simplified or abridged, a characteristic that has been strongly criticized by many whole-language theorists (e.g., Goodman, 1986; Routman, 1988).

Basal programs have some advantages that may help to explain their enduring popularity in American education. Among other things, they combine at least a modicum of direct instruction in word-recognition skills with instruction in comprehension; they provide teachers with a curriculum to follow in teaching reading; and they provide ready-made materials. These advantages are not insignificant, especially for novice teachers or for teachers who have large numbers of students. In contrast, some whole-language programs do not involve commercially published sets of materials but, rather, require teachers to develop most of their own materials as well as, in some cases, an entire curriculum. For beginning teachers, or for teachers who are developing a program independently (i.e., instead of as part of a school or district-wide initiative), these requirements may be very difficult to implement.

Underlying Philosophical Differences Between Approaches. Thus far, we have highlighted some of the principal instructional features differentiating the code-emphasis and whole-language approaches to reading instruction. But note that there are also many underlying theoretical and philosophical differences that separate advocates of the two approaches. For example, as we have already mentioned, whole-language advocates emphasize authenticity, meaningfulness, and choice. In addition, they lean more toward guided discovery methods of teaching than toward direct instruction. By contrast, code-emphasis advocates tend to believe in the importance of direct instruction, especially in basic skills.

Perhaps most fundamental of all, advocates of the two approaches often have very different views of reading acquisition. On the one hand, many advocates of whole-language instruction view reading acquisition in the same way as do some of the researchers interested in emergent literacy, a view that we discussed in Chapter 4. Whole-language advocates generally conceptualize reading acquisition as a "natural" process, similar to oral language acquisition. Margaret Richeck (see Lerner, Cousin, & Richeck, 1992) provides a good example of this theoretical view:

> A postulation of whole language is that learning to read is as natural as learning to speak. Through exposure to and participation in many experiences involving written language, children become proficient language users. Phonics instruction which is isolated and systematic is viewed as unnecessary and even harmful, because it is literacy without communication. (p. 227)

On the other hand, code-emphasis advocates tend to view reading acquisition not as being effortless and "natural" like oral language acquisition but, rather, as requiring some kind of formal instruction:

> Code Emphasis agrees that a child need not be a linguist in order to speak. But it holds that to use an alphabetic writing system properly, the child must be led to the same linguistic insight—and it was a linguistic insight—that underlay the development of the alphabet. Becoming enough of a linguist to appreciate that all words have an internal structure need not be a disagreeable task . . . but, agreeable or not, it is a necessary achievement for anyone who would take advantage of the alphabetic mode for the purpose of reading and writing. (Liberman & Liberman, 1990, p. 60)

As already indicated, we do not support the "reading-is-natural" theory of reading acquisition, a theory that lacks scientific evidence. Accordingly, our view of reading acquisition is much more similar to that of Liberman and Liberman (1990) than to the view espoused by Richeck in Lerner, Cousin, and Richeck (1992). Moreover, if there is any group for whom reading acquisition manifestly is *not* "natural" and effortless, it is the children with RD, who struggle with learning basic reading skills so much more than do other children.

Which Approach Is Better?

There is abundant evidence that, especially for children with reading disability, but also for poor or at-risk readers in general, systematic instruction in learning to decode—in other words, the kind of decoding instruction characteristic of code-emphasis programs—is critical (e.g., Adams, 1990; Anderson et al., 1985; Blachman, 1989, 1994; Chall, 1967, 1983; Christenson, Ysseldyke, & Thurlow, 1989; Felton, 1993). Adams (1990) has further concluded that explicit (i.e., synthetic) phonics is more effective than is exclusive use of implicit (i.e., analytic) phonics. Given the fact that word-recognition difficulties are central to reading disability, it is not surprising that instructional approaches emphasizing decoding skills would benefit children with RD. A number of authors have expressed concern about the use of whole-language programs, particularly with poor readers or with at-risk populations, such as low-SES youngsters, because of the lack of emphasis on systematic teaching of word-recognition skills found in many such programs (e.g., Chall, 1989; Liberman & Liberman, 1990; Stahl & Miller, 1989).

Critics have raised even broader concerns about the lack of emphasis in whole-language programs on direct instruction, period. For example, Pearson (1989) argues that techniques such as modeling, clear feedback about errors, and sequencing of tasks are important components of *comprehension* instruction—even in constructivist models of comprehension instruction—and expresses the concern that whole-language theorists seem to have a bias against the use of these techniques. Gersten and Dimino (1993) suggest that, particularly if the teacher is not highly skilled, low-achieving students may flounder in whole-language classrooms; for instance, they might repeatedly select books that are too difficult for themselves. And Delpit (1988) contends that instructional approaches such as whole language deprive minority students of the direct instruction they need to learn the implicit rules of the majority culture.

In contrast, other authors (e.g., Goodman, 1986, 1989; Lyons, 1989) have argued that whole-language programs are exactly what good readers, but also poor and at-risk readers, need—because of the emphasis of such programs on meaning, on authenticity, and on reading in context. Whole-language advocates note that many poor readers spend large amounts of time practicing isolated word-recognition skills and little time on higher-level comprehension or on reading interesting stories or books. As we ourselves have contended, an instructional program that overemphasizes isolated drills on word-recognition skills—at the expense of activities that engage children and foster higher-level comprehension—is not likely to produce motivated readers who view reading in the same way as do other literate people. Also, some whole-language programs encourage the integration of reading instruction with instruction in spelling and content areas; if done well, these integrated programs may be of particular benefit to poor readers, both because they are efficient and because they help children to see the usefulness of reading.

Clearly, there are many positive aspects to whole language. Consider those documented by Fisher and Hiebert (1990), who did an extensive observational study of whole-language classrooms in grades two and six. These investigators found that, compared with students in more traditional classrooms, students in whole-language classrooms spent more time writing, were given more challenging assignments, and had much more choice about what they would read or write. Other authors (e.g., Gersten & Dimino, 1993; Routman, 1988) have noted that the whole-language movement has helped many teachers to bring greater joy and enthusiasm to reading instruction, and to develop the view that even poor or at-risk readers can be active, engaged learners.

Thus, in the debate about which instructional approach is better, each of the opposing camps makes some legitimate points. However, framing the question as a choice between two approaches—code emphasis versus whole language—is, we think, misguided. That the question frequently *has* been framed in this wrong way may be all too apparent to many practitioners, who experience the tensions between advocates of the two approaches in their working lives. However, just in case there are any readers who think we are setting up straw men, consider the titles of some relatively recent articles on the subject of reading instruction: "Debunking the Great Phonics Myth" (Carbo, 1988); "Learning to Read: The Great Debate 20 Years Later—A Response to 'Debunking the Great Phonics Myth'" (Chall, 1989); "Filling the Hole in Whole Language" (Heymsfeld, 1989); "Whole Language *Is* Whole: A Response to Heymsfeld" (Goodman, 1989); and "Whole Language Versus Code Emphasis: Underlying Assumptions and Their Implications for Reading Instruction" (Liberman & Liberman, 1990). Then there's the title of a *Newsweek* article about the controversies in reading instruction, "The Reading Wars" (Kantrowitz, 1990), which sums up the situation in some quarters rather well. Or, as another observer put it, "The Montagues and the Capulets had nothing on the irreconcilable clans slugging it out over the right way to teach reading" (Rothman, 1990, p. 40). Clearly, much of the debate over optimal methods of reading instruction has been framed as an either-or choice between code emphasis and meaning emphasis, or between their alter egos, phonics and whole language.

After examining some of the debate, one might fear that, in the realm of reading instruction as well as in the book of Ecclesiastes, there is nothing new under the sun. Not only has the debate about reading instruction often been framed as an either-or choice, but essentially the same two options (under varying names and in varying versions, to be sure, but differing more in details than in substance), as well as many of the same kinds of arguments, have been put forth for decades. For instance, in 1955, when Rudolf Flesch published *Why Johnny Can't Read,* an emotional critique of the meaning-emphasis method then popular in American schools, the code-emphasis versus meaning-emphasis controversy was already an old one. More than twenty-five years later, he wrote *Why Johnny Still Can't Read* (Flesch, 1981), arguing that reading programs were continuing to do an inadequate job of teaching phonics. Of course, rejoinders to Flesch's pronouncements—such as "It's only a Flesch wound" (Johns, 1980)—and to those of other, much more moderate phonics advocates, abounded.

We discussed a similar stalemate in Chapter 2, where the history of the intrinsic and extrinsic perspectives on reading disability is described. In both cases, it appears unlikely that more of the same kind of controversy, with the same two choices, will be helpful in the future. Does this stalemate mean that the reading-methods debate is irrelevant to practitioners, as some writers (e.g., Johns, 1991) have suggested? We do not think so. However, we do believe that the underlying question addressed in that debate—as to which approach is better—needs to be reframed.

Reframing the Question

In our view, the two major approaches to reading instruction are a bit like the Republican and Democratic parties, to use an appropriately political analogy—although we will not attempt to specify which instructional approach corresponds to which political party. (Some reading authorities have argued that reading instruction is indeed deeply political; see, for example, Adams et al., 1991.) Just as one cannot understand the American system of government without knowing something about these two major parties, one cannot understand how reading typically is taught, or what the major issues in reading instruction are, without knowing something about these two overall approaches to instruction—code emphasis or phonics, on the one hand, and meaning emphasis, whole word, or whole language, on the other. Just as there are real philosophical differences between different political parties, so too are there meaningful differences between the adherents of different instructional approaches to reading. Differences between advocates of the two instructional approaches are meaningful as well, because they stem from more fundamental philosophical and theoretical differences, and because they involve differences in instructional emphasis that may be quite important, particularly for children with RD and for other poor or at-risk readers. Therefore, we do not agree that the debate between the advocates of different approaches—interminable though it may seem—is simply irrelevant to practitioners and should be ignored.

Still, for a number of reasons it is imperative to reframe the question as to which of the two overall approaches—code emphasis or whole language—is superior. For one thing, there is a certain artificiality to the question. Just as we cannot necessarily predict an individual's stand on a political issue by knowing whether he or she is a Democrat or a Republican (although we might be able to make an educated guess), we cannot necessarily predict a specific characteristic of an instructional program by knowing whether the program is categorized as code emphasis or whole language. This difficulty in prediction exists because there is a wide range of variation not only between but also *within* approaches. For instance, as we have mentioned, whole-language programs vary considerably in the extent to which decoding skills are taught directly. Similarly, some code-emphasis programs provide children with a wide variety of reading materials, such as trade books and children's literature.

In addition, each of the two broad instructional approaches has numerous instructional features. The features that tend to be associated primarily with whole-language programs include reading in trade books, the use of invented spelling, and a nonsystematic approach to decoding instruction; those that tend to be associated primarily with code-emphasis programs include reading of phonetically controlled materials and a highly systematic approach to decoding instruction. Obviously, different instructional features might facilitate success in different areas of reading—for example, in word recognition as opposed to reading comprehension. Moreover, some features might interact with one another to improve reading achievement. For instance, an instructional feature such as invented spelling might be more effective in promoting growth in word recognition if combined with some other feature, such as direct instruction in decoding. Finally, some instructional features might be more effective with some youngsters than with others, depending on the cognitive characteristics of the children and on their level of skill in reading.

Thus, we share the viewpoint of many other investigators (e.g., Adams, 1990; Gersten & Dimino, 1993; Stahl, McKenna, & Pugnucco, 1994; Stahl & Miller, 1989) that it is time to look beyond broad approaches to teaching reading and examine the specific features of each approach that facilitate success in various areas of reading. Neither approach is uniformly "better" than the other for all purposes. Rather, as we will discuss next, all children—whether they are normally achieving readers or not—need a combination of approaches, with different instructional features emphasized for different children.

Instruction to Help Children Along the Road to Proficient Reading

As we pointed out in Chapter 4, typical reading development is a crucial reference point for practitioners interested in reading disability. Ultimately, we want to help all children, whether they have RD or not, along the road to proficient reading. Thus, before considering the instructional needs of children with RD, we must consider what constitutes effective reading instruction for normally achieving readers.

Like many other investigators whose work we have reviewed, we conceptualize reading acquisition as a developmental process involving a sequence of phases. Reading is different for a normally achieving five-year-old than for a ten-year-old or for a proficient adult reader. The kind of instructional emphasis that children require varies—depending, in part, upon their phase of development (just as the appropriateness or effectiveness of any activity varies with development). A one-year-old might enjoy peek-a-boo games, but no one would expect a four-year-old to be thrilled by such games; and whereas crayons and paper are very appropriate for three- or four-year-olds, a one-year-old might prefer eating them to drawing with them. Similarly, a particular instructional feature—such as the use of invented spelling or systematic instruction in decoding—might be more or less effective depending upon children's phase of development.

For example, children in the phase of visual-cue word recognition—generally, preschoolers and kindergartners, or children through the age of about five—may benefit from many of the instructional features typical of whole-language programs. Activities such as listening to children's literature, pretend-reading books with predictable text, and experimenting with writing provide a motivating way for young children to learn basic concepts about print (e.g., that printed words are separated by spaces). Similarly, the use of invented spelling, combined with instruction in letter names and sounds, may help children to attain alphabetic insight and phonetic-cue word recognition.

However, children in the phase of phonetic-cue word recognition—usually first-graders, or children approximately six years old—make only partial use of phonetic cues and letter information in word recognition. These children need to acquire phonological-reading and orthographic skills in order to move along the road to proficient reading. Direct and systematic instruction in word-recognition skills, which is more characteristic of code-emphasis than of whole-language programs, is important for children in the phase of phonetic-cue word recognition.

Normally achieving readers have acquired basic word-recognition skills by the time they've reached the phase of automatic word recognition—typically, by the end of third grade, about the age of eight. At this point, nondisabled readers no longer need basic instruction in *decoding,* although they still require instruction in other "basic-skill" areas of literacy, such as spelling and the mechanics of written expression. However, in reading, these children need more of an emphasis on comprehension. Thus, many of the features of whole-language programs—such as the emphasis on meaning, on reading in context, and on varied reading materials—again may be particularly effective for them.

A number of research findings support the idea that the effectiveness of an instructional approach, or of a particular instructional feature, may vary with children's phase of reading acquisition. For example, Fisher and Hiebert (1990) concluded that, for students who could read well independently, the whole-language approach was beneficial, whereas for students still struggling with basic reading skills, such as word recognition, this approach was not particularly effective. In contrast, other evidence (e.g., Chall, 1983; Williams, 1985) suggests that the code-emphasis approach is especially effective in developing word-recognition skills.

Stahl and Miller (1989) did a literature review comparing basal reading programs with whole-language and language-experience approaches to beginning reading instruction. (Language experience is an older instructional approach with many similarities to whole language, although there are some differences as well; see, for example, McGee and Lomax, 1990, as well as Stahl and Miller, 1989.) Stahl and Miller concluded that the whole-language approach was more effective with kindergartners than with first-graders. These authors suggest that, once children are in first grade, they need more systematic instruction in word-recognition skills than is characteristic of most whole-language programs. A subsequent, updated meta-analysis (Stahl et al., 1994) reached similar conclusions.

Snow et al. (1991) found that different classroom practices facilitated different aspects of reading. A structured program of decoding instruction, such as that found in the code-emphasis approach, was important for children's learning of word-recognition skills. And the presence of a wide variety of reading materials in the classroom—as might be found in whole-language programs—was important for reading comprehension as well as for stimulating practice reading in context.

Indeed, both word recognition and reading comprehension are important in reading achievement. However, as we argued in Chapter 4, word-recognition skills are particularly crucial in the early phases of reading acquisition, whereas comprehension is particularly crucial in the later phases. Thus, on the one hand, instructional features that facilitate gains in word recognition would be most important early in reading acquisition, especially at the point when children are expected to begin to learn to decode—most commonly, in first grade. On the other hand, instructional features that facilitate gains in reading comprehension would be especially important somewhat later in reading acquisition, around the start of the middle elementary years.

It is not that kindergartners need whole language, first-graders need code emphasis, and so on. Rather, in all phases, children need a *combination* of instructional features that tend to be characteristic of different approaches. Yet precisely which features need to be emphasized change depending on the children's phase of development (as well as on other factors, of course, such as individual strengths and weaknesses). For example, as we have suggested, children in the phase of phonetic-cue word recognition benefit particularly from an emphasis on systematic instruction in decoding. Obviously, however, they also need activities to develop comprehension and exposure to varied reading materials. And even when children have acquired basic word-recognition skills and benefit from more of an emphasis on comprehension, they still require some direct instruction in other "basic-skill" areas of literacy, such as spelling. In our view, these areas do not simply "emerge" spontaneously in all children, any more than reading does. In both examples, children need a combination of code-emphasis and whole-language instructional features, but different features need to be emphasized depending on their phase of development.

Marilyn Adams (in Adams et al., 1991), who argues for a combination of instructional approaches, has addressed the debate between advocates of whole language and those of code emphasis with particular eloquence:

> [Questions about beginning reading instruction] were clearly questions that warranted objective, scientific study. Further, the more I studied them, the more convinced I became that both sides of the debate were right. They were right, moreover, not in frivolous dismissible ways, but in certain deeply and vitally important ways, and they were right, not as alternatives to one another, but as necessary complements, effective and realizable only in complex interdependency with one another. (p. 372)

Several pages later, in a discussion of reading acquisition in normally achieving readers, Adams points out that "effective literacy growth depends on a delicate balance between extending one's confidence with the code of text (where that includes its syntax as well as the spellings and meanings of its words) and expanding one's appreciation of its larger forms, functions, and values" (Adams et al., 1991, p. 394). In other words, children's acquisition of word-recognition skills does not stand alone, in some kind of vacuum; on the contrary, it interacts with their developing comprehension abilities and their growing appreciation for reading. Children must indeed acquire accurate and automatic word-recognition skills in order to progress in reading acquisition, as we have stressed; but their engagement with text and their interest in reading also push forward their decoding skills. Surely these ideas are just as true for children with reading disability as they are for normally achieving readers. Regardless of whether they have reading disability, children become "hooked" not on phonics but on stories, books, and ideas.

Instruction to Help Children with Reading Disability

In our model of reading disability, children with RD are not a monolithic group. Rather, at any given time, they may fall into one of four patterns—nonalphabetic, compensatory, nonautomatic, or delayed readers—each of which diverges from the road to proficient reading at a different point. Just as normally achieving readers need a combination of instructional approaches, with different emphases that depend upon the phase of reading acquisition, children with reading disability also require a combination of instructional approaches, with different emphases that depend upon the pattern of reading disability.

In short, like normally achieving readers, children with reading disability have areas of strength and areas of weakness. For both groups of youngsters, instruction needs to capitalize on children's strengths and to remediate weaknesses. In the case of children with RD, and depending upon the pattern of reading disability, there are some predictable weaknesses that need to be remediated, as well as some strengths that can be capitalized upon.

Weaknesses of Children with RD. As we discussed in Chapter 5, acquisition of word-recognition skills is much more difficult for children with RD than for normally achieving children and, perhaps, even than for other poor readers (Shinn, Tindal, & Stein, 1988). Relative to younger, normally achieving readers matched to them on reading level, children with RD appear to have deficits in phonological processing (e.g., phonological awareness) that are related to their difficulties in developing word-recognition skills. In addition, some children with RD appear to have particular difficulty with automatization of word recognition. These areas involving word-recognition skills clearly demand special remedial attention. However, as in the case of normally achieving readers, the instructional needs of children with RD—whatever the pattern of reading disability—are best met not through any single instructional approach but, rather, through a combination of approaches.

For instance, nonalphabetic readers and compensatory readers, who have not achieved accuracy in basic word-recognition skills, need an emphasis on direct, systematic instruction in decoding. For these youngsters, instruction that gives short shrift to word-recognition skills or that takes a nonsystematic approach—as do many whole-language programs—would be disastrous. Furthermore, as we will discuss in the next chapter, many nonalphabetic and compensatory readers may need more intensive instruction in phonological skills than typically is provided even in many code-emphasis programs. Of course, the word-recognition needs of these youngsters also must be integrated with good comprehension instruction and with reading materials that are engaging and motivating, or the whole point of learning to read will be lost on them.

Nonautomatic readers do not need decoding instruction that is aimed at word-recognition *accuracy,* because their word-recognition skills are adequate in this respect. However, they do need training to develop *automatization* of word recognition. This training, which we will describe in Chapter 7, involves the kind of isolated skill instruction that is anathema to whole-language advocates. But motivation and practice also are important to the development of automatization. In this regard, nonautomatic readers might benefit from some of the typical features of whole language, such as the emphasis on choice and on reading in context, if these features are implemented in such a way as to increase the students' motivation as well as their practice on appropriate types of texts.

Finally, delayed readers have acquired accurate and automatic word-recognition skills, but they need an emphasis on comprehension, on reading in context, and on strategy use. These needs may be at least partially accommodated by the whole-language approach. However, we should point out that, although delayed readers do not require systematic word-recognition instruction, they probably will need systematic instruction in other basic-skill areas of literacy such as spelling. For example, Bruck (1990), whose study of college students labeled as dyslexic in childhood, which we discussed in Chapter 5, found that spelling problems were virtually universal among her subjects—even among those who had attained relatively high levels of reading-comprehension skill.

Low Motivation, Limited Practice, Negative Expectations. In our model of reading disability, there are three negative factors in particular that affect all children with RD and greatly exacerbate their initial difficulties in reading. We have referred to these factors as the "swamp" of lowered motivation, lowered levels of practice, and lowered expectations. Thus, instructional approaches that enhance motivation, provide a high level of practice, and communicate positive expectations are even more important for children with RD than they are for normally achieving readers. Obviously, both the code-emphasis and the whole-language approaches can be effective—or can fall short—in these areas.

Nevertheless, we will hazard a few generalizations about how code emphasis and whole language compare in the areas of practice and motivation. On the one hand, typical code-emphasis programs may be particularly effective in providing practice on specific decoding skills, because of their systematic approach to decoding instruction. On the other hand, typical whole-language programs may be more likely than their code-emphasis counterparts to provide a large amount of practice reading in context. Of course, the extent to which either type of practice benefits children with RD hinges upon the appropriateness of the materials. For example, children will not benefit from practice struggling through texts that are much too difficult for them, nor will they benefit from excessive drill on isolated words that they already can decode with a reasonable degree of accuracy.

With regard to motivation, we agree with other authors that systematic code-emphasis instruction does not necessarily have to be joyless drudgery (Liberman & Liberman, 1990) and that whole-language programs are not necessarily motivating to the students who are floundering in them (Stein & Osborn, 1993). Nevertheless, we do think that many features of whole language have the potential to engage students with RD and to increase their motivation—in particular, the emphases on using a wide range of reading materials, on ensuring authenticity of reading experiences, and on accommodating students' choices in reading and writing.

Strengths of Children with RD. Children with reading disability also have some predictable areas of strength that may be exploited in instruction. For instance, relative to garden-variety poor readers, with whom they share similar kinds of word-recognition difficulties, children with RD may have strengths in the higher-level cognitive areas that are tapped heavily by IQ tests—such as nonverbal reasoning, problem solving, and vocabulary (Torgesen, 1991; but also see Fletcher et al., 1994). Because the two groups initially are defined in terms of IQ, these cognitive differences are not surprising. Nevertheless, some investigators (e.g., Torgesen, Dahlem, & Greenstein, 1987) have suggested that the greater strengths of some children with RD in higher-level cognitive areas may enable them to benefit from instructional techniques that would be less effective with garden-variety poor readers, such as the use of recorded textbooks to enhance comprehension.

Another relative area of strength for children with RD is listening comprehension. Children with the cognitive profile typical of RD are characterized by good listening comprehension as compared with reading comprehension. Very young normally achieving readers also have better listening comprehension than reading comprehension; for example, a normally achieving first-grader can comprehend much more sophisticated material in a listening mode than in a reading mode. However, among normally achieving readers, reading comprehension becomes an increasingly important vehicle for learning compared to listening comprehension, and the disparity between reading comprehension and listening comprehension lessens over time. In fact, older children and adults sometimes comprehend information *better* in a reading mode than in a listening mode—for instance, when the information is highly technical or unfamiliar.

For children with RD, by contrast, the disparity between listening comprehension and reading comprehension generally continues over time. There *are* exceptions; as we have discussed, because of Matthew effects a long-standing reading disability eventually may erode the original disparity between listening comprehension and reading comprehension in some individuals with RD. Nevertheless, for many individuals, it is unlikely that this disparity will vanish completely. For example, an adult with reading disability who has achieved only a third-grade level in reading comprehension probably will have better listening-comprehension skills than the average eight-year-old. Of course, listening-comprehension skills may vary across individuals with reading disability, such that some have unusually strong listening comprehension and others have weaker listening comprehension.

In the context of instruction, what does the preceding discussion imply for children with reading disability? Although the reading comprehension of such children is impaired, listening comprehension continues to be an important vehicle for learning, especially among youngsters possessing strong listening-comprehension skills. Listening-comprehension activities can be used not only to impart information that children with RD would be unable to read, as in content subjects like social studies and science, but also to stimulate comprehension abilities that may eventually transfer to reading and, above all, to enhance motivation for reading. In general, the whole-language approach probably places more emphasis on listening comprehension than does the code-emphasis approach. However, our experience has suggested that, even in whole-language programs, listening-comprehension activities are more commonly used with young beginning readers than with older children.

In the preceding discussion, we have focused on areas of relative strength for nearly all children with reading disability. Obviously, however, individual children also have their own particular strengths and interests; one may be musically talented, another may have an aptitude for mathematics, yet another may be a good athlete, and so on. Incorporating these areas into the programs of individual children, in the manner employed in many whole-language and in some code-emphasis programs—for example, providing stories and books about musicians to a child with a strong interest in music—is one way to offset some of the motivational difficulties experienced by many children with RD.

Conclusions

In our view, a "purist" version of either instructional approach, whether code emphasis or whole language (or some other version of meaning emphasis), is obviously inadequate for normally achieving readers as well as for children with reading disability. Here, we summarize our objections to the use of either approach by itself.

Whether or not whole language has an inherent bias against basic-skill instruction—and, in our opinion, many whole-language advocates do demonstrate such a bias, one that tends to follow from their theoretical view of reading acquisition—it indisputably has a bias against *isolated* skill instruction. Consider, for example, Reid (1993), a whole-language advocate who argues that the issue is not about whether direct instruction in word-recognition skills should be provided but, rather, concerns the contextualization of that instruction:

> Clearly, we cannot abandon our *instructional* role, a role that explicitly and intensively addresses the way one processes information, the way one works on problems, the way one organizes, plans, and monitors learning. But being explicit and intensive

does not necessarily mean using hierarchical sequences, teaching phonics in isolation, or preparing comprehension questions. (p. 15)

Reid goes on to give some examples of contextualized, as opposed to isolated, activities for teaching phonological and word-recognition skills:

> Contextualized, meaningful practice can be achieved through rhyming games, writing activities, reading highly repetitious and/or highly predictable books, explicitly noting letter-sound correspondences in real words in real text, talking about how to spell words that are needed to communicate in meaningful writing, and so forth. The possibilities are endless. (p. 16)

We certainly do not object either to the kinds of activities that Reid uses as examples or to the idea that basic-skill instruction must be integrated with meaningful activities, such as reading interesting stories and books. However, we do object to the notion that *all* skill instruction must be contextualized. For one thing, the distinction between isolated and contextualized skill instruction strikes us as somewhat artificial. For example, suppose that a child stumbles on a specific word while reading a text, and the teacher wants to help the child decode it. This scenario involves the sort of contextualized instruction of which Reid and other whole-language advocates approve. But, in some sense, the word must be considered in isolation in order for the child to learn how to decode it—that is, unless the teacher encourages the child to guess at the word based on contextual cues, rather than prompting the child to decode the word completely. The former technique, commonly recommended by whole-language advocates (e.g., Goodman, 1986), is one to which we also object, because it discourages children from attending closely to the sequence of letters in a word and from applying their decoding skills in context.

Most important, contextualized skill instruction frequently is inefficient and ineffective, as researchers interested in automatization training (e.g., Frederiksen, et al., 1983; Schneider, 1984) have pointed out. When children read in context, they have to meet many cognitive demands—not just recognizing the individual words in the text but also comprehending what they are reading, attending to punctuation, using appropriate expression in oral reading, and so on. Also, the individual words in the text may vary greatly in terms of phonetic structure. Thus, children may receive very limited practice on any single word type or sound-symbol relationship, and the attention that they are able to allocate to learning word-recognition skills may be depleted by many other competing demands. In this situation, children—especially those who are having difficulty—may easily become overwhelmed and discouraged.

When one learns to play a musical instrument, part of the instruction often involves isolated exercises to develop technical skill with the instrument; similarly, many athletes (e.g., runners or football players) do isolated exercises, such as those involved in weight training, to improve muscle strength. We believe that, in reading, there is also a place for instruction in isolated skills—so long as this instruction is only *one part* of a total program that includes more meaningful activities, and so long as the skill instruction is well integrated with the other parts of the program. Both normally achieving readers and children with RD require such integration of isolated skill work with other, contextualized activities. However, children with reading disability have problems that center on basic skills, and, by definition, they lag behind normally achieving readers; thus, a program that eschews basic-skill instruction, or that delivers basic-skill instruction in an ineffective, inefficient manner, is particularly damaging to youngsters with RD.

Unfortunately, code-emphasis programs often contain too much isolated skill instruction, yet not enough of the kinds of activities that will enable children to see what the point of the skill instruction is or that will engage them and motivate them to keep reading. These reading programs are like music instruction that consists of finger exercises but no playing of real music, or like athletic coaching in which the athlete never actually gets to play in a game or to run in a race. Obviously, this kind of instruction is detrimental to normally achieving readers as well as to children with reading disability; again, however, it is especially detrimental to children with RD, who are likely to experience more severe motivational problems and to take longer in learning word-recognition skills than do nondisabled readers.

Furthermore, children with RD need *age-appropriate,* not reading-level-appropriate, comprehension instruction. Otherwise, while they are in the difficult and often lengthy process of acquiring word-recognition skills, their comprehension abilities may atrophy from lack of use. For many children with RD, this kind of higher-level comprehension development may need to be accomplished through listening activities as well as through reading activities, but heavy use of listening-comprehension activities is not characteristic of many code-emphasis programs.

Advocates of either approach sometimes respond to critics—and to negative data—by saying that it is not the approach itself but, rather, some implementations of the approach that are faulty. For instance, Reid (1993) admits that, in some cases, "whole language has been poorly implemented" (p. 15) and suggests that this outcome has arisen from "efforts to foist whole language instruction on a cadre of professionals who are dedicated and well-meaning, but in many instances and in many ways (through no fault of their own) unprepared to implement it" (p. 16)—that is, because they have been inadequately trained. In a similar vein, Liberman and Liberman (1990) acknowledge the value of many practices encouraged by whole-language advocates, such as reading to children, the use of predictable texts, and the integration of reading and writing. However, they go on to assert that these practices are not distinctive to whole language but, rather, "have been part of every good teacher's repertoire since the teaching of reading began" (p. 53). The implication is that "good" code-emphasis teachers have been using these so-called whole-language practices all along; only the "poor" code-emphasis teachers have not.

Of course, there are always good and poor implementations of any model. Nevertheless, we think that the problems with either instructional approach—code emphasis or whole language—cannot be dismissed merely as problems of implementation, because some of them stem from the underlying theoretical and philosophical views of each approach as well as from the instructional methods promoted by each approach.

The theoretical assumption of many whole-language advocates that reading and writing skills spontaneously "emerge," given sufficient experience with meaningful activities, provides few tools for teachers to use when such skills do not arise. Indeed, some of the techniques promoted by whole-language advocates— such as encouraging children to rely heavily on contextual cues in reading rather than to apply decoding skills in context, or ignoring children's oral reading "miscues" (i.e., word-recognition errors) unless they dramatically alter the meaning of the text—clearly convey the message to all but the most obtuse that basic skills are not important.

Furthermore, in our view, the aversion of whole-language theorists to isolated skill instruction and to the use of predetermined skill sequences not only is ineffective for many children but also puts an unrealistic burden on teachers. Most teachers work with groups, often rather large groups, of children. Attempting to work on all skills in a contextualized manner, without some kind of predetermined sequence of instruction, makes it extremely difficult for teachers to keep track of the progress and the needs of individual children, much less to meet all of those needs. Inevitably, some youngsters are lost in the shuffle.

At the same time, we think that even many "good" code-emphasis teachers fail to take advantage of positive practices encouraged by whole-language advocates, such as the use of varied kinds of texts, the use of listening-comprehension activities, and the integration of basic-skill instruction with more meaningful activities. These flaws, too, are not just poor implementations of an ideal model; rather, they accrue in part from the model itself.

As indicated, we share the theoretical view of code-emphasis advocates that acquisition of word-recognition skills is crucial to progress in reading for most youngsters with reading disability as well as for young nondisabled readers. We further agree with code-emphasis advocates that acquisition of word-recognition skills often does not spontaneously "emerge" but, rather, requires some kind of direct instruction. Indeed, we think that these conclusions are inescapable for anyone who looks at the experimental literature on reading acquisition with a reasonably objective eye. For these reasons, we share the concerns of code-emphasis advocates regarding not only the lack of emphasis on word-recognition skills in many whole-language programs but also the use of some highly questionable whole-language techniques, such as urging children to guess at words based on contextual cues.

We must also note, however, that code-emphasis programs frequently give short shrift to the importance of meaning and comprehension. Consider the following example. Although we recognize that not all phonetically controlled materials are unappealing, and also that some code-emphasis approaches use varied texts, many of the texts used in code-emphasis programs do not lend themselves easily to the development of higher-level comprehension skills. It is difficult, for instance, to generate interesting discussions about Dan's tan fan or about Nat the fat cat. Moreover, listening-comprehension activities, which might be used to stimulate the comprehension abilities of youngsters with limited reading skills, do not play a central role in most code-emphasis programs. Indeed, in some of these programs, by the time the teacher gets the children through the word-recognition activities, there is little time left for any comprehension at all.

As Adams (1990) points out, children's word-recognition skills develop not in a vacuum but, rather, in the context of their interest in and engagement with print. Like normally achieving readers, children with reading disability must acquire accurate and automatic word-recognition skills in order to become proficient readers. In our view, as we have discussed, the use of some isolated word-recognition instruction is a much more effective, efficient way to help children acquire word-recognition skills than is wholly contextualized instruction. But skill instruction alone is obviously not enough, either for children with RD or for normally achieving readers. Without sufficient stimulation of their comprehension abilities, and without a level of interest in reading that is far more likely to be spurred by engaging texts and by child-centered, meaningful activities than by isolated word-recognition instruction, children with RD cannot return to the road to proficient reading—or, like nondisabled readers, progress along it. Even more important, they will never really understand the uses of reading or experience its joys.

Combinations of the code-emphasis and whole-language approaches have been very effectively implemented with first-grade poor readers (e.g., Clay, 1985; Hiebert, Colt, Catto, & Gury, 1992). Such combinations might be achieved in a variety of ways, using a variety of materials—and with older children as well as with first-graders. For instance, they might be achieved by supplementing a literacy-based basal program with systematic word-recognition instruction, or by interweaving a good decoding program with reading in varied materials and with extensive writing activities.

The debates between advocates of different approaches to reading instruction—whether they center on the needs of children with RD or on the needs of normally achieving readers—are not likely to end in the near future. The differences between these approaches are rooted in fundamental theoretical convictions and in deeply held philosophical beliefs. Even if the debates become recast in other terms or areas of agreement are found, there is little reason to anticipate a real resolution. The reaction to Adams's (1990) book on reading acquisition and instruction (see, for example, Adams et al., 1991) is a case in point. Although Adams tried harder than many writers to be fair to both sides in the code-emphasis versus whole-language controversy, her work was met not only with objective criticisms but also with disagreements that came close to being personal attacks.

An end to this controversy will certainly not be hastened by the extremists on both sides, nor by the persistent refusal of some authorities—a few of whom apparently want to dispatch the scientific method along with phonics instruction (see F. Smith, 1992)—to acknowledge well-established experimental findings. For example, one of the founding fathers of whole language in the United States was quoted in *Education Week* as saying that an emphasis on decoding in reading instruction was "outmoded" and that only "a small group of people thinks that making sense of text depends first on identifying words" (Rothman, 1992). Presumably this group includes people like ourselves and the "small" number of researchers whose work we have cited.

Although practitioners need to understand and to appreciate the genuine differences between instructional approaches, they cannot afford to wait for all of the extremists to put aside their rhetoric; that wait would likely be exceedingly long. Rather, for teachers the immediate concern is exactly how to implement the kind of combined instructional approach that we have discussed, in the way that is best for each particular child. For practitioners in general, and especially for those who work with children with reading disability, achieving this combination in practice—for instance, integrating basic word-recognition instruction with appropriate comprehension instruction, using activities that engage and motivate children—often will not be easy. The actual methods by which this combination of approaches might be achieved, with appropriate emphases for each of the four patterns of reading disability, are the topic of the next chapter.

References

Adams, M. J. (1990). *Beginning to read: Thinking and learning about print.* Cambridge, MA: MIT Press.

Adams, M. J., Allington, R. L., Chaney, J. H., Goodman, Y. M., Kapinus, B. A., McGee, L. M., Richgels, D. J., Schwartz, S. J., Shannon, P., Smitten, B., & Williams, J. P. (1991). Beginning to read: A critique by literacy professionals and a response by Marilyn Jager Adams. *Reading Teacher, 44,* 370–395.

Anderson, R., Hiebert, E., Scott, J., & Wilkinson, I. (1985). *Becoming a nation of readers: The report of the Commission on Reading.* Champaign, IL: Center for the Study of Reading.

Beckwith, L., & Rodning, C. (1991). Intellectual functioning in children born preterm: Recent research. In L. Okagaki & R. J. Sternberg (Eds.), *Directors of development: Influences on the development of children's thinking* (pp. 25–58). Hillsdale, NJ: Erlbaum.

Blachman, B. A. (1989). Phonological awareness and word recognition: Assessment and intervention. In A. Kamhi & H. Catts (Eds.), *Reading disabilities: A developmental language perspective* (pp. 133–158). Boston, MA: College-Hill.

———. (1994). What we have learned from longitudinal studies of phonological processing and reading, and some unanswered questions: A response to Torgesen, Wagner, and Rashotte. *Journal of Learning Disabilities, 27,* 287–291.

Bruck, M. (1990). Word-recognition skills of adults with childhood diagnoses of dyslexia. *Developmental Psychology, 26,* 439–454.

Carbo, M. (1988). Debunking the great phonics myth. *Phi Delta Kappan, 70,* 226–240.

Chall, J. (1967). *Learning to read: The great debate.* New York: McGraw-Hill.

———. (1983). *Learning to read: The great debate (revised).* New York: McGraw-Hill.

———. (1989). Learning to read: The great debate 20 years later—A response to "Debunking the Great Phonics Myth." *Phi Delta Kappan, 70,* 521–538.

Christenson, S. L., Ysseldyke, J. E., & Thurlow, M. L. (1989). Critical instructional factors for students with mild handicaps: An integrative review. *Remedial and Special Education, 10,* 21–31.

Clarke, L. K. (1988). Invented versus traditional spelling in first graders' writings: Effects on learning to spell and read. *Research in the Teaching of English, 22,* 281–309.

Clay, M. M. (1985). *The early detection of reading difficulties,* 3rd ed. Portsmouth, NH: Heinemann.

Delpit, L. D. (1988). The silenced dialogue: Power and pedagogy in educating other people's children. *Harvard Educational Review, 58,* 280–298.

Felton, R. H. (1993). Effects of instruction on the decoding skills of children with phonological-processing problems. *Journal of Learning Disabilities, 26,* 583–589.

Fisher, C. W., & Hiebert, E. H. (1990). Characteristics of tasks in two approaches to literacy instruction. *The Elementary School Journal, 91,* 3–18.

Flesch, R. (1955). *Why Johnny can't read.* New York: Harper & Row.

———. (1981). *Why Johnny still can't read.* New York: Harper & Row.

Fletcher, J. M., Shaywitz, S. E., Shankweiler, D. P., Katz, L., Liberman, I. Y., Stuebing, K. K., Francis, D. J., Fowler, A. E., & Shaywitz, B. A. (1994). Cognitive profiles of reading disability: Comparisons of discrepancy and low achievement definitions. *Journal of Educational Psychology, 86,* 6–23.

Frederiksen, J. R., Weaver, P. A., Warren, B. M., Gillotte, H. P., Rosebery, A. S., Freeman, B., & Goodman, L. (1983). *A componential approach to training reading skills* (Final Report 5295). Cambridge, MA: Bolt, Beranek and Newman, Inc.

Gersten, R., & Dimino, J. (1993). Visions and revisions: A special education perspective on the whole language controversy. *Remedial and Special Education, 14,* 5–13.

Goodman, K. S. (1986). *What's whole in whole language: A parent-teacher guide.* Portsmouth, NH: Heinemann.

———. (1989). Whole language *is* whole: A response to Heymsfeld. *Educational Leadership, 46,* 69–70.

Hargrove, L. J., & Poteet, J. A. (1984). *Assessment in special education.* Englewood Cliffs, NJ: Prentice-Hall.

Heymsfeld, C. R. (1989). Filling the hole in whole language. *Educational Leadership, 46,* 65–68.

Hiebert, E. H., Colt, J. M., Catto, S. L., & Gury, E. C. (1992). Reading and writing of first-grade students in a restructured Chapter 1 program. *American Educational Research Journal, 29,* 545–572.

Johns, J. L. (1980, March). It's only a Flesch wound. *Illinois Reading Council Journal, 8,* 3–4, 10.

———. (1991). Helping readers at risk: Beyond whole language, whole word, and phonics. *Reading, Writing, and Learning Disabilities, 7,* 59–67.

Kantrowitz, B. (1990, Fall/Winter). The reading wars. *Newsweek* (Special Edition), 8–9, 12, 14.

Lerner, J. W., Cousin, P. T., & Richeck, M. (1992). Critical issues in learning disabilities: Whole language learning. *Learning Disabilities Research and Practice, 7,* 226–230.

Liberman, I. Y., & Liberman, A. M. (1990). Whole language versus code emphasis: Underlying assumptions and their implications for reading instruction. *Annals of Dyslexia, 40,* 51–76.

Lyons, C. A. (1989). Reading recovery: A preventative for mislabeling young "at-risk" learners. *Urban Education, 24,* 125–139.

Mann, V. A., Tobin, P., & Wilson, R. (1987). Measuring phonological awareness through the invented spellings of kindergarten children. *Merrill-Palmer Quarterly, 33,* 365–391.

McGee, L. M., & Lomax, R. G. (1990). On combining apples and oranges: A response to Stahl and Miller. *Review of Educational Research, 60,* 133–140.

Pearson, P. D. (1989). Reading the whole-language movement. *The Elementary School Journal, 90,* 231–241.

Reid, D. K. (1993). Another vision of "Visions and Revisions." *Remedial and Special Education, 14,* 14–16, 25.

Rothman, R. (1990, January). Both ends against the middle? *Teacher Magazine,* 40–41.

———. (1992, January 8). Studies cast doubt on benefits of using only whole language to teach reading. *Education Week.*

Routman, R. (1988). *Transitions: From literature to literacy.* Portsmouth, NH: Heinemann.

Schneider, W. (1984). *Training high-performance skills: Fallacies and guidelines* (Final Report HARL-ONR-8301). Champaign, IL: University of Illinois, Human Attention Research Laboratory.

Shinn, M. R., Tindal, G. A., & Stein, S. (1988). Curriculum-based measurement and the identification of mildly handicapped students: A research review. *Professional School Psychology, 3,* 69–85.

Smith, C. R. (1991). *Learning disabilities: The interaction of learner, task, and setting.* Needham Heights, MA: Allyn and Bacon.

Smith, F. (1992, February). Learning to read: The never-ending debate. *Phi Delta Kappan,* 431–442.

Snow, C. E., Barnes, W. S., Chandler, J., Goodman, J. F., & Hemphill, L. (1991). *Unfulfilled expectations: Home and school influences on literacy.* Cambridge, MA: Harvard University Press.

Stahl, S. A., McKenna, M. C., & Pagnucco, J. R. (1994). The effects of whole-language instruction: An update and a reappraisal. *Educational Psychologist, 29,* 175–185.

Stahl, S. A., & Miller, P. D. (1989). Whole language and language experience approaches for beginning reading: A quantitative research synthesis. *Review of Educational Research, 59,* 87–116.

Stein, M., & Osborn, J. (1993). Revising the revisions. *Remedial and Special Education, 14,* 17–18, 25.

Torgesen, J. K. (1991). Learning disabilities: Historical and conceptual issues. In B. Y. L. Wong (Ed.), *Learning about learning disabilities* (pp. 3–37). San Diego, CA: Academic Press.

Torgesen, J. K., Dahlem, W. E., & Greenstein, J. (1987). Using verbatim text recordings to enhance reading comprehension in learning disabled adolescents. *Learning Disabilities Focus, 3,* 30–38.

Uhry, J. K., & Shepherd, M. J. (1993). Segmentation/spelling instruction as part of a first-grade reading program: Effects on several measures of reading. *Reading Research Quarterly, 28,* 218–233.

Williams, J. P. (1985). The case for explicit decoding instruction. In J. Osborn, P. Wilson, & R. Anderson (Eds.), *Reading education: Foundations for a literate America* (pp. 205–213). Lexington, MA: D. C. Heath.

7 Educational Practices for Children with Reading Disability

REMEMBER Megan, James, Calvin, and Stacy, the four children we discussed in connection with our model of reading disability? The preceding chapter suggested some important broad educational implications of our model for these children and the many others like them who have been categorized as having RD. Regarding identification and assessment of reading disability, these implications included the prominence of linguistic and phonological measures (as opposed to, for example, visual-processing measures) as well as the need to set reasonably ambitious goals to keep children from becoming hopelessly mired in the "swamp" of lowered motivation, limited practice, and negative expectations. And regarding instruction, our discussion of implications focused on the necessity of combining the code-emphasis and meaning-emphasis approaches to teaching all children with RD, though with varying emphases depending upon the pattern of reading disability.

The preceding chapter forms a crucial backdrop for the present one. Nevertheless, educational planning typically requires a finer level of analysis than we employed in the previous chapter. For example, teachers frequently are sympathetic to the idea that children with RD require a combination of instructional approaches. But exactly what should be combined—and how? Answering this question is the principal focus of the present chapter. In our view, the answers to the question depend, at least in part, upon where children have gone astray in the process of reading acquisition. For instance, children who have wandered off the road to proficient reading at the earliest possible point, in the phase of visual-cue word recognition (i.e., nonalphabetic readers such as Megan), require some different instructional emphases than do children who have gone astray somewhat later, in, say, the phase of phonetic-cue word recognition (i.e., compensatory readers such as James).

Thus, in this chapter we elaborate on specific implications of our model for planning a comprehensive instructional program in reading for children with RD. In discussing these implications, we follow the approach outlined at the beginning of the previous chapter. That is, although we provide many examples of

tests, programs, and activities that teachers might use, we emphasize basic principles and guidelines rather than endorsements of particular tests or programs; and
we encourage readers to bear in mind the necessity for teacher judgment in implementing these, or any other, guidelines. Nevertheless, we intend to provide a
discussion detailed enough that the teachers of children like Megan, James,
Calvin, and Stacy will be able to use our guidelines in planning and implementing
educational programs of their own.

When we say that different patterns of reading disability require different instructional emphases, our choice of the word *emphases* is deliberate. We do not
mean that the different patterns of RD involve radically different educational programs. For instance, both nonalphabetic and compensatory readers benefit from
instruction in basic word-recognition skills. Thus, some of the same instructional
techniques and activities are appropriate for both of these patterns of reading disability, and, in some cases, nonalphabetic and compensatory readers may be
grouped together for instruction. On the other hand, what differentiates nonalphabetic from compensatory readers in our model is that the latter have achieved
alphabetic insight and the ability to use phonetic cues in word recognition,
whereas the former have not. Instructionally, then, nonalphabetic readers require
an emphasis on activities that will lead them toward the attainment of alphabetic
insight. But as compensatory readers already have this insight they require more
of an emphasis on achieving full *accuracy* in word recognition. In each case,
somewhat different emphases are necessary to help children find their way back
onto the road to proficient reading. Of course, toward this end, all children with
reading disability, whatever the pattern, also need a number of other benefits,
such as engagement in meaningful reading activities, instruction in comprehension, and exposure to a wide variety of texts.

We must acknowledge that many of the activities and programs used as examples in this chapter were developed for children, sometimes rather young children. Therefore, some activities may not be appropriate for older, but severely impaired, readers. For example, a fifteen-year-old who is a nonalphabetic reader may
respond with something less than delight to alphabet books as a means of learning letter-sound correspondences. However, virtually all of the activities discussed
here can be adapted in such a way as to be less juvenile for older students, yet nevertheless accomplish the desired purposes.

In addition, we should emphasize that any instructional program in reading
must be part of a much broader program for developing literacy, including skills
in areas such as spelling and written expression. As we pointed out in the first
chapter of this book, we have chosen to focus specifically on reading, because the
research literatures on reading acquisition, reading disability, and reading instruction are vast. However, all of these literacy skills are linked to one another and
must therefore be integrated in any instructional program.

We have organized this chapter thematically, with the first four major sections
corresponding to four broad skill areas that must be considered in planning an
instructional program in reading: phonological-processing skills, word-recogni-

tion skills, reading in context, and reading comprehension. With reference to the children described in Chapter 5, we discuss specific assessment and instructional techniques for each of these four areas, which may receive varying kinds of emphases depending upon the pattern of reading disability. The fifth and final section of the chapter contains sample instructional plans for Megan, James, Calvin, and Stacy.

Phonological-Processing Skills

In previous chapters, we reviewed research showing that progress in reading acquisition is linked to a family of phonological-processing skills and that children with RD generally are deficient in these kinds of skills. One such skill, phonological awareness, has received a tremendous amount of attention from researchers and, to date, is the only phonological-processing skill for which there is evidence of trainability and transfer to reading. Thus, in this section, we will focus primarily on assessment of and instruction in phonological awareness. First, however, we would like to say a few words about one other important phonological-processing skill: naming speed.

Naming Speed

Naming-speed tasks are used to measure phonological processes in lexical access—that is, the ability to access phonological information, such as letters and words, quickly and easily in long-term memory (Torgesen, Wagner, & Rashotte, 1994). Naming speed, like phonological awareness, is a strong predictor of reading achievement; it is also a skill in which some children with RD appear to be deficient (Blachman, 1994; Torgesen et al., 1994; Wolf, 1991). Naming-speed deficiencies can affect reading acquisition in a number of ways. For instance, difficulty in rapidly accessing letter sounds stored in memory may impair decoding skills. In addition, even when decoding skills are accurate, if words cannot be quickly accessed in memory, automatization of decoding may be adversely affected. Thus, naming-speed deficiencies may be found in nonalphabetic, compensatory, and nonautomatic readers.

In experiments, researchers have often measured naming speed by having children name, as rapidly as possible, a series of thirty to fifty items that are printed on a page. These items can be pictures of objects, colors, numbers (single digits), or letters. A test that has been widely used experimentally is the Rapid Automatic Naming Test (Denckla & Rudel, 1976). Unfortunately, we know of no commercially published or standardized test of serial naming speed. Also, we must emphasize that there is no evidence that naming speed itself can be trained. As Blachman (1994) points out, whereas children with phonological-awareness deficits can readily be helped, there is currently little hard evidence about how best to help children with naming-speed deficits. However, later in this chapter, we will offer some instructional suggestions regarding word-recognition skills, such as automatization of word recognition, that may be affected by naming-speed problems.

Phonological Awareness

A rudimentary level of phonological awareness is a crucial prerequisite for developing word-recognition skills in an alphabetic language such as English. Nonalphabetic readers are especially likely to lack phonological awareness and to benefit from activities that develop this awareness. By contrast, both nonautomatic and delayed readers, who have acquired accurate word-recognition skills, are unlikely to require instruction aimed at phonological awareness.

Compensatory readers may or may not need training in phonological awareness. Because they have achieved alphabetic insight, all compensatory readers must have at least a rudimentary level of phonological awareness. Nevertheless, some compensatory readers might benefit from further development in this area. On the one hand, for example, a compensatory reader who consistently makes use of initial and final consonant sounds in trying to recognize words, but who cannot decode the other parts of most words, may lack phoneme-segmentation ability and thus benefit from activities to develop this ability. On the other hand, a compensatory reader with somewhat more sophisticated decoding skills may already have sufficient phonological awareness for learning to decode and therefore may not require phonological-awareness training.

Assessment of Phonological Awareness. Considering the prominence of phonological awareness as an area of research, commercially published tests of phonological awareness are surprisingly scarce. Most researchers either have developed their own tests of phonological awareness or have adapted or borrowed measures used by other researchers. These measures are quite adequate for research purposes, but they are not standardized or normed as are, for instance, tests of reading achievement. However, there are signs that this situation may be changing, such as the recent publication of the *Test of Phonological Awareness,* or TOPA (Torgesen & Bryant, 1994a). An older commercially published measure of phonological awareness is the *Lindamood Auditory Conceptualization Test* (Lindamood & Lindamood, 1979).

Some practitioners may wish to develop their own informal measures of phonological awareness. Following are some general guidelines, but readers may also consult sources such as Adams (1990), Blachman (1989), and Yopp (1988) for further information.

In testing phonological awareness, practitioners need to keep several points in mind. First, phonological-awareness tasks involve *spoken,* not written, words; thus, they generally do not require children to do actual reading or writing. Second, phonological-awareness tasks vary considerably in level of difficulty. The easier tasks appear to measure the kind of rudimentary awareness that is a prerequisite for learning to read an alphabetic language, whereas skill on the harder tasks may be at least partly a consequence, not just a cause, of learning to read (Stanovich, 1992). Third, before the testing begins, practitioners should run through examples of all these tasks with children, including feedback, in order to be sure that the children understand what they are expected to do. Some phonological-awareness tasks that may be useful in assessment are listed in Table 7.1.

Among the easiest phonological-awareness tasks are those involving rhyming (e.g., the child is asked to name words that rhyme with *bean*) and alliteration (e.g., the child is asked to name words that begin with the same sound as *bean*). Oddity or sound-categorization tasks (Bradley & Bryant, 1985) that do not require children to generate their own responses can also be used to test rhyming

TABLE 7.1 Examples of Phonological-Awareness Tasks

Phonological-Awareness Task	*Examples*
Rhyming	Children name as many words as they can that rhyme with *coat* (rhyme-generation task).
	Children tell which of the following words does not go with the others: *goat, boat, cup, coat* (sound-categorization task).
Alliteration	Children name as many words as they can that begin with the same sound as *moon* (generation task).
	Children tell which of the following words does not go with the others: *knife, moon, mud, money* (sound-categorization task).
Phoneme segmentation	Children segment the word *sun* into phonemes, saying the word slowly and putting down a block for each of the 3 sounds in the word: /s/, /u/, /n/.
	Children segment the word *lamp* into phonemes, saying the word slowly and putting down a block for each of the 4 sounds in the word: /l/, /a/, /m/, /p/.
Phoneme counting	Children count the number of sounds in the word *ship* (i.e., 3).
Phoneme blending	Children listen to the teacher say the sounds /f/, /i/, /sh/; children repeat the sounds; children blend the sounds to form the word *fish*.
Phoneme deletion	Children are told to "say *boat*; now say *boat* without the /b/" (i.e., *oat*).
	Children are told to "say *feet*; now say *feet* without the /t/" (i.e., *fee*).
	Children are told to "say *snail*; now say *snail* without the /n/" (i.e., *sail*).

and alliteration. For example, for rhyming, a child might be asked to select the word that "does not go with the others" from the following list spoken by the examiner: *bean, fall, green, mean.*

Tasks involving rhyming and alliteration can be seen as measures of onset-rime awareness rather than as measures tapping full awareness of phonemes. As we discussed in Chapter 4, onsets and rimes are intrasyllabic units—that is, units intermediate in size between syllables and phonemes. The onset of a word is the initial consonant or consonant cluster, whereas the rime consists of the vowel and any final consonants. Thus, in a word such as *black,* the letters *bl* represent the onset and the letters *ack* represent the rime. Some words (e.g., *ate, ear*) have no onset and consist only of a rime. Onset-rime awareness is easier for young children to achieve than is phonological awareness (Adams, 1990; Treiman, 1992).

Other, more difficult tasks that require a deeper awareness of phonemes also may be useful in assessment. These tasks include phoneme segmentation (e.g., the child is asked to say the word *lake* slowly and to put down a block or other counter for each sound in the word); phoneme counting (e.g., the child is asked to tell the number of sounds in the word *lake*); phoneme blending (e.g., the examiner says the separate sounds in the word *lake* and the child must blend them to form the word); and phoneme deletion (e.g., the child is asked to say *lake* without the /k/). An example of a test involving phoneme deletion is the *Test of Auditory Analysis Skills* (see Rosner, 1979).

How should one interpret performance on these tasks? Most children can do rhyming and alliteration tasks in kindergarten, or at about the age of five, if not before then. In fact, even some children as young as three can do certain kinds of rhyming or alliteration tasks (Maclean, Bryant, & Bradley, 1987). Phoneme counting appears to be acquired by the majority of children—about 70 percent— by the end of first grade, or at about age six (Mann, 1991). Easier phoneme-deletion tasks, such as those requiring children to delete an initial phoneme, may be accomplished by some kindergartners (Treiman, 1992); however, harder phoneme deletion tasks, such as those requiring children to delete a phoneme that is not initial or final (e.g., "say *snail* without the /n/"), may be too difficult even for second-graders (Rosner, 1979).

Megan, the third-grade nonalphabetic reader we described in Chapter 5, has difficulty in listening for initial consonant sounds (i.e., alliteration). Thus, she lacks even this very rudimentary level of phonological awareness, and phoneme-counting or phoneme-segmentation tasks probably would be impossible for her to accomplish without training. By contrast, James, our example of a compensatory reader, can decode many one-syllable words and functions at a second-grade level in reading. Thus, James might perform adequately on many tests of phonological awareness, especially those involving rhyming, alliteration, easy phoneme deletion, and even phoneme counting.

Finally, observations of children's invented spelling, which now is widely used in many schools in the beginning elementary grades, can be helpful in gauging children's phonological awareness. Mann, Tobin, and Wilson (1987) developed a system for scoring kindergartners' invented spellings of a list of dictated words.

For example, for the word *name*, a conventionally correct spelling merited the highest score of four points; a spelling that captured the entire phonological structure of the word but was not conventionally correct (e.g., *nam*) merited three points; a spelling that captured part of the phonological structure of the word (e.g., *na* or *nme*) was awarded two points; and spelling of only the initial phoneme (e.g., *n* for *name*) merited one point. Scores on the test of invented spelling predicted first-grade reading achievement and correlated with a measure of phonological-processing skill.

Measures involving invented spelling confound letter-sound knowledge with phonological awareness. For instance, does the child who writes *na* for *name* lack awareness of the last phoneme in the word, or lack memory for the letter that represents the sound /m/? Thus, an important adjunct to interpreting children's invented spelling involves measures of letter-sound knowledge. Some standardized test batteries for reading (e.g., lower levels of the *Stanford Diagnostic Reading Test*; see Karlsen, Madden, & Gardner, 1985) contain subtests that measure letter-sound knowledge.

However, most standardized tests of letter knowledge measure letter recognition (e.g., selecting from an array of letters one named by the examiner) or letter identification (e.g., naming a letter shown by the examiner). These kinds of measures do not necessarily tap knowledge of letter *sounds*. Also, they may not tap the kind of memory for letters that is required in order to write a letter from memory and appears to be critical to the acquisition of word-recognition skills (Ehri & Sweet, 1991). Thus, informal tests of memory for letters are a useful supplement to many standardized tests. For example, a child might be asked to write the letter that says the sound /s/, the letter that says the sound /m/, and so forth.

Instruction to Develop Phonological Awareness. To begin on a cautionary note, we should acknowledge that not all investigators have been equally sanguine about the potential benefits of phonological-awareness training. For example, Wagner et al. (1994) performed an extensive longitudinal study of the phonological-processing and reading skills of a group of regular-classroom youngsters, from kindergarten through second grade. Although this study confirmed the causal role of phonological-processing skills (including phonological awareness) in early reading achievement, and specifically in learning to decode words, the evidence also suggested that individual differences in phonological processing were quite stable over the two-year time span of the study. Wagner et al. suggest that this stability may make it difficult to alter phonological-processing skills through training. They also point to the mixed results of studies attempting to demonstrate the efficacy of phonological-awareness training by itself—that is, apart from formal reading instruction—in improving reading achievement. (Also see Crowder & Wagner, 1991.)

Note, however, that Wagner et al. (1994) did not actually attempt to alter children's phonological awareness through training. A number of studies have indicated that, especially when combined with formal reading instruction (e.g., instruction in letter-sound correspondences), phonological-awareness training can benefit poor readers, including children categorized as having reading disability (Blachman, 1989, 1994; Bradley, 1987; Bradley & Bryant, 1983, 1985). As we discussed in Chapter 5, *both* letter knowledge and phonological awareness appear to be necessary in order for children to achieve alphabetic insight; they also appear to work together in a complementary way (Byrne, 1992). Thus, it is not surprising that phonological-awareness training would be more effective in improving reading achievement when it is combined with formal reading instruction (see, for instance, Hatcher, Hulme, Ellis, 1994).

We must acknowledge that, even among the many phonological-awareness training studies in which trained groups significantly outperform control groups, there is often a significant percentage of children in the trained groups who fail to respond, or at least fail to respond dramatically, to training. For example, Torgesen et al. (1994) note that, in their training studies with at-risk youngsters, approximately 30 percent of the children showed little or no improvement in phonological awareness after training, which ranged in length from eight to twelve weeks. On the other hand, about 70 percent of youngsters *did* respond to training. Blachman (1994) suggests that the longer and more intensive the intervention—comprising formal reading instruction as well as phonological-awareness training—the fewer the children who become "treatment resisters."

Clearly, phonological-awareness training is not a magic wand to make reading disability vanish in a puff of smoke. Children can be expected to vary considerably in their responses to this training. Nevertheless, in our opinion, phonological-awareness training is warranted for children with RD who lack phonological awareness—as one part of a broader program of formal reading instruction. Next, we describe some examples of activities for training phonological awareness. Additional examples of such training, and of the integration of phonological-awareness training with reading instruction, may be found in Adams (1990), Blachman (1987, 1989), Engelmann (1969), Liberman, Shankweiler, and Liberman (1989), and Uhry and Shepherd (1993). Readers also may wish to examine two commercially published programs for training phonological awareness: *Phonological Awareness Training for Reading* (Torgesen & Bryant, 1994b) and *Auditory Discrimination in Depth* (Lindamood & Lindamood, 1975).

Rhyming and alliteration may be developed, among other ways, by reading poetry and nursery rhymes to children, by playing word games, and by singing songs. Some investigators (e.g., Treiman, 1992) have also made use of puppetry in the testing and training of phonological awareness, especially with very young children. For instance, children might be told that the puppet likes only words that rhyme with *take*. Children must then decide whether the puppet will like the words *shake, snake, bike,* and so on. In addition, rhyming activities can be integrated with formal reading instruction by using word families consistent with the words that children can rhyme. Phonological-awareness training and reading instruction might begin at this level with Megan, who appears to have very low phonological-awareness skills. Eventually, however, children like Megan should be taught to analyze rhyming and other words at the phoneme level, because this level of awareness is required for decoding an alphabetic language.

A phoneme-level technique that eventually might be used with Megan is D. B. Elkonin's (1973) phoneme-segmentation activity. In this procedure, children are given a picture—for instance, a picture of the sun—along with blocks to represent the sounds in the pictured word. Children are taught to say the word slowly and, as they do so, to put down a block every time they hear another sound. Eventually, they are taught to use blocks of different colors, one for consonants and another for vowels. Finally, letters are attached to the blocks so that the children may spell the word as they segment it.

In these early phonological-awareness, spelling, and decoding activities, some types of words are easier for children than are others (Liberman et al., 1989). Specifically, words that begin with a fricative, liquid, or nasal consonant—such as *s*, *f*, or *m*—are easier for children than are words that begin with a stop consonant—such as *b*, *g*, or *c*. Another way of putting it is that words beginning with sounds that can be articulated continuously are easier than words beginning with sounds that cannot be articulated continuously. Thus, words like *sat* and *mat* are easier than *bat* or *cat*.

Some children may benefit from encouragement in the use of sensory cues to develop phonological awareness. For instance, children who have difficulty deciding whether or not *mouse* and *night* start with the same sound might be encouraged to watch the teacher's lips as he or she says the word, or to think about how the word "feels" as they say the word themselves. In a program developed by Lindamood and Lindamood (1975), Auditory Discrimination in Depth, students are taught to use sensory cues in a highly systematic way to aid in the development of phonological awareness. For example, using mirrors to observe their own speech, children learn to categorize the sounds /b/ and /p/ as "lip poppers" because of the way the lips are moved in making these sounds. The sound /p/ is further categorized as the "quiet" (i.e., unvoiced) lip popper.

In a small clinical study, Alexander, Andersen, Heilman, Voeller, and Torgesen (1991) found the Lindamood program to be very successful in improving the phonological-awareness and decoding skills of a group of children with reading disability, all of whom began the training program with severe word-recognition deficits. However, these results must be regarded with caution, because the sample was small—ten children—and no control group was used. Alexander et al. are now in the process of trying to replicate their initial findings with a much larger, controlled study.

Another pair of investigators (Kennedy & Backman, 1993) also used the Lindamood program with ten very poor readers categorized as having LD. In this study, a second group of poor readers who were not exposed to the Lindamood program served as controls. Both groups of children received the same comprehensive, code-emphasis remedial program in reading and spelling. The results indicated that the children who underwent the Lindamood program made greater gains in phonological awareness and in the use of phonetic spelling strategies than did the second group of children. However, these differences did not translate into superior performance on standardized reading and spelling tests for the Lindamood group.

We can summarize thus far by saying that, in training children's phonological awareness, teachers may find it helpful to encourage children to make use of sensory cues. Still uncertain, however, is whether more intensive and systematic teaching about sensory cues—as in the Lindamood program—benefits reading and spelling achievement.

Another approach that might be tried with youngsters who have severe difficulties with phonological awareness—including, perhaps, Megan—involves the initial use of onsets and rimes, rather than phonemes, as units. In this approach (e.g., Treiman, 1992), consonant blends—like *st, br, cl,* and so forth—would initially be learned as units, in much the same way that consonant digraphs such as *sh* would be learned. Similarly, common rimes, such as *ack, ick,* and *ake,* would initially be learned as units (i.e., like word families, as in our previous discussion of rhyming words). If these onsets and rimes were carefully selected, children would be able to read a reasonable variety of simple words, with many fewer demands on their abilities to blend and to segment phonemes. Later, they would learn to analyze onsets and rimes into their constituent phonemes.

Word-Recognition Skills

Nonalphabetic, compensatory, and nonautomatic readers all are deficient in basic word-recognition skills, though in varying ways. Nonalphabetic readers like Megan have not achieved alphabetic insight and must recognize words on a visual basis. In short, they have essentially *no* decoding skills at all. Nonalphabetic readers also are unlikely to amass a large sight vocabulary; because they must recognize words on a visual basis, it becomes increasingly difficult for them to find a salient visual cue for each new word. Thus, their level of word recognition is extremely limited.

Compensatory readers have achieved alphabetic insight but lack full accuracy in word recognition. They do not make use of all the letter information in words, although their ability to use partial phonetic cues in word recognition may allow them to acquire a large sight vocabulary. Thus, these youngsters exhibit a considerable range of reading skill. At one end of the spectrum, a compensatory reader who can decode only one-syllable short *a* words, and who has a limited sight vocabulary, functions at a very low reading level. In between, a compensatory reader like James, who can decode many one-syllable words, functions at a somewhat higher level. And at the opposite end of the spectrum, other compensatory readers, such as some of the college students studied by Bruck (1990), may have even higher levels of word-recognition skill.

Unlike compensatory readers, nonautomatic readers such as Calvin have accurate word-recognition skills relative to other children of their age, at least according to commonly used educational measures. However, nonautomatic readers are deficient on measures involving speed and fluency of word recognition. Some nonautomatic readers may demonstrate highly disfluent reading of nearly all words, whereas other nonautomatic readers may have automatic recognition of short or very common words but not of longer or less common words. Thus, like compensatory readers, nonautomatic readers may exhibit a range of reading skill.

Only delayed readers have achieved accurate and automatic word-recognition skills according to conventional educational measures. However, we should point out that delayed readers, like normally achieving readers, must continue to develop knowledge of word *meanings*. This knowledge is critical to academic success—especially in content areas such as science or history. Furthermore, as we discussed in the previous chapter, most delayed readers probably continue to require instruction in basic skills related to spelling and written expression.

In the following sections, we discuss four areas that are important in teaching word-recognition skills: assessment of word-recognition skills; helping children to achieve alphabetic insight; helping children to develop accurate word-recognition skills; and helping children to develop automatic word recognition.

Assessment of Word-Recognition Skills

A multitude of standardized tests may be used for measuring word-recognition skills, in the areas of both decoding and sight vocabulary. Two examples of standardized diagnostic test batteries with subtests measuring word recognition, both of which have good reliability and validity, are the *Stanford Diagnostic Reading Test* (Karlsen, Madden, & Gardner, 1985) and the *Woodcock Reading Mastery Tests—Revised* (Woodcock, 1987). Of course, for instructional planning, teachers may also need to supplement standardized testing with informal and criterion-referenced measures.

In assessing children's word recognition, practitioners should bear in mind that decoding, or phonological-reading, skills are the central problem area for youngsters with RD. In other words, although both sight vocabulary and decoding should be addressed instructionally, a youngster with deficient decoding skills and an adequate sight vocabulary is more worrisome than is a youngster with adequate decoding skills and a deficient sight vocabulary (Byrne, Freebody, & Gates, 1992).

Measuring automatization of word recognition has proven to be somewhat problematic for researchers, as we discussed in Chapter 4. In any case, the laboratory measures of automatization typically employed by researchers are not available or feasible for use in educational settings. For teachers, the most practical—though admittedly rough—indicators of automatization consist of standardized tests of word-recognition speed (e.g., upper levels of the *Stanford Diagnostic Reading Test;* see Karlsen et al., 1985) and observations of oral reading fluency. Calvin, who could decode accurately most words in his spoken vocabulary but demonstrated slow, disfluent oral reading when reading in context, is a typical nonautomatic reader.

Helping Children to Achieve Alphabetic Insight

Whereas compensatory, nonautomatic, and delayed readers have already achieved alphabetic insight, nonalphabetic readers like Megan are still crucially in need of this insight. Thus, in order to get nonalphabetic readers back onto the road to proficient reading, instruction must promote alphabetic insight—as part of a well-rounded reading program that also includes ample reading of texts, development of comprehension, and teaching of sight vocabulary. In turn, the achievement of alphabetic insight depends both on phonological awareness, which we have already discussed, and on letter-sound knowledge, which we discuss next.

Developing Letter-Sound Knowledge. Alphabet books are an appealing way to develop letter-sound knowledge and, because a wide range of such books is available, may be effective even with children as old as ten or eleven. (See Chaney, 1993, for some suggestions, as well as for an annotated bibliography.) Other techniques useful for developing letter-sound knowledge involve multisensory activities in which children trace and say a letter repeatedly, along with a "key word" to help them remember the letter sound. For example, in Slingerland's (1976) program, children learn a letter such as *s* by repeatedly writing the letter in the air, simultaneously saying the letter name, then its key word, and finally its sound: *s, sun, /s/*. Also helpful are pictorial displays of letters that provide mnemonic cues for the letter sound—for instance, a picture of a snake in the shape of an *s* (Adams, 1990). Finally, the use of invented spelling may develop children's memory for letters, by providing repeated practice in the of linking of letters and sounds.

We have stressed the importance of memory for letters and letter sounds in children's acquisition of word-recognition skills. However, this idea should not be interpreted to mean that letter-sound knowledge must be flawless before children actually are allowed to read texts. Rather, these isolated letter-sound activities should be only one small part of a total reading program, in which the texts that are used provide practice with the letters that the children have been learning.

In addition to learning letter-sound relationships and developing phonological awareness, children need to be encouraged to apply these skills in reading words. What must be conveyed to children is the idea that the letters in written words roughly map onto sounds in spoken words; therefore, reading a word requires close attention to the sequence of letters in the word. Instructional techniques that convey the opposite message—for instance, that paying attention to the letters in words is unimportant—would be disastrous for nonalphabetic readers as well as for other children with reading disability. In our view, as we discussed in the previous chapter, some of the techniques recommended by certain whole-language theorists convey this erroneous message. For example, if children repeatedly are encouraged to guess at words based on contextual cues, rather than to look closely at the letters in words to try to decode them, they will be misled about what is necessary for word recognition.

Furthermore, even if they have letter-sound knowledge and phonological awareness, they may fail to put these skills into practice in the actual reading of words.

Fortunately, there are several reading programs that do communicate the appropriate message about what is required for reading words, without excessive belaboring of phonic rules or an exclusive focus on word recognition. One example is provided by Beth Slingerland (1976). In Slingerland's program, children are encouraged to take a highly systematic approach to word recognition, whether they are reading words in isolation or encountering an unfamiliar word in context. First, they "unlock" (i.e., determine) the vowel sound, usually the most difficult part of the word, and then they decode the word, using their knowledge about letter-sound relationships, from left to right. Guessing at words is strongly discouraged. Rather, the message communicated to children is that written English involves a code that can be systematically deciphered. (Keep in mind that these word-recognition activities form only one part of a total reading program that also entails considerable reading of texts and the development of comprehension.) Reading Recovery (Clay, 1985) is another example of a program that integrates instruction in basic word-recognition skills and in phonological awareness with the reading of meaningful texts and with writing activities.

Helping Children to Acquire Accurate Word-Recognition Skills

Both nonalphabetic and compensatory readers need an emphasis on developing accurate word-recognition skills. For compensatory readers like James, who have already achieved alphabetic insight, this emphasis is the major one required for helping them to get back onto the road to proficient reading. The skills that these children must acquire in order to develop accurate word recognition include the ability to make full use of the phonological information in a word, orthographic and word-specific knowledge, and recognition of longer, more sophisticated words. We will deal with each of these areas in turn.

Using Phonological Information in Words. Compensatory readers who routinely use only initial and final letters to recognize words, thus ignoring the middle of the word, or who make errors such as reading *cap* for *clap* and *mit* for *mint,* are not making full use of the phonological information in words. Such youngsters may need to learn letter-sound relationships; they may also benefit from phonological-awareness training. In addition, of course, these children need to be encouraged to pay close attention to the sequence of letters in words.

One technique that may be helpful for children who fail to use all of the phonological information in words is to write down their mispronunciation of a word and to compare it to the word being read. For example, for the child who reads *cap* for *clap,* the teacher might write down the word *cap,* saying, "This is what you said." Then, placing the word *cap* next to the word *clap*, the teacher encourages the child to compare the two words, to notice the letter *l* in the word *clap*, and to try to read the word *clap* again.

Acquiring Orthographic and Word-Specific Knowledge. Orthographic knowledge is knowledge about spelling patterns that are common in English. For instance, in most English words, there is no one-to-one correspondence between letters and sounds; rather, combinations of letters—orthographic units—frequently map onto given sounds. Table 7.2 lists some examples of common orthographic units involving vowels, sounds that the orthographic units map onto, and examples of words containing the units. For example, an orthographic unit such as *ai* usually maps onto the long *a* sound, as in *rain* and *paid*. Furthermore, a particular orthographic unit may map onto more than one sound. For instance, the unit *ow* maps onto the long *o* in *snow* but also onto the sound /ow/ in *cow*.

In the case of units like *ow* that have more than one sound, often there is no "rule" or generalization that can be used to determine which sound the unit will have in a specific word. Rather, readers need to acquire word-specific knowledge in order to pronounce *snow* to rhyme with *slow* rather than with *now*. Word-specific knowledge also is needed for differentiating common homophones, such as *two*, *to*, and *too*.

To teach common orthographic units, practitioners can use the approach employed in many code-emphasis programs, such as those of Gillingham and Stillman (1970), Traub and Bloom (1992), and Slingerland (1976). In this approach, orthographic units are taught in the same way that sounds for single letters, such as *m* or *t*, would be taught. For instance, children might learn *ai* as a unit by using tracing activities and a "key word" such as *rain*. When they are fa-

TABLE 7.2 Examples of Orthographic Units

Orthographic Unit	Sound(s)	Examples of Words
ai	long *a*	*rain, train, pail, aid, wait, chain*
ay	long *a*	*may, pay, play, say, stay, gray, hay, tray*
augh	/aw/	*taught, caught, daughter*
igh	long *i*	*sigh, light, bright, fright, sight, thigh*
ie	long *i*	*pie, tie, tried, flies*
	long *e*	*piece, chief, believe*
oa	long *o*	*boat, oak, groan, road*
ow	long *o*	*slow, own, flown*
	/ow/	*cow, clown, frown, crowd*
ee	long *e*	*tree, eel, creek, speed*
ea	long *e*	*seat, east, bead, tea*
	short *e*	*head, bread, instead*
	long *a*	*break, steak*
eigh	long *a*	*sleigh, eight, freight*

miliar with the orthographic unit in isolation, children would be taught to look for the unit embedded within words; for example, they might be given a list of words such as *train, pail,* and *aid,* and then be asked to circle and pronounce the *ai* units. Finally, they would be asked to decode entire words.

For orthographic units with multiple pronunciations, such as *ow,* many code-emphasis programs teach children to try more than one sound to see which one makes a "real" word, or to use contextual cues to determine the correct pronunciation. These strategies are adequate for making an initial pass at an unfamiliar word, especially in context; however, in order to acquire fully accurate recognition of these words, in or out of context, children must develop word-specific knowledge (as discussed earlier). To develop word-specific knowledge, whole-word tracing activities, such as those described by Fernald (1943), or the repeated use of the words in writing activities, such as those described by Clay (1985), may be helpful. In addition, for very common words, including common homophones, mnemonic strategies may be taught; see Traub and Bloom (1992) for some suggestions.

Recognizing Longer Words. Children must also acquire certain skills necessary for reading the longer, more sophisticated words that increasingly are encountered from the middle elementary grades onward. For instance, structural analysis involves analyzing long words for meaningful units, such as prefixes (e.g., *un, re,* and *dis*); suffixes (e.g., *tion, ment,* and *ous*); and root words (e.g., *danger* in the word *endangered*). A number of programs are available for teaching the skills involved in structural analysis (e.g., Rule, 1984).

When children encounter longer, more sophisticated words, vocabulary knowledge also begins to play an important role in decoding (Chall et al., 1990; Snow, Barnes, Chandler, Goodman, & Hemphill, 1991). For example, many simple one-syllable words such as *tarn* (a small mountain lake) and *drake* (a male duck), can be decoded accurately even if one has never heard the words and does not know their meaning. However, many multisyllabic words, such as *category* and *intrepid,* are very difficult to decode accurately if one lacks familiarity with the words as they are spoken. Thus, by this point, if not earlier, decoding instruction must be combined with an increased emphasis on instruction in word meanings. Teaching structural analysis is one way to increase students' knowledge of word meanings (White, Power, & White, 1989; White, Sowell, & Yanagihara, 1989).

Phonic Generalizations. Many code-emphasis programs teach word-recognition skills through the use of phonic rules or generalizations. Examples of phonic generalizations include the closed syllable rule (i.e., when a syllable has only one vowel and ends in a consonant, the vowel sound is usually short); the silent-e rule (i.e., when a syllable ends in a vowel-consonant-e pattern, the vowel sound is usually long and the *e* is silent); and rules for syllabicating multisyllable words (e.g., when a word contains a vowel-consonant-consonant-vowel pattern, the word is generally divided between the two consonants).

As we have discussed, it clearly is possible to go overboard in teaching phonic rules. But it's also true that, because English does not involve a simple one-to-one correspondence between letters and sounds, phonic generalizations can sensitize children to common letter patterns in English, such as the silent-e pattern, and can provide some strategies for children to use in recognizing unfamiliar words. For instance, a youngster like James, who appears to have few strategies for recognizing long words, might benefit from learning three or four generalizations for syllabicating multisyllable words. Following are some brief guidelines for teaching phonic generalizations. (See Adams, 1990, and Anderson et al., 1985, for further discussion.)

First, teach generalizations in the spirit of providing children with helpful tools for recognizing unfamiliar words; they should not be the overriding emphasis of the program. Second, teach a small number of the most useful generalizations. For example, generalizations such as the closed syllable rule and the silent-e rule do apply to many common words and would seem to provide useful strategies for children who cannot yet recognize these kinds of words. However, long-winded rules that apply to relatively few words are best avoided. Third, emphasize application rather than verbalization of the rule. For instance, James's ability to apply syllabication rules in decoding multisyllable words is much more important than is his ability to recite these rules to the teacher. And fourth, keep in mind that once children can read the kinds of words to which the rules apply, the rules themselves become superfluous and no longer need attention in an instructional program.

Helping Children to Develop Automatic Word Recognition

As we have discussed, nonalphabetic, compensatory, and nonautomatic readers all need to develop automatic word-recognition skills. For nonautomatic readers, whose word-recognition skills already are accurate, automatization needs particular emphasis—but, again, only as one part of a broader program of reading instruction.

At present, unfortunately, less is known about how to develop automatic word recognition than about how to develop accurate word recognition. As noted earlier in this chapter, some children with RD appear to have deficits in naming speed, a phonological process that has been associated with the development of automatic word recognition. Yet, at least for now, there is no evidence that naming speed can be trained. Furthermore, some contemporary cognitive theories of reading—in particular, the instance-based theories that we mentioned in Chapter 4—view speed of word recognition merely as a by-product of high-quality mental representations of specific words in memory. According to this approach, speed of word recognition is not something that can or should be trained. Thus, our instructional suggestions in this section must be regarded more tentatively than those in the previous one.

Nevertheless, some investigators have studied the development of automatic processes (e.g., Frederiksen et al., 1983; Schneider, 1984) and have made suggestions for promoting automatization in a number of areas, including reading. Active participation in a task (as opposed to passive observation), repeated trials of a task, and mild speed pressure all may be helpful in promoting automatization. One technique that utilizes these suggestions involves speed drills on isolated words. Children are encouraged to read the words on the drills as rapidly as they can without greatly sacrificing accuracy. Like speed drills on letter sounds, which we discussed previously, speed drills on words should be brief (e.g., one minute long); should involve types of words already familiar to children (e.g., consonant-vowel-consonant words with short *a*); and should entail comparisons with children's own previous performance, not comparisons across children. Words may be presented on flash cards or listed on a sheet of paper (see, e.g., Gallistel, Fischer, & Blackburn, 1977).

For James, who can decode many one-syllable words, speed drills might involve a familiar category of one-syllable words, such as short vowel words. For Calvin, who can decode multisyllable words, more difficult words might be used on speed drills. For either boy, separate speed drills consisting of sight vocabulary, selected from an appropriate source (e.g., for Calvin, a content-area text), also could be used. The number of words read correctly in one minute for each speed drill would be determined, with the resulting scores recorded over time to show progress. These speed drills would consume only a few minutes of instructional time each day.

In these tasks, the goal should involve a *reasonable* level of accuracy, not perfect accuracy. For example, on a speed drill, Calvin may encounter a difficult word and skip it or occasionally make an error on a word; but if perfect accuracy were demanded, he and other children like him might have great difficulty developing automatization.

Computer programs for improving automatization of word recognition also have been developed. For example, Jones, Torgesen, and Sexton (1987) used a computer program called *Hint and Hunt* for fifteen minutes a day over a ten-week training period with a group of poor readers categorized as learning disabled. The *Hint* portion of the program emphasized accuracy of decoding a set of one-syllable, phonetically regular words, whereas the *Hunt* portion emphasized speed. Jones et al. found the program to be effective in improving the children's speed and accuracy of reading not only the words in the program but also unpracticed, phonetically similar words.

Another technique for developing automatization involves repeated readings of familiar material (Adams, 1990). In repeated readings, students read short texts repeatedly until a predetermined level of accuracy and fluency has been reached. Repeated readings are more effective if the texts share many of the same words rather than if they use very different words (Rashotte & Torgesen, 1985). Some variations on the repeated-readings technique include imitative reading, in which the teacher reads the passage first, modeling good expression and fluency, and the student rereads it; paired reading, in which students take turns reading in pairs and keep track of each other's accuracy and speed; and the use of audio support, in which a student reads along with a taped version of the passage (Gelzheiser & Clark, 1991).

Investigators interested in automatization have noted the importance of motivation to the development of this skill. As Schneider (1984) points out, there is little that could be considered intrinsically motivating about automatization training involving isolated skills, such as speed drills. For these kinds of tasks, motivation may need to be external—a matter of trying to "beat" one's previous score, playing computer games, and so on. However, in a broader sense, motivation for persisting on isolated-skills tasks also comes from an understanding of the point of these tasks and from the desire to learn to read. In other words, if automatization training is only one part of a much broader program of reading instruction in which students also are engaged in more meaningful and intrinsically enjoyable activities, such as reading interesting texts, they may have more motivation for automatization training.

Finally, for investigators with instance-based theories of reading, rapid and effortless word recognition is a function of having high-quality mental representations of words. Spelling has been suggested as a good measure of the quality of a word's mental representation in memory (Perfetti, 1992). That is, in order to spell a given word correctly, reliably, and with little effort, one must have a high-quality mental representation of that word. In this view, activities that promote spelling skill—in this case, conventional spelling as opposed to invented spelling—might be expected to promote automatization of word recognition.

Other authorities (e.g., Adams, 1990), too, have maintained that the development of spelling skill is an important part of an instructional program in reading. Spelling skill may be developed not only by direct instruction in spelling but also, as we discussed in Chapter 4, through exposure to text. Thus, repeated readings of text might promote automatic word recognition not so much because they facilitate a generic type of automatic processing but because they facilitate the development of high-quality mental representations of specific words.

The preceding discussion provides yet another example of how particular instructional activities may be more beneficial during one phase of development than during another. As we have discussed, activities involving invented spelling may be very beneficial in developing phonological awareness and letter-sound knowledge. However, for youngsters who are beyond the earliest phases of reading acquisition—specifically, for those who have generally accurate word recognition but who need to develop more automatic word recognition—it appears that activities involving conventional rather than invented spelling are most helpful.

A program for Calvin should include speed drills and computer games for developing automatization on isolated words, activities to develop conventional spelling skill, and, especially, reading and rereading texts of interest to him.

(Because Calvin has a strong interest in cars, this topic is an obvious one to explore in terms of reading material.) In addition, Calvin might benefit from being asked to read aloud to younger, less able readers. Calvin currently reads at about a beginning fourth-grade level, so reading some easy texts to younger children certainly would be feasible for him. Children with reading disability usually are among the least competent readers in a classroom. Being cast in the role of competent readers, even for a little while, can be a heady—and motivating—experience for them.

Reading in Context

Like normally achieving readers, all children with reading disability need ample practice reading in context. In this section, we begin by discussing assessment of reading in context. Next, we turn to a number of instructional issues: encouraging children to apply their word-recognition skills in context; integrating word-recognition instruction with children's reading in context, and selecting texts for children to read.

Assessment of Children's Reading in Context

Assessment of children's reading in context typically involves having children read text—often a series of graded passages—aloud, after which they answer a series of oral comprehension questions. Children's accuracy in both word recognition and comprehension for each passage is then determined. In addition, the examiner observes characteristics such as children's speed and fluency of reading, expression, and use of contextual cues. Assessment of reading in context may employ published tests (e.g., the *Gray Oral Reading Test—Revised;* see Wiederholt & Bryant, 1986) or an informal reading inventory developed by the teacher (see Hargrove & Poteet, 1984, for some detailed guidelines on developing informal reading inventories).

Delayed readers, who have accurate and automatic word-recognition skills, can read fluently in context, though not necessarily with good comprehension. At the other extreme are nonalphabetic readers, who have such poor word-recognition skills that their abilities to read in context may be very limited; in effect, there is often little "context" for them to use in attempting to read sentences. Finally, compensatory and nonautomatic readers tend to use contextual cues to compensate for their deficiencies in word recognition. A heavy reliance on contextual cues may not impair their comprehension at early grade levels, when the text demands are relatively easy. However, when the text demands escalate in the middle and upper elementary grades, their word-recognition deficiencies result in impaired comprehension.

To analyze children's use of contextual cues in reading, practitioners can examine their oral-reading errors in a procedure sometimes called "miscue analysis"

(Goodman, 1973). When children who use contextual cues make oral-reading errors, they tend to substitute real words that fit the surrounding context of the sentence. For instance, such children might substitute the word *woods* for *forest* or the word *mommy* for *mother*. In contrast, children who do not use contextual cues tend to substitute words that do not fit the context, or words that are not real words at all (e.g., *fors* for *forest*).

Of course, the types of oral-reading errors that children make reflect not only their own patterns of abilities but also the nature of the instruction they have received. A child who has been exposed to a strong code-emphasis approach is more likely to make the *fors* for *forest* error—that is, the kind of error that comes out of an attempt to decode the word. By contrast, children who have been exposed to a strong meaning-emphasis approach may be more likely to substitute real words when they make oral-reading errors.

Keep in mind that what is detrimental is not the simple fact of using contextual cues but, rather, the routine use of these cues to *compensate* for faulty word-recognition skills. We are not suggesting that children—regardless of whether they have reading disability—should ignore the meaning of what they are reading to focus exclusively on recognizing words. On the contrary, our point is that if children cannot use skilled word-recognition abilities *in conjunction with* context but instead, like James, must use context to compensate for poor word recognition, they will eventually run into trouble in comprehension.

Encouraging Children to Apply Word-Recognition Skills in Context

Nonalphabetic, compensatory, and nonautomatic readers all must be encouraged to apply their developing word-recognition skills when they are reading in context. Of great value toward this end is a well-integrated reading program—that is, a program in which the more contextualized activities, such as reading in context, make high use of the skills being developed in isolation. A well-integrated program encourages children to apply their word-recognition skills in context because it provides them with numerous opportunities to use the skills that they have learned. In the next subsection, we will suggest some specific methods by which teachers can integrate isolated word-recognition activities with more contextualized activities.

In addition, teachers can encourage children to apply their word-recognition skills in context by the manner in which they respond to children's mistakes in oral reading. If teachers foster the routine use of contextual cues instead of the application of word-recognition strategies, or if they frequently ignore word-recognition errors, children will be less likely to apply their word-recognition skills in context. To put it another way, encouraging heavy reliance on contextual cues in word recognition is like teaching children to use crutches when they could be taught how to walk. Moreover, contextual cues are not particularly good crutches, because they are unreliable in predicting individual words in text (Gough, 1983).

Instead, teachers can respond to children's word-recognition errors in the following way. Suppose that James stumbles on a long word while reading in context. James's teacher might encourage him to examine the word closely and to apply decoding strategies (e.g., to divide between two consonants in a word with a vowel-consonant-consonant-vowel pattern). If necessary, the teacher can provide cues to James (e.g., by pointing out the vowel-consonant-consonant-vowel pattern to James if he does not notice it himself), but she should not tell him the word unless it becomes clear that he will not be able to decode it even after numerous attempts. Finally, once James has decoded the word or, as a last resort, the teacher has told James the word, he should reread the entire sentence to establish comprehension.

When is it appropriate to encourage children to use contextual cues? There are two answers to this question. First, children should be encouraged to use contextual cues to determine word *meanings* (e.g., Sternberg & Powell, 1983; Sternberg, Powell, & Kaye, 1983). For example, practitioners can help children to differentiate the meanings of common homophones (e.g., *to, two,* and *too*) by drawing their attention to the different ways that these words are used in context. Second, as we have mentioned, children's use of contextual cues in conjunction with word-recognition skills is highly appropriate. Nicholson, Bailey, and McArthur (1991) point out that some children actually may make use of contextual cues to improve their word-recognition skills—as when they initially use contextual cues to recognize a word but then closely examine the sequence of letters in the word for future reference. Nicholson et al. also note that this use of context is a desirable one.

Integrating Word-Recognition Instruction with Reading in Context

As we have repeatedly emphasized, it is important to integrate isolated work on skills with more meaningful, contextualized activities. Thus, the word-recognition activities that we have described must be integrated with children's reading in context. If isolated word-recognition activities are not properly integrated with the other parts of the child's instructional program, then the program will be fragmented and inefficient, and the point of learning the skills will remain completely obscure to the child.

To accomplish this integration, practitioners should start by analyzing the text they want children to be able to read. In other words, after selecting the text, they should examine it in terms of the specific skills—such as sight words and letter-sound relationships—that need to be taught. For example, James can practice syllabicating multisyllable words in isolation using words that have been selected from texts that he will be reading. Planning in this fashion generally is more effective than teaching from a sequence of skills and then trying to find a text that fits the sequence. Furthermore, in daily reading lessons, the isolated word-recognition activities should precede reading in context, because the former should facilitate the latter.

We should point out, however, that the text itself must be chosen with care. In Megan's case, for instance, text that does not involve numerous repetitions of some common letter-sound relationships—such as several short *a* words or several words with *sh*—would be difficult to combine with decoding instruction, thus providing Megan with little practice on the kinds of words that she is learning to decode in isolation. The same is true for all children with RD: The text should be selected so as to provide a reasonable level of practice on the specific skills that are being developed in the other parts of the program.

Of course, word-recognition instruction also must be integrated with spelling and with meaningful writing activities. For example, children who are learning to read words with orthographic units such as *ai* can simultaneously be learning to spell words with the same pattern. In addition, children should be encouraged to apply their orthographic knowledge in spontaneous writing; in this regard, sentence-dictation activities can be used for more structured practice. Even children functioning at very low levels of skill in reading and spelling can be engaged in meaningful writing activities through the use of invented spelling.

We conclude this subsection with one particularly crucial point. Even in a well-integrated instructional program, work on isolated skills should not consume an excessive amount of time in a given lesson. Although it seems sensible to provide these skill activities early in the lesson to facilitate children's reading and writing in context, there is a danger that the later activities will get short shrift simply *because* they come at the end. Note, too, that the skill activities we discuss do not need to be lengthy in order to be useful; for that matter, one activity can sometimes be used to develop a combination of skills. For example, letter-sound activities and phonological-awareness training might be combined into a ten-minute segment at the beginning of every lesson, using techniques such as Elkonin's (1973) procedure. Lessons can be organized and implemented in a variety of ways, but the important point is that isolated-skills work should not crowd more contextualized activities out of the child's program. Rather, the isolated-skills work should be the "warm-up," and the contextualized activities—such as reading in context, meaningful writing, and listening comprehension—should be the main events.

Selecting Texts

Without experiences involving connected texts and books, activities that focus on letters and on isolated words are not likely to engage children or even to make sense to them (Dyson, 1984). Like all children, youngsters with reading disability need to be exposed to a variety of engaging, stimulating texts. Like all children, they need practice not just reading, but *rereading*, familiar texts. As Anderson et al. (1985) point out, we would never expect a musician to play a piece flawlessly without repeated practice—but too often, this is exactly what children are expected to do in reading.

However, because the reading skills of many children with reading disability are severely limited, finding appropriate texts for these children to read may pose a considerable challenge. Initially, for instance, many nonalphabetic readers, as well as some compensatory readers, may need to read the kinds of phonetically controlled materials found in most code-emphasis programs. Although the interest level of some of these readers is abysmal, phonetically controlled materials that are attractive and appealing do exist. Phonetically controlled texts have the advantage of providing a high level of practice in decoding specific word types that the children have learned in isolation. Furthermore, for some children with RD, phonetically uncontrolled materials, such as most children's trade books and basal readers, may be too difficult to read at first, because they make too many demands on word recognition. Indeed, for some youngsters, *any* commercially published text may be too difficult to read at first. Rather, for the first few lessons, teachers may need to write their own short texts, tailored to fit the kinds of words that the children can recognize.

"Big books" with predictable texts, which are popular in many whole-language programs, also may be helpful with children whose word-recognition skills are very limited, such as nonalphabetic and some compensatory readers. "Big books" are enlarged versions of books that can be read aloud by the teacher and easily seen by a group of children. Predictable texts involve the repetition of specific phrases and sentences, or the recurrence of certain story structures. One example of a popular big book with predictable text is *Mrs. Wishy-Washy* (Cowley, 1990). Also, many familiar fairy tales and children's books (e.g., *The Three Bears, The Three Little Pigs, The Gingerbread Man*) involve predictable text. Predictable text is helpful because it lessens the word-recognition demands on the reader. In addition, many of these texts are very engaging and appealing to young children.

An activity that frequently employs big books and predictable texts is fingerpoint-reading, as in the "shared book experience" of Holdaway (1979). As we discussed in Chapter 4, in fingerpoint-reading, a text is read repeatedly to children by the teacher, and the children are taught to point word by word as they recite the text verbatim from memory. In Holdaway's approach, fingerpoint-reading involves a considerable amount of structured guidance from the teacher. For instance, the teacher models fingerpoint-reading for the children and systematically draws the children's attention to letter-sound relationships in the text. One advantage of fingerpoint-reading is that it may permit children with limited reading skills to begin reading interesting and naturalistic texts right away.

Nevertheless, as we also discussed in Chapter 4, children who lack letter-sound knowledge and phonological awareness—as do many nonalphabetic readers— may have a great deal of difficulty with fingerpoint-reading. Furthermore, without phonological awareness, letter-sound knowledge, and at least a small stock of sight words, most children cannot be expected to move into independent word recognition from fingerpoint-reading alone (Ehri & Sweet, 1991). Still, fingerpoint-reading may be used to communicate some basic concepts about print to nonalphabetic readers—that printed words are separated by spaces, that print is read from left to right, and so on—and to expose nonalphabetic readers to more varied kinds of texts.

Thus, fingerpoint-reading may be useful with nonalphabetic readers, but it must be supplemented with many other kinds of activities if nonalphabetic readers are to achieve alphabetic insight and to develop independent word-recognition skills. In contrast, for young compensatory readers, who have more word-recognition skills than do nonalphabetic readers, fingerpoint-reading may be easier to accomplish and more likely to lead to independent word recognition.

Selecting texts of an appropriate level of difficulty is important for all children. Children with RD probably benefit from reading texts that are somewhat challenging in terms of *comprehension*, because these kinds of texts may be more interesting and more effective in developing comprehension skills than are very "easy" texts. However, texts that are overly challenging in terms of *word recognition* present some special difficulties for students with RD, particularly for nonalphabetic, compensatory, and nonautomatic readers. For instance, such texts may prevent compensatory readers from applying their word-recognition skills in context or impede the development of automatization in nonautomatic readers. Obviously, the kind of approach to oral-reading errors that we discussed earlier, using James as an example—that is, having James analyze the letters in a difficult word, decode it, and reread the sentence—would not be feasible if James stumbled on every other word.

In reading groups, moreover, the assignment of texts that are too demanding in terms of word recognition can spark a chain of negative events. For example, Chinn, Waggoner, Anderson, Schommer, and Wilkinson (1993) found that, when poor readers in second- and third-grade reading groups struggled too much in decoding a text, other children in the groups became restless and inattentive. In order to keep all of the children on task and to preserve the meaning of the text for these other children, teachers tended not to provide hints or cues to struggling readers, or to give them more time to figure out a word, but rather just supplied difficult words quickly. Although this kind of terminal feedback may enable teachers to meet the overall needs of a particular group, it is not particularly helpful in improving poor readers' decoding skills. Chinn et al. suggested that teachers who work with groups of poor readers should be sure to use texts that are easy enough for the children. Similarly, Adams (1990) concluded that children's word-recognition error rates should not exceed about 5 percent in the materials they are given for reading instruction. According to Adams's guidelines, a youngster like James, reading a text of two hundred words, should make errors on no more than ten words.

Finally, like all youngsters (e.g., Anderson et al., 1985), children with reading disability should be encouraged to do independent reading. In the school setting, teachers can set aside classroom time on a regular basis for independent reading and provide guidance to children in picking books of an appropriate level of difficulty. And outside of school, parents can foster independent reading by establishing TV rules, having children read regularly to other members of the household, making trips to the library, and so on. In time, independent reading can yield some specific dividends in terms of skills and knowledge. For instance, as we discussed in Chapter 4, skills such as orthographic knowledge and vocabulary appear to accrue in part from exposure to text. These are skills that children like James need in order to develop word-recognition accuracy and to get back onto the road to proficient reading. Finally, for youngsters like Calvin, independent reading in materials that have low word-recognition demands may help to promote automatization.

Reading Comprehension

Reading-comprehension activities are a crucial part of any instructional program for reading, because skilled reading comprehension is the ultimate goal of the program. The other objectives of the program—phonological awareness, word recognition, and reading in context—are important not as ends in themselves but as factors upon which skilled reading comprehension depends.

Reading-comprehension difficulties are characteristic of all patterns of reading disability. The reading-comprehension deficits of nonalphabetic, compensatory, and nonautomatic readers are linked to their ongoing problems with word recognition. In the case of nonalphabetic readers, who have extremely limited word recognition skills, reading-comprehension problems are particularly severe. Compensatory and nonautomatic readers may achieve much higher levels of reading comprehension than do nonalphabetic readers, depending upon, among other things, their specific word-recognition skills and their talents in using contextual skills. Thus, when the text demands are relatively low, compensatory and nonautomatic readers may appear to have adequate reading comprehension. However, their comprehension deteriorates rapidly in more demanding texts.

Delayed readers are children who, after much time and effort, finally have acquired fluent word-recognition skills. However, these children labored so long to acquire word-recognition skills that they failed to develop certain higher-level skills in reading, such as strategic abilities and content-area knowledge. For instance, while delayed readers like Stacy were struggling to learn basic decoding skills in the elementary grades, good readers were moving on to read more complex texts, to do more independent reading, to acquire more sophisticated vocabulary from reading, and to develop and apply comprehension strategies. Although students like Stacy no longer demonstrate significant word-recognition deficits, their current difficulties in reading comprehension must be understood as a direct result of their early, prolonged difficulties in acquiring word-recognition skills. In order to return to the road to proficient reading, such students need particular emphasis on acquiring content-area knowledge and on using strategies in reading.

In this section, we discuss four areas that are particularly relevant to reading-comprehension instruction: assessment of reading comprehension, the role of listening-comprehension activities in developing comprehension, reading instruction in content-area subjects such as science and social studies, and encouraging children to become strategic readers.

Assessment of Reading Comprehension

Many standardized test batteries contain subtests for measuring reading comprehension; examples include the *Stanford Diagnostic Reading Test* (Karlsen et al., 1985) and the *Woodcock-Johnson Psycho-Educational Battery* (Woodcock, 1978). In addition, there are a few standardized tests that focus exclusively on reading comprehension, such as the *Test of Reading Comprehension* (Brown, Hammill, & Wiederholt, 1986). Like a number of other standardized tests, the *Test of Reading Comprehension* has subtests to measure knowledge of content-area vocabulary as well as literal and inferential comprehension of paragraphs.

Standardized tests can be useful in assessing comprehension, because they provide a relatively easy way to measure children's comprehension skills compared with those of other children of the same age and grade level. Nevertheless, standardized tests do not provide a deep or thorough measure of comprehension (Anderson et al., 1985). For instance, the kinds of skills involved in reading long texts, such as plot analysis and summarization, do not lend themselves to the format typical of most standardized tests, which entails reading short paragraphs and answering multiple-choice questions, picking the picture that best illustrates a sentence, filling in the blank in a sentence, and so on. Furthermore, most standardized tests provide little information about students' understanding or use of comprehension strategies, although some standardized tests might be adapted to provide this kind of information. For example, after formal testing is complete, an examiner might ask a child to "think aloud" while completing selected items (Pressley, Borkowski, Forrest-Pressley, Gaskins, & Wile, 1993). One commercially published test that does attempt to measure strategic knowledge in a variety of academic domains, including reading, is collectively known as the *Surveys of Problem-Solving & Educational Skills* (Meltzer, 1987).

Informal measures of reading comprehension and strategic knowledge are important adjuncts to standardized tests. These informal measures might involve having children read and summarize selections from school texts, including content-area texts; observing children's use of strategies, such as their abilities to skim text, monitor comprehension, and apply fix-up strategies; and keeping records of children's independent reading.

Listening-Comprehension Activities

Listening-comprehension activities can play an important role in developing the comprehension skills of children with reading disability. As we have discussed, a long-standing reading disability eventually may erode listening comprehension through Matthew effects (Stanovich, 1986). However, for most individuals with RD, listening comprehension remains a relatively strong vehicle for learning, especially as compared with reading comprehension.

Listening-comprehension activities should utilize a wide variety of interesting, stimulating texts that are age-appropriate for children. In our view, the goals behind the use of these activities are twofold. First, they should engage children and motivate them to become readers. Second, they should expose children to vocabulary, ideas, syntactic structures, and other elements of written language that children cannot yet read themselves. In other words, the listening-comprehension activities should be used to compensate, at least partially, for children's current lack of reading skills, and to ameliorate the loss of motivation for reading that tends to lead children with RD farther and farther away from the road to proficient reading. Thus, the use of well-designed listening-comprehension activities, over time, actually may help to prevent poor reading from eroding listening comprehension.

For children with extremely limited reading skills (e.g., nonalphabetic readers such as Megan), listening-comprehension activities often are the most feasible way to ensure exposure to a variety of texts and to develop age-appropriate comprehension skills. However, even older students with higher levels of achievement in reading (e.g., delayed readers such as Stacy) can benefit from the use of listening-comprehension activities. Jim Trelease (1989) offers some excellent suggestions for reading aloud to children, including older ones, along with recommendations of books for use at various age levels. He points out, for example, that books and other texts should always be previewed by the teacher, with an eye toward words or passages that may need to be explained or elaborated. Also, the teacher may wish to shorten or skip some passages, such as lengthy descriptions. If children have difficulty just sitting still and listening, they might be allowed to draw while the teacher reads. As Trelease notes, mood is indeed important in reading aloud to children. A relaxed, comfortable atmosphere conveys the idea that reading is fun, not a chore, and is more conducive to good listening than continually admonishing children to sit still and pay attention.

Trelease further suggests that a novel already seen by children on television or at the movies is not a good choice for reading aloud, because once children know the outcome of the story, much of their motivation for listening is lost. However, a novel might be read to children *prior* to its appearance on television; then the children could contrast the book with its television version. Moreover, if the material being read is expository rather than narrative in nature—for example, a science selection about snakes—some television programs (e.g., the public-television sion progam *NOVA*) may actually be a very useful complement to the reading.

Of course, listening-comprehension activities cannot substitute for children's own reading of text; rather, they should supplement children's reading in context and reading-comprehension development. For older students like Stacy, listening comprehension—class discussions, listening to tapes, and so on—may be an important aid for learning in subjects such as history or science, where the texts may be particularly demanding. Obviously, however, the long-term goal of the program must be to develop such students' reading skills sufficiently that they can read and comprehend content texts themselves.

In addition, listening-comprehension activities may be combined with students' reading in context, through the use of activities such as paired or alternating reading. For example, in Stacy's case, a text from one of the classes in which she is mainstreamed might be used. Stacy and the teacher could alternate between reading sections of the text and engaging in ongoing discussion. The portions of text read by the teacher would tap Stacy's listening-comprehension skills, ease the reading demands on Stacy, and provide a model of skilled reading. At times, Stacy also might be paired with another student, rather than with the teacher, for alternating reading.

Reading in Content Areas

All text, of course, has "content." In this section, we address the issue of reading instruction in subjects such as social studies, history, and science, which commonly are called *content areas*. In the early elementary grades, the reading demands in content areas typically are low, but as children progress into the middle and upper elementary grades, they are expected to do increasing amounts of reading in content areas. Even normally achieving readers may have some difficulty making the transition to content-area reading (Anderson et al., 1985; Chall et al., 1990). As students move into middle school and high school, academic success depends more and more heavily on their abilities to read and write in content-area subjects.

For children with reading disability, reading in content areas tends to be especially problematic, given not only the demanding nature of many content-area texts but also the fact that students with RD may be particularly lacking in experiences involving these kinds of texts. Both Calvin and Stacy, the two older children we introduced in Chapter 5, were experiencing significant academic difficulties involving content-area reading. In contrast, content-area reading was not yet a major issue for Megan and James—but it eventually will be, if they are ever to be placed in mainstream classes and to progress academically. What can teachers do to help children with RD function in content areas, when so many of these youngsters struggle merely with reading the words on a page?

First, like normally achieving readers (e.g., Anderson et al., 1985), children with reading disability should be exposed very early to varied texts, including the expository types of texts that predominate in content areas. The structure of expository texts tends to be different from that of narratives. For example, a science text about the life cycle of monarch butterflies would have a different kind of organization than would a story involving specific characters and a plot line. Also, expository texts frequently involve specialized vocabularies; for instance, the text about monarch butterflies may contain words such as *pupa* and *migration*. Early exposure to expository text structure as well as to the kinds of vocabulary and information contained in expository texts facilitates the transition to content-area reading required of children as they progress in school. For children with very limited reading comprehension, like Megan, this exposure initially might be implemented through listening rather than through reading.

Second, although integrating instruction in basic reading skills with content-area reading is crucial, sometimes this integration is not carried out in practice (Anderson et al., 1985). For instance, children may be assigned phonics workbooks in which there is little overlap between the words used and the vocabulary found in their content-area texts, or children may be asked to practice reading-comprehension skills such as "finding the main idea" using isolated paragraphs that bear little relation to the texts employed in their history or science classes.

Instead, a youngster like James, who still is developing accuracy in word recognition, could be asked to practice dividing words or using structural analysis on words selected directly from content-area texts. Calvin could be helped to develop automatic recognition of important words from his content-area texts (e.g., through speed drills), which in turn would facilitate his reading comprehension in those texts. And Stacy, who needs to develop reading strategies, could learn these strategies in the context of content-area demands, not contrived activities.

Finally, explicit teaching of certain skills involved in comprehending text can be very helpful to children with reading disability. These skills include not only knowledge about expository text structure and vocabulary but also activation of one's *prior* knowledge in reading or summarizing text. Some of these skills may be conceptualized as strategies to aid comprehension, a topic to which we turn next.

Encouraging Strategic Reading

Dole, Duffy, Roehler, and Pearson (1991) discuss traditional, task-analytic views of reading comprehension and their influence on instruction. In these traditional views, good reading comprehension involves mastering a set of discrete skills such as "finding the main idea," "drawing inferences," and "remembering details." Furthermore, some skills may be seen as prerequisites for others. For example, these views advocate that literal comprehension—understanding and recalling information explicitly stated in the text—should be "mastered" before children move on to inferential skills. Most teachers are familiar with instructional programs based on these views of comprehension, because such programs continue to be used in many schools.

Dole et al. (1991) suggest an instructional approach based upon a very different view of comprehension. This approach emphasizes the strategic nature of skilled reading and is fairly congruent with the later phases of our own model of reading acquisition. The alternative comprehension curriculum involves teaching a set of basic strategies applicable to a variety of texts—for example, summarizing, generating questions, and applying fix-up strategies when comprehension fails—and helping students to adapt the strategies to any text that they read. Inferential comprehension is emphasized from the start.

Strategy interventions currently are quite popular in some schools, especially those serving adolescents with LD. There is evidence that strategy instruction can benefit not only students with learning problems but normally achieving readers as well (Anderson et al., 1985; Dole et al., 1991; Harris & Pressley, 1991). In this subsection, we discuss some examples of strategy interventions, some problems and issues surrounding these interventions, and our own recommendations for strategy instruction with students with RD.

Examples of Strategy Interventions. Although early work on strategy training emphasized very general kinds of strategies, researchers have more recently tended to emphasize integrating strategy instruction into content domains in order to facilitate content-area learning (Wong, 1993). Two examples of models integrating strategy instruction and content-area learning, both of which have been developed with students with LD in mind, are the strategies instruction model of the Kansas University Institute of Research in LD (e.g., Deshler, Warner, Schumaker, & Alley, 1983) and Ellis's integrative strategy instruction model (e.g., Ellis, 1993).

Table 7.3 lists some examples of strategies that may be taught in intervention programs. Some of these strategies, such as fix-up strategies and mental imagery, are quite general and may be applied across a wide variety of situations. Others,

TABLE 7.3 Examples of Strategies in Intervention Programs

Strategy	Purpose	Description
Fix-up strategies (e.g., Anderson, Hiebert, Scott, & Wilkinson, 1985)	To achieve understanding when comprehension has failed	Student is taught to use strategies such as reading ahead, rereading, or consulting an external source.
Mental imagery (e.g., Pressley, 1976)	To aid recall	Student is taught to form a mental picture after reading a segment of text.
PREP (Ellis, 1993)	To prepare for class	Student is taught to *prepare* materials, *review* what he or she knows, *establish* a positive mind-set, and *pinpoint* goals.
PARTS (Ellis, 1993)	To peruse text	Student is taught to *perform* goal setting, *analyze* little parts (e.g., title, headings), *review* big parts (e.g., introduction, summary), *think* of questions, and *state* relationships (e.g., to what he or she already knows).
FIRST-letter mnemonic strategy (Nagel, Schumaker, & Deshler, 1986)	To recall details or lists of information	Student is taught to form a word using the first letter of a list of items; this word then serves as a mnemonic.
ACE guessing technique (Hughes, Schumaker, Deshler, & Mercer, 1988)	To use on multiple-choice test items for which student does not know the answer (part of a broader test-taking strategy)	Student is taught to *avoid* absolutes (e.g., choices with words like "never" and "always"), to *choose* the longest, most detailed option, and to *eliminate* similar choices.

such as PREP (Ellis, 1993), are much more specific. PREP, a strategy that students use to prepare for classes, is the acronym for *preparing* materials (e.g., notebook, textbook, pencil); *reviewing* what the students already know; *establishing* a positive mind-set; and *pinpointing* goals (e.g., what the students want to learn).

Much strategy training involves explicit teaching of strategies that successful students appear to generate on their own. In some cases, furthermore, developers of strategy interventions have taken a rather pragmatic view of what is involved in academic success. For example, in the ACE guessing technique, which is part of a broader test-taking strategy (Hughes, Schumaker, Deshler, & Mercer, 1988), students explicitly are taught strategies for guessing answers to multiple-choice test items that they do not know.

Problems and Issues in Strategy Instruction. A particularly thorny problem in strategy instruction concerns maintenance and generalization of strategies (Harris & Pressley, 1991). Specifically, students may use a strategy effectively when they are doing one particular task or attending the classroom of one particular teacher, but fail to apply the strategy in other contexts. To facilitate maintenance and generalization of strategies, Harris and Pressley (1991) emphasize, among other things, involving students in instructional planning, having students practice strategies in a wide array of materials and settings, monitoring long-term strategy use, and involving special-education and regular-education teachers in collaboration with each other.

A related problem concerns the role of motivation and attributional beliefs in strategy use. Students may have strategic knowledge that they fail to put into practice for a number of reasons, such as the belief that they are "stupid" or that their efforts will not make a difference (Garner, 1990). Being a strategic reader involves being "planful," being flexible, and exerting conscious control over the task at hand, characteristics that are not highly compatible with the low motivation and maladaptive attributional beliefs of many students with RD. Indeed, for strategy training to be effective, these motivational and attributional issues must be addressed. Helping students to perceive the effectiveness of reading strategies is critical, because students have little motivation to continue using a strategy that they do not perceive as effective. In addition, strategy instruction must be individualized to some extent, as a particular strategy probably will not be equally effective for all students.

Owing to a lack of data, many current strategy-training programs are yet to be validated (Wong, 1993). We know that skilled reading is strategic, that poor readers can be helped to become more strategic, and that teaching strategies can be an effective way to improve students' comprehension. However, the long-term effectiveness of elaborate or intensive instruction involving "packages" of strategies remains uncertain.

Recommendations. In our view, some of the same suggestions we made in discussing the teaching of phonic generalizations also may be applied to strategy instruction. First, keep it simple. Basic fix-up strategies, such as looking up words in a dictionary or rereading when comprehension fails, have wide utility and are not difficult to remember. The same is true of the strategies discussed by Dole et al. (1991). However, other strategies taught in intervention programs involve seven or eight steps; some even entail strategies embedded within strategies. These complex strategies strike us as being a bit like teaching children to memorize the six different sounds of *ough*—perhaps more trouble than they are worth for many students.

Second, as Harris and Pressley (1991) point out, strategy instruction is not a cure-all. Just as phonic generalizations are but one tool to aid students in word recognition, so reading strategies are just one tool to aid students in reading comprehension. Strategies can be particularly powerful tools for readers, but there is clearly more to skilled reading comprehension than knowing and using strategies. Among other things, vocabulary, an extensive knowledge base, and independent reading in a variety of materials also are important to skilled reading comprehension.

Third, in strategy instruction, as in decoding instruction, the essential thing is to convey a particular kind of message to students. In decoding instruction, this message is that written words involve a systematic code and that attention to the letters within words is important. In strategy instruction, the bottom-line message is that skilled reading is "planful," flexible, and self-regulated. Conveying this underlying message to students is more important than the particular strategies one chooses to teach. Indeed, if the wrong underlying message is comminicated— for instance, if strategies are taught in an inflexible, rote, mechanistic way—then the strategy instruction is doomed to fail.

How can teachers convey the appropriate underlying message to students in strategy instruction? One effective way they can do so is through explicit teaching and modeling of strategies (Anderson et al., 1985; Dole et al., 1991). However, this explicit teaching and modeling should not involve rote drill. Rather, teachers need to "think aloud"—for instance, to describe how they are activating their prior knowledge about a text or generating questions as they read—in order to communicate the kinds of processes involved in strategic reading to their students. The flexibility and adaptability of strategies, rather than rigid adherence to a set of steps, should be emphasized. Many researchers also have suggested that strategy instruction should entail a kind of scaffolding on the part of the teacher. In other words, strategy instruction initially involves a set of supports and cues that gradually are diminished as the student acquires more competence in using the strategy.

Another way of conveying the appropriate underlying message about strategy instruction is for teachers to engage students in partnerships with themselves. Students cannot become "self"-regulated if the teacher is always in charge. For example, Brown and Palincsar (1989) used an approach to developing strategic knowledge called *reciprocal teaching*. In reciprocal teaching, teachers and students take turns leading a dialogue about a text. The dialogue focuses on summarizing portions of the text, generating questions, clarifying difficult parts of the text, and making predictions about what will come next. Reciprocal teaching is effective in improving not only poor readers' comprehension but also their use of strategies; moreover, these gains are maintained over time and generalize beyond the experimental setting (Palincsar, Winn, David, Snyder, & Stevens, 1993). Recently, Palincsar and her colleagues have developed an even more student-centered approach to reading-comprehension instruction called *collaborative problem-solving* (Palincsar et al., 1993). In collaborative problem-solving, as compared with reciprocal teaching, students are given a greater role in generating and evaluating the effectiveness of strategies.

An instructional program for delayed readers such as Stacy should emphasize the learning of useful strategies in the context of everyday academic activities. For instance, because Stacy is inclined to give up when reading difficult material, she probably would benefit from learning some fix-up strategies; moreover, some basic study strategies might make the demands of her content-area classes seem less overwhelming. These strategies, and others, can be modeled by the teacher in the context of daily reading lessons—for instance, during alternating reading of Stacy's content-area texts. Control over generating and using strategies gradually should be ceded to Stacy.

However, for the strategy instruction to be effective, the teacher must also address Stacy's low motivation for reading—perhaps by giving Stacy some choices in reading material and in instructional activities. The strategy instruction would be even more likely to improve Stacy's performance in content-area classes if her content-area teachers become involved in her instructional program (e.g., if they monitor and reinforce strategic reading) and if the instruction itself utilizes the texts and academic tasks employed in her content-area classes.

Although delayed readers require a particular emphasis on strategic learning, we are not suggesting that *only* delayed readers should be encouraged to be strategic in reading. For example, learning some basic strategies may permit nonautomatic readers such as Calvin to comprehend content-area texts much better than they would otherwise. Clearly, even children like Megan and James should be encouraged to employ strategies such as activating prior knowledge, monitoring comprehension, and applying fix-up strategies.

We conclude this subsection by returning to the issue of literal versus inferential comprehension raised by Dole et al. (1991). We agree with these investigators that the development of inferential comprehension should not await some arbitrary level of "mastery" in literal comprehension but, rather, should be emphasized from the start. Moreover, we believe that this issue is particularly critical for youngsters with RD, who, because of their limited reading skills, frequently are assigned texts that are not conducive to the development of inferential comprehension (e.g., "Nat the cat sat on the tan mat"). Even when children with RD are given more naturalistic or challenging texts, the instruction may tend to deemphasize inferential comprehension in favor of word recognition and literal comprehension. But in our view, all youngsters with reading disability—whether they are nonalphabetic readers like Megan or delayed readers like Stacy—need comprehension instruction that emphasizes inferential, and not just literal, skills.

Sample Instructional Plans

Tables 7.4, 7.5, 7.6, and 7.7 present sample instructional plans in reading for Megan, James, Calvin, and Stacy. The tables are intended to summarize the kinds of instructional emphases that are needed for each of these youngsters and for each pattern of reading disability. In addition, the tables list some examples of instructional activities that might be used with each child.

Three points need to be made regarding the interpretation of these tables. First, because the tables summarize the *varying* instructional emphases associated with the four patterns of reading disability, we have excluded certain areas that are highly similar across all four patterns, such as listening comprehension and independent reading. The absence of these areas should not be construed as meaning that they are unimportant instructionally. (Nor are the tables themselves meant to represent detailed or exhaustive educational plans.) Second, readers should keep in mind that activities used as examples in one youngster's instructional plan might also be applicable to other patterns of reading disability. As we indicated at the outset of this chapter, the various patterns of RD involve not completely distinct instructional programs but, rather, areas of overlap. And third, the examples of instructional activities are just that—examples. Many activities not listed here might be equally appropriate for a given youngster and equally effective in accomplishing a particular goal.

Although we have not focused on spelling and writing instruction in these tables (indeed, a complete instructional program for these two areas is well beyond the scope of this book), we have provided examples of spelling and writing activities that might be integrated with reading instruction. Also, we have tried to indicate how these activities might vary depending upon the pattern of reading disability. In the case of a young nonalphabetic reader like Megan, invented spelling is a very useful technique for reinforcing letter-sound knowledge and for developing alphabetic insight. More generally, however, as children develop skill in reading, they must also be helped to make the transition to conventional spelling—for instance, through instruction in spelling generalizations or strategies such as looking up words in a dictionary.

Finally, beyond the more pragmatic issues involved in instructional programming, there are some fundamental questions. Why do children like Megan, James, Calvin, and Stacy wander from the road to proficient reading in the first place? In other words, what are the ultimate causes of RD? We explore the complex issues surrounding causation of reading disability in the next chapter.

TABLE 7.4 Sample Instructional Plan for Megan

Skill Area	Sample Activities	Instructional Emphases
I. Phonological awareness	Use onset-rime tasks (e.g., ask Megan to circle pictures of words that share the same onset and to match with appropriate letter[s]).	Emphasize onset-rime tasks involving letter-sound relationships that Megan has learned or currently is learning.
II. Word recognition a. Letter-sound knowledge	a. Review familiar sounds with flash cards of letters.	Emphasize attention to letters within words.
	Teach a new sound using multisensory techniques and a key word.	Encourage application of phonological-awareness skills and letter-sound knowledge to develop alphabetic insight.
b. Reading/ spelling words	b. Using letter cards to form words, read and spell simple short-vowel words.	In isolated-word activities, select as many words as possible from the text that Megan is reading.
	Teach words that Megan cannot decode as sight vocabulary, using flash cards or multisensory techniques.	
III. Reading in context	Preview difficult vocabulary and hard-to-decode words.	Emphasize development and application of word-recognition skills in context.
	Read selections from phonetically controlled reader(s): one familiar selection, one new selection.	
IV. Reading comprehension	Discuss today's reading. Draw a picture about something connected to today's reading and label it, using invented spelling.	Emphase inferential as well as literal comprehension.
		Use invented spelling in writing activities to develop alphabetic insight.

TABLE 7.5 Sample Instructional Plan for James

Skill Area	Sample Activities	Instructional Emphases
I. Phonological awareness	Check phoneme-segmentation skills; train if necessary, using Elkonin's procedure.	If training is needed, focus on the kinds of words James needs to learn to read and spell (e.g., words with common orthographic units).
II. Word recognition		
a. Letter-sound knowledge	a. Review familiar orthographic units with flash cards of letters.	Emphasize a systematic approach to word recognition and attention to all of the letters in words to develop accuracy.
	Teach new unit (e.g., *augh*) using multisensory techniques and a key word.	
b. Reading/ spelling words	b. Read and write words using both familiar and new orthographic units.	In isolated-word activities, select as many words as possible from the text James is reading.
	Teach useful generalizations for dividing long words.	
	Teach words that James cannot yet decode as sight vocabulary, using flash cards or multisensory techniques.	
III. Reading in context	Preview difficult vocabulary and hard-to-decode words.	Emphasize application of word-recognition skills in context rather than overrelying on contextual cues.
	Read in children's trade book(s) of appropriate level of difficulty: one familiar selection, one new selection.	

(continues)

TABLE 7.5 (continued)

Skill Area	Sample Activities	Instructional Emphases
IV. Reading comprehension	Discuss today's reading. Write in journal about a topic related to today's reading.	Emphasize inferential as well as literal comprehension; accuracy in word recognition should not come at the price of comprehension. In writing activities, emphasize application of previously learned spelling skills (e.g., spelling of familiar orthographic units). Use invented spelling only for difficult, unfamiliar words.

TABLE 7.6 Sample Instructional Plan for Calvin

Skill Area	Sample Activities	Instructional Emphases
I. Phonological awareness	———	———
II. Word recognition a. Letter-sound knowledge	———	
b. Reading/spelling words	b. Perform two speed drills: one on phonetically regular words, one on difficult words selected from content texts. Use supplemental computer games to develop automatization. Teach useful generalizations for spelling (e.g., "*i* before *e* except after *c*").	Emphasize automatization of word recognition; goals are speed and fluency along with a reasonable degree of accuracy. In isolated-word activities, select as many words as possible from the texts Calvin is reading (including content texts).

(continues)

TABLE 7.6 (continued)

Skill Area	Sample Activities	Instructional Emphases
III. Reading in context	Perform a repeated-reading activity (using an appropriate text that Calvin has helped to pick out).	Emphasize application of word-recognition skills in context and a high degree of fluency.
	For all reading in context, preview difficult vocabulary words on which Calvin is not yet automatic.	Teacher should provide a model of fluent reading to Calvin.
IV. Reading comprehension	Discuss today's reading.	Emphasize inferential as well as literal comprehension; fluency should not come at the expense of comprehension.
	Write in journal about a topic related to today's reading.	
	Write answers to written questions about content reading.	In writing activities, emphasize application of previously learned spelling skills; for unfamiliar words, teach strategies such as looking up words in a dictionary.

TABLE 7.7 Sample Instructional Plan for Stacy

Skill Area	Sample Activities	Instructional Emphases
I. Phonological awareness	———	———
II. Word recognition a. Letter-sound knowledge	———	

(continues)

TABLE 7.7 (continued)

Skill Area	Sample Activities	Instructional Emphases
b. Reading/ spelling words	b. Discuss meanings of words from content and other texts. Spell, in isolation, words from content texts and words needed in writing. Teach useful generalizations for spelling.	In isolated-word activities, select as many words as possible from the texts Stacy is reading (including content texts).
III. Reading in context	Preview difficult vocabulary. Use PREP strategy (Ellis, 1993). Alternate with Stacy the oral reading of a selection from Stacy's science text; include ongoing discussion; allow Stacy to finish reading the selection silently.	Emphasize application of strategies during reading in context. When teacher reads, emphasize modeling of strategies to aid comprehension.
IV. Reading comprehension	Discuss today's reading. Teach summarization strategy: Ask Stacy to orally summarize and then to write a summary of today's selection. Teach note-taking and study strategies.	Emphasize inferential as well as literal comprehension, use of strategies to aid comprehension, and acquisition of content knowledge. In writing activities, emphasize application of learned skills and strategies, such as procedures for using a dictionary, a computer spell-checker, etc.

References

Adams, M. J. (1990). *Beginning to read: Thinking and learning about print.* Cambridge, MA: MIT Press.

Alexander, A. W., Andersen, H. G., Heilman, P. C., Voeller, K., & Torgesen, J. K. (1991). Phonological awareness training and remediation of analytic decoding deficits in a group of severe dyslexics. *Annals of Dyslexia, 41,* 193–206.

Anderson, R. C., Hiebert, E. H., Scott, J. A., & Wilkinson, I. A. G. (1985). *Becoming a nation of readers: The report of the Commission on Reading.* Champaign, IL: Center for the Study of Reading.

Blachman, B. A. (1987). An alternative classroom reading program for learning disabled and other low-achieving children. In W. Ellis (Ed.), *Intimacy with language: A forgotten basic in teacher education* (pp. 49–55). Baltimore, MD: Orton Dyslexia Society.

———. (1989). Phonological awareness and word recognition: Assessment and intervention. In A. Kamhi & H. Catts (Eds.), *Reading disabilities: A developmental language perspective* (pp. 133–158). Boston, MA: College-Hill.

———. (1994). What we have learned from longitudinal studies of phonological processing and reading, and some unanswered questions: A response to Torgesen, Wagner, and Rashotte. *Journal of Learning Disabilities, 27,* 287–291.

Bradley, L. (1987, November). *Rhyme recognition and reading and spelling in young children.* Paper presented at the Early Childhood Symposium on Preschool Prevention of Reading Failure at the meeting of the Orton Dyslexia Society, San Francisco, CA.

Bradley, L., & Bryant, P. E. (1983). Categorizing sounds and learning to read—A causal connection. *Nature, 301,* 419–421.

———. (1985). *Rhyme and reason in reading and spelling.* Ann Arbor, MI: University of Michigan Press.

Brown, A. L., & Palincsar, A. S. (1989). Guided cooperative learning and individual knowledge acquisition. In L. Resnick (Ed.), *Knowing and learning: Issues for a cognitive psychology of learning. Essays in honor of Robert Glaser.* Hillsdale, NJ: Erlbaum.

Brown, V. L., Hammill, D. D., & Wiederholt, J. L. (1986). *Test of reading comprehension* (revised). Austin, TX: Pro-Ed.

Bruck, M. (1990). Word-recognition skills of adults with childhood diagnoses of dyslexia. *Developmental Psychology, 26,* 439–454.

Byrne, B. (1992). Studies in the acquisition procedure for reading: Rationale, hypotheses, and data. In P. B. Gough, L. C. Ehri, & R. Treiman (Eds.), *Reading acquisition* (pp. 1–34). Hillsdale, NJ: Erlbaum.

Byrne, B., Freebody, P., & Gates, A. (1992). Longitudinal data on the relations of word-reading strategies to comprehension. *Reading Research Quarterly, 27,* 140–151.

Chall, J., Jacobs, V. A., & Baldwin, L. E. (1990). *The reading crisis: Why poor children fall behind.* Cambridge, MA: Harvard University Press.

Chaney, J. H. (1993). Alphabet books: Resources for learning. *The Reading Teacher, 47,* 96–104.

Chinn, C. A., Waggoner, M. A., Anderson, R. C., Schommer, M. & Wilkinson, I. A. G. (1993). Situated actions during reading lessons: A microanalysis of oral reading error episodes. *American Educational Research Journal, 30,* 361–392.

Clay, M. M. (1985). *The early detection of reading difficulties,* 3rd ed. Portsmouth, NH: Heinemann.

Cowley, J. (1990). *Mrs. Wishy-Washy.* San Diego, CA: Wright Group.

Crowder, R. G., & Wagner, R. K. (1991). *The psychology of reading: An introduction.* New York: Oxford University Press.

Denckla, M. B., & Rudel, R. (1976). Rapid automatized naming (RAN): Dyslexia differentiated from other learning disabilities. *Neuropsychologia, 14,* 471–479.

Deshler, D. D., Warner, M. M., Schumaker, J. B., & Alley, G. R. (1983). The learning strategies intervention model: Key components and current status. In J. D. McKinney & L. Feagans (Eds.), *Current topics in learning disabilities* (Vol. 1). Norwood, NJ: Ablex.

Dole, J. A., Duffy, G. G., Roehler, L. R., & Pearson, P. D. (1991). Moving from the old to the new: Research on reading comprehension instruction. *Review of Educational Research, 61,* 239–264.

Dyson, A. H. (1984). Reading, writing, and language: Young children solving the written language puzzle. In J. M. Jensen (Ed.), *Composing and comprehending* (pp. 165–175). Urbana, IL: National Conference on Research in English and ERIC Clearinghouse on Reading and Communication Skills.

Ehri, L. C., & Sweet, J. (1991). Fingerpoint-reading of memorized text: What enables beginners to process the print? *Reading Research Quarterly, 26,* 442–462.

Elkonin, D. B. (1973). USSR. In J. Downing (Ed.), *Comparative reading.* New York: Macmillan.

Ellis, E. S. (1993). Integrative strategy instruction: A potential model for teaching content area subjects to adolescents with learning disabilities. *Journal of Learning Disabilities, 26,* 358–383, 398.

Engelmann, S. (1969). *Preventing failure in the primary grades.* Chicago, IL: Science Research Associates.

Fernald, G. (1943). *Remedial techniques in basic school subjects.* New York: McGraw-Hill

Frederiksen, J. R., Weaver, P. A., Warren, B. M., Gillotte, H. P., Rosebery, A. S., Freeman, B., & Goodman, L. (1983). *A componential approach to training reading skills* (Final Report 5295). Cambridge, MA: Bolt, Beranek and Newman, Inc.

Gallistel, E., Fischer, P., & Blackburn, M. (1977). *Sequence of objectives for teaching and testing reading.* Hamden, CT: Montage Press.

Garner, R. (1990). When children and adults do not use learning strategies: Toward a theory of settings. *Review of Educational Research, 60,* 517–529.

Gelzheiser, L. M., & Clark, D. B. (1991). Early reading and instruction. In B. Y. L. Wong (Ed.), *Learning about learning disabilities* (pp. 261–281). San Diego, CA: Academic Press.

Gillingham, A., & Stillman, B. (1970). *Remedial training for children with specific disability in reading, spelling, and penmanship.* Cambridge, MA: Educator's Publishing Service.

Goodman, K. S. (1973). Analysis of oral reading miscues: Applied psycholinguistics. In F. Smith (Ed.), *Psycholinguistics and reading* (pp. 158–176). Toronto: Holt, Rinehart, & Winston.

Gough, P. B. (1983). Context, form, and interaction. In K. Rayner (Ed.), *Eye movements in reading: Perceptual and language processes* (pp. 203–211). New York: Academic Press.

Hargrove, L. J., & Poteet, J. A. (1984). *Assessment in special education.* Englewood Cliffs, NJ: Prentice-Hall.

Harris, K. R., & Pressley, M. (1991). The nature of cognitive strategy instruction: Interactive strategy construction. *Exceptional Children, 57,* 392–404.

Hatcher, P. J., Hulme, C., & Ellis, A. W. (1994). Ameliorating early reading failure by integrating the teaching of reading and phonological skills: The phonological linkage hypothesis. *Child Development, 65,* 41–57.

Holdaway, D. (1979). *The foundations of literacy.* Sidney, Australia: Ashton Scholastic.

Hughes, C. A., Schumaker, J. B., Deshler, D. D., & Mercer, C. (1988). *The Test-Taking Strategy: The instructor's manual.* Lawrence, KS: Edge Enterprises.

Jones, K. M., Torgesen, J. K., & Sexton, M. A. (1987). Using computer guided practice to increase decoding fluency in learning disabled children: A study using the Hint and Hunt I program. *Journal of Learning Disabilities, 20,* 122–128.

Karlsen, B. M., Madden, R., & Gardner, E. (1985). *The Stanford Diagnostic Reading Test, Third Edition.* Cleveland, OH: Psychological Corporation.

Kennedy, K. M., & Backman, J. (1993). Effectiveness of the Lindamood Auditory Discrimination in Depth program with students with learning disabilities. *Learning Disabilities Research & Practice, 8,* 253–259.

Liberman, I. Y., Shankweiler, D., & Liberman, A. M. (1989). The alphabetic principle and learning to read. In D. Shankweiler & I. Y. Liberman (Eds.), *Phonology and reading disability: Solving the reading puzzle.* Ann Arbor, MI: University of Michigan Press.

Lindamood, C. H., & Lindamood, P. C. (1975). *Auditory Discrimination in Depth.* Hingham, MA: Teaching Resources Corporation.

———. (1979). *Lindamood Auditory Conceptualization Test.* Hingham, MA: Teaching Resources Corporation.

Maclean, M., Bryant, P., & Bradley, L. (1987). Rhymes, nursery rhymes, and reading in early childhood. *Merrill-Palmer Quarterly, 33,* 255–281.

Mann, V. A. (1991). Language problems: A key to early reading problems. In B. Y. L. Wong (Ed.), *Learning about learning disabilities* (pp. 129–162). San Diego, CA: Academic Press.

Mann, V. A., Tobin, P., & Wilson, R. (1987). Measuring phonological awareness through the invented spellings of kindergarten children. *Merrill-Palmer Quarterly, 33,* 365–391.

Meltzer, L. J. (1987). *Surveys of problem-solving & educational skills.* Cambridge, MA: Educators Publishing Service.

Nagel, D., Schumaker, J. B., & Deshler, D. D. (1986). *The FIRST-letter Mnemonic Strategy: Instructor's manual.* Lawrence, KS: Edge Enterprises.

Nicholson, T., Bailey, J., & McArthur, J. (1991). Context cues in reading: The gap between research and popular opinion. *Reading, Writing, and Learning Disabilities, 7,* 33–41.

Palincsar, A. W., Winn, J., David, Y., Snyder, B., & Stevens, D. (1993). Approaches to strategic reading instruction reflecting different assumptions regarding teaching and learning. In L. J. Meltzer (Ed.), *Strategy assessment and instruction for students with learning disabilities* (pp. 247–270). Austin, TX: Pro-Ed.

Perfetti, C. A. (1992). The representation problem in reading acquisition. In P. B. Gough, L. C. Ehri, & R. Treiman (Eds.), *Reading acquisition* (pp. 145–174). Hillsdale, NJ: Erlbaum.

Pressley, M. (1976). Mental imagery helps eight-year-olds remember what they read. *Journal of Educational Psychology, 68,* 355–359.

Pressley, M., Borkowski, J. G., Forrest-Pressley, D., Gaskins, I. W., & Wile, D. (1993). Closing thoughts on strategy instruction for individuals with learning disabilities: The good information-processing perspective. In L. J. Meltzer (Ed.), *Strategy assessment and instruction for students with learning disabilities* (pp. 355–377). Austin, TX: Pro-Ed.

Rashotte, C. A., & Torgesen, J. K. (1985). Repeated reading and reading fluency in reading disabled children. *Reading Research Quarterly, 20,* 180–188.

Rosner, J. (1979). *Helping children overcome learning difficulties.* New York: Walker.

Rule, J. M. (1984). *The structure of words.* Cambridge, MA: Educators Publishing Service.

Schneider, W. (1984). *Training high performance skills: Fallacies and guidelines* (Final Report HARL-ONR-8301). Champaign, IL: University of Illinois, Human Attention Research Laboratory.

Slingerland, B. H. (1976). *A multisensory approach to language arts for specific language disability children.* Cambridge, MA: Educators Publishing Service.

Snow, C. E., Barnes, W. S., Chandler, J., Goodman, J. F., & Hemphill, L. (1991). *Unfulfilled expectations: Home and school influences on literacy.* Cambridge, MA: Harvard University Press.

Stanovich, K. E. (1986). Matthew effects in reading: Some consequences of individual differences in the acquisition of literacy. *Reading Research Quarterly, 21,* 360–406.

———. (1992). Speculations on the causes and consequences of individual differences in early reading acquisition. In P. B. Gough, L. C. Ehri, & R. Treiman (Eds.), *Reading acquisition* (pp. 307–342). Hillsdale, NJ: Erlbaum.

Sternberg, R. J., & Powell, J. S. (1983). Comprehending verbal comprehension. *American Psychologist, 38,* 878–893.

Sternberg, R. J., Powell, J. S., & Kaye, D. B. (1983). Teaching vocabulary-building skills: A contextual approach. In A. C. Wilkinson (Ed.), *Classroom computers and cognitive science.* New York: Academic Press.

Torgesen, J. K., & Bryant, B. R. (1994a). *Test of Phonological Awareness.* Austin, TX: Pro-Ed.

———. (1994b). *Phonological Awareness Training for Reading.* Austin, TX: Pro-Ed.

Torgesen, J. K., Wagner, R. K., & Rashotte, C. A. (1994). Longitudinal studies of phonological processing and reading. *Journal of Learning Disabilities, 27,* 276–286.

Traub, N., & Bloom, F. (1992). *Recipe for reading,* 3rd ed. Cambridge, MA: Educators Publishing Service.

Treiman, R. (1992). The role of intrasyllabic units in learning to read and spell. In P. B. Gough, L. C. Ehri, & R. Treiman (Eds.), *Reading acquisition* (pp. 65–106). Hillsdale, NJ: Erlbaum.

Trelease, J. (1989). *The new read-aloud handbook.* New York: Penguin Books.

Uhry, J. K., & Shepherd, M. J. (1993). Segmentation/spelling instruction as part of a first-grade reading program: Effects on several measures of reading. *Reading Research Quarterly, 28,* 218–233.

Wagner, R. K., Torgesen, J. K., & Rashotte, C. A. (1994). The development of reading-related phonological processing abilities: New evidence of bidirectional causality from a latent variable longitudinal study. *Developmental Psychology, 30,* 73–87.

White, T. G., Power, M. A., & White, S. (1989). Morphological analysis: Implications for teaching and understanding vocabulary growth. *Reading Research Quarterly, 24,* 283–304.

White, T. G., Sowell, J., & Yanagihara, A. (1989). Teaching elementary students to use word-part clues. *The Reading Teacher, 42,* 302–308.

Wiederholt, J. L., & Bryant, B. R. (1986). *The Gray Oral Reading Test—Revised.* Austin, TX: Pro-Ed.

Wolf, M. (1991). Naming speed and reading: The contribution of the cognitive neurosciences. *Reading Research Quarterly, 26,* 123–141.

Wong, B. Y. L. (1991). The relevance of metacognition to learning disabilities. In B. Y. L. Wong (Ed.), *Learning about learning disabilities* (pp. 231–258). San Diego, CA: Academic Press.

————. (1993). Pursuing an elusive goal: Molding strategic teachers and learners. *Journal of Learning Disabilities, 26,* 354–357.

Wong, B. Y. L., & Wong, R. (1986). Study behavior as a function of metacognitive knowledge about critical task variables: An investigation of above average, average, and learning-disabled readers. *Learning Disabilities Research, 1,* 101–111.

Woodcock, R. W. (1978). *Woodcock-Johnson Psychoeducational Battery.* Hingham, MA: Teaching Resources Corporation.

————. (1987). *Woodcock Reading Mastery Tests—Revised.* Circle Pines, MN: American Guidance Service.

Yopp, H. K. (1988). The validity and reliability of phonemic awareness tests. *Reading Research Quarterly, 23,* 159–177.

8 Possible Causes of Reading Disability

WHEN PEOPLE in the LD field, and sometimes those outside of it as well, think about possible causes of RD, they generally think about defective genes or about dysfunctional brains—in short, about biology. Yet, in our experience, teachers tend to have mixed feelings about biological research on reading disability, because this research rarely has any immediate practical utility. Textbooks on learning disabilities, which almost invariably include a section on biological research, must take pains to provide reasons why teachers should care about this research. Most of these reasons are somewhat less than compelling. For instance, in the words of some textbooks, teachers should know about biological research because "the mysteries of the human brain and learning are fascinating in themselves" (Lerner, 1993, p. 217); because "teachers must understand the vocabulary and concepts of medical subspecialties to interpret medical reports" (Lerner, 1993, p. 216); because teachers should play "a cooperative role in medically related matters" (Gearheart & Gearheart, 1989, p. 49); or because "knowledge about brain patterns may someday become linked to valid instructional approaches" (C. R. Smith, 1991, p. 111).

For teachers who find brain research less than fascinating or are not often called upon to interpret medical reports, the promise of a practical payoff "someday" still may hold considerable allure. After all, the popular press is filled with reports about the miraculous advancements of science and technology. Could new methods of visualizing the brain, such as computed tomography (CT) scanning and magnetic resonance imaging (MRI), aid in the diagnosis of reading disability? Could these "hard-science" approaches to diagnosis settle once and for all the controversies about differentiating children with RD from other kinds of poor readers? Might there someday be a genetic test for reading disability, with the possibility of prenatal diagnosis of children with a vulnerability to RD? What would parents do with this kind of prenatal information?

As we will show, any practical dividends of biological research on RD, and their attendant ethical problems, are likely still a long way off. Although biological research on RD certainly may yield practical benefits "someday," we think that teachers should be familiar with this research for another, more immediate reason. As many teachers know, when parents are told that a child has a reading disability, they have an understandable desire to seek answers about causation. Older children with RD frequently ask about causation as well. Thus, in our view, teachers should know about biological research on RD because it is natural—for parents, for children, and also for teachers themselves—to seek answers about the causes of reading difficulties, and because biology provides *one part* of the answer.

Unfortunately, however, the role of biology in causing RD often has been misinterpreted and placed in the wrong context. Those with an intrinsic perspective on RD have sometimes overemphasized the role of biology, creating, as it were, a kind of one-person show, or at least a show in which all of the other players' roles are exceedingly minor. And those with an extrinsic perspective have been inclined to the opposite extreme, dropping biology from the cast entirely. But there's a third, more balanced perspective: Putting the role of biology in context requires the examination of environmental, as well as biological, influences on causation. Furthermore, because biology and environment continually shape each other, it is crucial that we try to understand the interaction of these two broad kinds of influences in causing reading disability, rather than considering the influences in isolation.

Throughout this book, we have maintained that this interactive perspective—one that emphasizes the interaction between factors within the child and the environment outside of the child—is the most educationally useful way to understand reading disability. In our view, RD cannot be reduced to a single cause, and unraveling the interplay of factors that results in an individual case of reading disability is extremely difficult, or even impossible. Nevertheless, enough is now known about reading acquisition and reading disability that we can generate some reasonable hypotheses about the multiple causes of RD. Knowledge about causation—with the role of biology set in an appropriate context, as only one player in a larger cast—is important both because there is a natural "need to know" and because this knowledge has practical implications. Furthermore, although scientific knowledge about the causes of RD is far from complete, it is nevertheless sufficient to dispel some misconceptions about RD—for example, that reading disability is exclusively the result of unfortunate genetic inheritance, of immutable brain defects, or of inadequate instruction.

In this chapter, we examine research evidence pertaining to some of the possible causal factors in reading disability. In the first major section of the chapter we draw upon research from an intrinsic perspective, and in the second section we draw upon research from an extrinsic perspective. These bodies of research show that both intrinsic biological differences *and* environmental factors play a role in the causation of reading disability. For instance, there are cases in which studies cited to support a genetic explanation of reading disability could also be cited to support an environmental explanation, and vice versa. We do not wish to pit biological accounts of RD against environmental accounts. Rather, we use the research evidence to explore, in the third and final section of this chapter, how an interactive perspective can provide the most accurate, as well as the most educationally useful, account of the genesis of RD. Why do children with RD go off track in reading in the first place? And why do some children go astray at a particular point—for instance, in the phase of phonetic-cue word recognition, becoming compensatory readers—rather than earlier or later in reading acquisition? These are the kinds of questions to which we ultimately hazard some answers.

Biological Influences on RD

It would be astonishing indeed if the broad, complex set of mental processes involved in reading had no connection to biology, or if wide variations in reading skill did not reflect any underlying biological differences. In fact, research done from an intrinsic perspective does document some biological factors that may play a role in reading disability. In this section, we review three kinds of biological differences that have been associated with RD: genetic differences, structural differences in the brain, and differences in brain functioning. We then draw some general conclusions about the role played by these differences in RD.

Our use of the word *differences* in this chapter and elsewhere is deliberate. Certain biological differences may make a particular youngster vulnerable to reading disability. However, as we will see, there is little evidence that these differences constitute actual neurological abnormalities or brain defects. Rather, we will argue that, in most cases, these biological differences are best conceptualized as being part of a normal continuum that includes both other poor readers and normally achieving readers. Moreover, the biological differences that have been associated with RD clearly do not preclude learning to read, sometimes at a high level of achievement.

Before we begin, we should acknowledge that for most readers as well as for the authors topics such as genetics and neuroanatomy are not exactly light reading. Moreover, a full treatment of these topics, and of their relationship to reading disability, could easily take up a volume of its own. We have tried to convey essential points in comprehensible language without sacrificing basic accuracy. However, for more detail than we provide here, readers may wish to consult sources such as Hynd and Semrud-Clikeman (1989), Plomin (1989, 1991), Plomin, DeFries, and McClearn (1990), and S. D. Smith (1986).

Genetic Differences

It has long been known that reading disability has a tendency to run in some families (DeFries, Vogler, & LaBuda, 1985). Yet the fact that RD recurs in families does not necessarily mean that the cause for RD in these families is genetic; the family resemblance could instead be due to shared environmental characteristics, such as a lack of exposure to books or to certain kinds of verbal stimulation. On the other hand, given that a wide range of specific cognitive skills as well as academic achievement show significant genetic influence (Plomin, 1989), it is reasonable to suppose that there might be genetic effects in reading disability as well.

Twin Studies and Modes of Inheritance. In attempting to ascertain the extent of genetic influence in RD, most studies have employed the twin design. Twin studies, in which at least one member of each twin pair has RD, compare identical twins with fraternal twins. Studies of this kind assume that environmental influences are similar across the two different types of twins. Note, however, that identical twins share identical genetic material, whereas fraternal twins, on average, share only 50 percent of their genes, the same percentage as do other siblings. Thus, a greater concordance rate, or similarity, between identical as compared with fraternal twins would suggest genetic influence in RD.

Twin studies of reading disability do indicate a significantly higher concordance rate for identical than for fraternal twins (Decker & Bender, 1988; DeFries, Fulker, & LaBuda, 1987; Pennington, Gilger, Pauls, S. A. Smith, S. D. Smith, & DeFries, 1991; Plomin, Owen, & McGuffin, 1994; S. D. Smith, Pennington, Kimberling, & Ing, 1990). In other words, as compared with fraternal twins, identical twins are more likely to have a similar status—such that both have RD or both are good readers. However, although these findings suggest that genes do play a role in many cases of reading disability, the mode of genetic transmission in RD is a matter of considerable debate.

Some investigators (e.g., Pennington et al., 1991; S. D. Smith et al., 1990) have suggested that RD may be inherited in an autosomal dominant fashion, in a manner similar to the genetic transmission of disorders such as neurofibromatosis or Tourette's syndrome. In this view, RD could be passed on via a single gene, whose location in the human genome might eventually be specified; research suggests possible locations on either chromosome 6 or chromosome 15 (S. D. Smith, Kimberling, Pennington, & Lubs, 1993; S. D. Smith et al., 1990). However, other investigators (e.g., Plomin, 1989, 1991) have argued that, to the extent that RD is "hereditary," inheritance is much more likely to be influenced by multiple genes acting together.

Knowing the mode of genetic transmission is important for practical as well as for theoretical reasons. In particular, although the fact that multiple genes influence a trait does not rule out identifying at least some of those genes (Plomin et al., 1994), scientists have been most successful in identifying and in developing diagnostic tests for single, major gene disorders. Furthermore, even developing a genetic test for a single-gene disorder with straightforward Mendelian inheritance—such as the test for Huntington's disease that emerged in the 1980s—is akin to looking for the proverbial needle in the haystack. To the extent that RD is influenced by many genes rather than by one major gene, developing a diagnostic genetic test for RD is likely to be particularly difficult and time consuming.

Like other attempts to link specific genes to complex behavioral disorders, the initial findings linking RD to chromosome 15 have been plagued by serious problems with replication (see C. Mann, 1994), and the claims of linkage to chromosome 6 could well meet the same fate. In any case, virtually all of the investigators interested in the genetics of reading disability acknowledge that RD may be transmitted in multiple ways. In other words, even if the mode of genetic transmission involves a single gene in some families, it is clear that many families do not fit the single-gene model. Of course, these observations barely even begin to address a host of other issues, such as the fact that not all children with RD demonstrate a family history of reading problems. Thus, the development of a genetic test for RD, and especially one that would apply to a broad population, seems unlikely in the foreseeable future.

Heritabilities of Specific Cognitive Skills. Twin studies also are used to derive a statistic termed *heritability*. In fact, research on reading disability often has emphasized a particular type of heritability known as *group heritability*. Group heritability describes the proportion of the difference between individuals with RD and the unselected population that can be ascribed to genetic differences (Plomin, 1991). However, group heritability for a particular characteristic among individuals with RD (e.g., word-recognition skills) may differ from the heritability for individual differences in the normal population (Olson, Rack, Conners, DeFries, & Fulker, 1991).

Although research indicates that genes play some role in many cases of reading disability, heritabilities vary depending upon the specific reading or cognitive skill examined. For instance, among individuals with reading disability, word-recognition skills appear to be more heritable than reading comprehension (DeFries et al., 1987; Olson, Wise, Conners, Rack, & Fulker, 1989), and phonological-reading skill has a much higher heritability than orthographic skill (Olson et al., 1991). The heritability of word-recognition skills may be mediated largely by the high heritability of phonological reading (Plomin, 1991). Thus, one of the cognitive-processing deficits central to reading disability—phonological-reading skill—shows particularly strong genetic influence.

In short, one of the multiple causes of reading disability appears to involve an inherited weakness in a phonological-processing skill crucial to reading acquisition in an alphabetic language. Whether or not other phonological-processing skills, such as naming speed and phonological awareness, will show similar genetic influence remains to be seen. Nevertheless, given that there are stable individual differences in phonological-processing skills in young children (Wagner, Torgesen, & Rashotte, 1994), and given that RD does not appear to constitute a distinctive, separate syndrome of poor reading (Fletcher et al., 1994; Shaywitz, Escobar, Shaywitz, Fletcher, & Makuch, 1992), it is quite possible that most cases of reading disability represent the extreme of a normal continuum of phonological processing. Data on the heritabilities of various phonological-processing skills in nondisabled readers as well as in children with RD are still needed to confirm this view (Plomin, 1991).

Structural Differences in the Brain

Research on possible structural differences in the brains of individuals with reading disability has employed two major methods: postmortem studies and neuroimaging techniques. In postmortem studies, the brains of individuals thought to have RD are autopsied after their deaths. These autopsies generally include extensive sectioning of the brain, with microscopic examination for evidence of differences at the cellular level. The second method, neuroimaging, involves techniques such as computed tomography scanning and magnetic resonance imaging, which yield images of the brain in living subjects.

Many, though not all, of these studies of structural differences in the brain have focused on adult subjects rather than on children. Fortunately, there are few children with RD available for autopsy. Also, neuroimaging techniques do not lend themselves to routine use with children: CT scanning involves radiation, and MRI requires subjects to lie in a confining chamber, which some children find difficult to tolerate.

Two basic findings of research on structural brain differences in RD are widely cited. The first finding involves the presence, among some individuals with RD, of unusual symmetry in a brain structure called the *planum temporale*. The planum temporale is an area on the surface of each temporal lobe behind the primary auditory cortex that is thought to be involved in language processing (Flowers, 1993). In the general population, the left planum temporale usually is larger than the right one, reflecting not only the greater incidence of right-handedness in the general population (Steinmetz, Volkmann, Jancke, & Freund, 1990) but also, presumably, the greater involvement of the left hemisphere in language processing. However, in many individuals with RD, the two plana appear to be more equal in size (Flowers, 1993; Galaburda, Sherman, Rosen, Aboitiz, & Geschwind, 1985; Galaburda, Corsiglia, Rosen, & Sherman, 1987; Hynd & Semrud-Clikeman, 1989; Larsen, Hoien, Lundberg, & Odegaard, 1990), although not all investigators have found this pattern (e.g., Denckla, LeMay, & Chapman, 1985). Galaburda et al. (1987) further suggest that the apparent symmetry arises from a larger-than-usual right planum temporale, not a smaller-than-usual left planum temporale, although studies also conflict on this latter point (e.g., Hynd, Semrud-Clikeman, Lorys, Novey, & Eliopulos, 1990).

The second finding, from postmortem studies, involves apparent microscopic differences in some of the brains of individuals with reading disability. In these brains, there were more misplaced and unusually organized cells—particularly, though not exclusively, in the left-hemisphere regions of the brain involved in language processing (Galaburda et al., 1985). Galaburda and his colleagues have suggested that these anomalies in cell organization arise during fetal development. In addition, Geschwind and Galaburda (1985) have argued that such differences in brain morphology—both the cellular anomalies and the unusual brain symmetries just described—may be linked to a number of other factors, including an increased incidence of autoimmune disease.

In summary, there is evidence to indicate that structural brain differences, especially in areas of the brain involved in language processing, are associated with *some* instances of reading disability. However, beyond this one affirmative statement, there is abundant speculation but little hard evidence. For instance, the questions of whether these structural brain differences exist in *most* individuals with RD, of how structural brain differences arise, and of whether they bear a relationship, if any, to other problems such as autoimmune disease all are highly debatable. In their extensive review of the literature, Hynd and Semrud-Clikeman (1989) conclude that the available evidence is suggestive and warrants further study, but that structural brain differences cannot yet be said to characterize reading disability.

Furthermore, even if structural differences do turn out to characterize reading disability, their precise effect on cognitive functioning remains unclear. Flowers (1993) discusses some unpublished data (Wood & Flowers, 1991) indicating that MRI measurements of the right planum temporale correlate negatively with serial naming speed and with verbal memory, but there is little evidence delineating how structural differences in the brain might correspond to the specific differences in cognitive functioning that are typical of reading disability. Also, the way in which the genetic differences mentioned in the previous section relate to structural brain differences, if they do so at all, is uncertain. These many unanswered questions suggest that we are a long way from being able to use neuroimaging techniques to diagnose individual cases of reading disability.

Functional Brain Differences

Another way to consider brain differences is to examine how the brain works rather than how it is built. Individuals with reading disability might differ from nondisabled readers not so much in terms of their basic brain structures, as in terms of their brain functioning. Of course, in the most obvious sense, individuals with RD must differ from nondisabled individuals in brain functioning, because reading involves the brain and individuals with RD have deficient reading skills. However, researchers interested in brain functioning and reading disability have tried to specify functional differences at the biological level.

Numerous techniques exist for examining brain functioning. Here, we will briefly consider four techniques that specifically have been used to measure brain functioning in subjects with reading disability: positron emission tomography (PET), measurements of regional cerebral blood flow (rCBF), evoked potentials, and brain electrical activity mapping (BEAM).

PET is a radiological technique related to CT scanning. It has been employed to measure a variety of brain functions, including glucose metabolism, oxygen consumption, and blood flow. Of these three indicators of moment-to-moment brain function, blood flow appears to be the most reliable (Raichle, 1994). When PET is used to measure regional cerebral blood flow, water labeled with oxygen-15, a radioisotope of ordinary oxygen, is administered into a blood vessel; from there it travels to the brain, where it provides multiple pictures of blood flow as the subject performs a variety of cognitive tasks. Although few people relish the idea of a brain full of radioactive water, PET is considered to be safe because oxygen-15 decays very rapidly and only low doses of the radioisotope are necessary. Another technique for measuring regional cerebral blood flow involves the use of xenon-133 as a radioactive tracer, administered by inhalation (Flowers, 1993).

Evoked potentials involve electroencephalographic (EEG) data recorded while the subject responds to a variety of stimuli, such as flashes of light or spoken words, or performs a cognitive task, such as reading a word. In the BEAM technique, EEG and evoked-potential data are used to create a color-coded, moving visual display of electrical activity in the brain. As both the evoked-potential and BEAM techniques have the advantages of being noninvasive and nonradiological in nature, unlike PET and rCBF, they are more feasible to use with children. However, the interpretation of evoked-potential data and of data from BEAM stands out as being particularly complex and controversial (Flowers, 1993; Lyon, Newby, Recht, & Caldwell, 1991), in a domain already more complex and controversial than most.

Data from these four sources—PET, rCBF, evoked potentials, and BEAM—do suggest some possible differences in brain functioning among individuals with RD. For instance, while performing language and reading tasks, subjects with RD appear to differ from nondisabled readers in brain electrical activity associated with the left parietal area, the left temporal area, and the medial frontal area of the brain (Duffy & McAnulty, 1985). Rumsey et al. (1992) used PET to measure blood flow in a group of male subjects with RD and found that, unlike nondisabled controls, the subjects with RD failed to activate a particular region of the brain (the left temporoparietal cortex) while performing a rhyme-detection task. In other studies, Flowers and her colleagues (Flowers, 1993; Flowers, Wood, & Naylor, 1991) have used xenon-inhalation rCBF with a group of adult subjects diagnosed as having RD in childhood. These investigators found that, when performing an orthographic task, subjects with a history of RD showed a pattern of blood flow different from that found in nondisabled subjects, specifically in two brain areas heavily involved in language processing: Wernicke's area and the angular gyrus. Furthermore, this different pattern of blood flow was present regardless of the reading level of the subjects with RD. In other words, adults whose reading difficulties had been remediated showed the same blood flow pattern as did those with persistent reading problems. This last finding is particularly interesting because it suggests the possibility of a stable pattern of functional brain differences in some individuals with RD.

Such techniques do have something to offer in advancing our understanding of brain functioning, of the biological correlates of various cognitive processes, and, perhaps in time, of reading disability itself. For instance, should a stable pattern of brain functioning emerge as characteristic of RD, some of these techniques might prove useful diagnostically—"someday." However, even if certain functional brain differences do characterize reading disability, their causal relationship to RD is far from certain. Do individuals have RD because their brains function differently? Or do their brains function differently because they have RD? In other words, even if the brains of individuals with RD do function differently, these functional differences might not be a cause of their poor reading but, rather, might only reflect either the poor reading itself or some other, underlying cause.

Methodological Issues

Methodological shortcomings characterize much of the research on biological differences in reading disability. These shortcomings make it impossible to draw conclusions more definite than the ones we have already discussed. For example, research in behavioral genetics has been criticized on a number of counts, including bias in selecting subjects and controls, inadequate definition of the trait being studied (i.e., reading disability), and misuse of statistical methods (C. Mann, 1994). Many of the studies on brain functioning are open to similar criticisms. Moreover, these studies on brain functioning tend to be particularly difficult to interpret, because so many variables, such as attention, motivation, and practice, may influence experimental outcomes. The problem of interpretation is exacerbated by the fact that many of the functional neuroimaging techniques we described here are relatively new.

The studies on structural differences in the brain have also come under heavy criticism (e.g., Hynd & Semrud-Clikeman, 1989) for problems such as failure to appraise handedness in subjects, failure to describe subjects adequately, and questionable classification of some subjects as having RD. An especially important problem (Hynd & Semrud-Clikeman, 1989) has involved the failure to demonstrate that structural differences—such as greater symmetry in the planum temporale—are unique to RD and thus do not also exist in individuals with other developmental disorders, such as mild mental retardation or attention-deficit hyperactivity disorder (ADHD). In addition, although the findings of Galaburda and his colleagues regarding microscopic structural differences in cell organization have been widely cited, they involve only a very small number of cases and lack independent verification (Coles, 1987; Hynd & Semrud-Clikeman, 1989).

Conclusions

These methodological issues aside, we think it likely that some intrinsic biological differences do play a causal role in many cases of reading disability. We find the evidence regarding the role of genetic differences in RD to be most convincing, because it converges with two very substantial bodies of research. The first of these has generated evidence supporting the importance of phonological-processing skills in reading disability, which we have reviewed at length in this book. And the second points to the strong influence of genetics in a wide range of human cognitive abilities, temperamental characteristics, and personality. (This latter body of literature is well beyond the scope of the present book, but interested readers may wish to consult sources such as Bouchard, 1984, 1994; Plomin, 1988; and Scarr, 1992.) To what extent structural or functional brain differences also characterize reading disability, and how (or even whether) structural or functional differences relate to genetic differences and to each other, remains to be seen.

However, as we indicated at the outset of this section, evidence that RD involves intrinsic biological differences does not necessarily mean that these differences constitute a "disease" or "defect," or that they doom children to a lifetime of poor reading. Nevertheless, evidence about biological differences in reading disability frequently is interpreted in just these erroneous ways.

Differences Versus Defects. With regard to the issue of differences versus defects, there is little evidence to suggest that the structural or functional brain differences seen in some individuals with RD constitute actual abnormalities. For instance, although in most normally achieving readers the left planum temporale is larger than the right, a significant percentage of these readers demonstrate reversed asymmetry, or symmetrical plana—just like the subjects with RD (Galaburda & Kemper, 1979; Lyon et al., 1991). Although apparent structural differences have been documented in the brains of subjects with RD, the finding of clear-cut abnormalities is rare (e.g., Denckla et al., 1985). And as we noted earlier, many functional neuroimaging techniques, such as BEAM, are so new that individual differences in nondisabled readers have not yet even been explored (Lyon et al., 1991).

In the realm of genetics, it may turn out that a single-gene "defect" characterizes a minority of families with RD. Currently, however, the evidence for such a defect, even in a minority of families, is limited at best. We are inclined to agree with Plomin (1991) that genetic effects in most cases of RD probably involve multiple genes and are part of a normal continuum of individual differences rather than etiologically distinct characteristics.

Biology Does Not "Determine" Reading Skill. Even more important, from a practitioner's perspective, is our other point: The biological differences associated with reading disability clearly do not preclude learning to read, at least not in the vast majority of instances. In other words, biology does not act alone to "determine" reading skill, in youngsters with RD or in anyone else. How do we know that this contention is true? We know it in part from research on the role of environmental factors in reading disability, which we will address in the next section of this chapter. But we also know it from the research on biological differences that we have just reviewed.

For instance, most of the work on biological differences in reading disability includes, within the RD group, adults with a wide range of reading skill. Pennington et al. (1991) use the term *compensated adults* to refer to these individuals, who possess a history of reading difficulty but nevertheless have attained a relatively high level of achievement in reading as adults. Similarly, recall the findings of Flowers and her colleagues regarding an apparently stable pattern of functional brain differences in remediated as well as in low-achieving subjects with RD. Even if this stable pattern of functional brain differences holds up under further experimental scrutiny, the pattern obviously does not rule out learning to read!

Some authorities (e.g., Plomin, 1991) suggest that the heritability of reading disability may be as high as 50 percent. In other words, genetic influences may account for as much as half the variance for RD. But another way of stating the same hypothesis is to say that at least 50 percent of the variance is accounted for by environmental influences. That is, environmental influences on reading disability are at least as important as are genetic influences.

The heritabilities of some specific cognitive skills, such as phonological reading, could be even higher than 50 percent (e.g., Olson et al., 1991). However, as Stephen Jay Gould points out in his discussion of heritability and human intelligence (Gould, 1981), heritabilities, no matter how high the percentages, say nothing about the extent to which a characteristic may be modified by the environment. Gould uses vision as an example. Certain weaknesses in vision may show strong genetic influence, yet someone who has inherited a weakness in vision may see quite normally with glasses. Thus, the term *heritable* is most definitely not a synonym for *inevitable* or *predetermined*.

Consider an analogy involving height. Like phonological-processing skills and many other cognitive skills involved in reading, height involves a continuum. Adult females who are three feet tall, or those who are seven feet tall, probably have growth abnormalities. However, in our view, most youngsters with RD are more like a woman who is five feet tall, perhaps with a mother or a grandmother who was also five feet tall. The woman who is five feet tall does not have a biological abnormality with respect to height; she is just short. Being short might make it more difficult, but not necessarily impossible, for her to succeed in certain kinds of endeavors in which height is important, as in some sports. Similarly, many youngsters with RD may bring to reading acquisition certain biological differences that make it more difficult—but by no means impossible—for them to learn to read.

A Final Caveat. Biological research on human cognitive abilities and behavior has not enjoyed a pristine past, often serving conveniently to confirm what some people thought was "obvious" all along—that blacks are inferior to whites, that women are inferior to men, that Jews are inferior to non-Jews, and so on. Or, as another writer put it, "The history of brain research does not exactly reveal a noble and impartial quest for truth. ...Typically, when scientists haven't found the differences they were seeking, they haven't abandoned the goal or the belief that such differences exist; they just moved to another part of the anatomy or another corner of the brain" (Tavris, 1992, p. 44). Coles (1987) argues a similar point about the dogged pursuit by researchers of biological evidence to confirm the preexisting assumption of a biological cause for reading disability. Although certainly the intent of most researchers is to help people and not to harm them, it is clear that the potential for misuse and misinterpretation of biological research on complex behaviors, including reading disability, is enormous.

Consider, for example, the issue of *Science* dated June 17, 1994, which highlights the field of behavioral genetics. One article in this issue (C. Mann, 1994) refers to a report linking a rare genetic mutation to violent or aggressive behavior in some individuals who carry the mutation. In the article, members of the research team that published the report describe their dismay at some of the public reaction to the research. One researcher received phone calls from lawyers eager to test clients on Death Row for the mutated gene in order to exonerate them for criminal behavior; talk-show hosts suggested the possibility of sterilizing people who carry the gene. It does not take an overactive imagination to envision similarly disturbing scenarios involving an "RD gene." Would the intricacies of research on biological differences in RD be discussed on the talk-show circuit and elsewhere? Or would many people view the research as confirming that some children simply are predestined to be poor readers?

Of course, all research can be misinterpreted, and science and technology can be used toward good as well as toward bad ends. The extreme found among some critics of biological research—who merely deny the existence of biological differences—is not helpful either. Anyway, this head-in-the-sand approach is increasingly untenable in the face of mounting evidence for biological influences on a wide range of human abilities and behaviors. Rather, biological differences in reading disability must be viewed in context, as only one important set of influences on the reading achievement of individuals with RD. Next, we consider another important set of influences on reading disability—environmental influences.

Environmental Influences on RD

According to traditional definitions of learning disabilities (e.g., National Joint Committee on Learning Disabilities, 1988), environmental factors are not supposed to play a significant causal role in reading disability. Much of the research relevant to understanding environmental influences on RD has been done by investigators *outside* of the LD field—that is, from an extrinsic perspective, which emphasizes the importance of environmental factors in causing poor reading. These researchers have focused on causes of poor reading in general rather than on causes of reading disability in particular.

Nevertheless, we believe that this research is quite relevant to an understanding of RD, for several reasons. First, as we have discussed in previous chapters, children with RD are very similar to other poor readers in terms of the cognitive skills related to word recognition and perhaps some other cognitive areas as well (see, for example, Fletcher et al., 1994). Second, as we discussed in the initial section of this chapter, although some biological differences may characterize children with reading disability, there is little evidence that most children with RD suffer from a distinctive biological abnormality that makes them qualitatively different—from other kinds of poor readers or even from good readers. And finally, although the LD field assumes that environmental factors cannot account for reading disability, in actual practice the nature of the environment—for instance, the adequacy of instruction for a particular youngster—is rarely, if ever, assessed.

Environmental influences on reading achievement are abundant, including both influences in the home and at school. However, we should remember that environmental factors affecting achievement and cognitive development in very broad ways are not likely to provide a good theoretical account of reading disability, because RD involves a relatively specific deficit in reading. Rather, it is important to look for environmental influences on the particular cognitive deficits that are causally central to RD—for instance, deficits in areas such as phonological processing and word recognition. Although many practitioners tend to think of "cognitive deficits" and "processing disorders" as shaped entirely by biology, cognitive psychologists have pointed to the influence of the environment and of experience on cognitive processing (e.g., Spear & Sternberg, 1992; Sternberg, 1988; Vellutino & Scanlon, 1991).

Another place to look for possible environmental influences on RD involves differences in background knowledge related to reading and, specifically, to word-recognition skills. Because RD emerges early in schooling, these differences in background knowledge would have to be shaped in the home or at the very beginning of school—for instance, in kindergarten. Examples of background knowledge related to word recognition include letter knowledge and basic concepts about print (e.g., the knowledge that words are separated by spaces).

In this section, we discuss possible environmental influences on the cognitive deficits central to reading disability, first in terms of variables in the home, then in terms of variables in school. The periods we emphasize regarding these environmental influences are the preschool years, kindergarten, and first grade. (Because some of this research has been extensively reviewed in previous chapters, we only summarize here.) Third, we discuss the concept of nonshared environment and its possible application to understanding causation of reading disability. Finally, we draw some conclusions regarding the role of environmental causes in reading disability.

Influences in the Home

Many reading authorities (e.g., Adams, 1990; Anderson, Hiebert, Scott, & Wilkinson, 1985) have emphasized that reading aloud regularly to children in the preschool years plays a pivotal role in their later reading achievement. Adams (1990) suggests that among children entering kindergarten, differences in exposure to reading and to print may be vast, depending in great part upon the extent to which the children's parents have read aloud to them at home. Although Adams focuses on differences across socioeconomic status (SES) levels, there are clearly within-SES differences as well.

For example, Snow, Barnes, Chandler, Goodman, and Hemphill (1991) found that many low-SES families provided a highly literate home environment to their children, including frequent reading aloud to children. Low-SES children who came from more literate home environments had an initial advantage in reading achievement, specifically in word recognition, over those from less literate home environments. In fact, many of the former youngsters did extremely well in reading, especially in the early grades. Similarly, just as not all poor children lack exposure to reading and to print in the preschool years, not all middle-class youngsters receive equal exposure to reading and to print.

It is not just the fact of reading aloud to children, but also the way parents interact with their children during reading, that is important. Both Anderson et al. (1985) and Adams (1990) suggest that parents who actively engage children in stories, who ask thought-provoking questions, who elaborate upon word meanings, and who draw children's attention to features of the print (e.g., spaces between words, directionality in reading, and specific letters) provide the greatest benefit to their children. It is easy to see how drawing children's attention to features of the print might benefit word-recognition development. However, helping children to acquire knowledge in areas such as vocabulary also might benefit later word recognition. For example, children who have extensive vocabularies can devote more of their mental resources to acquiring word-recognition skills than to comprehension (Mason, 1992).

Children do enter school with large individual differences in background knowledge about letters and print, although these differences may be shaped in a variety of ways. Moreover, the differences exist both within and across socioeconomic levels, affecting not only poor families, as noted by Snow et al. (1991), but middle-class families as well. For instance, in one suburban school, Dreyer (1994) observed very wide differences in print-related knowledge among entering kindergartners, with some youngsters recognizing no letters or words at all and others able to read simple text. By the middle of the year, all of the children could recognize some letters and most could recognize at least a few words. However, Dreyer also noted substantial variation in progress. This progress was linked both to letter knowledge and to phonological-processing skills.

In Dreyer's (1994) study and that of others (e.g., Wagner et al., 1994), substantial individual differences in phonological processing appear to be present among entering kindergartners as well. As we have already discussed, differences in phonological processing may be partially attributable to biology. But what are the environmental influences on phonological processing?

Although environmental influences on phonological processing in the preschool years have not been widely studied, one possible influence is the extent to which children are read nursery rhymes or play rhyming or alliterative word games. For example, Maclean, Bryant, and Bradley (1987) found that children's knowledge of nursery rhymes at age three predicted later phonological awareness and later reading achievement. The relationship between phonological awareness and word recognition is clearly reciprocal, as we have noted in previous chapters, and the relationship between other phonological-processing skills and reading may be reciprocal as well (Spear & Sternberg, 1992). Thus, the beginning reading and writing skills that some children acquire at home—such as letter names and an occasional sight word—may also help to promote phonological processing.

Of course, we are not suggesting that parents should drill letters and sight vocabulary into three- and four-year-olds in order to promote later reading achievement. Rather, our point is that children enter school with wide individual differences in terms of the cognitive abilities and kinds of background knowledge that are central to acquiring word-recognition skills. One source of these differences involves experiences that children have in the preschool years.

Influences in School

In Chapter 6, we reviewed research indicating that a code-emphasis approach to reading instruction in the beginning elementary grades is especially beneficial in developing word-recognition skills. Moreover, children with learning difficulties appear to derive particular benefit from code-emphasis instruction in the early grades. V. Mann (1991) suggests that such instruction enhances phonological awareness, a suggestion that seems quite reasonable given the reciprocal relationship between phonological awareness and reading. Other research we reviewed indicated that phonological-awareness skills can be trained and that such training, particularly in combination with a program of formal reading instruction, can improve reading achievement.

Some authorities (Clay, 1990; Lyons, 1989) suggest that appropriate instructional interventions in the early elementary grades can prevent poor readers from being mislabeled as "learning disabled." However, the view of these authorities as to what constitutes appropriate instruction is somewhat different from that of authorities such as V. Mann (1991). The former writers contend that many youngsters classified as having LD have been taught to rely excessively on decoding skills in reading but insufficiently on other kinds of cues, such as contextual cues. Thus, in the view of authorities like Clay (1990) and Lyons (1989), what constitutes appropriate instruction is less code emphasis and more meaning emphasis.

In other words, in evaluating instructional causes of poor reading, whole-language advocates tend to believe that the problem is too much phonics, whereas code-emphasis advocates tend to believe that the problem is not enough phonics or not the right kind of phonics. We have contended that both views are wrong. Rather, all children—and especially poor readers—require *both* explicit word-recognition instruction, including some work on isolated skills, as typifies code-emphasis approaches, *and* more meaningful, engaging, comprehension-based activities, of the kind espoused by whole-language advocates. In addition, different children also require different instructional emphases, as we discussed in Chapters 6 and 7 and as we will discuss further in Chapter 9.

Many other variables in instruction may influence reading achievement in general and word-recognition skills in particular, especially in the early grades, when word recognition is most likely to be the focus of reading instruction. These other variables include the manner in which the teacher responds to word-recognition errors (Chinn, Waggoner, Anderson, Schommer, & Wilkinson, 1993; Hoffman, O'Neal, Kastler, Clements, Segel, & Nash, 1984); the amount of classroom time devoted to reading instruction, which can vary substantially from teacher to teacher (Rosenshine & Stevens, 1984); and the pace of instruction, which can also vary substantially from one teacher to another, even within the same grade (Gambrell, 1984).

Ability grouping in reading, which still is used in many schools, appears to be particularly detrimental to children in low reading groups (Anderson et al., 1985). Children in these groups tend to receive less effective instruction than do other children, because of a variety of factors, including less practice reading in context, lower expectations on the part of the teacher, and a higher incidence of behavior problems in low reading groups. Moving up to a higher reading group is possible in theory but occurs rarely in reality. Yet, as Anderson et al. (1985) point out, methods of determining initial reading-group placement are far from flawless. For instance, a youngster might be classified erroneously as a low-ability reader in first grade but live up (or rather down) to that classification in a self-fulfilling prophecy. It has even been suggested (Allington, 1983) that initial reading-group placement is a more important determinant of future reading achievement than is actual ability.

Nonshared Environment

In the past, environmental influences, whether in the home or at school, often were conceptualized in rather global terms. This relatively broad view of the environment emphasized environmental differences across families or communities. Examples of these broad environmental influences include differences in socioeconomic status, parental education, or cultural expectations.

More recently, however, psychologists and behavioral geneticists have emphasized a less global view of the environment. Specifically, they have emphasized the importance of *nonshared* environment in shaping differences among siblings (Plomin, 1989; Plomin & Daniels, 1987). Nonshared environment involves experiences at home, in school, and elsewhere that are specific to individual children rather than shared by children within the same family. Some examples of factors that contribute to nonshared environment are birth order (e.g., first-born children in a family have different experiences than do later-born children), gender (e.g., boys have different experiences than do girls), and schooling (e.g., children in the same family experience different teachers). In other words, environmental influences vary not only within and across socioeconomic classes but also within families, from one youngster to another.

The basic argument of many behavioral geneticists and psychologists (e.g., Bouchard, 1994; Plomin et al., 1994) is that the similarities among various members of the same family—in a number of personality, cognitive, and behavioral traits—tend to be due primarily to genetic influences, not to shared environmental influences such as those associated with socioeconomic status. Rather, important environmental influences tend to be of the nonshared type. These nonshared environmental influences also tend to contribute to *differences* rather than to similarities among family members. Of course, genetic influences, too, may contribute to differences among family members.

This position does not deny the importance of environmental influences in shaping cognitive abilities and behavior. Instead, it holds that these influences "do not operate on a family-by-family basis but rather on an individual-by-individual basis" (Plomin, 1989, p. 109) and that these influences tend to make family members different rather than similar. Most of us need only to think of our own families to realize that differences among members of the same family may be considerable. Indeed, sibling correlations for a variety of personality characteristics and cognitive abilities typically are only in the low to moderate range (Plomin, 1989).

Obviously, the environmental influences on RD that we have discussed—both those in the home, such as the extent to which children are read to or play rhyming games, and those at school, such as ability grouping or the nature of reading instruction—may vary widely for children who come from the same family. Thus, the fact that one youngster in a family has RD whereas a sibling is a good reader might owe as much or more to nonshared environmental influences as to genetic inheritance. For example, two siblings might inherit a similar genetic vulnerability to RD, but nonshared environmental influences might cause this vulnerability to be realized for only one of the children.

Conclusions

The specific cognitive deficits that are characteristic of RD, such as deficits in phonological processing and in word-recognition skills, are susceptible to environmental influences. As we have discussed, children enter kindergarten with wide individual differences in reading-related knowledge and in cognitive-processing skills, and these differences may be shaped, at least in part, by the environment. Early in schooling, there are many instructional variables that can exacerbate or even create poor word recognition. Moreover, even a genuine biological weakness (e.g., an inherited weakness in phonological processing) develops only in interaction with the environment. Thus, in our view, environmental influences are one of the multiple causes of reading disability.

These environmental influences are not particular to one socioeconomic class. In other words, a child need not come from a generally "disadvantaged" background in order to lack skills that are important for reading acquisition. By implication, as Coles (1987) aptly points out, a youngster who appears to meet exclusionary criteria and who is classified as having reading disability may have problems that actually stem largely from environmental causes.

Furthermore, as the concept of nonshared environment suggests, the influences even on different children within the same family may vary greatly. For instance, two siblings who come from a literate home environment may nevertheless have experienced different amounts of being read to or different kinds of interactions during reading. They certainly will have many different experiences in school, including different teachers, classroom environments, and friends.

We should underscore the fact that parents need not be "bad" parents, or teachers "bad" teachers, to exert an influence that is less than ideal on children's reading acquisition. For example, conscientious and concerned parents may be limited in the amount of time that they can spend reading to children because of the demands of making a living. And a highly competent teacher may be constrained by a required curriculum. In our experience, nearly all parents want to see their children succeed academically, and the vast majority of teachers sincerely want to help children learn.

As emphasized at the beginning of this book, we do not think the solution to the problem of reading disability lies in the extrinsic perspective alone, any more than it lies in the intrinsic perspective alone. Just as genetic differences do not develop in a vacuum, environmental variables do not write on a blank slate. Most important is the following point: Although in books it is often convenient to discuss biological and environmental influences separately, in everyday life these two broad kinds of influences never act in isolation. Rather, they continually interact.

For example, an interesting and seemingly paradoxical finding from behavioral genetics is that measures traditionally thought of as environmental (e.g., regarding parents' behavior toward their children) actually show significant genetic effects (Plomin, Reiss, Hetherington, & Howe, 1994). How can this be? The usual interpretation of this finding is that children shape their own environments based on certain genetically influenced characteristics (Plomin, Reiss, et al., 1994; Scarr, 1992; Scarr & McCartney, 1983). Parents of more than one child, as well as many teachers, can relate to this idea. For example, as we have noted, characteristics of temperament and personality show strong genetic influence; and in terms of environmental shaping, a child who is temperamentally placid and easygoing tends to elicit a different response from adults than does a youngster who is temperamentally more "difficult." Of course, these responses from adults may in turn influence children in a variety of ways.

Conversely, the environment and experience may alter biology. For instance, repeated practice with a cognitive task appears to change the way the brain organizes itself and the neural circuits that are recruited (Raichle, 1994). Thus, just as children shape their own experiences based in part on their own unique biology, the experiences they have may also shape their biology.

Exploring Causation from an Interactive Perspective

In our model of reading disability, there is a common road to good reading that consists of a series of developmental phases: visual-cue word recognition, phonetic-cue word recognition, controlled word recognition, automatic word recognition, strategic reading, and proficient reading. Reading disability is conceptualized as involving a departure from the road to proficient reading in one of the first four developmental phases pertaining to word recognition. Returning to the questions posed at the beginning of this chapter, we ask again, Why do children with RD wander off the road to proficient reading at all? And why might a particular youngster go astray in one phase rather than in another?

Answering these questions, as we have repeatedly argued, requires an interactive perspective. However, research on RD done from an interactive perspective is relatively scant. Some notable exceptions (e.g., Stanovich, 1986) have provided crucial insights about what happens to youngsters with RD, and to other poor readers as well, *after* initial failure in reading, but they do not address the issue of ultimate causation. Indeed, from an interactive perspective, the ultimate causation of reading disability is extremely difficult to test, because it involves multiple factors that may vary widely from one individual to another. Nevertheless, the research that we have reviewed to this point suggests several highly plausible ways in which intrinsic and extrinsic factors might interact to cause reading disability in a particular child. In this final section of the chapter, we summarize our views regarding the reasons why children with RD may stray from the path to proficient reading. These reasons always involve an interaction between children's intrinsic characteristics and environmental variables.

Sources of Cognitive Deficits Causally Involved in RD

Of the many intrinsic characteristics that might be causally related to reading disability, current evidence most strongly implicates phonological processes. Phonological processes involve a family of related but somewhat separate skills; children can have a severe weakness in one phonological-processing skill, such as phonological awareness, but be less deficient, or perhaps not deficient at all, in another, such as naming speed (e.g., Felton, 1993). At least some, and possibly all, phonological-processing skills are strongly influenced by genetic endowment (Olson et al., 1991). However, as we have seen, these skills also are influenced by the environment and by experience. Thus, in our view, although the phonological weaknesses of children with RD probably have a basis in biology, and specifically in genes, like all genetic characteristics these weaknesses develop only in interaction with the environment. Furthermore, we think it most likely that, in the majority of youngsters with reading disability, weaknesses in phonological processing are part of a normal continuum of individual differences rather than etiologically distinct characteristics.

Weaknesses in phonological processing are causally central to most cases of reading disability. However, as we discussed in Chapter 5, other cognitive weaknesses also may play a causal role in some cases of reading disability. For instance, young elementary-age youngsters show individual differences in orthographic processing that are accounted for in part—but only in part—by differences in exposure to text (Barker, Torgesen, & Wagner, 1992). Recall from Chapters 4 and 5 that orthographic skills clearly play a role in learning to read and that compared with nondisabled readers of their own age, children with RD are deficient in orthographic skills. As it turns out, the orthographic skills of individuals with reading disability show much more environmental influence than do their phonological-reading skills (Olson et al., 1991). Some of this environmental influence undoubtedly is attributable to the fact that children with reading disability receive less exposure to text than do nondisabled readers. But it is also possible that the orthographic weaknesses of some children with RD go beyond lack of exposure to text. In other words, some children with RD may begin reading acquisition with a specific weakness in orthographic processing.

Another example of an intrinsic characteristic that may play a causal role in some cases of reading disability involves reading-related knowledge—specifically, background knowledge important in acquiring word-recognition skills. Examples of this kind of background knowledge include knowledge about letter names, letter sounds, and basic concepts of print. Although environmental variables have an obvious influence on children's acquisition of any kind of knowledge, in that children must be exposed to the knowledge in the environment in order to acquire it, biology may play a role in knowledge acquisition as well, in that some children may be biologically predisposed to acquire new knowledge more readily than are others.

Of course, these important intrinsic characteristics—phonological-processing skills, orthographic-processing skills, and reading-related knowledge—are not completely independent of one another; rather, they are related. For instance, as we discussed in Chapters 4 and 5, orthographic-processing skills appear to be partially, but not entirely, dependent on phonological-processing skills. Weaknesses in phonological processing may affect children's ability to acquire knowledge about letter names and letter sounds. The reverse is true as well: Lack of knowledge about letters may affect phonological processing.

We conceptualize individual differences in all of these cognitive areas as a product of the interaction between biology and environment. However, the environment may have a relatively stronger influence on some kinds of cognitive weaknesses, such as those in orthographic processing, and biology may have a relatively stronger influence on other kinds of cognitive weaknesses, such as those in phonological processing. Or to put it another way, in some cases of RD, the environment may play a relatively stronger causal role, whereas in other cases of RD, biology may play a relatively stronger causal role.

In addition, as we discussed in the previous section, not only does the environment shape children but children also shape their own environments, based in part on genetically influenced characteristics. How might this notion—technically termed *genotype-environment correlation* (Scarr & McCartney, 1983)—apply to causation of reading disability? Consider the phonological-processing weaknesses that are causally prominent in RD. We know that at least some phonological processes show strong genetic influence. And it is possible that children with inborn weaknesses in phonological processing respond less readily to rhyming games, to alphabet games, or to certain kinds of word play. With these youngsters, parents may be less inclined to engage in the kinds of activities that would develop phonological skills, because of the youngsters' failure to respond. In school, moreover, these children's initial difficulties with decoding may lead to the erroneous conclusion that the children are "unable" to learn phonics or that they require a radically different approach to instruction, one in which decoding skills are not emphasized. In these ways, children with phonological-processing weaknesses may end up getting *less* experience with phonological activities, when what they really require is *more* experience with such activities.

Why Children Go Astray at a Particular Point

The point at which an individual youngster with RD goes astray in reading acquisition depends in part upon his or her profile of cognitive-processing weaknesses, because these weaknesses have somewhat different effects in the different phases of reading acquisition. For example, deficits in naming speed may have an impact somewhat later in reading acquisition than do deficits in phonological awareness (Blachman, 1994). Because children need at least a rudimentary level of phonological awareness in order to attain the phase of phonetic-cue word recognition, those who lack this level of awareness may go astray in the phase of visual-cue word recognition, becoming nonalphabetic readers. Naming speed is particularly important in achieving automatic word recognition; so children with naming-speed problems may be especially likely to go astray in the phase of controlled word recognition, becoming nonautomatic readers. And finally, weaknesses in orthographic processing may affect reading acquisition most strongly in the transition from phonetic-cue to controlled word recognition, because in order to achieve controlled word recognition, children have to acquire a great deal of orthographic knowledge.

Of course, the severity of children's cognitive-processing weaknesses is important, too. For instance, children who have *both* phonological-awareness and naming-speed weaknesses appear to be particularly impaired in reading (Blachman, 1994; Felton, 1993). These youngsters may be especially likely to become nonalphabetic or compensatory readers. Likewise, children whose naming-speed problems are so severe that they interfere with accuracy of decoding—for example, because of extreme slowness in retrieving letter sounds—may have great difficulty attaining the phase of controlled word recognition and become nonalphabetic or compensatory readers themselves.

As we have emphasized, the point at which a specific child with RD goes awry in reading acquisition also depends upon environmental variables, not only in the home but in school as well. We think that most children with RD begin school with a vulnerability for reading failure. However, what happens very early in schooling—in kindergarten and in first grade—may be pivotal in deciding whether or not an individual child's vulnerability to RD is realized as poor reading. For instance, kindergarten programs that emphasize letter knowledge and basic concepts about print, through engaging and age-appropriate activities, can help to compensate for some children's weaknesses in these areas. And first-grade programs that emphasize phonological skills, such as phonological awareness and phonological reading (decoding), can benefit children with phonological weaknesses. Although these kinds of instructional emphases are appropriate for all beginning readers, they appear to be especially crucial for youngsters with a vulnerability to RD.

The general point is not that teachers should focus exclusively on one set of skills at a particular grade level. Rather, teachers can help children to become good readers by being sensitive to individual differences, by understanding how these differences affect reading acquisition, and, to whatever extent possible, by addressing these differences instructionally. Occasionally, of course, a child's vulnerability to RD may be so great that he or she lags far behind in reading despite the best efforts of the teacher. However, we believe that this last scenario need not happen nearly as often as it currently does. Furthermore, even for youngsters with a severe vulnerability to RD, appropriate teaching may help to bring about a higher level of achievement than would otherwise be possible.

Garden-Variety Poor Reading Versus RD

In many respects, our view of causation is applicable not only to children with reading disability but to garden-variety poor readers as well. Like children with RD, garden-variety poor readers exhibit prominent phonological-processing weaknesses. They also may have weaknesses in orthographic processing and in reading-related knowledge. However, garden-variety poor readers bring to reading acquisition additional, broader weaknesses, in areas such as vocabulary and listening comprehension, that may likewise be causally related to their problems in reading. As we discussed in Chapter 5, these broader weaknesses may make it difficult for some garden-variety poor readers to achieve a high level of comprehension in reading even after their deficits in word recognition have been remediated.

Like the cognitive weaknesses of children with RD, those of garden-variety poor readers are produced by the interaction of both biological and environmental variables. Still uncertain, however, is whether the relative influences of biology and environment are the same for garden-variety poor readers as for children with reading disability. For instance, in their twin studies of reading disability, Olson et al. (1991) found that the heritability of word recognition tended to be somewhat higher for high-IQ poor readers than for low-IQ poor readers, although this trend did not attain statistical significance. These authors tentatively suggest that the genetic influence on word recognition may be relatively stronger in reading disability than in garden-variety poor reading, whereas environmental factors may be relatively more influential in garden-variety poor reading. In other words, although poor reading is never "determined" exclusively by genetic factors, genetic influences may be relatively stronger or weaker depending upon the underlying cognitive profile of reading difficulties.

We share the view of many investigators (e.g., Fletcher et al., 1994; Stanovich, 1990; Stanovich & Siegel, 1994) that most cases of RD are best conceptualized as being on a continuum with other instances of poor reading. Just as there are children who have distinctive "syndromes" of mental retardation (e.g., phenylketonuria), there may be a small number of children who have a distinctive "syndrome" of poor reading. However, as is becoming increasingly clear from the work of a variety of investigators, the concept of reading disability as a distinctive "syndrome" is not tenable for the vast majority of children who are identified in schools as having RD. The way that schools and many researchers define reading disability—in terms of a severe discrepancy between IQ and reading—involves a partitioning of continua that is both artificial and arbitrary.

We propose a different view—namely, that all children come to school with unique packages of individual differences, including differences in a variety of cognitive skills that are important in reading acquisition, such as phonological processing, broad intellectual abilities, listening comprehension, and so on. These various cognitive skills tend to be correlated with each other, but the correlations are far from perfect. Thus, there will always be some children who are relatively high on the continuum of intellectual abilities or of listening comprehension but relatively low on the continuum of phonological processing (or perhaps low in other areas of cognitive processing as well).

Unfortunately for children with weak phonological processes, these processes play a particularly critical role in the early phases of reading acquisition in an alphabetic language; thus, such children are likely to have difficulty in acquiring word-recognition skills, especially without educational intervention. Whether or not these children end up exhibiting potential-achievement discrepancies, and are therefore classified as having RD, will depend upon at least two factors: the measure of potential that is used (e.g., an IQ test or listening comprehension) and the point at which they fall along that continuum of potential relative to their weaknesses in word recognition. However, many youngsters who are poor readers fall in between the extremes of continua, and these poor readers do not appear to be qualitatively different from cases of poor reading that involve potential-achievement discrepancies.

Both for youngsters with RD and for garden-variety poor readers, initial difficulty in reading tends to ignite a chain of negative events, as captured by Keith Stanovich's (1986) concept of Matthew effects. These negative events constitute an important experiential influence on the development of RD and may be seen as another set of genotype-environment correlations (see Stanovich, 1986). For example, as discussed, the tendency of children with RD and of other poor readers not to read widely results in a relative lack of exposure to text, which in turn exerts a negative influence on certain cognitive processes, such as orthographic development. In order to limit these negative events, early intervention is crucial. Ideally, of course, reading failure would be prevented altogether. Indeed, as we have seen, many of the processes central to most cases of reading disability, such as phonological awareness, are amenable to environmental influence, a fact that raises the possibility of actual prevention of RD. We examine this possibility further in Chapter 10.

First, however, we wish to discuss another set of cognitive characteristics— those involved in intelligence and thinking styles—that are important in school achievement. These cognitive characteristics involve a broader level of analysis than do the cognitive processes emphasized so far, but, in some cases, they too may play a role in reading disability. In the next chapter, then, we consider the relationship among abilities, disabilities, and reading disability.

References

Adams, M. J. (1990). *Beginning to read: Thinking and learning about print.* Cambridge, MA: MIT Press.

Allington, R. L. (1983). The reading instruction provided readers of differing ability. *Elementary School Journal, 83,* 255–265.

Anderson, R., Hiebert, E., Scott, J., & Wilkinson, I. (1985). *Becoming a nation of readers: The report of the Commission on Reading.* Champaign, IL: Center for the Study of Reading.

Barker, T. A., Torgesen, J. K., & Wagner, R. K. (1992). The role of orthographic processing skills on five different reading tasks. *Reading Research Quarterly, 27,* 335–345.

Blachman, B. A. (1994). What we have learned from longitudinal studies of phonological processing and reading, and some unanswered questions: A response to Torgesen, Wagner, and Rashotte. *Journal of Learning Disabilities, 27,* 287–291.

Bouchard, T. J. (1984). Twins reared together and apart: What they tell us about human diversity. In S. W. Fox (Ed.), *Individuality and determinism* (pp. 147–178). New York: Plenum Press.

———. (1994). Genes, environment, and personality. *Science, 264,* 1700–1701.

Chinn, C. A., Waggoner, M. A., Anderson, R. C., Schommer, M. & Wilkinson, I. A. G. (1993). Situated actions during reading lessons: A microanalysis of oral reading error episodes. *American Educational Research Journal, 30,* 361–392.

Clay, M. M. (1990). Learning to be learning disabled. *ERS Spectrum, 8,* 3–8.

Coles, G. S. (1987). *The learning mystique: A critical look at "learning disabilities."* New York: Pantheon Books.

Decker, S. N., & Bender, B. G. (1988). Converging evidence for multiple genetic forms of reading disability. *Brain and Language, 33,* 197–215.

DeFries, J. C., Fulker, D. W., & LaBuda, M. C. (1987). Evidence for a genetic aetiology in reading disability in twins. *Nature, 329,* 537–539.

DeFries, J. C., Vogler, G. P., & LaBuda, M. C. (1985). Colorado Family Reading Study: An overview. In J. L. Fuller & E. C. Simmel (Eds.), *Behavior genetics: Principles and applications II* (pp. 357–368). Hillsdale, NJ: Lawrence Erlbaum Associates.

Denckla, M. B., LeMay, M., & Chapman, C. A. (1985). Few CT scan abnormalities found even in neurologically impaired learning disabled children. *Journal of Learning Disabilities, 18*, 132–135.

Dreyer, L. G. (1994, April). *The development of phonologic and orthographic knowledge in kindergarten children: Relationship to emerging word reading ability.* Paper presented at the annual meeting of the American Educational Research Association, New Orleans, LA.

Duffy, F. H., & McAnulty, G. B. (1985). Brain electrical activity mapping (BEAM): The search for a physiology signature of dyslexia. In F. H. Duffy & N. Geschwind (Eds.), *Dyslexia: A neuroscientific approach to clinical evaluation* (pp. 105–122). Boston, MA: Little, Brown.

Felton, R. H. (1993). Effects of instruction on the decoding skills of children with phonological-processing problems. *Journal of Learning Disabilities, 26*, 583–589.

Felton, R. H., & Brown, I. S. (1990). Phonological processes as predictors of specific reading skills in children at risk for reading failure. *Reading and Writing: An Interdisciplinary Journal, 2*, 39–59.

Felton, R. H., & Wood, F. B. (1992). A reading level match study of nonword reading skills in poor readers with varying IQ. *Journal of Learning Disabilities, 25*, 318–326.

Fletcher, J. M., Shaywitz, S. E., Shankweiler, D. P., Katz, L., Liberman, I. Y., Stuebing, K. K., Francis, D. J., Fowler, A. E., & Shaywitz, B. A. (1994). Cognitive profiles of reading disability: Comparisons of discrepancy and low achievement definitions. *Journal of Educational Psychology, 86*, 6–23.

Flowers, D. L. (1993). Brain basis for dyslexia: A summary of work in progress. *Journal of Learning Disabilities, 26*, 575–582.

Flowers, D. L., Wood, F. B., & Naylor, C. E. (1991). Regional cerebral blood flow correlates of language processes in reading disability. *Archives of Neurology, 48*, 637–643.

Galaburda, A. M., Corsiglia, J., Rosen, G. D., & Sherman, G. F. (1987). Planum temporale asymmetry: Reappraisal since Geschwind and Levitsky. *Neuropsychologia, 25*, 853–868.

Galaburda, A. M., & Kemper, T. L. (1979). Cytoarchitectonic abnormalities in developmental dyslexia: A case study. *Annals of Neurology, 6*, 94–100.

Galaburda, A. M., Sherman, G. F., Rosen, G. D., Aboitiz, F., & Geschwind, N. (1985). Developmental dyslexia: Four consecutive patients with cortical anomalies. *Annals of Neurology, 18*, 222–233.

Gambrell, L. B. (1984). How much time do children spend reading during teacher-directed reading instruction? In J. A. Niles & L. A. Harris (Eds.), *Changing perspectives on research in reading/language processing and instruction* (pp. 193–198). Rochester, NY: National Reading Conference.

Gearheart, B. R., & Gearheart, C. J. (1989). *Learning disabilities: Educational strategies.* Columbus, OH: Merrill Publishing Company.

Geschwind, N., & Galaburda, A. M. (1985). Cerebral lateralization: Biological mechanisms, associations, and pathology: I. A hypothesis and a program for research. *Archives of Neurology, 42*, 428–459.

Gould, S. J. (1981). *The mismeasure of man.* New York: Norton.

Hoffmann, J. V., O'Neal, S. F., Kastler, L. A., Clements, R. O., Segel, K. W., & Nash, M. F. (1984). Guided oral reading and miscue focused verbal feedback in second-grade classrooms. *Reading Research Quarterly, 19*, 367–384.

Hynd, G. W., & Semrud-Clikeman, M. (1989). Dyslexia and brain morphology. *Psychological Bulletin, 106*, 447–482.

Hynd, G. W., Semrud-Clikeman, M., Lorys, A. R., Novey, E. S., & Eliopulos, D. (1990). Brain morphology in developmental dyslexia and attention deficit disorder/hyperactivity. *Archives of Neurology, 47*, 919–926.

Larsen, J. P., Hoien, T., Lundberg, I., & Odegaard, H. (1990). MRI evaluation of the size and symmetry of the planum temporale in adolescents with developmental dyslexia. *Brain and Language, 39*, 1–12.

Lerner, J. W. (1993). *Learning disabilities: Theories, diagnosis, and teaching strategies.* Boston, MA: Houghton Mifflin Company.

Lyon, G. R., Newby, R. E., Recht, D., & Caldwell, J. (1991). Neuropsychology and learning disabilities. In B. Y. L. Wong (Ed.), *Learning about learning disabilities* (pp. 375–406). San Diego, CA: Academic Press.

Lyons, C. A. (1989). Reading Recovery: An effective early intervention program that can prevent mislabeling children as learning disabled. *ERS Spectrum, 7*, 3–9.

Maclean, M., Bryant, P., & Bradley, L. (1987). Rhymes, nursery rhymes, and reading in early childhood. *Merrill-Palmer Quarterly, 33*, 255–281.

Mann, C. (1994). Behavioral genetics in transition. *Science, 264*, 1686–1689.

Mann, V. (1991). Language problems: A key to early reading problems. In B. Y. L. Wong (Ed.), *Learning about learning disabilities* (pp. 129–162). San Diego, CA: Academic Press.

Mason, J. M. (1992). Reading stories to preliterate children: A proposed connection to reading. In P. B. Gough, L. C. Ehri, & R. Treiman (Eds.), *Reading acquisition* (pp. 215–241). Hillsdale, NJ: Erlbaum.

National Joint Committee on Learning Disabilities. (1988). Letter to NJCLD member organizations.

Olson, R. K., Rack, J. P., Conners, F. A., DeFries, J. C., & Fulker, D. W. (1991). Genetic etiology of individual differences in reading disability. In L. V. Feagans, E. J. Short, & L. J. Meltzer (Eds.), *Subtypes of learning disabilities: Theoretical perspectives and research* (pp. 113–135). Hillsdale, NJ: Lawrence Erlbaum Associates.

Olson, R. K., Wise, B., Conners, F., Rack, J., & Fulker, D. (1989). Specific deficits in component reading and language skills: Genetic and environmental influences. *Journal of Learning Disabilities, 22*, 339–348.

Pennington, B. F., Gilger, J. W., Pauls, D., Smith, S. A., Smith, S. D., & DeFries, J. C. (1991). Evidence for major gene transmission of developmental dyslexia. *Journal of the American Medical Association, 266*, 1527–1534.

Plomin, R. (1988). The nature and nurture of cognitive abilities. In R. J. Sternberg (Ed.), *Advances in the psychology of human intelligence* (Vol. 4, pp. 1–33). Hillsdale, NJ: Lawrence Erlbaum Associates.

————. (1989). Environment and genes: Determinants of behavior. *American Psychologist, 11*, 105–111.

————. (1991). A behavioral genetic approach to learning disabilities and their subtypes. In L. V. Feagans, E. J. Short, & L. J. Meltzer (Eds.), *Subtypes of learning disabilities: Theoretical perspectives and research* (pp. 83–109). Hillsdale, NJ: Lawrence Erlbaum Associates.

Plomin, R., & Daniels, D. (1987). Why are children in the same family so different from each other? *Behavioral and Brain Sciences, 10*, 1–16.

Plomin, R., DeFries, J. C., & McClearn, G. E. (1990). *Behavioral genetics: A primer*, 2nd ed. New York: W. H. Freeman.

Plomin, R., Owen, M. J., & McGuffin, P. (1994). The genetic basis of complex human behaviors. *Science, 264*, 1733–1739.

Plomin, R., Reiss, D., Hetherington, E. M., & Howe, G. W. (1994). Nature and nurture: Genetic contributions to measures of the family environment. *Developmental Psychology, 30*, 32–43.

Raichle, M. E. (1994). Visualizing the mind. *Scientific American, 270*, 58–64.

Rosenshine, B., & Stevens, R. (1984). Classroom instruction in reading. In P. D. Pearson, R. Barr, M. L. Kamil, & P. Mosenthal (Eds.), *Handbook of reading research* (pp. 745–799). New York: Longman.

Rumsey, J. M., Andreason, P., Zametkin, A. J., Aquino, T., King, A. C., Hamberger, S. D., Pikus, A., Rapoport, J. L., & Cohen, R. M. (1992). Failure to activate the left temporoparietal cortex in dyslexia. *Archives of Neurology, 49*, 527–534.

Scarr, S. (1992). Developmental theories for the 1990s: Development and individual differences. *Child Development, 63*, 1–19.

Scarr, S., & McCartney, K. (1983). How people make their own environments: A theory of genotype-environment effects. *Child Development, 54*, 424–435.

Shaywitz, S. E., Escobar, M. D., Shaywitz, B. A., Fletcher, J. M., & Makuch, R. (1992). Evidence that dyslexia may represent the lower tail of a normal distribution of reading ability. *New England Journal of Medicine, 326*, 145–150.

Shaywitz, S. E., Shaywitz, B. A., Fletcher, J. M., & Escobar, M. D. (1990). Prevalence of reading disability in boys and girls: Results of the Connecticut Longitudinal Study. *Journal of the American Medical Association, 264*, 998–1002.

Smith, C. R. (1991). *Learning disabilities: The interaction of learner, task, and setting*. Needham Heights, MA: Allyn and Bacon.

Smith, S. D. (1986). *Genetics and learning disabilities*. San Diego, CA: College-Hill.

Smith, S. D., Kimberling, W. J., Pennington, B. F., & Lubs, H. A. (1983). *Science, 219*, 1345.

Smith, S. D., Pennington, B. F., Kimberling, W. J., & Ing, P. S. (1990). Familial dyslexia: Use of genetic linkage data to define subtypes. *Journal of the American Academy of Child and Adolescent Psychiatry, 29*, 204–213.

Snow, C. E., Barnes, W. S., Chandler, J., Goodman, J. F., & Hemphill, L. (1991). *Unfulfilled expectations: Home and school influences on literacy*. Cambridge, MA: Harvard University Press.

Spear, L. C., & Sternberg, R. J. (1992). Information processing, experience, and reading disability. In D. J. Stein & J. E. Young (Eds.), *Cognitive science and clinical disorders* (pp. 313–336). San Diego, CA: Academic Press.

Stanovich, K. E. (1986). Matthew effects in reading: Some consequences of individual differences in the acquisition of literacy. *Reading Research Quarterly, 21*, 360–406.

————. (1990). Explaining the differences between the dyslexic and the garden-variety poor reader: The phonological-core variable-difference model. In J. K. Torgesen (Ed.), *Cognitive and behavioral characteristics of children with learning disabilities* (pp. 7–40). Austin, TX: Pro-Ed.

Stanovich, K. E., & Siegel, L. S. (1994). Phenotypic performance profile of children with reading disabilities: A regression-based test of the phonological-core variable-difference model. *Journal of Educational Psychology, 86*, 24–53.

Steinmetz, H., Volkmann, J., Jancke, L., & Freund, H. J. (1990). Anatomical left-right asymmetry of language-related temporal cortex is different in left- and right-handers. *Annals of Neurology, 29*, 315–319.

Sternberg, R. J. (1988). *The triarchic mind: A new theory of human intelligence.* New York: Viking.

Tavris, C. (1992). *The mismeasure of woman.* New York: Touchstone.

Vellutino, F. R., & Scanlon, D. M. (1987). Phonological coding, phonological awareness, and reading ability: Evidence from a longitudinal and experimental study. *Merrill-Palmer Quarterly, 33,* 321–363.

———. (1991). The effects of instructional bias on word identification. In L. Rieben & C. A. Perfetti (Eds.), *Learning to read: Basic research and its implications* (pp. 189–203). Hillsdale, NJ: Lawrence Erlbaum Associates.

Wagner, R. K., Torgesen, J. K., & Rashotte, C. A. (1994). The development of reading-related phonological processing abilities: New evidence of bidirectional causality from a latent variable longitudinal study. *Developmental Psychology, 30,* 73–87.

Wood, F. B., & Flowers, D. L. (1991). [Neuropsychological correlates of MRI measurements.] Unpublished raw data.

9 Abilities, Disabilities, and Reading Disability: How Are They Related?

WHY ARE SO MANY CHILDREN who once were labeled as "mentally retarded" today being labeled as "learning disabled"? Does the reason have to do with society's societal attempt to hide the truth with euphemisms? Are the mentally retarded really disappearing? Or are people who were once believed to be mentally retarded truly now seen as learning disabled?

What is the relation between learning disability and mental retardation, anyway? How about that between giftedness and learning disability? Can someone simultaneously be both gifted and reading disabled? Or is the label of "gifted learning disabled" yet another ploy to smooth over unpleasantness, in the way that the label of "sanitation engineer" is sometimes now applied to those who collect garbage or "canine officer" is now used to describe what was once pejoratively known as a "dogcatcher"?

These are just a few of the questions that will be addressed in this chapter. Our goal here is to present readers with modern views of abilities, and to discuss the relation of these views to the notion of reading disability in particular and to learning disabilities in general. Contemporary views of abilities actually do lead to a rather different perspective on learning disabilities than was the case for earlier views, so if our goal is to understand disabilities and, ultimately, to help remediate them, we need first to understand how current theories of abilities can help us accomplish these goals.

Although there are many and various contemporary views of abilities, their similarities are much more striking than their differences. Indeed, the views are largely complementary, a fact that is reflected in our treatment of two such views in this chapter. Our particular goal will be to discuss the relevance of these views for understanding reading disabilities.

Multiple Views of Multiple Abilities

Multiple Intelligences

One of the most influential current views of abilities has been proposed by Howard Gardner (1983), whose theory of multiple intelligences has revolutionized much of our thinking about the nature and organization of abilities. Gardner's basic premise is that there is not just one intelligence, measurable by conventional intelligence- and scholastic-aptitude tests, but rather multiple, distinct intelligences, each of which is relatively independent of the others.

Gardner has proposed the existence of at least seven such intelligences:

1. *Linguistic intelligence*, used in reading, writing, speaking, and hearing, is the intelligence most relevant to writing an essay, reading a book, or analyzing a speech.
2. *Logical-mathematical intelligence*, used in solving abstract mathematical and logical problems, and in various kinds of symbolic reasoning, is the intelligence most relevant to solving proofs in geometry, factoring an algebraic equation, or multiplying fractions.
3. *Spatial intelligence*, used to visualize objects and transformations of objects in space, is the intelligence most relevant to fitting suitcases into the limited space available in the trunk of a car, finding your way from one part of town to another, or imagining what an object would look like when seen from a different vantage point.
4. *Musical intelligence*, used to read and write music as well as to listen to or produce music, is the intelligence most relevant to singing a song, recognizing a tune, or playing the piano.
5. *Bodily-kinesthetic intelligence*, used to produce, coordinate, and refine one's bodily movements, is the intelligence most relevant to playing football or baseball, dancing with grace, or exercising in a gym.
6. *Interpersonal intelligence*, used to understand and interact with other people, is the intelligence most relevant to succeeding in a job interview, conversing effectively with a potential friend or romantic partner, or giving an effective presentation to the "opposition."
7. *Intrapersonal intelligence*, used to understand and evaluate oneself, is the intelligence most relevant to understanding why one is happy or sad, getting over depression, or recognizing both one's strengths and one's weaknesses.

Gardner's theory represents a modular view of mind. In this view, each intelligence operates with relative autonomy from the other intelligences and can be quite effective even when certain others are not. There is no "general intelligence," according to Gardner, although the intelligences working in tandem might give the appearance of such. Moreover, the intelligences can be developed both inside and outside the classroom (see Gardner, 1993).

The theory of multiple intelligences has direct and, indeed, profound implications for our understanding of reading disability in particular and of learning disabilities in general. For one thing, the condition traditionally labeled as "mental retardation" truly becomes a form of specific disability in Gardner's theory. According to Gardner, a low IQ score, one of the primary bases for labeling people as mentally retarded in the past, reflects little more than a low level of functioning in two or possibly three of the intelligences. Most conventional intelligence tests measure primarily linguistic and logical-mathematical abilities, and perhaps spatial abilities as well. But they almost never measure musical, bodily-kinesthetic, interpersonal, or intrapersonal intelligences. A person with a deficit in any one of the two or three typically measured intelligences may score low on an IQ test; however, this low score represents a fairly limited area of deficit, rather than the broad range of deficits typically supposed. Even if an assessment of low levels of adaptive behavior is incorporated into the identification of an individual as mentally retarded (and well it should be), there may still be other intelligences (such as musical and bodily-kinesthetic) that are not being addressed.

Gardner's point is even stronger, however. He argues that traditional tests rely largely on multiple-choice or other convergent forms of assessment. On such tests students are rarely given an opportunity to think divergently or to generate any kind of meaningful performance. One could thus be classified as mentally retarded on the basis of very limited kinds of information. For example, many very successful writers were, as students, neither the top scorers on verbal IQ tests nor even the best in their English classes. Indeed, we ourselves have taught a number of highly successful students (at Southern Connecticut State University and Yale University) who were labeled as learning disabled in childhood.

If one accepts even the basic notion of multiple intelligences, without necessarily accepting the particular intelligences Gardner has identified, it becomes quite difficult to distinguish between mental retardation and specific learning disabilities. The reason is that all "retarded" performance must then be viewed in terms of both the domain(s) in which the performance is observed and the way in which it is measured.

Gardner's theory does not totally eliminate the concept of generalized mental retardation. After all, it is statistically possible and even likely that at least some individuals will perform at very low levels in all seven of the domains of Gardner's theory, and perhaps in other domains as well. But, clearly, the proportion of individuals identified as mentally retarded in this way of thinking would be far smaller than that assessed by conventional test-based notions of a single intelligence.

Note, too, that Gardner's theory makes it quite easy to conceive of children as being both gifted and learning disabled. A brilliant musician might well have trouble reading novels, just as a brilliant novelist might have little ability to sing or write music. Just as the concept of general retardation seems to dissolve in the face of this theory, so does the concept of general intellectual giftedness. After all, people are typically gifted in some domains but not others. Yet those who are gifted in the linguistic and logical-mathematical domains may have been singled out in the past by conventional intelligence tests as having the most unusual gifts, whereas those gifted in, say, music or dance may never have been placed in any gifted classes if they could not also readily solve linguistic and mathematical problems.

It is further important to realize that a single intelligence represents a system of functioning in a given symbol system, not a unitary ability. Gardner well knows that the gifted reader is often not a gifted writer. Thus, we should not jump to the conclusion that the child with reading disability is deficient in all linguistic abilities. Although Gardner has not specified just what the various linguistic abilities are (nor exactly what the component abilities are in other domains), it is clear that to understand specific disabilities, we must understand more than just the domain in which the disability occurs.

Another implication of the theory of multiple intelligences is that there may be compensations for less of one intelligence with more of another. For example, someone with weaker linguistic skills but stronger logical skills might use logical analysis in an attempt to decode and understand what is being read. In some cases, however, such compensations can actually put a child at a disadvantage. For example, a youngster who develops compensatory strategies for deficits in certain linguistic abilities may not have the incentive to remediate the particular deficits.

We believe there is one further implication of Gardner's theory that is well worth mentioning. According to this theory, a person can be highly successful in many aspects of life, regardless of the particular disabilities he or she may have.

One of the coauthors heard the story of a highly successful industrialist in Mexico—a man who had achieved the greatest heights of financial and other forms of success—despite being unable to read. He started out in a low-level job in a shoe factory, a job that had no future and no promise of leading to a better life. The man's employer discovered, to his chagrin, that his employee was illiterate. Not wanting illiterates in his factory, he promptly fired the employee.

Left to his own devices, the man started his own small shoe business. The business prospered, and he eventually bought out his former employer's company. In the later years of his life, he was asked by a reporter if it wasn't rather sad that he had never learned to read. After all, the reporter suggested, he might have been even more successful if he had been literate. "On the contrary," the industrialist pointed out, "if I had learned how to read, I would still be on the assembly line in my former employer's shoe factory!"

Three Faces of Abilities

Another view of intelligence—the triarchic theory of intelligence (Sternberg, 1985, 1988)—is compatible with Gardner's theory, but it emphasizes processes rather than domains of intelligence. According to this triarchic theory, there are three key aspects of intelligence, which we will describe in turn.

Components of Intelligence. The first aspect is the set of component processes constituting intelligence. These processes are of three kinds: (1) higher order processes, or metacomponents, (2) performance components, and (3) knowledge-acquisition components. *Metacomponents* are used to plan what one is going to do, to monitor it as one is doing it, and to evaluate it after it is done. Included within this domain are processes such as defining the nature of a problem, setting up a strategy to solve the problem, representing information about the problem, and evaluating the solution to the problem after it is reached. When a child decides to read one book carefully because of an upcoming test on the book's contents and another book cursorily because there will be no such test, the child is exhibiting a kind of decision making that represents metacomponential processing. *Performance components* are used to execute the instructions of the metacomponents—for example, in decoding and encoding words or other stimuli, or in inferring the relation between the meanings of two words. Finally, *knowledge-acquisition components* are used to learn how to solve problems and perform tasks in the first place. For example, in the process of selective encoding, one distinguishes new information that is relevant for one's purposes from information that is not so relevant. And in selective comparison, one draws upon old information that is relevant to a task currently being faced. Selective encoding, for instance, is used to decide which aspects of one's reading material are important and which are not, whereas selective comparison is used to relate what one knows from the past to what one learns in the present.

Notice that the componential view presented here can be viewed as consistent with the view of multiple intelligences. The various processes of the triarchic theory could be described as being embedded within the various domains of the multiple intelligences—and indeed, researchers at Harvard and Yale have undertaken a joint research and development effort based on just this notion (Gardner et al., 1994). But we do not have to accept either view to accept the other. For example, we could view various kinds of processes as being more generalized than they would be viewed in Gardner's theory.

In the triarchic view, mental retardation is due primarily to deficient functioning of metacomponents—the planning, monitoring, and evaluation processes of the human mind. In order for the concept of mental retardation to be applicable to an individual, the deficit would have to be general—that is, exhibited across many domains. We believe that there is fairly compelling evidence to suggest that individuals who are accurately labeled as mentally retarded do show such generalized deficits and, moreover, that such individuals exist in small, but not vanishingly small, numbers (Borkowski & Cavanaugh, 1979; Butterfield & Belmont, 1977; Campione & Brown, 1979). In our own view, the theory of multiple intelligences is attractive in that it points out the multiple domains in which individuals can perform; but we do not believe that it should be interpreted to mean that no one is mentally retarded or no one intellectually gifted. Rather, these concepts should be recognized as less generalized than they were once thought to be.

Much more common than mental retardation are specific disabilities, which are due in part to inadequacies in the functioning of performance and knowledge-acquisition components. As children become older, top-down higher-order planning strategies become more and more central to reading, and thus metacomponents become more and more influential in affecting how the children read. But at the lower age levels, when bottom-up recognition and decoding operations are key to deciphering words, the performance components involved in these operations are key to success. Performance components tend to be much more specific to individual domains than are metacomponents, and the particular deficits in such components that someone exhibits in particular domains can lead to one form of disability or another. Thus, a person may be quite able to plan and evaluate his or her activities; but a performance-componential deficit in phonetic decoding might lead to a reading disability in this person, whereas a performance-componential deficit in quantitative comparison might lead to an arithmetical disability.

Children who show specific deficits in the bottom-up functioning necessary to learning a skill may later show more top-down deficits in the functioning needed to perform the skill at a higher level. Consider, for example, reading. A youngster who does not learn how to decode phonetically is likely to fall behind children who do learn such decoding. In effect, the child with a problem in this respect strays from the road to proficient reading. Later, when the child who remains on this road has mastered phonetic decoding, he or she is able to devote a full measure of mental resources to perfecting the top-down skills needed for proficient reading. But the child with the early, bottom-up deficit may continue to need to allocate mental resources to phonetic decoding and, hence, not have the mental resources left over to concentrate on larger questions of meaning. Accordingly, what started out as a localized, bottom-up deficit later appears as a global, top-down one. In fact, though, the child's reduced comprehension is due not to a lack of top-down resources but, rather, to his or her inability to exploit them.

Consider a simple analogy. Suppose you, an adult, are asked to read a fairly simple French text. But your knowledge of French is so limited that even this simple text is a challenge: You need to devote almost your full attention to figuring out what the words say and what they mean. Even though you may have marvelous comprehension skills in English, you would appear to be top-down deficient on a test of reading comprehension in French, because you would barely get to the top-down processes necessary for proficient reading in French. Some children confront in their first language the same problem you have encountered in this second language. Indeed, even adults may encounter such first-language problems.

From this analysis we can see the importance of assessing children not just at a global level—whether in terms of an overall reading score or even in terms of reading speed and comprehension scores—but also at the level of componential functioning. A child could appear to be deficient in comprehension processes when in fact he or she is deficient only in a few basic bottom-up processes. The one weak link in the chain of processes needed for reading makes the whole chain appear weak. Yet repair of just the single link would strengthen the chain. Indeed, a child could be gifted intellectually in a number of domains and still have a reading disability if even just one performance component functions at a low level.

In some cases, failure to analyze performance into its constituent components can lead to entirely fallacious conclusions. Consider the verbal-analogies test, for which performance is generally very highly correlated with that for a reading test. A child's low score on such a test might lead teachers and psychologists alike to conclude that the child is not very bright. A low reading score might be seen as clinching the argument. But performance on a test of verbal analogies is highly dependent on vocabulary, which in turn is dependent on word recognition (as well as on context, to be discussed later). If the child does not recognize the words, he or she may be labeled as a poor reasoner, when in fact reasoning is not the problem at all. Once again, we see the need for diagnosis at the level of information-processing components.

Intelligence and Experience. The second aspect of the triarchic theory of human intelligence deals with the relation of intelligence to experience. Experience with a task or situation can range from the extreme of total novelty to the extreme of total familiarity. According to this theory, then, two levels of experience are particularly relevant to understanding reading disability: the level of relative novelty and the level of automatization of information processing when a task is quite familiar.

Consider again the task you face if you have had relatively little experience in reading French but are presented with a reading comprehension test in this language. Could the same conclusion be drawn about you from this test as could be drawn for an adult who grew up in France and has read French all his or her life? Certainly not. In many respects, the test will be much more novel for you than for the individual who grew up in France. If you've ever visited a country whose language was foreign to you, you may well have felt "stupid" in the context of that country. But obviously your problem was not one of stupidity; rather, it was one of ignorance. You just could not have been expected to perform at the same level as would those who grew up in the country.

The problem applies not only across countries. It can apply within countries as well. Not all children get the same exposure to written or even oral language; hence, not all children go into the learning or testing of reading on an equal basis. What is fairly familiar for one child may be quite novel for another.

For example, Shirley Heath (1983) investigated children from three communities in North Carolina, which she referred to as Trackton, Roadville, and Gateway. Trackton was a black community; Roadville and Gateway, white communities. Heath discovered that in Trackton, there was much more emphasis on nonverbal modes of communication than in either Roadville or Gateway. Conversely, in the latter two communities, there was considerably more emphasis on verbal forms of communication.

When children from the various communities started to learn reading in school, they were by no means starting on an equal footing. For one thing, children in Roadville and Gateway had generally been socialized in ways that emphasized verbal communication. For another thing, homes in Gateway tended to have far more books, magazines, and other verbal resources than did homes in Roadville. So the children from Roadville and Gateway did not start reading on an equal footing either. Rather, they varied widely in terms of the degree to which the task of reading was familiar in their experience. But when the children were evaluated for reading readiness, and later for their actual reading ability, all of these differences in prior experience were essentially ignored.

In fact, any test of reading readiness or reading accomplishment would have been measuring different things for different children, because the children entered the testing situation at different points along the continuum of novelty. But these differences were not taken into account in North Carolina; indeed, such data rarely are, anywhere. When we hear talk of "culture-fair" tests, we can hardly take it seriously. We cannot equate what a test measures across the members of our own culture, much less across a variety of cultures. Clearly, people go into both instruction and assessment with varying amounts of prior knowledge; thus, differences in the acquisition of knowledge may in part be environmentally determined. But the common assumption is that instruction and testing present the same challenge to everyone. They don't.

At least as important as the role of novelty in reading is that of automatization. We suggest that reading disability, as well as other specific disabilities, may result from slow or limited automatization of skills (see also LaBerge & Samuels, 1974; Sternberg & Wagner, 1982). In particular, many individuals with learning disabilities must continue to perform in a controlled way (i.e., with conscious attention) tasks that a normally functioning individual would long ago have automatized. A person with a reading disability, for example, may have to devote attention to tasks and task components that others have already mastered. In this event, processing resources that in others have been freed up for use in mastering new tasks must, for the person with RD, still be directed to completion of the original tasks.

In normal functioning, controlled processing is eventually replaced by automatic processing. For example, when first learning to drive a car, you have to devote your full mental resources to driving safely. You cannot divide your attention, say, by concentrating on other things at the same time. But after you have been driving for even a few months, you may be able to drive, carry on a conversation, listen to the radio, and think about something else more or less simultaneously. The same applies to reading. What at first is a highly controlled and attention-absorbing process for most people eventually becomes a process that requires relatively less attention—except in the case of novel material, which must be processed in a careful and controlled fashion. Some individuals with reading disability, we believe, never automatize, with the result that they must continue to devote large amounts of attention to processes that for others are essentially ef-fortless.

Why doesn't a person with reading disability automatize the skills needed for proficient reading? Several possible reasons present themselves, one or more of which may be correct in a given case. First, the individual may be unable or un-willing to utilize specific symbol systems, such as words (or numbers, in the case of arithmetic disability). Perhaps the individual is afraid of the domain, or has no interest in the domain, or simply has difficulty processing symbols in the domain. Second, specific neuropsychological deficits may be involved, as discussed in the last chapter. Third, the individual may display an inability or unwillingness to re-code certain kinds of information into higher order units that then make possible the storage of greater amounts of information. For example, when first learning a new language, you are likely to encode words one at a time, translating each word as you go along. Over time, however, you start to attend more to higher-order units, such as groupings of words, sentences, and even paragraphs. The nonau-tomatized reader may not make these transitions. Fourth, the individual may have an acquired aversion to thinking in some domains, as seen in the cases of math-phobia or fear of reading. Finally, the individual may simply be unmotivated to learn in the domain, perhaps for lack of interest. In this event, the person may not want to read, or do math, or learn new skills in any particular domain.

In sum, we believe that some kinds of reading disability derive from automati-zation failure. Other kinds result from the contextual variables considered next.

The Role of Context. Throughout this book, we have emphasized the importance of context in disabilities. People who grow up in different environments have dif-ferent opportunities. Ultimately, we need to remember that the purpose of intelli-gence is adaptation to the environment. Note, however, that for most of the his-tory of humankind, reading was not a part of such adaptation. The construct of reading disability would not have made sense, and no one would have been la-beled as having this disability, when there was no written language to read. Even today, reading plays a variable role in different groups and for different individu-als. We need to take the environmental context into account, therefore, in deter-mining whether a reading disability is in part a response to demands of the envi-ronment that differ from those we suppose are present.

For instance, when diagnosing reading disability, we must consider the context in which the child has grown up and is living. As discussed in previous chapters, children who come from less literate environments may not have the prerequisites to learn reading as quickly as children who grow up in environments with more advantages for reading. And a further complication is that by jumping to a hasty conclusion about the former children's lack of reading ability, teachers or other practitioners could create a self-fulfilling prophecy. In short, reading ability, like other abilities, must be understood in the contexts in which it develops and man-ifests itself.

The Role of Intellectual Styles

Some, though certainly not all, psychologists distinguish between intelligence and a kind of construct that is variously referred to as "intellectual style," "thinking style," "learning style," or "cognitive style." We are among those psychologists who believe in the construct of styles; moreover, we think that styles have an important role to play in the development of reading disability in certain children. Specifically, styles become important in the context of the method or methods used to teach reading.

Earlier in the book, we made a distinction between "whole-language" and "code-emphasis" approaches to the teaching of reading. We also pointed out that, in our opinion, neither approach by itself is entirely effective. Good teaching would involve *both* the whole-language and the code-emphasis approaches. For whatever reason, however, educators often go to extremes in teaching; and as educators ourselves, we have watched the pendulum swing back and forth from one extreme to another. One era will see an almost total emphasis on mastery of the fundamentals; another will witness an equally strong emphasis on something else. These extreme positions may serve certain political agendas, but they hurt children.

Reading acquisition is a good example of an area in which children can be hurt. We believe that some children develop reading disability as an unfortunate by-product of adult political agendas. As of this writing, the whole-language movement is going strong, though not quite as strong as it was a few years ago. Some schools and many textbook publishers have jumped on the whole-language bandwagon in order to show that they are at least as modern as the next school or school district. Yet in another era, they might have jumped on the phonics bandwagon and completely ignored the notion of whole language.

The concept of intellectual styles, when applied to learning, implies that some children will learn better through one method and other children, through other methods. But the ideal method of teaching always involves a combination of techniques. When just one technique is used, only those children whose style of learning is consistent with this technique will benefit; the remaining children will suffer. Almost regardless of which theory of learning styles is being applied, then, the whole-language approach will be optimally effective only for some children and the code-emphasis approach only for others.

In the phraseology of one such theory, the whole-language approach is more global, the code-emphasis approach more local (see Sternberg, 1988, 1991, 1994). Other theories might capture the difference with other terminology. But unless we ensure that reading is taught by a variety of methods, we will inadvertently benefit some students at the expense of others. Moreover, different aspects of reading are highlighted by different methods of teaching reading. For example, the code-emphasis method focuses on the important component of word-recognition skills, whereas the whole-language method focuses on global word-comprehension skills.

The same principle holds true in any educational subject matter—not just in reading. For example, when one of the coauthors learned French in high school, he was taught exclusively through the "mimic-and-memorize" method. This method emphasizes drill and repetition. The teacher recites a phrase, and the children recite it back. Slowly, the children learn and begin to make variations on this phrase. By repeating the patterns intoned by the teacher, they eventually learn to create these patterns for themselves. The author's teacher commented to him one day that although he was quite intelligent in general, he had no real aptitude for foreign languages. The author took the teacher's comment to heart and, in college, made sure he took no foreign-language courses. Why study something for which you have no aptitude? And equally important, why risk a low grade and spoil your GPA, possibly compromising your chances of getting into a good graduate school? The author reached adulthood convinced that he was disabled, or at least lacking in the ability to learn foreign languages.

Years later, as an assistant professor, the author received a contract to devise a program for teaching intellectual skills to Venezuelan schoolchildren. It was obvious that he would have to learn at least some Spanish, as the program was to be in Spanish; moreover, he would have to interact with his hosts as well as the students in Venezuela, all of whom were Spanish-speaking. He therefore sought a tutor in Spanish, who taught him Spanish via what is called the "direct method." In this method, the foreign language is learned through natural contexts, rather than through mimicking and memorization. The upshot was that the author learned Spanish rapidly and, today, speaks and reads it fluently.

The key point here is that what a teacher took to be a "foreign-language disability," or at least a lack of ability, was a disability only with respect to the method of teaching being used. The style of teaching was a poor match to the author's style of learning. He did not learn to read or speak French well in high school but might have done so had a different method of teaching been used. Sometimes, then, a disability reflects not a genuine overall lack of ability but, rather, a lack of fit between a method of teaching and a student's preferred style of learning.

The same principle holds in mathematics. For years, one of the authors taught a course in statistics for psychology students. Some of the students seemed bright in statistics, others not so bright. Still others seemed genuinely "statistically disabled." The author taught the course in the standard algebraic way, which heavily emphasizes the use and derivation of equations.

One year, almost on a lark, the author retaught a lesson he had just completed. This time, however, he taught it using primarily geometric concepts. This was hard for him to do, because his own thinking is primarily algebraic. And, like many teachers, he tends to teach in a way that matches his own style of thinking (Sternberg, 1994). When he taught the lesson geometrically, an interesting thing happened. Many of the students who had been in the "don't-get-it" category suddenly understood the lesson for the first time. Conversely, some of the students who had always learned the concepts quickly when they were presented algebraically had difficulty when they were presented geometrically. Which students were more able, and which less so, changed as a function of the way the statistical concepts were taught.

The point we wish to emphasize is that, before classifying a child as disabled in any way, practitioners should ensure that more than one method of teaching that child has been tried. As we have seen, students who learn well via one method of teaching may learn poorly via another, and vice versa. Students who are taught to read or to write or to do arithmetic through only one method may indeed appear disabled—but their disability may extend only to the method of teaching that is being used, or to that method and others like it. Moreover, if we classify a child as disabled, and then try to remediate through the same method that has not worked before, we may compound the child's problem.

Of course, we are not claiming that all children classified as having a reading disability are so classified because their style of learning mismatches the method through which they have been taught to read. But as educators, we need to remember that disabilities tend to be cumulative; that if we start out teaching by just a single method, we may be inadvertently creating a cumulative deficit in some of our children. Later on, these children may in fact have difficulty learning, regardless of the method used, because they have gotten so far behind. So unless we teach children through a variety of methods from the very start, we risk creating artificial learning disabilities.

How Serious Is Reading Disability, Anyway?

To a carpenter, an apprentice who cannot use a hammer well will seem severely disabled, and quite possibly hopeless. To a seamstress, an apprentice who cannot use a needle and thread capably will appear to be similarly hopeless. To a teacher in the elementary school, a youngster with a reading disability may seem, if not hopeless, at least destined to a life of frustration.

Elementary school teachers are entrusted with teaching our children many subjects, but the "three R's"—reading, 'riting, and 'rithmetic—have always been at the core of the curriculum. And it is no coincidence that "reading" comes at the head of the group—nor, we believe, that it is the only one of the three R's that really begins with *r*. Reading is the core of the core. A person can't learn to write or do arithmetic without at least the fundamentals of reading in place.

Once a child is identified as having a reading disability, whether correctly or not, that child is likely to be perceived by teachers and other school personnel as something like the carpenter's unfortunate apprentice. But looked at from the standpoint of modern theories of abilities, reading and other disabilities are what their names say they are—*specific disabilities*. It is true that many things will be difficult to learn if you cannot read. But if you master a basic level of reading, even if you do so at a slow rate, then you can achieve almost any goal as an adult.

Some youngsters with reading disability may be slow in learning to read because of their disability, but they eventually reach a proficient reading level, or at least a level proficient enough to get them through their lives. Other youngsters with reading disability never reach proficiency but eventually are able to read at a reasonably high level. Either way, it is important to keep their reading disability in perspective.

First, whether we believe in conventional or modern theories of abilities, reading disability is not mental retardation. Indeed, the definition of RD ensures that youngsters, if classified correctly as such, will be distinguishable from those youngsters who are mentally retarded. For the majority of pursuits in life, intelligence is far more important than reading skill. It is no coincidence that the enormous psychometric literature that has grown up around the prediction of occupational success has used conventionally measured intelligence rather than reading skill as the predictor of job success. Intelligence is arguably an important predictor; reading is much less so. Indeed, some tests of intelligence are completely nonverbal. The two major individually administered intelligence tests require little reading, even among the verbal items. Rather, most of the verbal sections of these tests are completed by listening. Our point, quite simply, is that youngsters with reading disability typically have the intelligence they will need to succeed in life.

We are not saying that such youngsters, if unable to overcome their disability, will not be at a disadvantage. Obviously they will be. People with any kind of disability are at a disadvantage. Those who are hearing impaired constantly have to compensate for their difficulties in hearing. Those who cannot see well compensate for their lack of visual acuity. But the point to remember is that, as adults, individuals with reading disability will not be as incapacitated as those who are totally deaf or blind. They will be able to read—in some cases, even as well as most other adults.

Second, even if these individuals with reading disability do not achieve full reading proficiency, they can still succeed in most adult occupations. We can both remember undergraduate and graduate students who have done well in our programs despite reading disability; indeed, we have even observed successful adults in our own fields of psychology and education who were classified as having reading disability in their childhoods. This is not to suggest that those who lack high reading achievement can master any occupation. They might not be cut out to work as proofreaders or to spend their days abstracting technical articles in a university library. But there are ultimately few fields that will remain closed to them.

We are not attempting to downplay the importance or the seriousness of reading disability. After all, we have written a book about it! But we do think that teachers and parents need to keep a proper perspective. When children are growing up, it is only natural to compare them on the skills that are most central to the tasks of childhood. Reading is one such skill. But how often do we compare adults in their reading ability? As a child, you may have known the reading ability of every child in your class—through their classifications in a reading group, their performance in class oral readings, or whatever. But as an adult, do you know the reading ability of even one other adult with whom you come into contact? The answer is very likely no, because the tasks that we confront as adults are different from those we confront as children. Moreover, as adults, we can work out means of compensation to get by on those tasks that we do not perform well. And this, we believe, is the key to adult success. Indeed, according to the triarchic theory, persons with practical intelligence are those who figure out what they do really well and what they do really badly, and then devise means to capitalize on their strengths and compensate for or remediate their weaknesses so as to render themselves capable enough to meet the demands of their lives.

Thus, we believe that reading disability certainly is important, especially to those who have to deal with children with reading disability in school; but we also believe that a long-term perspective needs to be maintained. School success is not particularly indicative of life success, and success in a particular aspect of school—namely, reading—is even less indicative. Some of the most successful people in business, the arts, the sciences, and other occupations are those who as children were classified as having reading disability. As adults, they have found their own individual roads to success.

References

Borkowski, J. G., & Cavanaugh, J. C. (1979). Maintenance and generalization of skills and strategies by the retarded. In N. R. Ellis (Ed.), *Handbook of mental deficiency*, 2nd ed. Hillsdale, NJ: Erlbaum.

Butterfield, E. C., & Belmont, J. M. (1977). Assessing and improving the cognition of mentally retarded people. In I. Bialer & M. Sternlicht (Eds.), *Psychology of mental retardation: Issues and approaches.* New York: Psychological Dimensions.

Campione, J. C., & Brown, A. L. (1979). Toward a theory of intelligence: Contributions from research with retarded children. In R. J. Sternberg & D. K. Detterman (Eds.), *Human intelligence: Perspectives on its theory and measurement.* Norwood, NJ: Ablex.

Gardner, H. (1983). *Frames of mind: The theory of multiple intelligences.* New York: Basic.

———. (1993). *Multiple intelligences: The theory in practice.* New York: Basic.

Gardner, H., Krechevsky, M., & Sternberg, R. J. (1994). Intelligence in context: Enhancing students' practical intelligence for school. In K. McGilly (Ed.), *Classroom lessons: Integrating cognitive theory and classroom practice.* (pp. 105–127). Cambridge, MA: Bradford Books.

Heath, S. B. (1983). *Ways with words.* Cambridge University Press.

LaBerge, D., & Samuels, J. (1974). Toward a theory of automatic information processing in reading. *Cognitive Psychology, 6,* 293–323.

Sternberg, R. J. (1985). *Beyond IQ: A triarchic theory of human intelligence.* New York: Cambridge University Press.

———. (1988). *The triarchic mind: A new theory of human intelligence.* New York: Viking.

———. (1991). Are we reading too much into reading-comprehension tests? *Journal of Reading, 34*(7), 540–545.

————. (1994). Thinking styles: Theory and assessment at the interface between intelligence and personality. In R. J. Sternberg and P. Ruzgis (Eds.), *Personality and intelligence* (pp. 169–187). New York: Cambridge University Press.

Sternberg, R. J., & Wagner, R. K. (1982). Automatization failure in learning disabilities. *Topics in Learning & Learning Disabilities, 2,* 1–11.

10 Early Intervention and Prevention

CHILDREN WHO STRAY from the road to proficient reading should be brought back to it as soon as possible. The farther they go off track in reading, the more difficult it is to help them, because of the cognitive and motivational consequences of reading failure. As we discussed in the previous chapter, children who are poor readers in school can go on to have successful and productive lives in adulthood. Obviously, however, no one would choose to be a poor reader rather than a good reader. In some cases, long-term reading failure has disastrous effects on employment and on opportunities in adult life. Moreover, as we will discuss shortly, early failure in reading can be an emotionally devastating experience, even if the individual ultimately attains a high level of achievement in reading. Thus, there are some compelling reasons to intervene early with children who are experiencing reading difficulties and, if possible, to try to prevent these difficulties from happening in the first place.

Just as professionals sometimes become strongly wedded to purist versions of whole-language or code-emphasis instruction, they also may become wedded to one particular early intervention program. A couple of years ago, one of the coauthors attended a conference presentation aimed at recruiting teachers for participation in a well-known early intervention program in reading. This coauthor was startled to hear the presenters use the term *franchise* in describing the distribution of the program to different school districts. The word conjured up images of hamburger stands and fried-chicken restaurants, where harried-looking employees distribute food in prewrapped, standardized packages. The underlying tone of the presentation seemed to imply that there was one "right" way to do early intervention in reading and that, unless the procedures advocated by the developers of this particular program were followed down to the last detail, early intervention would be ineffective.

As we will see, certain key elements keep cropping up in the most successful early intervention programs in reading. In a broad sense, there *are* "right" and "wrong" ways to do early intervention. However, no one program owns a franchise on preventing reading failure, and there are many ways in which the broad characteristics of effective early intervention programs can be implemented.

We begin this section by discussing Jack, whose story illustrates the emotional toll of early failure in reading. We then explore some general issues: whom to target for early intervention, when to intervene, and what to avoid in early intervention. In the second major section of the chapter, we review a number of successful early intervention programs in reading. Finally, in the third section, we draw some conclusions about early intervention in reading and about preventing reading disability.

Jack's Story

Jack is a teacher in a residential facility for children with emotional and academic problems. He holds a master's degree and has an exemplary academic record at both the undergraduate and graduate levels. Jack is a very bright, articulate, and extremely conscientious individual; his written-expression skills, including spelling, are excellent. To all outward appearances, he is a typical high achiever.

However, despite his current level of academic achievement, Jack experienced serious reading difficulties in childhood. These difficulties conformed to the pattern common in reading disability, involving early deficiencies in word recognition and specifically in phonological-reading skills. Later in elementary school, Jack had difficulty with orthographic skills, as evidenced by poor spelling, and problems in reading comprehension that were related to his word-recognition deficits. By the time he was ready to enter the sixth grade, Jack was functioning only at a third-grade level on an informal reading inventory.

Jack entered elementary school in the early 1960s, well before the passage of P.L. 94-142. There does not appear to have been a learning-disabilities program in place in Jack's school. Instead, he received one-to-one tutoring help from a reading teacher hired privately by his parents. Jack was not as dramatically impaired in reading as are some children with RD; he was not a nonreader. However, his reading difficulties conform to the profile that is typical of RD; and, as we have seen, children with RD can vary in reading skill. Jack clearly views himself as having a reading disability. His childhood records suggest that he might well have been identified as having RD according to contemporary learning-disabilities guidelines used in public schools: He had seriously deficient reading skills, met exclusionary criteria, and tested in the high average range on a *Wechsler Intelligence Scale for Children* (WISC).

A number of factors appear to have contributed to Jack's eventual success in reading. First, he was a compliant and unusually motivated youngster. His teachers repeatedly praised his willingness to work hard, his attentiveness, and his eagerness to learn. Jack has described these personal qualities in somewhat more pragmatic terms; he says that he detested remedial classes in public school—where many of the students were behavior problems—and was willing to do whatever it took to get out of them. Second, Jack received a great deal of support from family members, who did their best to help him and never invidiously compared him with his high-achieving siblings. Third, Jack seems to have received an excellent remedial program from his private tutor. This remedial program combined an emphasis on direct instruction in word-recognition skills, vocabulary, and comprehension with an emphasis on independent reading for enjoyment.

Thus, in many ways, Jack's story can be seen as one of eventual success against formidable odds. In his case, early and ongoing difficulty in reading did *not* lead to the kinds of cognitive and motivational consequences predicted by the theory of Matthew effects in reading (Stanovich, 1986). On the contrary, Jack now has excellent cognitive abilities as well as excellent academic skills—neither of which would have been predicted by his early academic record or by his childhood WISC score. In addition to illustrating the limitations of traditional IQ tests in measuring cognitive abilities, Jack's story illustrates that, under the right kinds of circumstances and with the right kinds of support, children with RD can attain a high level of achievement.

Nevertheless, Jack's early reading difficulties have left an emotional legacy. Jack clearly thinks of himself as someone with limited abilities, who has done well strictly by dint of hard work. He still has sharp memories of many unhappy school experiences—such as of the class in which the teacher posted students' names along with a list of the books each student had read that year. The lists next to other students' names grew longer and longer, whereas Jack took almost an entire year to read one book. Jack continues to feel a great deal of anxiety about competing with other students in academic situations, despite the fact that he invariably performs well.

Early reading failure can be a powerful force in shaping children's visions of themselves. As Jack's story shows, these negative visions sometimes persist even in the face of eventual success. The emotional consequences of reading failure, and in some cases the cognitive and motivational consequences, can be avoided only if reading failure is addressed very early or prevented entirely. Later in this chapter, we will discuss some specific early intervention programs that might have prevented or at least ameliorated Jack's reading problems long before he entered the sixth grade. First, however, we need to consider some general issues. Specifically, who should be targeted for early intervention? And when is the best time to intervene?

Deciding Whom to Target for Early Intervention

In retrospect, it is obvious that Jack could have benefited from early intervention in reading. However, at the time that Jack entered school, the fact that he was going to have reading problems was not at all obvious. Indeed, because he was a particularly inquisitive preschooler, his mother thought that he might excel academically. How could the adults who were involved with Jack, and especially his teachers, have determined that he was at risk for reading disability?

Research reviewed in previous chapters provides some answers to the question of who should be targeted for intervention in reading. Because no unique biological or genetic profile has yet been found to characterize reading disability, early screening for RD must occur at the level of cognitive processes. As noted, cognitive skills that are especially predictive of early reading achievement are phonological-processing skills, such as phonological awareness and naming speed, and letter knowledge. For children who have received formal reading instruction (e.g., first-graders), failure to acquire decoding skills on schedule is an ominous sign. Difficulties with phonological-processing skills and with decoding also are particularly characteristic of reading disability. Thus, these areas—phonological-processing skills, letter knowledge, and decoding—should be emphasized in attempts to determine who is at risk for RD. In Chapter 7, we discussed some possible ways to assess these areas. Of course, because garden-variety poor readers also are characterized by phonological and word-recognition deficits, testing in these areas would identify not only children at risk for RD but those at risk for poor reading in general.

Early screening of children, especially in kindergarten, has become commonplace. Unfortunately, however, these screening procedures do not always emphasize the kinds of cognitive skills that best predict later reading achievement and that would be helpful in identifying children who are at risk for reading difficulties. In particular, tests of phonological awareness and of naming speed are conspicuously absent from many kindergarten screening batteries. Even more important, kindergarten screening often is misused. As McGill-Franzen (1994) points out, poor performance on screening measures frequently is attributed exclusively to innately low ability or to delayed cognitive development. By the same token, the role of experience in shaping the skills tapped by screening tends to be vastly underrated.

Screening should be used not to categorize children and not to set long-term expectations but, rather, for instructional purposes. Children who have weak phonological skills need an instructional emphasis on these kinds of skills in order to progress in reading acquisition. And children who lack reading-related knowledge, such as knowledge about letters and about basic concepts of print, need to be extensively engaged in literacy experiences that will help them to develop this knowledge. In fact, most children with RD will need both of these things—an instructional emphasis on phonological skills and extensive engagement in literacy experiences. What they do not need is to be labeled or stigmatized during their very first year in school.

Deciding When to Intervene

Just how early should early intervention occur? Researchers interested in early intervention with youngsters who are at risk in reading have been oriented toward school-based programs. Many of these programs are at the first-grade level (e.g., Clay, 1985; Hiebert, Colt, Catto, & Gury, 1992; Pinnell, Lyons, DeFord, Bryk, &

Seltzer, 1994; Taylor, Short, Frye, & Shearer, 1992). At this grade level, children usually are identified based on low initial achievement in reading and in reading subskills, such as knowledge of letter names and sounds.

Other intervention programs have been aimed at children of kindergarten age. These kindergarten programs tend to fall into two broad categories: programs involving phonological-awareness training (e.g., Bradley, 1987; Bradley & Bryant, 1983, 1985; Torgesen, Morgan, & Davis, 1992) and programs involving an "emergent literacy" style of emphasis on immersion in print, story reading, and the like (e.g., Martinez, Cheyney, McBroom, Hemmeter, & Teale, 1989; Pinnell & McCarrier, 1994). The former programs have examined the impact of phonological-awareness training both on phonological awareness itself and on later reading achievement, particularly the later reading achievement of children with phonological weaknesses. The latter programs have tended to focus on low-SES youngsters who have had relatively impoverished literacy experiences and who lack basic print-related knowledge. Although these two groups of children—children with phonological weaknesses and children who lack basic print-related knowledge—might appear to be quite distinct, in fact they probably overlap considerably. That is, children with phonological weaknesses may have difficulty acquiring print-related knowledge, and children who lack print-related knowledge may have phonological weaknesses.

In most preschool intervention programs, little attention has been directed to the area of literacy. We know of no commercially published intervention program aimed at the cognitive characteristics typical of reading disability, such as at specific reading-related phonological weaknesses, prior to kindergarten. Even compensatory education programs involving preschoolers, such as Head Start, have not focused on fostering literacy (Taylor & Hiebert, 1994), although many of the youngsters in these programs are at risk for reading failure. Much of this lack of attention to literacy seems to grow out of the perception that literacy activities are not developmentally appropriate for preschoolers. However, as Taylor and Hiebert (1994) point out, preschool children can be engaged in literacy activities in appropriate ways—for example, through shared reading of children's books rather than through rote or highly academic tasks.

It is possible to identify children who have had very limited experiences with literacy in the preschool years. However, currently it is far less feasible to identify other preschoolers with a specific vulnerability to RD, even using cognitive-processing measures. Existing measures of reading-related phonological-processing skills such as phonological awareness are designed for school-aged children rather than for preschoolers. Measures of letter knowledge generally are not appropriate for children below kindergarten age. New tests and new assessment techniques will be needed if preschool intervention efforts to help children with a specific vulnerability to RD are to be developed.

Also, there are some serious hazards in trying to identify children vulnerable to RD at the preschool level. Cognitive assessment tends to be less reliable with younger children. With preschoolers, then, it is likely that a significant number of children will be erroneously identified as being at risk for reading disability. As we have seen, when children are falsely identified as at risk, they may be subject to lowered expectations and to inappropriate kinds of programming. It also makes little sense to expend resources, financial and otherwise, on children who do not need them. These hazards must be kept in mind in targeting any group of youngsters for very early intervention.

Nevertheless, for those children who do bring to school a vulnerability to RD, intervention in the preschool years might still be desirable. Preschool intervention already is commonplace for broad kinds of language impairments, and children with RD have been conceptualized as having a milder or more specific form of language disability (see, for example, Stanovich & Siegel, 1994). Because the cognitive processes that are causally implicated in reading disability are at least partially amenable to environmental influence, intervention in the preschool years could benefit many children. This intervention could involve activities that are appropriate for and generally benefit all young children, but that might be especially beneficial to children with a vulnerability to RD. Such activities include listening to and retelling stories, playing rhyming and alliterative word games, and engaging children with letters, print, drawing, and writing.

Whether intervention occurs prior to kindergarten or early in schooling, parental involvement is very important. For example, parents can be encouraged to read to their children on a regular basis, to have children read to them regularly, to take children to libraries, and to limit television-watching. These, too, are activities that benefit all youngsters but might prove particularly advantageous to children who are at risk for reading failure. Furthermore, effective parental involvement requires something more than simply disseminating information. Rather, children's achievement benefits when parents are engaged in an active, ongoing fashion—for instance, when teachers regularly telephone parents, encourage parents to visit the classroom, or send home books and other assignments (Goldenberg, 1994).

Some Situations to Avoid in Early Intervention

Before beginning our review of successful early intervention programs, we would like to say a few words about what should *not* be done in early intervention in reading. At least three recommendations come to mind. First, as Adams (1990) points out, it is imperative that children deemed at risk for reading failure, such as those with weak phonological skills, not be routinely retained in kindergarten or otherwise held back in reading. For one thing, although it may be warranted in certain instances, kindergarten retention does not appear to be a generally effective form of intervention (Mantzicopoulos & Morrison, 1992). In addition, because assessment tends to be less reliable with younger children, and because no screening device is perfect, some young children who appear to be at risk actually are not at risk. Finally, and most important, learning to read itself helps to develop phonological skills and print-related knowledge. Thus, although children with weaknesses in these areas may have greater difficulty in learning to read, their introduction to formal reading instruction should not await some arbitrary level of readiness.

Our second recommendation regarding what not to do involves the idea that children with weak phonological skills may be unable to learn phonics and thus may require a predominantly sight-word approach to reading instruction (e.g., Lyon, Newby, Recht, & Caldwell, 1991). However, the disappointing results of research on the modality-method interaction approach, which we discussed in Chapter 2, as well as what we know about the process of reading acquisition in an alphabetic orthography, suggest that children cannot become proficient readers solely by memorizing sight words. Learning to read an alphabetic language without understanding how the alphabet works is like learning mathematics by memorizing numerals in lieu of understanding place value. On the other hand, whether they have strong or weak phonological-processing skills, children cannot become good readers just by learning phonics. Rather, all youngsters require a combination of instructional approaches, with different emphases for different children.

Our third caveat involves the need to allow for individual differences at both ends of the spectrum. In other words, reading instruction should encompass children who have strong phonological skills or excellent reading-related knowledge *as well as* those who are weak in these areas. By the same token, programming for youngsters who are at risk for reading failure should not come at the expense of youngsters who are not at risk, some of whom may enter school already knowing how to read. In short, instructional programming should be flexible enough that the needs of high achievers and those of low achievers or at-risk children can be accommodated.

Examples of Successful Early Intervention Programs in Reading

In this section, we review a number of intervention programs that have been successful in improving the reading skills of children who are at risk for reading failure, sometimes to the point of making these children indistinguishable from their normally achieving classmates. Some of these programs are aimed at poor readers in general; others are aimed more specifically at children considered to be at risk for reading disability. Because the instructional needs and many of the cognitive-processing characteristics of youngsters with RD do not differ dramatically from those of other poor readers (Fletcher et al., 1994; Stanovich & Siegel, 1994), we believe that both types of programs should be examined by practitioners who are interested in reading disability.

Table 10.1 summarizes some basic characteristics of the five intervention programs that we review: Reading Recovery (Clay, 1985), Success for All (Madden, Slavin, Karweit, & Livermon, 1987; Slavin, Madden, Karweit, Dolan, & Wasik, 1994), the restructured "Chapter 1" program of Elfrieda Hiebert and her colleagues (Hiebert et al., 1992), Early Intervention in Reading (Taylor et al., 1992), and the Bowman Gray Learning Disabilities Project (Brown & Felton, 1990; Felton, 1993; Felton & Wood, 1992). In addition, at the end of this section, we discuss some experimental interventions involving the training of phonological awareness in kindergartners at risk for reading failure.

We must acknowledge at the outset the uncertain efficacy of all these interventions in *permanently* preventing reading failure. There is considerable evidence that these programs do help to keep many children on the road to proficient reading in the early grades. But still unclear is whether an intervention at the kindergarten or first-grade level can chart some children's courses on the road to proficient reading through adulthood. We will return to this issue in the final section of the chapter.

As we will show, there are some striking similarities across these successful programs. However, these programs also vary considerably—not only regarding the intensity and duration of the intervention but also in terms of whether the intervention involves individual tutoring or groups of children, and whether a regular-classroom teacher or a different teacher provides the intervention. In other words, the programs vary with respect to features that go beyond actual instructional content or instructional approach. These features are important not only because they may affect the efficacy of the intervention but also for reasons such as cost. For instance, one-to-one tutoring tends to be a particularly expensive form of intervention, given the limited numbers of children that a teacher can serve at any one time.

Sometimes the costs of early intervention can be mitigated through the utilization of funds that are already in place. For instance, some intervention programs in schools with large numbers of low-income and minority students have drawn heavily upon "Chapter 1" funds as well as upon other sources such as funds from special education, bilingual education, and school desegregation lawsuits (e.g., Slavin et al., 1994). "Chapter 1" monies also have been used to fund Reading Recovery (Hiebert, 1994a). If the effects of early intervention are of a long-term nature, then the cost of the intervention might be covered by reductions in retention rates, reductions in special-education placements, and so on. Indeed, if these effects are essentially permanent in preventing reading failure, then the cost of the intervention might be a wise investment in terms of reducing the costs associated with social problems such as unemployment, delinquency, and welfare. Of course, cost is not the only issue in deciding whether to implement an early intervention program in reading. Some authors (e.g., Slavin et al., 1994) have argued that we now know enough to prevent most cases of reading failure and thus have a moral obligation to act on this knowledge—regardless of cost.

TABLE 10.1 Characteristics of Early Intervention Programs

	Intervention Program				
	RR	SA	RCH1	EIR	BG
When children are identified	Beginning of first grade	In first, second, or third grade, but most often in first	Beginning of first grade	Beginning of first grade	In kindergarten
How children are identified	Low reading skills	Low reading skills	Low reading skills	Low reading skills and poor phonological awareness	Weaknesses in phonological processing
Intensity and duration of intervention	1/2 hour per day for 12 to 20 weeks	20 minutes per day for as long as needed	1/2 hour per day for most of the school year	20 minutes per day for most of the school day	A total reading program for first and second grades
Intervention supplements regular-classroom instruction	Yes	Yes	Yes	Yes	No
Intervention involves one-to-one tutoring or small groups	Tutoring	Tutoring (as part of a schoolwide restructuring program)	Small groups	Small groups	Small groups
Providers of intervention	Trained RR teachers	Certified teachers familiar with the regular classroom SA program	Certified Chapter 1 teachers and aides	Regular first-grade teachers	Research teachers working in the regular first-grade classroom

Note: RR=Reading Recovery (Clay, 1985); SA=Success for All (e.g., Slavin et al., 1990); RCH1=Restructured "Chapter 1" (Hiebert et al., 1992); EIR=Early Intervention in Reading (Taylor et al., 1992); BG=Bowman Gray Learning Disabilities Project (e.g., Felton, 1993).

Reading Recovery

Of all the existing early intervention programs in reading, the most frequently cited, perhaps one of the most effective, and certainly one of the most controversial is Reading Recovery. Originally developed by Marie Clay (1985) in New Zealand, where it is in wide use, Reading Recovery was imported into the United States in the 1980s under the auspices of Ohio State University. The program is now used not only in Ohio but in many other states as well; indeed, its speed of implementation in the United States has been described as "phenomenal" (Hiebert, 1994a, p. 15).

Description. In Reading Recovery, children's reading skills are screened early in first grade using a Diagnostic Survey (Clay, 1985). Children who score in the lowest 20 percent of their classes are possible candidates for the program, but other factors, such as teacher judgment, also influence which children are selected. Reading Recovery involves one-to-one tutoring for thirty minutes a day in a pull-out program. All Reading Recovery teachers receive at least a year of intensive training that includes numerous opportunities for observation and feedback during actual teaching of children. Teachers are expected to continue their professional development after the training year through professional conferences and through regular contact with other Reading Recovery teachers. Both the tutorial aspect of the program and its emphasis on intensive, continuing teacher training are viewed by advocates of Reading Recovery as particularly crucial to its success (e.g., Pinnell, Short, Lyons, & Young, 1994).

Reading Recovery is conceptualized as a short-term intervention. Children remain in the program for a period of weeks or for several months, but Reading Recovery is not intended to be a long-term intervention spanning a year or more. Within twelve to twenty weeks, the majority of children do catch up to the oral reading levels of their first-grade classmates and are dismissed from the program. These youngsters are termed "discontinued." Children who do not catch up to their classmates in a few months' time also are released from the program but are termed "not discontinued."

Reading Recovery involves a whole-language approach to instruction. Although decoding skills are taught directly, the emphasis is overwhelmingly on the teaching of these skills in meaningful contexts—for example, through reading stories or writing messages—rather than in isolation. The thirty minutes per day of instruction are spent primarily on the following four activities: rereading familiar books; obtaining a running record of the child's reading in context, for use by the teacher in making instructional decisions; writing; and reading new books. Activities involving magnetic letters may be added for children who do not yet know the alphabet.

Pinnell, Fried, and Estice (1990) provide some good examples of typical activities used in Reading Recovery. We will discuss one such activity, involving writing, that is used daily in the program. The child is given a blank writing tablet opened and turned sideways, so that there is a page on the top and a page on the bottom. The child uses the bottom page to write a message involving a sentence or two, or, in some instances, even an entire story. The top page, called the practice page, is available for the child to work out the spellings of words that are unfamiliar. If the child is having difficulty figuring out the spelling of an unfamiliar word—for example, the word *bath*—the teacher might make three connected boxes on the practice page, to show the child that the word has three sounds in it. The child is encouraged to use his or her knowledge of sound-symbol correspondences or of other words (e.g., *math*) to fill in the boxes. Finally, when the child has completed the message on the bottom page, the teacher writes it on a separate strip of paper, cuts the words apart, and asks the child to reassemble the sentence.

Notice that although this activity is labeled as a writing activity (which, of course, it is), it also serves as an activity for developing word recognition skills, decoding knowledge, and phonological awareness. In fact, the use of the empty boxes to represent sounds in words is reminiscent of Elkonin's procedure for developing phonological awareness, which we described in Chapter 7. Reading Recovery makes extensive use of writing activities to focus children's attention on the details of print—that is, to teach, among other things, decoding and phonological-awareness skills.

As is typical of many whole-language programs, Reading Recovery does not employ a predetermined curriculum. Rather, teachers closely observe the reading skills that children already have and use these existing skills to build further competence in reading through an individually tailored program. Books are carefully selected to suit the instructional needs of a particular child and always involve natural language, not phonetically controlled or otherwise contrived texts.

Outcomes. Studies have reported significant gains for Reading Recovery children as compared with children in other interventions—such as in a tutorial intervention employing direct instruction in basic skills—or as compared with poor readers receiving "Chapter 1" services (DeFord et al., 1988; Pinnell, Lyons, DeFord, Bryk, & Seltzer, 1991; Pinnell, Short, Lyons, & Young, 1986; Pinnell et al., 1994). The percentages of Reading Recovery children who are "discontinued" because they have achieved grade-appropriate reading skills in a period of a few months are extremely impressive. In studies done in the United States, these percentages usually are around 80 or higher, especially after the first year of implementation (DeFord et al., 1988; Hiebert, 1994a; Smith-Burke & Jaggar, 1994). Wasik and Slavin (1993) conclude that the positive effects of the Reading Recovery intervention appear to be maintained for at least two years, and perhaps longer.

Comments. Given these results, what could possibly be controversial about Reading Recovery? For one thing, research on Reading Recovery has been criticized on a number of counts. First, both Wasik and Slavin (1993), whose overall evaluation of Reading Recovery is quite positive, and Hiebert (1994a), whose overall evaluation is more negative, point out serious flaws in early research on Reading Recovery in New Zealand (e.g., Clay, 1985)—research that is frequently cited as evidence of the effectiveness of the program. The inadequacies of the New Zealand research include the fact that it focuses only on the "discontinued" children, those who have been successful in the program. (By contrast, the U.S. studies cited in the preceding section provide data on both "not discontinued" and "discontinued" children.)

A second criticism is that, according to Wasik and Slavin (1993) as well as Hiebert (1994a), many Reading Recovery programs appear to have a policy of excluding certain children, such as those who have already been retained in first grade or who are receiving special-education services. Hiebert (1994a) suggests that, at least in the United States, Reading Recovery programs typically have serviced children in the fourth quintile in reading achievement according to national norms—not those in the lowest, or fifth, quintile. The policy of excluding certain children does not seem to be Clay's intent (see, for example, Clay, 1987). However, if the exclusion of the lowest achievers in reading from Reading Recovery is indeed commonplace, then this fact not only biases experimental findings but also undermines arguments about the cost-effectiveness of Reading Recovery. These arguments often revolve around the ability of Reading Recovery to prevent retention or to avoid the need for special-education services—and obviously, it is the lowest achievers in reading who are most likely to be retained or to end up in the special-education system.

A third criticism (Wasik & Slavin, 1993) concerns the strong relationship between the instructional orientation of Reading Recovery and many of the measures used to evaluate the program. It is not unreasonable to employ measures that are sensitive to the instructional emphases and underlying instructional philosophy of an educational program. However, such a relationship also might bias the results of the studies—in this case, because the Reading Recovery children were more familiar with the types of items emphasized in the assessment than were the children in the other groups. In addition, Hiebert (1994a) points out that the Reading Recovery measures rely heavily upon accuracy—specifically, accuracy of oral reading of text. But the measures do not reflect fluency of oral reading or comprehension, reading skills that become more crucial as children progress beyond the first-grade level.

Finally, the longitudinal data on the effectiveness of Reading Recovery have not gone unchallenged. Hiebert (1994a) maintains that these data, from the U.S. studies, are incomplete and unconvincing. For instance, DeFord, Pinnell, Lyons, and Place (1990) followed Reading Recovery students through the fourth grade and compared them with two other groups of students: other low achievers who, in the first grade, received regular "Chapter 1" services instead of Reading Recovery (called the Achievement Comparison group); and a group of more typical students representing a range of achievement levels at the Reading Recovery students' schools (the School Comparison group). At the fourth-grade level, Reading Recovery students performed better than did the Achievement Comparison group on an oral reading task, but the differences between the two groups, though substantial, did not attain statistical significance. On a standardized reading test, the Reading Recovery students performed similarly to the Achievement Comparison group; both groups performed significantly below the level of the School Comparison group.

In schools and among the general public, however, these research issues are not at the forefront of the controversy that surrounds Reading Recovery. Rather, the cost of the program and the limited numbers of children who can be served in a school year—due to the one-to-one model and the large amount of time spent in ongoing teacher training—are more frequent sources of criticism. A community newspaper, under the heading "Children in Tailored Reading Program Showing Results" (Sheridan, 1994), recently ran a story about a Reading Recovery program in a local school district with a large population of low-income and minority youngsters. Although the article emphasized the effectiveness of the program, it also included numerous complaints from those who saw the program as helping too few children for the number of dollars spent—a sort of "Porsche approach" to poor reading, they called it. A week later, in a letter to the editor, a local classroom teacher grumbled that she could be effective with children, too, if she could see all of them one-to-one.

Although one-to-one tutoring is a key component of Reading Recovery, this component alone does not account for the success of the program, contrary to what some people may think. Indeed, other key components of the program— such as the emphasis on integrating word-recognition strategies with the reading of connected text, as well as the emphasis on teacher development—also likely account for its effectiveness, at least at the first-grade level. Nevertheless, questions about the population of poor readers served, and about the long term efficacy of Reading Recovery, do undermine arguments about the cost-effectiveness of the program. Hiebert (1994a) suggests that Reading Recovery may be effective in meeting the needs of many suburban school districts where the overall levels of literacy are high and the number of poor readers relatively small. However, in school districts where large numbers of students need extra help—such as the one described in the community newspaper—Reading Recovery may not be the best way to utilize limited funds.

Success for All

Success for All (Madden et al., 1987) is a school restructuring program aimed primarily at schools with large numbers of economically disadvantaged students. A main goal of Success for All is to ensure that all students acquire basic academic skills, particularly in reading, from the beginning elementary years. The program involves a comprehensive package of services including family support services, preschool services, and one-to-one tutoring by certified teachers for students who are experiencing reading difficulties in first through third grades.

Description. The regular reading program in Success for All involves a number of important components. These components include grouping children for reading instruction based on their reading levels, sometimes across grades; cooperative learning; a combination of direct instruction in word-recognition and decoding skills with instruction in comprehension and comprehension strategies; the extensive use of listening-comprehension activities to develop comprehension skills, beginning in kindergarten; and strong encouragement of independent reading (Slavin et al., 1994).

Unlike Reading Recovery, Success for All uses texts that sometimes deviate from natural language or children's literature, particularly for beginning readers. Slavin et al. (1994) describe an interesting activity involving one such text (see also Beck et al., 1989). This activity entails shared story reading and is meant to be used with youngsters early in the first grade. At this grade level, phonetically regular words are emphasized in children's reading, in order to help children develop decoding skills. However, to avoid the stilted nature of many phonetically controlled texts, shared story books represent some words in small type and others in large type. The former words are read by the teacher, whereas the latter are read by students. In addition, to further reduce the decoding demands of the text, some words are represented by pictures. Later in first grade, children read more naturalistic types of texts.

Most of the youngsters who receive additional tutoring in reading are first-graders (Wasik & Slavin, 1993). Children are selected for tutoring based on low performance on an individually administered oral reading inventory and are seen every day for twenty minutes. Tutoring may last for a few weeks, months, the school year, or even longer if necessary. The goal of the tutoring program is to help children keep up with the regular-classroom program in reading. Thus, in contrast to Reading Recovery, where the intervention may not relate strongly to the regular-classroom reading program, Success for All provides strong integration of the tutoring program with the regular-classroom reading program.

All of the teachers and tutors in Success for All are certified, but their initial training in the program is fairly minimal, involving a few days of in-service presentations and distribution of written teachers' manuals. However, ongoing teacher training is also offered throughout the year. In particular, as Slavin et al. (1994) note, "the staff development model used in Success for All emphasizes relatively brief initial training with extensive classroom follow-up, coaching, and group discussion" (p. 137).

Outcomes. Because of the comprehensive, schoolwide nature of Success for All, it is difficult to evaluate the specific effect of the tutoring component of the program. However, students in the schools involved in Success for All have demonstrated dramatic improvements in reading achievement as compared with control students in other schools (Madden, Slavin, Karweit, Dolan, & Wasik, 1992; Slavin, Madden, Karweit, Livermon, & Dolan, 1990). Across programs in a number of different states, Success for All students performed, on average, at or near expected grade levels. In addition, the experimental schools approximately halved the numbers of students referred for special-education services and assigned to learning-disabilities services. Retentions were virtually eliminated (Slavin et al., 1990).

Comments. Success for All targets a population of children who, though not generally regarded as having reading disability, experience very high rates of reading failure—namely, low-income children in urban schools. In the schools where it has been used, Success for All has been very effective in bringing most of these children close to grade-level performance, in greatly reducing special-education placements, and in almost eliminating retentions. Given the track record of many other similar schools, these achievements are very impressive. Consider, for example, another low-income, urban school, not involved in Success for All, discussed by McGill-Franzen (1994). In this school, among a cohort of fifty-two children who entered kindergarten one year, only eighteen remained in the same school and managed to make it to the third grade on time—that is, without being retained or placed in special eduation. On the state-mandated achievement test given to third-graders, most of these eighteen youngsters scored in the bottom quartile in reading.

The positive effects of Success for All have not been attained without considerable cost, part of which can sometimes be covered by existing funds, such as those allocated to "Chapter 1" (Slavin et al., 1994). Like Reading Recovery, Success for All is expensive. However, there is evidence that, at least under certain circumstances, less expensive interventions involving small groups of children, rather than tutoring, also can help to prevent reading failure. We describe one such program next.

Restructured "Chapter 1" Services

"Chapter 1" is a federally funded program for poor children that began as Title 1 of the Elementary and Secondary Education Act of 1965 (McGill-Franzen, 1994). It is intended specifically to provide additional educational services to economically disadvantaged youngsters. Typically these additional services involve reading. Although Chapter 1 programs may vary considerably from one school or school district to another, in general these programs have not been very effective in preventing long-term reading failure among poor children (Hiebert, 1994b). Many Chapter 1 programs appear vulnerable to the same criticisms directed against special-education programs—namely, that they tend to focus on drills of isolated skills with little emphasis on reading connected text for meaning (Allington & McGill-Franzen, 1989). Elfrieda Hiebert and her colleagues (Hiebert, 1994b; Hiebert et al., 1992) designed a first-grade intervention program that utilized existing Chapter 1 services but also involved considerable restructuring of these services.

Description. Hiebert et al. (1992) selected children for this intervention based upon their low performance on a standardized reading-readiness test as well as upon low teacher ratings of reading readiness, criteria similar to those generally used for Chapter 1 programs. The intervention involved a pull-out program in which children were seen in groups of three by trained Chapter 1 teachers and their aides, for approximately half an hour per day for most of the school year. The regular-classroom reading program, in which all of the children also participated, used a whole-language approach.

The restructured Chapter 1 program emphasized three instructional activities: reading predictable texts, writing rhyming words and journal writing, and decoding instruction on isolated words that had been selected from the books that the children were reading. Thus, the reading instruction in the restructured program integrated isolated word-recognition instruction with a great deal of meaningful reading of text. For instance, after reading a text several times, children would be asked to find a particular word, such as *back,* in the text. Then they would form the word with magnetic letters or write it on an acetate sheet with felt-tip markers. Finally, they would be helped to generate words with similar patterns, such as *tack, sack,* and *shack.* Phonological-awareness activities, such as adaptations of Elkonin's procedure described in Chapter 7, were part of the instruction in word-recognition skills. In addition, children were encouraged to take books home and to read to their parents on a daily basis.

Outcomes. By the end of first grade, 77 percent of the children in the restructured Chapter 1 program could read a primer text fluently, and about 50 percent could read an end-of-first-grade-level text. The comparable percentages for the regular Chapter 1 program were 18 percent (primer level or better) and 6 percent (end-of-first-grade-level or better). The entering readiness scores of the regular Chapter 1 children were significantly lower than those of the children in the restructured program; but even when these differences were controlled statistically, the children in the restructured program still outperformed the children in the regular Chapter 1 program on all measures. In fact, the performance of the children in the restructured program was statistically indistinguishable from that of most of their classmates, with the exception of the highest achievers (namely, children who had begun first grade with readiness scores in the top fifth of the class).

Comments. In terms of instructional content, the group intervention of Hiebert et al. (1992) is fairly similar to Reading Recovery. Although existing data on the two programs are difficult to compare, they appear to be approximately equal in effectiveness at the first-grade level. Like Reading Recovery, the progam of Hiebert et al. (1992) emphasizes reading and rereading of connected text along with explicit instruction in word-recognition strategies. Of course, there also are some differences between the two programs. The group intervention of Hiebert and her colleagues places greater emphasis on word-recognition instruction in isolation, and less emphasis on intensive teacher training, than does Reading

Recovery. Also, it extends throughout most of the school year, whereas most Reading Recovery interventions last between twelve and twenty weeks.

Small-group interventions probably have the potential to be as effective as Reading Recovery, at least for some poor readers. However, one possible objection to all of the intervention programs we have discussed so far—Reading Recovery, Success for All, and the restructured Chapter 1 program of Hiebert et al. (1992)—concerns the nature of the population that they address. Although all of the programs target children with poor initial achievement in reading, one might argue that many of these children probably lack the cognitive profiles characteristic of RD. For example, they may be characterized not by weaknesses in phonological processing or word-recognition skills but, rather, by weaknesses in comprehension. In other words, many of the youngsters in these programs may not be "real" cases of reading disability.

In the first chapter, we indicated our reservations about this kind of reasoning, based on the fact that the line separating the "real" cases of RD from other kinds of reading failure is blurry at best. On the one hand, we believe that many of the youngsters in progams such as Reading Recovery or Chapter 1 might well be viewed as having RD. On the other hand, it is certainly important to examine the results of early interventions in reading that have been designed specifically for youngsters with the cognitive profiles typical of reading disability. A number of such studies have been done, primarily involving youngsters with weaknesses in phonological awareness. We describe several of these interventions next.

Early Intervention in Reading

Description. Barbara Taylor and her colleagues (Taylor et al., 1992; Taylor, Strait, & Medo, 1994) have reported the results of a small-group, first-grade intervention called Early Intervention in Reading (EIR). EIR was developed specifically for use by regular-classroom teachers. The identified children remained in the regular classroom and participated in the regular reading program, but they also received extra help from their teachers for about fifteen to twenty minutes per day, in a small group of five to seven children. Children were identified based not only upon low reading scores but also upon problems with phonological awareness. Classroom teachers had completed workshop training in the procedures involved in the EIR program; they also received feedback and suggestions from EIR project assistants during the course of the intervention, which lasted roughly from October through April of first grade.

Following are some typical instructional activities employed in the EIR program, as described by Taylor et al. (1994). Instruction involved a three-day cycle of activities using the same text for all three days. On the first day, the teacher began by reading the book to the children, using a chart or a "big book" format. An approach similar to Holdaway's (1979) shared book experience, which we discussed in Chapter 7, was also employed: The teacher pointed to each word while reading and drew children's attention to important features of the print such as letter-sound relationships, spaces between words, and so on. Over the three-day instructional cycle, children gradually were engaged in choral (i.e., group oral) reading and independent reading of the story, with the teacher assuming a secondary role and providing help only as needed. Children had many opportunities to practice rereading the story beyond their fifteen or twenty minutes of EIR time with the classroom teacher. For instance, classroom aides or volunteers listened to children read individually, and children received copies of the story to take home to read to their parents.

A number of instructional activities supplemented the story reading. For instance, on the first day of an instructional cycle, after the story had been read, the teacher selected several words from the story for the children to analyze in isolation. Children wrote each word by putting letters in boxes, with one box per phoneme—a technique similar to the one used in Reading Recovery. Then, on the second and third days of the instructional cycle, children wrote a sentence about the story.

Like Success for All, but unlike Reading Recovery, EIR made use of texts that were tailored specifically for instructional purposes. In the EIR program, these texts primarily involved retellings of children's literature. The retellings simplified and shortened the story—for instance, by omitting certain episodes—to make it easier for the children to read. Taylor et al. (1994) argue that, although unaltered children's books could have been used, the shorter retellings were important as they allowed children to experience success in the early stages of the program. Later in the first-grade year, actual trade books rather than retellings were used.

Outcomes. EIR has been employed in several different school districts and with several different kinds of regular-classroom reading programs, including both the code-emphasis and whole-language approaches. Not surprisingly, although children in all of the districts benefited from the EIR program, the outcomes of EIR varied somewhat depending upon the school district and the nature of the regular-classroom reading curriculum (Taylor et al., 1994). For instance, in a rural district that used a basal program for regular-classroom instruction, and in which many of the EIR children also received Chapter 1 services, the EIR youngsters fared particularly well; by the end of first grade, 73 percent were reading on grade level or better, as compared with only 20 percent of a comparison group of children. In a suburban district that used a literature-based program, and in which EIR children did not receive any other supplemental reading help, 40 percent of EIR youngsters were reading on grade level or better, as compared with 11 percent of a comparison group.

Comments. The instructional emphases of EIR are similar to those of several other programs we have discussed, such as Reading Recovery and the restructured Chapter 1 program of Hiebert et al. (1992). Like these other programs, EIR emphasizes reading connected text, rereading, writing activities, and the development of decoding skills. The most obvious difference between EIR and these other programs involves the fact that in EIR, instruction is provided entirely in the regular classroom, by the regular-classroom teacher. Although its results do not appear to be as dramatic as those for some other programs, such as Reading Recovery, EIR appears to be effective in preventing reading failure among many first-grade students. Programs such as EIR might thus be seen as a good initial measure to try with entering first-graders who are at risk for reading failure. For some children, no other intervention is likely to be necessary, whereas for others, a more intensive approach might eventually be needed.

Of course, the long-term effectiveness of programs like EIR depends heavily upon the willingness of regular-classroom teachers to continue to implement the program year after year. New programs that are funded by grants and that involve partnerships between public schools and universities may create considerable enthusiasm at first. Unfortunately, however, this enthusiasm may wane when the grant money dries up and the university support weakens or disappears entirely.

Taylor et al. (1994) surveyed teachers who had been involved in the first year of the EIR project and found that many of them did continue to use the program on their own, even without university support. These teachers frequently made their own adjustments to the program—for example, by having a special-education teacher function as a coordinator and support person for the program. However, the teachers generally thought that the benefits of the program were worth the extra effort it required, and they continued to follow the basic instructional procedures of EIR fairly closely.

Bowman Gray Learning Disabilities Project

Description. Another longitudinal intervention has been carried out by investigators involved with the Bowman Gray Learning Disabilities Project (e.g., Brown & Felton, 1990; Felton, 1993; Felton & Brown, 1990; Felton & Wood, 1992). In this intervention project, children were identified in kindergarten based upon teacher assessment as well as upon weaknesses in phonological processing. These weaknesses included problems in phonological awareness, naming speed, or both. A subset of the identified children was randomly assigned to one of two experimental interventions, a meaning-emphasis program or a code-emphasis program, for both first and second grades. All of the instruction involved in the interventions was provided by research teachers working with children in small groups within the regular classroom. A third group of identified children did not participate in either experimental intervention and constituted a control group. These children received only the regular-classroom reading program, which was also a meaning-emphasis program, but it was not the same one used as an experimental intervention, nor was it delivered by a research teacher.

Published basal reading programs were used in the experimental interventions. The Houghton Mifflin basal program (Houghton Mifflin Company, 1986) was employed as the meaning-emphasis intervention, and the Lippincott program (Macmillan Publishing Company, 1981) constituted the code-emphasis intervention. Because both of these basal programs—like basal reading programs in general—teach decoding skills, the main differences between the two interventions pertained to the *way* the decoding skills were taught, not to *whether* they were taught. In the meaning-emphasis program, children were encouraged to utilize contextual or picture cues to aid in decoding words. However, in the code-emphasis program, children were taught phonological-awareness skills and were encouraged to apply decoding skills to unfamiliar words. Guessing at words based on contextual or picture cues was strongly discouraged in the code-emphasis program. Also, the initial texts used in the code-emphasis program were phonetically controlled, whereas the initial texts in the meaning-emphasis program were not phonetically controlled.

Outcomes. At the end of both first and second grades, children in the code-emphasis intervention outperformed both the control children and the children in the meaning-emphasis intervention in decoding skills. At the end of second grade, the advantage of the code-emphasis intervention was largest for the most difficult kinds of words—that is, for multisyllabic real words and pseudowords. In fact, many of the children in the code-emphasis intervention were functioning at grade level in reading (Brown & Felton, 1990; Felton, 1993). Of particular interest was the finding that, whereas all of the children in the code-emphasis intervention had acquired at least some decoding skills by the end of second grade, several children in the meaning-emphasis intervention and in the control group had virtually no decoding skills, even after two years of instruction. These latter children continued to rely almost exclusively on sight-word knowledge and on contextual cues to recognize words.

Comments. The code-emphasis intervention used by the Bowman Gray group of investigators is, to say the least, "at odds with current trends in reading instruction" (Felton, 1993, p. 588). This code-emphasis intervention did include ample opportunities for reading connected text and for writing. It also emphasized teacher-student interaction rather than seatwork or workbooks. However, in a number of important ways, the intervention was very different from currently more popular programs such as Reading Recovery—specifically, in its use of a highly structured, systematic code-emphasis approach, with a predetermined sequence of instruction; in its use of phonetically controlled texts; and in its relatively heavy emphasis on isolated word-recognition activities. Nevertheless, as Felton (1993) points out, and as we ourselves suggest in Chapter 7, with thoughtful planning this kind of systematic code-emphasis instruction can be integrated with the reading of children's literature and with the more contextualized kinds of activities generally advocated by whole-language theorists.

The code-emphasis intervention carried out by the Bowman Gray investigators also is longer and more intensive—entailing at least two years of a complete reading program provided by a research teacher—than are any of the others that we have discussed thus far. The population targeted by these investigators involved youngsters with rather stringently defined weaknesses in phonological processing. Thus, as a group, these children may have been more severely at risk for reading failure than were children in some of the other interventions we have reviewed. Children with severe weaknesses in phonological processing may require a relatively long, intensive intervention in order to learn to read. Yet clearly, and more optimistically speaking, with the appropriate kind of intervention, learning to read *is* possible, even for those children who are most at risk for reading disability.

Training Phonological Awareness in Kindergartners

In all of the interventions we have discussed to this point, phonological-awareness training of some kind was provided—but not until first grade. Could training at an earlier age—for example, in kindergarten—be even more effective and avoid the need for first-grade intervention altogether? Although many researchers have attempted to train phonological-awareness skills prior to first grade, most of these researchers have not focused on youngsters with the cognitive characteristics typical of reading disability. However, a few studies do provide information about the impact of training phonological-awareness skills in kindergartners who are relatively weak in these skills or who are otherwise at risk for reading failure. These studies provide some preliminary evidence that phonological awareness can be trained even in young children with relatively weak phonological-awareness skills and, moreover, that training can benefit later reading achievement.

For instance, Torgesen and his colleagues (Torgesen, Morgan, & Davis, 1992; Torgesen, Davis, & Wagner, 1993) trained the phonological awareness of kindergartners who were at risk for reading failure, using programs that were eight weeks (Torgesen et al., 1992) and twelve weeks (Torgesen et al., 1993) in length. The training emphasized phoneme blending and phoneme segmenting tasks, using a variety of games and activities to maintain the interest of the children. Even with these relatively brief interventions, the investigators demonstrated large treatment effects favoring trained groups in phonological awareness.

Among the best-known studies of phonological awareness is that of Bradley and Bryant (1983, 1985). These researchers longitudinally examined the phonological-awareness skills of a large group of four- and five-year-olds, using a sound-categorization task. As part of the study, Bradley and Bryant also trained the phonological awareness of a subset of these children who were initially weak in sound categorization. These latter children were assigned to one of four conditions: sound-categorization training, sound-categorization training with teaching of letter-sound knowledge, semantic categorization (a control group), and no training (a second control group). Training was spread over a two-year period.

The sound-categorization training involved teaching children to group words according to shared sounds by using pictures of objects. For example, the words *cake* and *rake* can be grouped together because they rhyme; the words *cake* and *cat* can be grouped together because they share the same initial consonant sound.

Children in the first experimental condition received only this sound-categorization training, whereas children in the second experimental condition not only received sound-categorization training but also learned how to represent common sounds with letters of the alphabet. Children in the third experimental condition, who received semantic-categorization training, learned to group words by semantic categories rather than by sounds. For example, *cake* and *bread* can be grouped semantically because both are types of food. After two years, the children in the second condition—those who had received both phonological-awareness training and letter-sound instruction—were eight to ten months ahead of the semantic-categorization control group in reading, a very substantial difference at this early age.

Thus, it appears that training phonological awareness in young children with weak phonological skills can improve both phonological awareness and later reading achievement. However, at this point, we must sound at least two cautionary notes. First, in studies of phonological-awareness training, there typically is large variability in phonological awareness within trained groups, even after training. That is, a significant minority of children with weaknesses in phonological awareness do not appear to respond readily to training. In Torgesen et al. (1992), this number was about 30 percent; in Torgesen et al. (1993), about 30 percent of children showed little improvement on a segmenting task and about 10 percent showed little improvement on a blending task. These results mirror those of the first-grade intervention studies, in which a significant minority of children continued to have persistent reading difficulty despite intervention. It would be interesting indeed to know whether the 30 percent of children who did not respond readily to training in the Torgesen et al. (1992) study are the same children who would continue to experience reading difficulties despite a first-grade intervention program such as Reading Recovery.

Our second cautionary note concerns the fact that most of the studies that have examined the phonological-processing skills of very young children, and all of those involving training, have emphasized one specific phonological-processing skill: phonological awareness. Indeed, there is much less evidence available regarding how to help children with other kinds of phonological weaknesses, such as naming-speed deficits (Blachman, 1994) or difficulties with phonological coding in working memory. Similarly lacking is evidence regarding how to help very young children who may have specific orthographic-processing weaknesses.

Preventing Reading Disability Through Early Intervention

Although the success rates of different intervention programs vary, all of the programs reviewed here have helped many children. Reading Recovery has a particularly impressive track record at the first-grade level, and the addition of a more intensive phonological-awareness training component may boost the success rates of Reading Recovery even further (Iversen & Tunmer, 1993). However, no single program is the solution to preventing reading failure. No single program succeeds with all children, and effective early intervention can be accomplished in a variety of ways.

In this final section of the chapter, we consider two sets of conclusions. First, we examine similarities and differences among the early intervention programs that we have reviewed, and we draw some conclusions about how to design programs to prevent reading disability. Second, we draw some conclusions about the long-term efficacy of early intervention.

Designing Programs to Prevent Reading Disability

At least three broad characteristics are common to the intervention programs described in this chapter. In our view, these characteristics should be duplicated in any program designed to prevent reading disability. First, all successful intervention programs emphasize the importance of children's immediate and ongoing success in reading. For example, Reading Recovery teachers are repeatedly exhorted to find out what children already know, to realize that this knowledge often is considerable, and to build upon this knowledge in instruction. Other programs, such as Success for All and EIR, emphasize adapting texts in ways that will make them easier for children to read, thereby providing more opportunities for success in the initial stages of reading instruction. Second, the professionals who have developed and who implement these programs share the very strong conviction that *all* children can learn to read with appropriate instruction. No children, even those most seriously at risk for reading difficulties, are viewed as incapable of learning to read well. Third, successful intervention programs tend to be characterized by strong support for teachers and by ample opportunities for feedback from colleagues, a characteristic that is particularly salient in Reading Recovery but that is present to some degree in all of the programs. Moreover, these supports for teachers include opportunities to learn not only from colleagues of comparable expertise but also from more knowledgeable colleagues. For instance, in Success for All, an experienced, highly competent teacher is assigned to serve full time as the program facilitator in each school; and in Reading Recovery, university-based teacher trainers and teacher leaders assume the roles of highly knowledgeable colleagues.

One obvious difference among the interventions involves the issue of tutoring versus small-group instruction. Although tutoring tends to be an expensive form of intervention, a number of investigators (e.g., Pinnell et al., 1994; Slavin et al., 1994) have argued that one-to-one tutoring is most effective for children experiencing reading problems. Jack, whose story opened this chapter, attributed much of his eventual success in school to the efficacy of the instruction he received from a private tutor.

Should teachers who are trying to design intervention programs to prevent reading disability focus largely on one-to-one tutoring, despite its greater cost? We do not think so, although we agree that such instruction may be warranted for some children. For instance, children with very severe difficulties may require the kind of intensive intervention that can only be provided by a good one-to-one tutorial program. Certainly, when teachers work with groups of children they must make some instructional compromises, because no two children have exactly the same instructional needs. Also, behavior problems tend to interfere with instruction more in group situations than in one-to-one instruction. Nevertheless, as our review has indicated, well-designed small-group interventions can be very effective in preventing early reading failure—in some cases (e.g., Hiebert et al., 1992), perhaps as effective as well-designed tutorial approaches.

At the kindergarten level, screening of phonological-awareness skills, and training of these skills, clearly is warranted—particularly for youngsters with weaknesses in phonological awareness. Furthermore, the results of Bradley and Bryant (1983, 1985), as well as those of investigators who have worked with somewhat older children (e.g., Hatcher, Hulme, & Ellis, 1994), indicate that isolated phonological-awareness training is not maximally effective in improving reading. Rather, in order for phonological-awareness training to be most effective, it must be integrated with the teaching of reading skills, such as letter-sound knowledge and decoding. Phonological awareness and beginning reading skills can be successfully developed in the context of emergent-literacy kindergarten interventions that emphasize shared storybook reading and writing activities (e.g., Pinnell & McCarrier, 1994).

In terms of instructional content and approach, the successful intervention programs vary somewhat. For example, some of the programs, such as Reading Recovery, use only "real" children's texts, whereas others, such as Success for All and EIR, initially use texts that have been altered to make them easier for children to read. The programs also vary in terms of the extent to which word-recognition instruction is contextualized—from the most heavily contextualized (Reading Recovery) to the least (probably the code-emphasis intervention employed by the Bowman Gray group of investigators). However, despite these apparent differences, the programs also share many important similarities in instructional content and instructional approach. These similarities should be noted by those interested in designing a program to prevent RD: All of the successful interventions emphasize teacher-student interaction rather than passive seatwork activities; all provide children with large amounts of practice reading and writing in meaningful contexts; all provide explicit instruction in word-recognition skills and, at least to some extent, in phonological awareness. Thus, these successful intervention programs provide the synthesis of the whole-language and code-emphasis approaches for which we and other writers (e.g., Adams, 1990) have repeatedly argued.

In other words, preventing or at least ameliorating many cases of reading disability, and of poor reading generally, simply may involve engaging children, from their earliest years in school, in the kind of instructional program that we have already argued is optimal for youngsters with RD. Moreover, this kind of program is not radically different from what normally achieving young readers need. Of course, as we have discussed, children with RD may require different instructional emphases, such as a greater emphasis on phonological awareness, than do other children. Nevertheless, some of these different emphases might be accommodated through regular-classroom programming, with flexibility to accommodate also those children who are not at risk. For example, the phonological-awareness training carried out by Torgesen et al. (1993) involved four twenty-minute sessions per week, conducted with small groups of children. This kind of training would be quite feasible to incorporate—especially with the help of a teacher's aide, reading consultant, or special-education consultant—as a routine part of regular kindergarten or first-grade instruction for children who need it. Another example is the program of Taylor et al. (1992), which was delivered entirely by regular-classroom teachers in a regular first-grade setting.

Some of these suggestions about what to include in programs designed to prevent RD may appear so obvious as to be glossed over with little thought. After all, who would deliberately design a program in such a way as to provide children with lots of failure experiences rather than with successes? Who would intentionally design a program that bored children with endless workbook activities? The point, of course, is not that teachers have malevolent intentions but, rather, that one can unwittingly create programs that accomplish the opposite of what is intended. For instance, if beautifully written children's texts are selected for use in a program but the texts are too difficult for the children to read, then the program will promote failure rather than success; similarly, if good word-recognition activities are used but are allowed to crowd more contextualized activities from the program, then the reasons for learning to read at all will be lost on the children.

The Long-Term Efficacy of Early Intervention

As we noted earlier in this chapter, we do not yet know whether even the most successful intervention programs can prevent reading failure in the long term—for instance, through high school or even through elementary school. Given what is currently known about the cognitive processes involved in reading acquisition and in reading disability, it would hardly be surprising if a single intervention at a single grade level failed to ensure permanent success for some youngsters. After all, children must successfully negotiate many phases of development in order to become proficient readers, and those with reading disability may go astray in more than one phase. For instance, children with phonological-processing weaknesses may be successful in negotiating the earliest phases of reading acquisition with the right kind of intervention, yet go astray in a later phase without continuing support.

Our model of reading disability, along with those of other investigators, certainly suggests that intervention beyond the kindergarten or first-grade level will be necessary in order to prevent some cases of reading disability. For instance, among nondisabled readers, as we discussed in Chapters 4 and 5, the transition to automatic word recognition commonly occurs approximately at a second- to third-grade level; children who go astray in reading acquisition at this point become nonautomatic readers. At these grade levels, it is particularly crucial that children receive both the kind of practice in reading connected text and the kind of direct instruction in orthographic skills that are required to develop fully accurate, automatic word recognition. In addition, children need experience with varied texts—expository texts as well as narratives—in order to facilitate the transition to reading in the later grades, when many demands on reading in content areas are made.

Again, although children with RD may require different instructional emphases than do nondisabled children in some of these areas—for instance, more practice to acquire orthographic skills—their instructional needs may in many cases be accommodated in the regular classroom. Indeed, as is true at the kindergarten and first-grade levels, excellent regular-classroom instruction at these later grade levels actually may prevent the emergence of many reading difficulties in the first place.

Undoubtedly, some children's needs cannot be met solely by short-term interventions or by high-quality instruction in the regular classroom. For a significant minority of youngsters, such as those with very severe weaknesses in phonological processing, learning to read may require the type of intensive, long-term support that has been supplied traditionally by special education; with this kind of intensive support, even these youngsters *can* learn to read well. However, for many other children, including some of those with the cognitive profiles typical of reading disability, relatively short-term kindergarten or first-grade interventions can prevent early reading failure. In our view, excellent reading instruction in the regular classroom, combined with relatively short-term early intervention programs for at-risk children, can go a long way toward keeping most children on the road to proficient reading.

References

Adams, M. J. (1990). *Beginning to read: Thinking and learning about print.* Cambridge, MA: MIT Press.

Allington, R. L., & McGill-Franzen, A. (1989). School response to reading failure: Instruction for Chapter 1 and special education students in grades two, four, and eight. *The Elementary School Journal, 89,* 529–542.

Beck, I. L., Ringler, L. H., Ogle, D. M., Raphael, T. E., Armbruster, B. B., & McKeown, M. G. (1989). *Reading today and tomorrow.* Austin, TX: Holt, Rinehart, and Winston.

Blachman, B. A. (1989). Phonological awareness and word recognition: Assessment and intervention. In A. Kamhi & H. Catts (Eds.), *Reading disabilities: A developmental language perspective* (pp. 133–158). Boston, MA: College-Hill.

———. (1994). What we have learned from longitudinal studies of phonological processing and reading, and some unanswered questions: A response to Torgesen, Wagner, and Rashotte. *Journal of Learning Disabilities, 27,* 287–291.

Bradley, L. (1987, November). *Rhyme recognition and reading and spelling in young children.* Paper presented at the Early Childhood Symposium on Preschool Prevention of Reading Failure at the meeting of the Orton Dyslexia Society, San Francisco, CA.

Bradley, L., & Bryant, P. E. (1983). Categorizing sounds and learning to read—A causal connection. *Nature, 301,* 419–421.

————. (1985). *Rhyme and reason in reading and spelling.* Ann Arbor, MI: University of Michigan Press.

Brown, I. S., & Felton, R. H. (1990). Effects of instruction on beginning reading skills in children at risk for reading disability. *Reading and Writing: An Interdisciplinary Journal, 2,* 223–241.

Clay, M. M. (1985). *The early detection of reading difficulties,* 3rd. ed. Portsmouth, NH: Heinemann.

————. (1987). Implementing Reading Recovery: Systemic adaptations to an educational innovation. *New Zealand Journal of Educational Studies, 22,* 35–58.

————. (1990). The Reading Recovery Programme, 1984–8: Coverage, outcomes, and education board district figures. *New Zealand Journal of Educational Studies, 25,* 61–70.

DeFord, D. (1991). On noble thoughts, or toward a clarification of theory and practice within a whole language framework. In W. Ellis (Ed.), *All language and creation of literacy* (pp. 27–39). Baltimore, MD: Orton Dyslexia Society.

DeFord, D., Pinnell, G. S., Lyons, C., & Place, A. W. (1990). *The reading recovery follow-up study: Volume XI.* Columbus, OH: Ohio State University.

DeFord, D., Pinnell, G. S., Lyons, C., & Young, P. (1988). *The reading recovery follow-up study: Volume IX.* Columbus, OH: Ohio State University.

Felton, R. H. (1993). Effects of instruction on the decoding skills of children with phonological-processing problems. *Journal of Learning Disabilities, 26,* 583–589.

Felton, R. H., & Brown, I. S. (1990). Phonological processes as predictors of specific reading skills in children at risk for reading failure. *Reading and Writing: An Interdisciplinary Journal, 2,* 39–59.

Felton, R. H., & Wood, F. B. (1992). A reading level match study of nonword reading skills in poor readers with varying IQ. *Journal of Learning Disabilities, 25,* 318–326.

Fletcher, J. M., Shaywitz, S. E., Shankweiler, D. P., Katz, L., Liberman, I. Y., Stuebing, K. K., Francis, D. J., Fowler, A. E., & Shaywitz, B. A. (1994). Cognitive profiles of reading disability: Comparisons of discrepancy and low achievement definitions. *Journal of Educational Psychology, 86,* 6–23.

Goldenberg, C. (1994). Promoting early literacy development among Spanish-speaking children. In E. H. Hiebert & B. M. Taylor (Eds.), *Getting reading right from the start: Effective early literacy interventions* (pp. 171–199). Boston, MA: Allyn and Bacon.

Hatcher, P. J., Hulme, C., & Ellis, A. W. (1994). Ameliorating early reading failure by integrating the teaching of reading and phonological skills: The phonological linkage hypothesis. *Child Development, 65,* 41–57.

Hiebert, E. H. (1994a). Reading Recovery in the United States: What difference does it make to an age cohort? *Educational Researcher, 23,* 15–25.

————. (1994b). A small-group literacy intervention with Chapter 1 students. In E. H. Hiebert & B. M. Taylor (Eds.), *Getting reading right from the start: Effective early literacy interventions* (pp. 85–106). Boston, MA: Allyn and Bacon.

Hiebert, E. H., Colt, J. M., Catto, S. L., & Gury, E. C. (1992). Reading and writing of first-grade students in a restructured Chapter 1 program. *American Educational Research Journal, 29,* 545–572.

Holdaway, D. (1979). *The foundations of literacy.* Sidney, Australia: Ashton Scholastic.

Houghton Mifflin Company. (1986). *Houghton Mifflin reading.* Boston, MA: Author.

Iversen, S., & Tunmer, W. E. (1993). Phonological processing and the Reading Recovery Program. *Journal of Educational Psychology, 85,* 112–126.

Lyon, G. R., Newby, R. E., Recht, D., & Caldwell, J. (1991). Neuropsychology and learning disabilities. In B. Y. L. Wong (Ed.), *Learning about learning disabilities* (pp. 375–406). San Diego, CA: Academic Press.

Macmillan Publishing Company. (1981). *Lippincott basic reading.* Riverside, NJ: Author.

Madden, N. A., Slavin, R. E., Karweit, N. L., Dolan, L. J., & Wasik, B. A. (1992, April). *Success for All: Longitudinal effects of a restructuring program for inner-city elementary schools.* Paper presented at the annual meeting of the American Educational Research Association, San Francisco, CA.

Madden, N. A., Slavin, R. E., Karweit, N. L., & Livermon, B. (1987). *Success for All: Teacher's manual for reading.* Baltimore, MD: Johns Hopkins University, Center for Research on Elementary and Middle Schools.

Mantzicopoulos, P., & Morrison, D. (1992). Kindergarten retention: Academic and behavioral outcomes through the end of second grade. *American Educational Research Journal, 29,* 182–198.

Martinez, M. G., Cheyney, M., McBroom, C., Hemmeter, A., & Teale, W. H. (1989). No-risk kindergarten literacy environments for at-risk children. In J. Allen & J. M. Mason (Eds.), *Risk makers, risk takers, risk breakers: Reducing the risks for young literacy learners* (pp. 93–124). Portsmouth, NH: Heinemann.

McGill-Franzen, A. (1994). Compensatory and special education: Is there accountability for learning and belief in children's potential? In E. H. Hiebert & B. M. Taylor (Eds.), *Getting reading right from the start: Effective early literacy interventions* (pp. 13–35). Boston, MA: Allyn and Bacon.

Pinnell, G. S., Fried, M. D., & Estice, R. M. (1990). Reading Recovery: Learning how to make a difference. In D. DeFord, C. A. Lyons, & G. S. Pinnell (Eds.), *Bridges to literacy: Learning from Reading Recovery* (pp. 11–35). Portsmouth, NH: Heinemann.

Pinnell, G. S., Lyons, C. A., DeFord, D. E., Bryk, A. S., & Seltzer, M. (1991). *Studying the effectiveness of early intervention approaches for first grade children having difficulty in reading.* Columbus, OH: Ohio State University, Martha L. King Language and Literacy Center.

————. (1994). Comparing instructional models for the literacy education of high-risk first graders. *Reading Research Quarterly, 29,* 8–37.

Pinnell, G. S., & McCarrier, A. (1994). Interactive writing: A transition tool for assisting children in learning to read and write. In E. H. Hiebert & B. M. Taylor (Eds.), *Getting reading right from the start: Effective early literacy interventions* (pp. 149–170). Boston, MA: Allyn and Bacon.

Pinnell, G. S., Short, A. G., Lyons, C. A., & Young, P. (1986). *The Reading Recovery project in Columbus, Ohio. Year 1: 1985–1986.* Columbus, OH: Ohio State University.

Sheridan, C. (1994, June 26). Children in tailored reading program showing results. *The Hartford Courant,* B1–B2.

Slavin, R. E., Madden, N. A., Karweit, N. L., Dolan, L., & Wasik, B. (1994). Success for All: Getting reading right the first time. In E. H. Hiebert & B. M. Taylor (Eds.), *Getting reading right from the start: Effective early literacy interventions* (pp. 125–147). Boston, MA: Allyn and Bacon.

Slavin, R. E., Madden, N. A., Karweit, N. L., Livermon, B. J., & Dolan, L. (1990). Success for All: First-year outcomes of a comprehensive plan for reforming urban education. *American Educational Research Journal, 27,* 255–278.

Smith-Burke, M. T., & Jaggar, A. M. (1994). Implementing Reading Recovery in New York: Insights from the first two years. In E. H. Hiebert & B. M. Taylor (Eds.), *Getting reading right from the start: Effective early literacy interventions* (pp. 63–84). Boston, MA: Allyn and Bacon.

Snow, C. E., Barnes, W. S., Chandler, J., Goodman, J. F., & Hemphill, L. (1991). *Unfulfilled expectations: Home and school influences on literacy.* Cambridge, MA: Harvard University Press.

Stanovich, K. E. (1986). Matthew effects in reading: Some consequences of individual differences in the acquisition of literacy. *Reading Research Quarterly, 21,* 360–406.

Stanovich, K. E., & Siegel, L. S. (1994). Phenotypic performance profile of children with reading disabilities: A regression-based test of the phonological-core variable-difference model. *Journal of Educational Psychology, 86,* 24–53.

Taylor, B. M., & Hiebert, E. H. (1994). Early literacy interventions: Aims and issues. In E. H. Hiebert & B. M. Taylor (Eds.), *Getting reading right from the start: Effective early literacy interventions* (pp. 3–11). Boston, MA: Allyn and Bacon.

Taylor, B. M., Short, R. A., Frye, B. J., & Shearer, B. A. (1992). Classroom teachers prevent reading failure among low-achieving first-grade students. *The Reading Teacher, 45,* 592–597.

Taylor, B. M., Strait, J., & Medo, M. A. (1994). Early intervention in reading: Supplemental instruction for groups of low-achieving students provided by first-grade teachers. In E. H. Hiebert & B. M. Taylor (Eds.), *Getting reading right from the start: Effective early literacy interventions* (pp. 107–121). Boston, MA: Allyn and Bacon.

Torgesen, J. K., Davis, C., & Wagner, R. K. (1993, April). *Individual difference variables that predict response to training in phonological awareness.* Paper presented at the annual meeting of the American Educational Research Association, Atlanta, GA.

Torgesen, J. K., Morgan, S., & Davis, C. (1992). The effects of two types of phonological awareness training on word learning in kindergarten children. *Journal of Educational Psychology, 84,* 364–370.

Torgesen, J. K., Wagner, R. K., & Rashotte, C. A. (1994). Longitudinal studies of phonological processing and reading. *Journal of Learning Disabilities, 27,* 276–286.

Wade, B. (1992). Reading Recovery: Myth and reality. *British Journal of Special Education, 19,* 48–51.

Wagner, R. K., Torgesen, J. K., & Rashotte, C. A. (1994). The development of reading-related phonological processing abilities: New evidence of bidirectional causality from a latent variable longitudinal study. *Developmental Psychology, 30,* 73–87.

Wasik, B. A., & Slavin, R. E. (1993). Preventing early reading failure with one-to-one tutoring: A review of five programs. *Reading Research Quarterly, 28,* 178–200.

11 Toward Another Way of Thinking About Reading Difficulties

Throughout this book, we have maintained that those who wish to help children with reading difficulties need to begin by shelving the traditional concept of reading disability—a concept that has long outlived its usefulness. Doing so, however, does not necessarily mean disposing of the field of learning disabilities, as an area of either scientific inquiry or educational practice. Scientific study of the kinds of children who have been labeled as having RD—children with normal intelligence, normal listening-comprehension skills, and reading problems that center on word-recognition and phonological skills—is both legitimate and worthwhile. Moreover, despite our many criticisms, we do not think that eradicating the field of learning disabilities in the area of educational practice is either necessary or desirable; instead, as we will show, what is needed are some fundamental changes in educational practice and in the roles of learning-disabilities specialists. The important point is this: For both areas of learning disabilities—scientific inquiry and the field of educational practice—the old concept of reading disability, with an IQ-achievement discrepancy as its cornerstone, is an outmoded one that needs to be abandoned in order for real progress to occur.

At one time, the concept of reading disability may have served to highlight the fact that children who are intellectually normal, and sometimes even unusually bright, can have serious problems in learning to read. However, most educators—and, we hope, the general public as well—grasped this fact long ago. From the wide variety of research findings reviewed in this book, it is obvious that the traditional concept of reading disability is not valid for the vast majority of youngsters who are categorized as having RD. The traditional concept does not serve either to help children or to advance scientific knowledge about poor reading. In its place we need another way of conceptualizing reading problems. This idea—that the traditional concept of reading disability needs to be replaced by a different way of thinking about reading difficulties—is our most important "take-home" message, the one we most want readers to remember long after they have finished the book.

In this final chapter, we use the research evidence reviewed throughout to draw conclusions about three major issues. First, we discuss why the traditional concept of reading disability needs to be abandoned. Second, we discuss a different—and, in our opinion, much better—way of conceptualizing reading difficulties. The basic components of this alternative view certainly did not originate with the coauthors. Nor, unfortunately, have they influenced most people's thinking about reading disability or about poor reading generally, either in educational circles or in the popular press. We hope that this book has encouraged educators to discard the traditional concept of reading disability in favor of a better way of conceptualizing reading problems. Thus, in the last section of this chapter, we present our suggestions as to where the field of learning disabilities, as an area of educational practice, should be going.

Why We Should Abandon the Concept of RD

Although views of reading disability certainly have varied from one authority to the next, some key elements have long characterized the traditional concept of reading disability. These key elements include the ideas that reading disability is caused by a biological abnormality; that reading disability involves a unique syndrome of poor reading; that a discrepancy between children's true potential in reading and their actual reading achievement, widely operationalized as an IQ-achievement discrepancy, is fundamental to RD; and that children with RD require educational treatment that differs significantly from the instruction needed by other children. However, the research that we have reviewed in this book seriously refutes *all* of these key elements. Among other things, current research shows that most children with RD are biologically "normal"; that RD typically does not involve a unique or distinctive syndrome of poor reading; and that children with RD can learn to read well with instruction that is similar in many (though not all) ways to that required by other children. We now consider each of these points in turn, followed by a summary of our views about why the traditional concept of reading disability should be abandoned.

Most Children with RD Are Biologically "Normal"

As we saw in Chapter 8, findings of clear-cut neurological or other biological abnormalities in children with RD are rare (e.g., Denckla, LeMay, & Chapman, 1985). A few specific studies, such as the autopsy studies of Galaburda and his colleagues (e.g., Galaburda, Sherman, Rosen, Aboitiz, & Geschwind, 1985), are repeatedly cited by some authorities in the learning-disabilities field to support the assumption that RD is caused by a biological disorder. However, these studies involve very small numbers of subjects and are clouded by methodological issues. Although one certainly cannot rule out the possibility of a tiny proportion of poor readers who have a genuine biological disorder, the assumption of biological abnormality clearly is incorrect for most children who are labeled as having RD.

The very term *disability* in the label of "reading disability" implies that children with RD have an intrinsic abnormality. However, as RD is defined educationally at present—primarily in terms of exclusionary criteria and an IQ-achievement discrepancy—it merely means poor reading that cannot be readily accounted for by other known causes, such as low intelligence, hearing or visual impairment, obvious economic disadvantage, and so on. If having low skill of uncertain cause in a particular domain is enough to constitute a disability, then we ourselves would have a few disabilities—and so, we suspect, would most of our readers.

Of course, the reading difficulties of children with RD are genuine. Furthermore, in saying that most children with RD are biologically "normal" we do not mean that biology has no role in reading disability. Indeed, as we discussed in Chapter 8, biological differences do appear to play a role in most cases of RD. For instance, at least some of the phonological-processing weaknesses prominent in RD are characterized by a strong genetic influence. The point is that these biological differences appear to be part of a continuum of individual differences that includes normally achieving children. Like the rest of us, individuals with RD are biological creatures whose temperaments and abilities, among other things, are influenced by biology. However, in most cases, they do not have an actual biological disorder or defect.

RD Is Not a Unique Syndrome of Poor Reading

Rather than exhibiting a unique syndrome of poor reading, children with RD are similar in many ways to garden-variety poor readers, who lack the IQ-achievement discrepancy that is central to the identification of reading disability. Both types of poor readers—those with this discrepancy and those without—appear to have similar instructional needs as well as similar cognitive profiles, especially with regard to word recognition. When both types of poor readers at the same word-recognition level are compared, it is clear that they share a core of phonological deficits (Stanovich & Siegel, 1994); when the two groups of poor readers are matched on chronological age rather than on word-recognition level, the cognitive similarities between them are even greater (Fletcher et al., 1994). Many investigators (e.g., Shaywitz, Escobar, Shaywitz, Fletcher, & Makuch, 1992) acknowledge that a rare distinctive syndrome of poor reading may exist, a position with which we concur. However, there is overwhelming evidence that most school-identified children with RD do not exhibit this unique syndrome.

Furthermore, as we discussed at length in Chapters 1 and 3, in school situations the classification of poor readers as learning disabled may have little to do with children's actual cognitive profiles. Rather, LD classification is strongly influenced by factors such as gender, classroom behavior, and socioeconomic status. For instance, Shaywitz, Shaywitz, Fletcher, and Escobar (1990) found that boys and girls were about equally likely to have a significant IQ-achievement discrepancy in reading. However, boys were much more likely than were girls to be identified as learning disabled, evidently because boys were more likely to be perceived as behavior problems. Indeed, Shaywitz et al. (1990) found that a significant number of children who had been classified as learning disabled did not even meet discrepancy criteria when the effects of regression were taken into account.

In short, educators sometimes ignore stringent discrepancy criteria in deciding whom to classify as having LD or RD—but even the rigorous application of discrepancy criteria would not differentiate a group of youngsters with unique cognitive profiles in reading.

Children with RD Can Learn to Read Well

Despite the pessimistic connotations of the term *reading disability*, there is little evidence to suggest that children with RD are inevitably doomed to lifelong reading failure. On the contrary, evidence reviewed throughout this book, especially in Chapters 8 and 10, suggests that most, and perhaps all, children with RD can learn to read well with appropriate instruction.

In order to learn to read well, children with RD, like other children, require a combination of instructional approaches involving both code emphasis and meaning emphasis. This combination of instructional approaches is necessary for at least two reasons. First, all children—whether they have reading difficulties or not—must acquire both word-recognition skills and comprehension skills if they are to learn to read well. And as we discussed in Chapters 6 and 7, the acquisition of accurate, automatic word recognition should be accomplished primarily, though not necessarily exclusively, in the context of engaging activities that are meaningful to children. Obviously, neither code-emphasis nor meaning-emphasis programs have ownership of any particular skill area. However, code-emphasis programs tend to be more effective in developing certain skills, such as word recognition (e.g., Chall, 1983), whereas meaning-emphasis programs tend to be more effective in, for instance, providing children with large amounts of practice in contextualized activities (e.g., Fisher & Hiebert, 1990).

A second reason for using a combination of instructional approaches is that, as we discussed in Chapter 9, children have a variety of thinking styles. A given instructional approach always constitutes a better "fit" with some children's thinking styles than with those of others. Thus, exclusive reliance on one approach invariably creates problems for some children. In some instances, it may even contribute to or cause poor reading.

In their need for a combination of instructional approaches, children with RD are not different from other poor readers, or even from normally achieving readers. However, as compared with normally achieving youngsters, children with RD do require some different instructional emphases. For example, some children with RD may benefit from much more intensive and lengthy phonological-awareness training than do young normally achieving readers (Blachman, 1994). This example is consistent with our argument that the instructional needs of children with RD involve different emphases—such as greater intensity or duration—rather than a dramatically different approach to instruction.

As a way of helping children with RD and other poor readers to attain a high level of reading achievement, early intervention is also very important, though not indispensable. Through early intervention, many of the cognitive and motivational consequences of long-term reading failure can be avoided. First-grade intervention programs such as Reading Recovery appear to be successful in preventing early reading failure in many youngsters, including some of those with the cognitive profiles typical of RD (e.g., Pinnell, Lyons, DeFord, Bryk, & Seltzer, 1994). Other children with RD may require longer-term and more intensive support; but with this support, they too can learn to read well (e.g., Blachman, 1994; Felton, 1993).

Summary: Why the Concept of Reading Disability Should Be Abandoned

The old way of conceptualizing RD, with an IQ-achievement discrepancy at its core, does not work on multiple levels: biological, psychological, or educational. At the biological level, the concept of reading disability does not work because many children labeled as having RD do not have a biological disorder or a medical ailment. Although these children's reading problems may well have been influenced by biological factors, such as genetic inheritance, these factors are better conceptualized as part of a continuum that includes both other poor readers and normally achieving readers than as a distinctive defect or disease.

At the psychological level, the traditional concept of RD is at least equally flawed. For one thing, children with RD (i.e., children with an IQ-achievement discrepancy) do not appear to differ substantially from other poor readers (i.e., those without this discrepancy) in terms of the underlying cognitive abilities related to reading, especially word recognition. Second, the discrepancy construct is inherently problematic because of statistical difficulties involving regression effects and the interpretation of difference scores (Cronbach & Furby, 1970).

Even more problematic is the issue of IQ. As we discussed in Chapter 9, many contemporary researchers share a broad, multidimensional view of intelligence. The idea that overall intellectual potential can be captured in a single number such as an IQ score is not only limiting (to say the least) but also inconsistent with this contemporary theoretical view.

Of course, as noted in Chapter 3, some investigators (e.g., Stanovich, 1991) have suggested—though with something less than wild enthusiasm—the possibility of using alternative measures of potential in reading, such as listening comprehension. This alternative replaces the IQ-achievement discrepancy with a listening comprehension–achievement discrepancy. The use of listening comprehension rather than IQ as an indicator of potential does appear to be more effective in identifying a group of poor readers who are somewhat distinct from garden-variety poor readers, although the cognitive differences between the resulting two groups of poor readers remain relatively small (e.g., Fletcher et al., 1994).

Basically, however, the concept of listening comprehension–achievement discrepancy has the same flaws as that of IQ-achievement discrepancy. Regardless of which measure of potential is used, the discrepancy construct (1) fails to relate reading difficulties to the process of learning to read; (2) involves an artificial and arbitrary partitioning of two continua, potential and achievement; and (3) does not identify a group of poor readers whose instructional needs are so dramatically different from those of other children as to require separate educational classification or treatment.

In short, the traditional concept of RD is flawed in educational terms because it does not define a group of children who need distinctive educational treatment. Nothing about this concept offers any insight regarding how to teach children who have been labeled as having RD. Indeed, by implying that children with RD have an intrinsic and immutable defect, the traditional concept actually may worsen rather than improve the quality of children's education (McGill-Franzen, 1994).

Our own model of reading disability has relatively little to do with potential-achievement discrepancies and everything to do with the underlying cognitive processes involved in learning to read. Moreover, the same is true of nearly all other contemporary theoretical models of reading disability, including those of the Haskins Laboratories group of researchers (e.g., Shankweiler, Crain, Brady, & Macaruso, 1992), Stanovich (1990), Willows (1991), and Frith (1985). Our claim, of course, is not that broad intellectual or language abilities are irrelevant to reading. Rather, we argue that the old construct of reading disability, with its emphasis on a potential-achievement discrepancy, simply is not the right way to conceptualize reading difficulties. In the following section, we present another way of doing so.

A Better Way of Thinking About Reading Difficulties

In this book, we have suggested a number of basic conclusions about reading disability that we believe to be of primary importance. These conclusions include the ideas that reading disability is best understood from an interactive perspective; that RD also must be understood in relation to development in normally achieving readers; that RD involves various patterns of performance; and that reading is not the only, or even the most important, skill related to success in adulthood. We now examine each of these points in turn.

RD Is Best Understood from an Interactive Perspective

Two major perspectives, which we term *intrinsic* and *extrinsic*, typify research and practice on reading disability. The intrinsic perspective ascribes RD largely to causes within the child, such as brain dysfunction or an unfortunate genetic inheritance, whereas the extrinsic perspective emphasizes the role of environmental variables, such as poor instruction, in reading failure. Each of these two perspectives tends to overemphasize one set of factors—intrinsic or extrinsic—at the expense of the other. Even more important, neither perspective takes into account the ways in which the two sets of factors continually interact with one another.

As we discussed in Chapter 2, the history of the LD field has mainly involved new renditions of the same old intrinsic tune, with an eternal chorus of criticism from advocates of the extrinsic point of view. It is now clear that neither the intrinsic nor the extrinsic perspective is likely to provide any fresh insights about reading difficulties or the solutions to them.

Accordingly, we have argued that a third perspective, which we term the *interactive* perspective, is the most accurate, and educationally useful, way to conceptualize reading disability. The interactive perspective recognizes that children bring to reading acquisition individual differences in cognitive abilities, and that individual differences in certain cognitive abilities—such as phonological processing—play a vital role in reading acquisition and in reading failure. Indeed, the interactive perspective emphasizes that individual differences do not develop in a vacuum but, rather, can be understood only in terms of their interaction with contextual variables.

Consider, for example, the phonological-processing weaknesses that appear to be causally central to many cases of RD. Cognitive psychologists may attempt to isolate phonological processes on a variety of tasks, behavioral geneticists may study genetic influences in phonological processing, and neurologists may attempt to find a neurological substrate for deficiencies in phonological processing. Of course, all of these endeavors are scientifically legitimate and may add to scientific knowledge about difficulties in reading. However, in everyday life, a given child's phonological-processing weakness is just one factor among many. For Jack, whose story we told in the previous chapter, these other factors include a strong will to succeed, an inquisitive nature, and a good relationship with his parents and his tutor. In other words, his phonological-processing weakness does not exist in isolation. Although phonological-processing skills are pivotal in reading acquisition, Jack's case provides a good example of the way in which other factors can help some individuals to overcome early weaknesses in phonological processing and, ultimately, to be successful in reading.

RD Must Be Understood with Reference to Development in Normally Achieving Readers

Special-education teachers sometimes comment that, after years of working exclusively with youngsters who have academic difficulties, they lose track of what normally achieving children can do. In states where special-education teachers are not required to have dual certification as regular-classroom teachers—such as the state of Connecticut—special educators' formal knowledge about the development of nondisabled youngsters may be relatively limited from the start. Furthermore, even regular-classroom teachers are not always knowledgeable about the cognitive processes involved in reading acquisition in normally achieving children. Yet knowledge about reading acquisition in normally achieving readers is essential for both special educators and for regular-classroom teachers.

Normally achieving readers undergo a series of developmental changes in which the cognitive skills that are most important to reading acquisition gradually shift over time. Throughout the process of reading acquisition, from early childhood through adulthood, both word recognition and comprehension play important roles. In general, however, word-recognition processes are most central to the early phases of reading acquisition, whereas comprehension processes are most central to the later phases.

For several reasons, reading disability can be understood only in relation to this process of reading acquisition in normally achieving youngsters. First, although reading problems may emerge at any point in development, the reading problems typical of reading disability emerge early in schooling and revolve around word-recognition processes. In terms of our model, children with RD go astray in one of the first four phases of reading acquisition: visual-cue word recognition, phonetic-cue word recognition, controlled word recognition, or automatic word recognition. Although in some cases reading disability may not be "diagnosed" until the children are of middle-school age or even older, in hindsight it is generally evident that these children have struggled in reading from the early elementary grades.

A second reason has to do with the cognitive weaknesses involved in reading disability. Often certain cognitive weaknesses or error patterns—such as reversal errors—have been viewed as uniquely characteristic of reading disability, when in fact they merely typify a beginning level of reading achievement. Conversely, a cognitive weakness that is pronounced in children with RD, even relative to younger, normally achieving readers, may be causally more central to reading disability. One example of this kind of causally central cognitive weakness is phonological-reading skill.

Finally, knowledge about reading acquisition in normally achieving readers is important both for planning instruction and for setting goals. For instance, some children with RD may require several years of intensive instruction in order to acquire basic word-recognition skills (e.g., Felton, 1993). Remember, however, that normally achieving readers acquire accurate word-recognition skills by the end of second grade and automatic word-recognition skills by the end of third grade. If word recognition is the exclusive focus of a remedial program year after year, then most children with RD will continue to lag far behind their normally achieving peers. Very limited IEP goals—"Will master consonant-vowel-consonant words with *a*," "Will master twenty new sight words," and so on—will never close the gap between children with RD and normally achieving readers.

RD Involves Various Patterns of Performance

Reading disability involves not just one pattern of cognitive and reading deficits but, rather, several different patterns. Our model of RD proposes four patterns of reading disability—nonalphabetic, compensatory, nonautomatic, and delayed reading—that depend upon the point at which children go astray in reading acquisition. Nonalphabetic readers lack a basic knowledge of the alphabetic code and have particularly impaired reading skills. Compensatory readers have some word-recognition skills, but these skills are not fully accurate. Nonautomatic readers have accurate, but nonautomatic, word-recognition skills. And finally, delayed readers have accurate, automatic word recognition—acquired later than usual and with great effort—but they lack comprehension skills, such as the effective use of strategies to aid comprehension.

As emphasized, we do not view these different patterns of performance as etiological subtypes; in this respect we differ from Boder (1973), for example. Technically, our view of RD is compatible both with unitary-deficit views of RD (e.g., Shankweiler, Crain, Brady, & Macaruso, 1992) and with multiple-deficit views of RD (e.g., Willows, 1991). At present, the bulk of the evidence clearly favors the view that phonological deficits play a central role in *most* cases of reading disability. However, the views of investigators such as Willows (1991), who suggests that some cases of RD may be causally related to a visual deficit rather than, or in addition to, a phonological deficit, cannot be completely dismissed. The question of whether there are etiological subtypes of RD involving different cognitive deficits, such as visual versus phonological deficits, is one we must leave open for now. The important point, however, is that cognitive deficits develop only in interaction with the environment. Thus, even a unitary deficit, such as a deficit in phonological processing, may give rise to various patterns of performance, because this unitary deficit may interact with environmental variables in numerous ways. Or, to put it a little differently, in our view any individual case of RD always involves multiple causes, because RD arises from the interaction between environmental factors and the child's intrinsic characteristics.

For educators, the different patterns of performance that we have described are important in both assessment and instruction. In assessment, the different patterns indicate the need for a variety of assessment procedures. Assessment that emphasizes one particular cognitive area too heavily will miss some instances of reading disability. For example, although tests of phonological awareness are extremely useful for identifying young children at risk for RD, they may miss some compensatory readers, who already have developed at least a rudimentary level of phonological awareness, and they probably will not be useful at all for identifying nonautomatic or delayed readers. Similarly, with regard to instruction, children with RD need different instructional emphases that depend, at least in part, on the particular pattern of reading disability (as discussed at length in Chapter 7).

Reading Is Not the Only Skill Important to Success in Adulthood

Learning to read well certainly is important. In a highly literate society such as ours, inability to read well carries considerable stigma and creates many barriers in higher education, employment, and so on. However, as we pointed out in Chapter 9, there are many abilities—such as practical intelligence and creativity—that are equally, and even more, important to success in adulthood than is reading skill, especially if the individual is at least functionally literate.

This last assertion does *not* mean that parents, teachers, and other educational professionals should be unconcerned about reading failure, or that children's reading problems do not need vigorous educational attention. It's simply that reading disability must be kept in some perspective, as a problem that, though serious, does not automatically sentence an individual to a lifetime of failure and misery. In most schools, cognitive abilities tend to be defined very narrowly, either in terms of academic skills or on the basis of the relatively limited range of verbal, spatial, and mathematical abilities measured by traditional IQ tests. But this narrow definition ignores a wide range of other abilities—practical intelligence, creativity, interpersonal skills, artistic or musical talent—some of which are more important to success in adulthood than are "school smarts." If these other abilities were more broadly appreciated and utilized in school, then all children would benefit—not just those with reading difficulties.

Summary: A Better Way of Thinking About Reading Difficulties

Finding ways to criticize the LD field is all too easy. However, it is undeniably the case that some children experience unusual difficulty in learning to read and that the problems of these children need to be addressed educationally. In the absence of another way of conceptualizing children's reading difficulties, criticisms of the old concept of RD are not helpful.

In this section, we describe a better way of conceptualizing youngsters who currently are labeled as having reading disability. This alternative approach does not ignore the cognitive processes implicated in reading failure; nor does it deny or downplay the fact that children exhibit individual differences in the cognitive skills that are central to reading acquisition. Rather, it considers reading difficulties and their cognitive underpinnings from an interactive perspective and in relation to typical reading development. In addition, it encourages a broad view of cognitive abilities, one in which an IQ or reading test is not the last word in evaluating children's aptitudes.

Throughout this book we have focused on the kinds of children who typically are labeled as having reading disability in contemporary research and in educational practice. Our model of reading disability, which we discussed in Chapters 4 and 5, is intended specifically for these youngsters. However, the conceptualization of reading difficulties that we have just outlined applies to poor readers in general—not just to those who have the cognitive profiles typical of RD. All poor readers may be conceptualized from an interactive perspective and with reference to typical reading development. And all poor readers, not only those who have been labeled as having RD, may have unappreciated or untapped abilities in areas such as practical intelligence or interpersonal skills.

Of course, poor readers may differ in terms of the cognitive underpinnings and developmental course of their poor reading. For instance, some poor readers— those with the cognitive profiles typical of RD—are characterized by early phonological-processing and word-recognition deficits. Other poor readers—those who have been termed "garden-variety poor readers"—may have broad language deficits as well as phonological-processing and word-recognition deficits. These differences may have important ramifications in numerous areas—for example, in planning instruction. Nevertheless, it is the underlying cognitive profile, not the presence or absence of a potential-achievement discrepancy, that is significant. Unlike the old concept of RD, the approach to reading difficulties that we have described does not artificially distinguish among poor readers based on the biologically, psychologically, and educationally irrelevant characteristic of potential-achievement discrepancy. Rather, it provides a more inclusive, more valid, and more educationally useful way of thinking about the problems of poor readers, whether or not they have the cognitive profiles typical of reading disability.

Consider an analogy in a domain other than reading. One of the coauthors has been rather unsuccessful in learning to play tennis. Now, the coauthor is quite willing to concede that this lack of success is probably related, at least in part, to an intrinsically low aptitude for racket sports. Nevertheless, it is unlikely that scanning the coauthor's brain for abnormalities or searching her chromosomes for an unusual genetic defect would yield much insight into these poor tennis skills. Furthermore, despite a relative lack of aptitude for tennis, the coauthor might learn to play reasonably well with effort and with the right kind of coaching.

Let us think about what would help anyone, including the coauthor, learn to play tennis. Would relating an individual's poor tennis skills to some other measure—to one, say, that is supposed to predict overall athletic aptitude—provide much insight into these difficulties? Probably not. Rather, what would be helpful is a knowledge of how people ordinarily progress from being beginners to being experts in tennis, of which underlying processes are important in this progression, of the specific underlying processes in which the individual is weak, and of the best ways to develop these underlying processes.

In our view, children come to school with relative strengths and relative weaknesses in a wide array of cognitive abilities. For all youngsters, the goals of schooling should include both exploiting their strengths and improving their weaknesses. Luckily for the coauthor, learning to read rather than learning to play tennis is at the center of schooling. But for children with cognitive weaknesses in areas that are crucial to reading acquisition, instruction that addresses these weaknesses is essential. The alternative approach to reading problems presented here does not deny the fact that some children find learning to read intrinsically more difficult. It also does not ignore children's underlying cognitive weaknesses or try to relate these weaknesses to an artificial construct such as an IQ-achievement discrepancy. Rather, it examines these weaknesses in relation to the process of learning to read itself.

Where Should the LD Field Be Going?

The research findings that we have reviewed in this book do not support many current educational practices in the field of learning disabilities. In the area of instruction, they certainly do not support the extremes found in some special-education (as well as some regular-education) programs—purist versions of whole language, with little or no explicit instruction in word recognition, on the one hand, and purist versions of code emphasis, with an excessive focus on isolated word-recognition drills, on the other. But even more problematic for those in the LD field are findings that undermine the traditional construct of reading disability itself. These findings shake the fundamental assumption of practitioners in the LD field—namely, that children with RD need separate educational diagnosis and distinctive treatment—to the point of near collapse. Of course, even a structure with a weak foundation can remain standing for a surprisingly long period of time. Nowhere is this observation more true than in the realm of education. However, regardless of whether those in the LD field change their educational practices, it is clear that they ought to. Specifically, then, where should the LD field be going?

Although plenty of recommendations have been put forth in behalf of the LD field's future, these recommendations have varied widely across authorities. Typical of advocates of the intrinsic perspective is an almost carefree confidence that continued scientific progress will support the search for the "real" cases of reading disability. According to this view, the future largely involves working out certain practical problems having to do with inclusion, instruction, and operationalization of discrepancy definitions of LD and RD. For example, Hammill

(1993), who concludes that "much progress [has] been made recently in developing an acceptable theoretical definition" of learning disabilities, suggests that "the time has come for persons who are interested in definitions to focus their attention on developing criteria for making definitions of learning disabilities operational" (p. 305).

Other authorities, though far from carefree about the scientific and theoretical foundations of current educational practices in the LD field, nevertheless hold out some hope for the future. For example, Moats and Lyon (1993) suggest that "if advocates, clinicians, and researchers press for validated theories, definitions, and methods, the field might possibly thrive. To preserve the gains we have made in public recognition of LD, program funding, and legal safeguards, we need to redouble our efforts to put science in the driver's seat" (p. 291).

By contrast, many authorities with an extrinsic perspective seem to believe that, at least in the area of educational practice, the field of learning disabilities should be dispatched with all deliberate speed. For instance, Allington and McGill-Franzen (1990) maintain:

> It is time that we stopped focusing on the unnecessary labeling of children as a prerequisite to their receiving instructional support. We have the knowledge, the research, and the demonstratively effective programs that can virtually eliminate reading failure. What is needed is to concentrate our knowledge, resources, and attention on providing all children with far more responsive and effective instructional programs that diagnose and correct reading problems in the early years of schooling. (p. 9)

Christensen (1992), whose recommendations for the future of the LD field we previously noted in Chapter 3, dispatches the field of learning disabilities not only in the context of educational practice but also as a legitimate area of scientific inquiry: "After 30 years of fruitless endeavour, surely it is morally and ethically encumbent upon researchers to acknowledge that the way ahead does not lie in the continued search for the 'true' learning disabled child, but rather in a search for specific instructional solutions to reading failure" (p. 278).

Despite his strong critique of the field of learning disabilities, Coles (1987) does not press for its dissolution. Instead, he urges educators in the field to adopt a "two-pronged approach," one that not only addresses practical issues such as providing children with the most effective instruction available but one that also "examine[s] and contest[s] the social organization, power, practices, and ideology that shape the conditions for educational failure" (p. 209). In short, Coles criticizes the narrow knowledge base of many professionals in the LD field and argues that these professionals must be "partisans," advocates for broader societal and systemic change.

We agree heartily with Coles's view that professionals in the LD field tend to lack a broad knowledge base, as do professionals in many other specialized domains. Addressing this narrowness was part of our motivation for writing this book. And certainly we agree that broad systemic changes are warranted—indeed, we will soon suggest some of our own. Unfortunately, however, broad changes in "the system" are largely beyond the control of any *individual* teacher, and the wheels of such changes usually grind exceedingly slowly.

Most important, the conceptualization of poor reading should not involve focusing on the problems in "the system" to the exclusion of examining children's intrinsic cognitive characteristics and the role of these characteristics in reading failure. This extrinsic perspective on poor reading is as flawed as is the traditional construct of reading disability. Rather, a fruitful way of conceptualizing reading difficulties fully incorporates *both* contextual variables, including broad systemic factors such as poverty, *and* children's intrinsic characteristics, such as cognitive-processing skills. From this alternative perspective, furthermore, the two broad sets of variables are viewed interactively rather than as isolated entities. Such a conceptualization also has the advantage of providing teachers with some immediate ideas about how to teach individual children, instead of requiring them to wait for their social activism to yield practical results.

In our view, the LD field should not be disbanded because some youngsters are always going to need more help than even the most capable regular-classroom teachers can provide. On the one hand, specially trained teachers may play a valuable role in enabling schools to more effectively meet the educational needs of all children. On the other hand, however, it is painfully obvious that some dramatic alterations are needed in the LD field as it presently exists. In the following subsections, we summarize our views about the most essential changes needed specifically in educational practice, organizing our discussion around four main areas: changes in terminology, in diagnostic procedures, in instruction, and in funding practices. Fundamental to change in all of these areas is the abandonment of the traditional construct of reading disability.

Changes in Terminology

In recent years, terminology in the field of learning disabilities, and in that of special education generally, has undergone yet another shift. In this latest phase, professionals are urged literally to put the child before the disability. Specifically, one is now supposed to eschew terms such as *learning-disabled children* and *reading-disabled youngsters* in favor of *children with learning disabilities* and *youngsters with reading disability.* This switch in terminology strikes us as exactly the kind of hairsplitting change that those in the LD field tend to mistake for real progress—rather like trying to bail out the *Titanic* with a tablespoon instead of a teaspoon. Rather than making a minor change in syntax, we really need to abandon the old construct of RD in favor of an entirely different way of thinking about reading problems.

Some authorities (e.g., Ysseldyke & Algozzine, 1983) have maintained that quibbling about terminology draws attention away from more important educational issues, such as the nature of instruction. Because trivial definitional disputes often have characterized the LD field, this "What's in a name?" philosophy does have something to recommend it. However, in our view, even though not all youngsters are affected negatively by the LD label, terminology is important. Labels may affect not only how children think of themselves but also how they are perceived by others.

Because there is little evidence that most school-labeled children with RD suffer from an intrinsic abnormality, the terms *reading disability* and *learning disability* are at best misleading; at worst, as we discussed in Chapter 1, they actually may aggravate rather than resolve children's problems. In our opinion, children who are currently called "learning disabled" or "reading disabled" should receive labels using purely descriptive terminology, as in "poor readers," "children with reading difficulties," "children with word-recognition problems," and the like. Along with this change in terminology would come a fundamental change in the conceptualization of reading difficulties, as we have discussed.

Changes in Diagnostic Procedures

Obviously, current educational procedures for classifying poor readers as LD, with their heavy reliance on discrepancy criteria, should be dropped. The energy, time, and financial resources consumed by RD diagnosis could be more effectively devoted to instruction as well as to more educationally relevant kinds of assessment—such as that of basic reading skills and of reading-related cognitive processes. Rather than being singled out through the use of potential-achievement discrepancies, children with the cognitive profiles typical of reading disability might be identified simply on the basis of low achievement in reading, like other poor readers. Of course, as we have repeatedly emphasized, the cognitive underpinnings and the developmental course of children's poor reading also remain important considerations. For instance, the specific instructional needs of children with word-recognition deficits differ from the specific instructional needs of youngsters with good word-recognition skills but poor comprehension. However, for the purpose of determining eligibility for special services, these distinctions should be irrelevant, because both types of children need educational help.

The use of low achievement as a criterion for educational services comes with some problems of its own; for instance, decisions have to be made about where to set cutoffs and what to do about borderline cases of poor reading (see, e.g., Fletcher et al., 1994). Of course, the use of discrepancy definitions of RD does not avoid these problems either, and it has the additional glaring inadequacies that we previously elaborated.

With the elimination of the educational distinction between "LD" poor readers and other poor readers, professionals in the field of learning disabilities will need to resolve some "turf" issues with certain other professional groups, such as reading specialists. However, in most schools that we have seen, there are enough youngsters with difficulties in reading to continue keeping everyone very busy. "Turf" issues can be resolved in a variety of ways (indeed, in some schools they already are being resolved, on an informal basis). For example, children might be assigned to one specialist or another on the basis of severity, with those who are especially low-achieving in reading going to, say, a learning-disabilities specialist and the somewhat higher-functioning children seeing a reading specialist. Alternatively, one specialist might serve as a consultant to regular-classroom teachers whereas the other might focus on providing pull-out remediation to children who require it. Not only can "turf" issues be resolved, but the resolution can occur in ways that give educators greater flexibility and the opportunity to use resources more effectively than the current system allows.

Thus, in this revised version of the LD field, learning-disabilities specialists will no longer be charged with diagnosing reading "disability" or, for that matter, other learning "disabilities." They will not be assigned the spurious task of distinguishing "LD" poor readers from other poor readers. Instead, learning-disabilities specialists—who obviously will require a new name—might specialize in and serve as resources for other, more educationally relevant kinds of knowledge. For example, they might specialize in knowledge about individual differences in reading acquisition (as well as in other areas, such as mathematics) and about the cognitive processes underlying poor achievement. Also, of course, they will continue to play a valuable role in instruction—specifically, in the ways that we have outlined in discussing "turf" issues.

Changes in Instruction

As we have seen, the old concept of reading disability interferes with improvements in instruction in numerous respects. Because of the assumption of biological abnormality that is embedded in the old concept, teachers and parents may, in some cases, develop low expectations for children who have been labeled as having RD. In turn, the expectations and motivation of the children themselves may be decreased. Discrepancy criteria provide few insights about how to teach children with RD and, furthermore, as we will discuss, tend to work against early intervention.

The alternative conceptualization of reading difficulties that we have presented recognizes that learning to read is inherently more difficult for some children. Virtually any complex task, whether it involves learning a sport, learning to play a musical instrument, learning mathematics, or learning to read, is more difficult for some individuals than for others. However, by emphasizing that the cognitive processes involved in learning to read are shaped by experience as well as by biology, by eschewing the invalid and stigmatizing notion of a biological defect, and by having a broad perspective on reading difficulties, this other conceptualization embodies a much more positive outlook on reading difficulties than does the old concept of RD. Perhaps most important from an educator's point of view, in emphasizing the specific cognitive processes involved in reading, the new concept leads to numerous implications for instruction, such as those we discussed at length in Chapter 7. Next, we turn to some of the issues involved in implementing these instructional changes.

The Need for Collaboration. Both normally achieving readers and children with reading difficulties benefit from a combination of the code-emphasis and meaning-emphasis instructional approaches in reading. Ideally, this combination of instructional approaches should be employed in regular-classroom settings as well as in special-education programs. On the one hand, for instance, if a combination of approaches is used in special education settings but the regular classroom continues to employ, say, a purist whole-language approach, then some children will not receive the explicit word-recognition instruction that they need. Thus, some children whose reading problems might have been prevented or ameliorated will continue to require intensive special-education services. On the other hand, if a combination of instructional approaches is used in the regular classroom, but the special-education program is a purist version of, for example, code emphasis, then many children in the special-education program may not receive the practice that they need in reading meaningful connected texts. In this event, children who might otherwise have caught up with their normally achieving peers will continue to languish in special education. Clearly, for such instructional programming to be most effective, these changes must involve a collaborative effort between regular and special educators.

Feasibility and Cost. Although there are some extremists when it comes to the issue of instructional approaches, especially in the domain of reading, many educators are quite sympathetic to the idea that a combination of approaches is necessary. For these teachers, the most immediate challenges involve the details of *implementing* this combined approach, with the right balance of emphases for a particular youngster in a particular situation. These challenges should not be glossed over or underrated. Consider, for example, the case of children with extremely limited word-recognition skills, such as nonalphabetic readers: Finding appealing texts for these children to read, and accommodating their instructional needs in group settings, may be quite difficult.

Yet such improvements in instruction do not necessarily require tremendous additional expenditures of money or effort. In fact, they may prove less costly and more feasible than the programs already in place. For instance, one of the coauthors recently met with a group of special-education teachers from a local school district who were interested in improving the quality of their reading instruction. The teachers were considering the purchase of an additional basal program, different from the one being used in the regular classroom. The purpose of the second basal program was to provide the children receiving special-education services with appropriate seatwork activities and with easier text to read, because the regular-classroom basal program was much too difficult for most of these youngsters. The teachers recognized that the children should not be spending long stretches of time in independent seatwork, but they also felt that the children needed to have "something to do" while the teachers were busy working with other children. In particular, they argued that it simply was not feasible for teachers to develop independent activities for every youngster.

These teachers also were concerned about the expense of the second basal program, which was considerable. The coauthor pointed out that the teachers could purchase a wide variety of trade books and educational texts, ranging in difficulty level and in subject matter, for much less than the cost of the basal program. Even very low-achieving youngsters would then have texts they could use for independent reading in the classroom, an activity that would be much more beneficial to them than completing large numbers of workbook pages. An important task for the teachers would thus be to devise a system for monitoring the children's independent reading—to make sure that the children were selecting appropriate texts and were getting something out of them. As this task would be no more difficult than monitoring and correcting children's seatwork, instructional improvements, in this case, could be achieved at relatively low cost and without making unrealistic demands on teachers.

Early Intervention. As we have repeatedly emphasized, early intervention with poor or at-risk readers is important. The current use of discrepancy definitions of RD makes early intervention difficult inasmuch as children need to fail in reading for some time before they can accumulate discrepancies. The use of low-achievement measures to identify children as needing educational services, which we suggested in the previous section, avoids some of the problems of discrepancy definitions. However, in order to identify at-risk children early, criteria other than low achievement—in particular, measures of cognitive processing—also must be used. For example, measures of phonological processing and of knowledge about basic print concepts are more useful in identification of at-risk kindergartners than are tests of reading achievement.

Finally, we believe that the current emphasis in the research literature on early intervention in reading certainly is appropriate and, indeed, that more could be done in many schools to identify poor readers early. However, the current emphasis on early intervention sometimes leaves the impression that all children identified in the later grades are doomed to be poor readers for life. It must be remembered that—as Jack's story shows—even older children and adults with serious reading problems can be helped. Early intervention is important, but individuals also can learn to read well at any age.

Changes in Funding Practices

Many of the improvements we have suggested are at least partially dependent upon changes in funding practices. As we discussed in Chapter 1, children often are identified as "LD" readers for pragmatic reasons—not so much because educators are convinced that particular youngsters have an intrinsic "disability" but, rather, because labeling children is the only, or the most feasible, way to provide them with extra help. Several improvements outlined here cannot be implemented, then, if funding to local school districts continues to be linked to the current process of diagnosing and labeling youngsters as "LD."

Funding practices in education are a complex issue, and changes in such practices frequently yield unanticipated results (e.g., Kozol, 1991). Nevertheless, we will suggest a few basic points to keep in mind. First, funding based on low achievement certainly is reasonable, but only as a starting point. For example, schools might receive funds for additional educational services for all youngsters scoring below a given percentile—say, below the 20th percentile—on state mastery testing in reading or on another standardized test (e.g., Reynolds, Zetlin, & Wang, 1993). Of course, factors other than standardized-test performance are important, too. For instance, a youngster with "test anxiety" who scores at the 18th percentile on standardized testing but does average work in reading on an everyday basis probably has no need for additional educational services, whereas a youngster who scores at the 23rd percentile on standardized testing, who is doing poorly on an everyday basis in the classroom, and who acts frustrated and upset probably does require such services. Thus, whatever system for funding special-education services is put in place, educators must have some discretion to make decisions about individual cases.

In addition, as Hiebert and Taylor (1994) point out in their discussion of "Chapter 1" funding, funding practices sometimes unintentionally work against early intervention and prevention. For example, if low achievement were the sole criterion for providing funds, then schools that concentrated their efforts on kindergarten and first-grade intervention programs might soon find themselves with fewer funds—and perhaps with none at all for continuing early intervention! Clearly, any system for funding special-education services must avoid penalizing districts for developing effective early-intervention programs.

Of course, we are not suggesting that only youngsters with low achievement should qualify for special-education services. Children with emotional problems or physical handicaps, for example, may also require special-education services even though they are not necessarily low achievers. Still, low achievement is a reasonable criterion for children who are the purview of this book—namely, those who are poor readers.

Some Concluding Thoughts

Those in the learning-disabilities field have always been steeped in controversy and in criticism—a situation that seems likely to continue, at least in the near future. Some practitioners seem oblivious to the growing cracks in the foundation of the LD field. However, to other educators—including, perhaps, some of the readers of this book—the flaws in the field may appear so serious as to preclude remedy.

To say that the LD field is vulnerable to legitimate criticism is a vast understatement. However, we believe that there is an important place for specialists in education, and that the elimination of these specialists would do nothing to help children with difficulties in learning to read. We urge educators in the field of learning disabilities not to go blithely on their current way, nor to give up in despair, but rather to play their part in making the fundamental changes that clearly are essential. The most fundamental change of all, which must precede the others, involves letting go of the old concept of reading disability.

Although we have focused here on recommendations for educators rather than for researchers, many of the latter already have moved away from the traditional concept of RD, especially insofar as it is operationalized through discrepancy criteria. For example, a number of investigators have attacked the validity of discrepancy criteria in diagnosing reading disability (e.g., Fletcher et al., 1994; Siegel, 1988, 1989, 1992; Stanovich, 1991). And other investigators (e.g., Olson, Rack, Conners, DeFries, & Fulker, 1991) have urged that poor readers should not be excluded either from research or from remedial services based on the lack of an IQ-achievement discrepancy. This scientific criticism has begun to influence prominent U.S. learning-disabilities organizations, several of which proposed, in May 1995, that the discrepancy requirement in federal regulations on LD be dropped, at least for grades three and below. Of course, we applaud this proposal, but we hope that it will be only the begining of even more profound changes in how educators conceptualize difficulties in reading and in other academic areas.

There is nothing about the old concept of RD that provides real insight into the problems of any of the poor readers whose stories we have told in this book, from Kim in Chapter 1 to Jack in Chapter 10. Like many "scientific" concepts that once were popular but proved to be false—such as the idea that bumps on the head tell us something about a person's abilities or the idea that bad humors in the body cause disease—the concept of reading disability belongs in the history of science, not at the forefront of contemporary educational practice and research. Long overdue is the time to move toward another way of thinking about problems in learning to read.

References

Allington, R. L., & McGill-Franzen, A. (1990). Children with reading problems: How we wrongfully classify them and fail to teach many to read. *ERS Spectrum, 8,* 3–9.

Blachman, B. A. (1994). What we have learned from longitudinal studies of phonological processing and reading, and some unanswered questions: A response to Torgesen, Wagner, and Rashotte. *Journal of Learning Disabilities, 27,* 287–291.

Boder, E. (1973). Developmental dyslexia: A diagnostic approach based on three atypical reading-spelling patterns. *Developmental Medicine and Child Neurology, 15,* 663–687.

Chall, J. (1983). *Learning to read: The great debate,* rev. ed. New York: McGraw-Hill.

Christensen, C. A. (1992). Discrepancy definitions of reading disability: Has the quest led us astray? A response to Stanovich. *Reading Research Quarterly, 27,* 276–278.

Coles, G. S. (1987). *The learning mystique: A critical look at "learning disabilities."* New York: Pantheon Books.

Cronbach, L. J., & Furby, L. (1970). How we should measure "change"—or should we? *Psychological Bulletin, 74,* 68–80.

Denckla, M. B., LeMay, M., & Chapman, C. A. (1985). Few CT scan abnormalities found even in neurologically impaired learning disabled children. *Journal of Learning Disabilities, 18,* 132–135.

Felton, R. H. (1993). Effects of instruction on the decoding skills of children with phonological-processing problems. *Journal of Learning Disabilities, 26,* 583–589.

Fisher, C. W., & Hiebert, E. H. (1990). Characteristics of tasks in two approaches to literacy instruction. *The Elementary School Journal, 91,* 3–18.

Fletcher, J. M., Shaywitz, S. E., Shankweiler, D. P., Katz, L., Liberman, I. Y., Stuebing, K. K., Francis, D. J., Fowler, A. E., & Shaywitz, B. A. (1994). Cognitive profiles of reading disability: Comparisons of discrepancy and low achievement definitions. *Journal of Educational Psychology, 86,* 6–23.

Frith, U. (1985). Beneath the surface of developmental dyslexia. In K. Patterson, J. Marshall, & M. Coltheart (Eds.), *Surface dyslexia* (pp. 301–330). London: Erlbaum.

Galaburda, A. M., Sherman, G. F., Rosen, G. D., Aboitiz, F., & Geschwind, N. (1985). Developmental dyslexia: Four consecutive patients with cortical anomalies. *Annals of Neurology, 18,* 222–223.

Hammill, D. D. (1993). A brief look at the learning disabilities movement in the United States. *Journal of Learning Disabilities, 26,* 295–310.

Hiebert, E. H., & Taylor, B. M. (1994). Interventions and the restructuring of American literacy instruction. In E. H. Hiebert & B. M. Taylor (Eds.), *Getting reading right from the start: Effective early literacy interventions* (pp. 201–217). Needham Heights, MA: Allyn and Bacon.

Kozol, J. (1991). *Savage inequalities: Children in America's schools.* New York: Crown.

McGill-Franzen, A. (1994). Compensatory and special education: Is there accountability for learning and belief in children's potential? In E. H. Hiebert & B. M. Taylor (Eds.), *Getting reading right from the start: Effective early literacy interventions* (pp. 13–35). Boston, MA: Allyn and Bacon.

Moats, L. C., & Lyon, G. R. (1993). Learning disabilities in the United States: Advocacy, science, and the future of the field. *Journal of Learning Disabilities, 26,* 282–294.

Olson, R. K., Rack, J. P., Conners, F. A., DeFries, J. C., & Fulker, D. W. (1991). Genetic etiology of individual differences in reading disability. In L. V. Feagans, E. J. Short, & L. J. Meltzer (Eds.), *Subtypes of learning disabilities: Theoretical perspectives and research* (pp. 113–135). Hillsdale, NJ: Lawrence Erlbaum Associates.

Pinnell, G. S., Lyons, C. A., DeFord, D. E., Bryk, A. S., & Seltzer, M. (1994). Comparing instructional models for the literacy education of high-risk first graders. *Reading Research Quarterly, 29,* 8–37.

Reynolds, M. C., Zetlin, A. G., & Wang, M. C. (1993). 20/20 analysis: Taking a close look at the margins. *Exceptional Children, 59,* 294–300.

Shankweiler, D., Crain, S., Brady, S., & Macaruso, P. (1992). Identifying the causes of reading disability. In P. B. Gough, L. C. Ehri, & R. Treiman (Eds.), *Reading acquisition* (pp. 275–305). Hillsdale, NJ: Lawrence Erlbaum Associates.

Shaywitz, S. E., Escobar, M. D., Shaywitz, B. A., Fletcher, J. M., & Makuch, R. (1992). Evidence that dyslexia may represent the lower tail of a normal distribution of reading ability. *New England Journal of Medicine, 326,* 145–150.

Shaywitz, S. E., Shaywitz, B. A., Fletcher, J. M., & Escobar, M. D. (1990). Prevalence of reading disability in boys and girls: Results of the Connecticut Longitudinal Study. *Journal of the American Medical Association, 264,* 998–1002.

Siegel, L. S. (1988). Evidence that IQ scores are irrelevant to the definition and analysis of reading disability. *Canadian Journal of Psychology, 42,* 201–215.

———. (1989). IQ is irrelevant to the definition of learning disabilities. *Journal of Learning Disabilities, 22,* 469–479.

———. (1992). An evaluation of the discrepancy definition of dyslexia. *Journal of Learning Disabilities, 25,* 618–629.

Stanovich, K. E. (1990). Explaining the differences between the dyslexic and the garden-variety poor reader: The phonological-core variable-difference model. In J. K. Torgesen (Ed.), *Cognitive and behavioral characteristics of children with learning disabilities* (pp. 7–40). Austin, TX: Pro-Ed.

———. (1991). Discrepancy definitions of reading disability: Has intelligence led us astray? *Reading Research Quarterly, 26,* 7–29.

Stanovich, K. E., & Siegel, L. S. (1994). Phenotypic performance profile of children with reading disabilities: A regression-based test of the phonological-core variable-difference model. *Journal of Educational Psychology, 86,* 24–53.

Torgesen, J. K. (1991). Learning disabilities: Historical and conceptual issues. In B. Y. L. Wong (Ed.), *Learning about learning disabilities* (pp. 3–37). San Diego, CA: Academic Press.

Willows, D. (1991). Visual processes in learning disabilities. In B. Y. L. Wong (Ed.), *Learning about learning disabilities* (pp. 163–193). San Diego, CA: Academic Press.

Ysseldyke, J. E., & Algozzine, B. (1983). LD or not LD: That's not the question! *Journal of Learning Disabilities, 16,* 29–31.

About the Book and Authors

The identification of poor readers as "learning disabled" can be the first of many steps toward consigning students to a lifetime of reading failure. The very label that is meant to help children often becomes a burden that works against effective learning throughout their schooling.

In this book, the authors identify the dangers of labeling children as reading or learning disabled, contending that a "reading disability" is not a unitary phenomenon. In order to diagnose and help children, educators and parents need to understand the multiple sources of reading difficulty before they can choose appropriate means to correct it.

Drawing on recent research in cognitive psychology, the authors present a new theoretical model of reading disability that integrates a wide variety of findings across age and grade spans. Laid out in terms that are readily comprehensible to parents and practitioners, the model outlines the phases that are characteristic of the path to proficient reading, then describes four ways in which disabled readers may stray from this path. The key to the authors' work lies in the fact that youngsters who stray from the path of typical reading acquisition often are not distinguishable from other children who are classified as "poor readers" rather than as "learning disabled." This model is an especially useful one for practitioners because it both provides a broader view of reading disability than have many previous models and shows how reading disability relates to typical reading acquisition. Using illustrative case studies, the authors describe the four patterns of reading disability, explain how to properly assess them, and suggest ways to conquer them.

Louise Spear-Swerling, Associate Professor of Special Education at Southern Connecticut State University, has taught both special education and regular classes in public schools. **Robert J. Sternberg** is IBM Professor of Psychology and Education in the Department of Psychology at Yale University. He is the author of several well-known books, including *The Triarchic Mind: A New Theory of Human Intelligence* and *Defying the Crowd: Cultivating Creativity in a Culture of Conformity* (with Todd Lubart).

Index

AAMD. *See* American Association on Mental Deficiency
Abilities, 257–270
  and intellectual styles, 266–268
  multiple intelligences theory, 48, 64, 258–260
  and reading success possibility, 268–270
  triarchic intelligence theory, 48, 64, 260–265
Ability grouping, 12, 244
Aboitiz, F., 234, 305
Accuracy- vs. rate-disabled readers, 141
ACE guessing technique, 215
ACLD. *See* Association for Children with Learning Disabilities
Acquired reading disorders, 31–32, 85
Adams, Marilyn J., 22, 79, 80, 81, 82, 85, 88, 96, 125, 164, 168, 170, 171, 173–174, 181, 188, 190, 192, 196, 200, 201, 202, 208, 241–242, 278, 296
Adaptive behavior, 259
Adelman, H. S., 38
Adelman, K. A., 38
Adelman, P. B., 142
ADHD. *See* Attention-deficit hyperactivity disorder
Adult reading. *See* Proficient adult reading
Advocacy, 8–9, 36–37, 37, 53
"Affliction of geniuses" perception, 38
Age/grade levels, 139–141
Alegria, J., 95
Alexander, A. W., 123, 193
Alexander, P. A., 102, 129
Algozzine, B., 7, 68, 316
Alley, G. R., 214
Allington, Richard L., 11, 131, 132, 244, 287, 315
Alliteration, 82, 95, 96, 192, 242
  assessment, 189–190
Alphabet books, 196
Alphabetic insight, 126, 196–197, 279
  and typical reading acquisition, 93, 94, 95, 96
  See also Nonalphabetic readers; Phonetic-cue word · recognition
American Academy of Ophthamology, 41–42
American Association on Mental Deficiency (AAMD), 67–68
Analytic phonics, 164, 165, 168
Andersen, H. G., 123, 193
Anderson, R. C., 12, 20, 87, 98, 101, 103, 129, 137, 141, 164, 165, 168, 200, 206, 208, 210, 212, 213, 216, 241, 242 ,244
Arter, J., 46
Assessment, 158–161, 187, 188–191, 195, 203–204, 210
  and early intervention, 276
  phonological awareness, 188–191
  and reading disability routes model, 311–312
  test types, 159–161
  See also School identification

Association for Children with Learning Disabilities (ACLD), 35. *See also* Learning Disabilities Association of America
Attention-deficit hyperactivity disorder (ADHD), 38, 237
Attributional patterns, 10, 130, 215
Audio support, 202
Auditory Discrimination in Depth, 192
Auditory perception skills, 35
Authenticity, 167, 168
Automatic word recognition, 99–101, 102, 107, 195
  educational practice for, 200–203
  and reading comprehension, 99, 172
  and reading practice, 128–129
  and triarchic intelligence theory, 264–265
  See also Nonautomatic readers

Backman, J., 123, 193
Bailey, J., 205
Baldwin, L. E., 79
Barker, T. A., 97, 98, 143, 248
Barnes, W. S., 67, 105, 153, 199, 242
Basal reading programs, 166–167, 172, 291–292, 319–320
Bateman, B., 8, 40, 41, 44
BEAM. *See* Brain electrical activity mapping
Beck, I. L., 95, 286
Beckwith, L., 153
Behavioral genetics, 16
Behavioral psychology, 40–41
Bell, L. C., 95, 104
Bellamy, G. T., 12
Belmont, J. M., 261
Bender, B. G., 232
Bender, L., 59
Bender Visual-Motor Gestalt Test, 59
Bereiter, C., 102
Bertelson, P., 95
"Big books," 207, 289–290
Biological abnormality theories, 22, 34, 41, 42
  ethical issues, 13
  history of, 30–33
  and school identification, 6–7, 65–66
  weakness of, 7–8, 48, 231, 238, 304–305
  See also Biological differences; Intrinsic perspective
Biological differences, 231–240
  conclusions, 237–240
  functional brain differences, 235–237, 239
  genetic differences, 16, 231–234, 237–238, 239, 246, 305
  methodological issues, 237, 305
  relevance of, 229–230
  research bias danger, 239–240

ALBERTSON COLLEGE OF IDAHO

3 5556 0016 1294 4

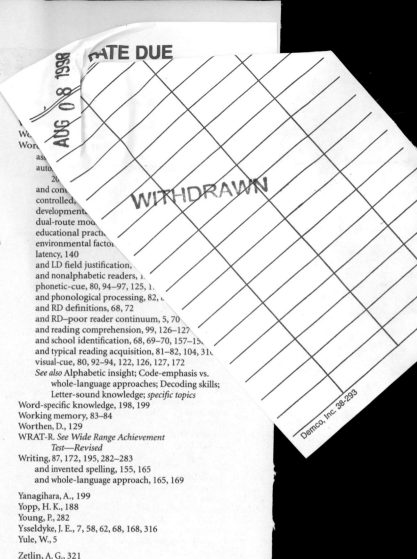

DATE DUE

AUG 08 1998

WITHDRAWN

Demco, Inc. 38-293